ENCYCLOPEDIA OF PUNK MUSIC AND CULTURE

ENCYCLOPEDIA OF PUNK MUSIC AND CULTURE

BRIAN COGAN

GREENWOOD PRESS
Westport, Connecticut ◆ London
OCM 63660128

Library of Congress Cataloging-in-Publication Data

Cogan, Brian, 1967–
    Encyclopedia of punk music and culture/ Brian Cogan.
        p. cm.
    Includes bibliographical references and index.
    ISBN 0–313–33340–8
    1. Punk rock music—Encyclopedias.   I. Title.
    ML102.R6C64   2006
    781.66—dc22   2006002440

British Library Cataloguing in Publication Data is available.

Library of Congress Catalog Card Number: 2006002440
ISBN: 0–313–33340–8

First published in 2006

Greenwood Press, 88 Post Road West, Westport, CT 06881
An imprint of Greenwood Publishing Group, Inc.
www.greenwood.com

Printed in the United States of America

The paper used in this book complies with the
Permanent Paper Standard issued by the National
Information Standards Organization (Z39.48–1984).

10 9 8 7 6 5 4 3 2 1

CONTENTS

LIST OF ENTRIES

GUIDE TO RELATED TOPICS

Punk Rock Personalities

Albini, Steve
Allin, G.G.
Bangs, Lester
Beahm, Paul
Belushi, John
Biafra, Jello
Biggs, Ronnie
Bingenheimer, Rodney
Bowie, David
Bromely Contingent
Captain Beefheart
Carroll, Jim
Childers, Leee Black
Cooper-Clarke, John
County, Wayne/Jayne
Darby Crash
Doe, John
Fields, Danny
Fowley, Kim
Fury, Don
Ginn, Greg
Hanna, Kathleen
Hell, Richard
Holmstrom, John
Hooley, Terri
Iggy Pop
Kent, Nick

Kristal, Hilly
Letts, Don
Livermore, Larry
Lunch, Lydia
Lydon, John
Lynman, Kevin
MacKaye, Ian
McLaren, Malcolm
McNeil, Legs
Nico
Peel, John
Pettibon, Raymond
Ramone, Dee Dee
Ramone, Joey
Reagan, Ronald
Reed, Lou
Reid, Jamie
Robinson, Tom
Robo
Rollins, Henry
Rotten, Johnny
Shaw, Greg
Smith, Patti
Smith, Winston
Strummer, Joe
Tabb, George
Thunders, Johnny
Top Jimmy

Good Vibrations
Hellcat Records
Jade Tree Records
Kill Rock Stars
K Records
Lookout Records
Mordam Records
Mr. Lady Records
Outpunk Records
Queercorps
Resistance Records
Revelation Records
Roir Records
Rough Trade
SST
Stiff Records
Touch and Go
2 Tone

Punk Clubs and Locations

ABC No Rio
Akron, Ohio
Anthrax
Anti-Club
A7
Boston
Canadian Punk
Canterbury Apartments
Cathay de Grande
CBGB's
Cleveland
Gilman Street
Irish Punk
London
Los Angeles
Madame Wong's
Masque
Max's Kansas City
New York
New Zealand
100 Club
Orange County
Rat
Roxy
Washington, D.C.
Whiskey a-Go-Go
Zero Club

Punk Culture

Acme Attractions
Advertising, Use of Punk in
Anarchy
Better Youth Organization
Blasting Concept
Body Art
Doc Martens
Drugs
Flyers
Gender and Punk
Glue
Gobbing
Heroin
Homosexuality
Krishna, Hare
KROQ
L.A.P.D.
MainMan
Maoism
MTV
National Front
Nazi Punks
Nihilism
Parents of Punkers
Pit
Pogo
Positive Force
Punk and Mass Media Representations
Punk and Race
Punk and Technology
Punk Books
Punk Fashion
Punk Is Dead
Punk Movies
Punk's Not Dead
Punk Rock Aerobics
Punkvoter.com
Pyramid Belts
Quaaludes
Radio Tokyo
RAR (Rock against Racism)
Revolution Summer
Scenes
Situationists
Skank
Skateboarding

Spike
Spiked Hair
Squats
Stage Diving
Tattoos
True till Death
Vans Warped Tour
Vegans
Vegetarians
Vinyl
Violence
Zines

Punk Bands and Songs

Accused
Adicts
Adolescents
Adverts
Agent Orange
Agnostic Front
All
Alternative TV
"Anarchy in the UK"
Angelic Upstarts
Angry Samoans
Anti-Flag
Anti-Nowhere League
Anti-Pasti
AOD
Avail
Avengers
Bad Brains
Bad Religion
Bags
Battalion of Saints
Beat Happening
Beefeater
Big Black
Big Boys
Big Drill Car
Bikini Kill
Black Flag
Black Randy and the Metrosquad
Black Train Jack
Black Velvet Flag
"Blank Generation"
Bl'ast!
Blisters
"Blitzkrieg Bop"

Blondie
Bold
Boris the Sprinkler
Bouncing Souls
Boys
Bracket
Bratmobile
Broken Bones
Butchies, the
Butthole Surfers
Buzzcocks
Can
Celibate Rifles
Chalk Circle
Chelsea
CH3
Chumbawumba
Circle Jerks
Civ
Clash
Cockney Rejects
Conflict
Corrosion of Conformity
Cramps
Crass
Crime
Crippled Youth
Cro-Mags
Crucifucks
Dag Nasty
Damned
Dead Boys
Dead Kennedys
Dead Milkmen
Deep Wound
Descendents
Devil Dogs
Devo
D Generation
DI
Dickies
Dicks
Dictators
Die Toten Hosen
Dils
Dim Stars
Discharge
DOA

PREFACE

This book was a labor of love and also enormously difficult. I do not mean difficult in the sense of doing the research but difficult in the sense of "releasing" to the general public something of which I had always been very possessive. When I was young, punk gave me a sense of identity and belonging that I could not find elsewhere, and it was an epiphany when I discovered that there were other outcasts such as myself. When I first came to know punk in the early eighties, it was not something that was marketed—it was truly an underground phenomenon, and we felt that it should stay that way. We loved punk, obsessed about it, fought over it, and held it close to us as if it were some sacred talisman that would lose its magic if revealed to the masses. Punk was something my friends and I regarded as ours alone. When we encountered other members of punk culture on the street, we would nod in silent recognition of a shared bond and way of looking at the world. It seems strange to write about punk in a critical way for "outsiders," as I am largely doing here. As Maria Raha wrote in her book *Cinderella's Big Score*, "it feels a bit traitorous to criticize a community in which I have invested so much" (ix), and to a certain extent that is what I am doing. In writing about punk and "revealing" it to the public, there is the inescapable feeling that one has betrayed the other members of a private club. But then again, optimist that I am, I firmly believe that for the hundreds of thousands of people who do not fit in with mainstream culture, and who have felt outside of the mainstream for years, discovering punk rock might help in some small way to help them get through high school, college, or just the mundanity of everyday life.

For those of you still in high school and college, this book contains some very valuable information. Not only do all entries come with discographies, but the encyclopedia also includes a list of print and electronic sources for further reading, with copious cross-references in bold— something that would have helped me quite a bit when I was young.

Most encyclopedias are written by committee; this one was written by this extremely tired person and aided and abetted by a cast of seemingly thousands. I do not have the space to list all the people who contributed via conversation, information, guidance, or other aid, but the following people were instrumental in the birth of this book, and, therefore, it would be remiss of me not to mention the enormous debt I owe them. For research help, which took several years and endless hours, I would like to thank especially Cynthia Conti, my chief researcher and frequent intellectual debater. Her help in organizing and finding vast amount of information and for sitting for hours in coffee shops talking me through this are much appreciated. Also thanks beyond the call of duty go to Robert Conway, my photo researcher, who helped me when I had no idea what a "right" or a "clearance" was (I have subsequently forgotten) and is responsible for most of the photos used in this work. Special thanks go also to my original research assistant, Lauren Jablonski, who helped get me started and also acted as an informant to modern punk fashion and music. The book would have had far more mistakes and errors in grammar were it not for the amazing Vanessa Weiman, who can spot a mistake miles away and did the initial copyedit and has always been a very good friend. I'd also like to thank the many people who talked me through this for free (or occasionally for beer), including John Lisa (who was even more punk than me!); my old friend and band mate John Pillarella; Maria Raha, the ever-generous author of the insightful *Cinderella's Big Score*, the best book on punk and gender; Marvin Taylor, who curates the downtown archives of New York University's Fales Library; John Holmstrom for his time and patience; Johnny Whoa-Oh; Mikey Erg; Legs McNeil; Richard Hell; El Hefe; Thomas King for additional guidance and patience and his killer steaks and Tater Tots; Andrew Barber, always a huge help; Mike Faloon, a great writer and friend; Bert Aldridge, who helped me on the New Zealand sections and in articulating my version of punk; Sal Cannestra for years of support and for naming his kid Milo, a very punk name; Robert Francos, photographer extraordinaire; Brendan Gilmartin, although he is now a sports yuppie; Sean Cogan for keeping me on the punk straight and narrow; Eloise Pillarella, who is the youngest and coolest punk I know; the old Staten Island punk crew from Neri's place; the Saint John's punk crew who got me through college; Jon Zimmerman of New York University for especial encouragement; my colleagues M. J. Robinson, Marion Wrenn, Bill Phillips, Cheryl Casey, Sue Collins, Samuel Howard-Spink and Devon Powers, Mike Grabowski, and Laura Tropp, all of whom encouraged me in too many ways to count; the Molloy College Communications Department and its chair, Alice Byrnes; the Molloy College faculty professional center for their generous grant to continue this research; and my editor, Debra Adams, for her patience and guidance. I would like to give special thanks to all past and present members of my band, In Crowd, for making me as punk as I am today. To my family, my father, Joseph Cogan, and my mother, Ann Cogan, who never got the punk thing but were glad I wasn't doing drugs and supported me anyway; my brothers, Joe and Sean, and their wonderful wives; my nieces and nephews; and my cousins/sisters Gina and Claudia, who have always been an inspiration. Also special thanks to my wonderful and loving wife, Lisa, who supported me throughout and helped me though this wonderful and difficult project. I would also like to dedicate this book to the memory of my late, great mentor, Neil Postman, of New York University, who would have despised any punk music he heard but whose ability as a teacher, mentor, and friend taught me how to write for an audience and how to think critically.

Also to any who helped me not mentioned here, my sincerest thanks, and I'll leave it at this: See you in the pit.

INTRODUCTION

In writing about punk rock, certain limitations and contradictions must be considered, especially because almost no two scholars or punks agree on an exact definition of the term, when punk began, and if punk currently still exists or if current punk is simply an imitation of a dead art form. These are legitimate questions, and punk scholars and zines have been debating them for years, to little or no consensus. Although I do not wish to add fuel to the fire, or fuel the ire of the many in the punk community who believe that to write about punk for public consumption is an act of selling out—the cardinal punk sin—I nonetheless believe that this book will provide a necessary resource for historians, students, and others who share a fascination with punk. This work examines the huge scope of punk rock, and it is not so much an effort to be the definitive work on punk rock but instead to provide a guide to the vast expanse of work that has been labeled punk rock and to provide an entry point and reference to those who want to know more about punk rock and its subcultures. Although punk rock is a vast and extraordinarily difficult subject to document in all its complexity, this work attempts to be a comprehensive guide to the subject.

There are many who argue over the scope of *when* punk occurred. Many scholars in both British and U.S. academic circles look at punk as a cultural and musical movement that started roughly in the early 1970s and concluded during the early 1980s when other popular musical movements, such as postpunk, hardcore, and new wave, became the dominant musical forms of the day and many of the early members of the punk scene left punk behind (as in the case of Johnny Rotten, who readopted his birth name of John Lydon and helped to pioneer postpunk within his band Public Image Limited). This book does not regard punk as so static and examines punk in all its complexity, contradictions, inconsistency, and power. This book regards punk as an ongoing and evolving subcultural, social, and political movement that is not simply a museum piece that can be examined from a historical viewpoint but one that is constantly changing and evolving, sometimes far beyond the scope of the original creator's intent. To examine punk rock is not to ask, "What happened and when?" but to ask, "What is going on, and where is it going now?"

PUNK AND THEORY

There have been numerous books written on punk rock over the last 30 years, many of a historical nature. The works of Heylin (1993), McNeil and McCain (1996), Azerad (2002), Blush (2001), Andersen and Jenkins (2001), Spitz and Mullen (2001), and Savage (1992) are among the most prominent histories of punk rock. There are also numerous works of scholarship into the nature of punk rock written from an academic perspective or for a largely academic audience, such as Sabin (1999), Hebdige (1979, 1987), Traber (2001), Taylor (2003), and Thompson (2004), as well as those that specialize in aspects of punk, such as Lahickey's work on Straight Edge (1997), Leblanc's work on gender (2002), Raha (2005), and Arnold (1997). These works and others have provided a rigorous critical history of punk rock from a variety of perspectives that are also sometimes contradictory. Most of these works also concentrate on a specific time period or try to define punk by rather narrow parameters and exclude other versions of the punk mythology, either due to space or to ideological limitations. Although all of these books are necessary additions to the shelf of any scholar of punk rock and subculture, they all (justly) concentrate on their area of specialization to the exclusion of other areas. This work serves not only as an addition to the fine scholarship done on punk rock but also ties together the disparate threads of punk rock and tries to organize the vast field of study into a cohesive whole that can be appreciated not only by scholars but also by those within the community seeking information on punk history. Where those previously mentioned works specialized, this work provides an overview of the entire subject.

WHAT IS PUNK ROCK?

The question of what punk rock is is not easily answered. To many, punk rock is a specific movement that was a result of the number of similar-minded experimental and artistic bands that started playing at CBGB's on New York's Lower East Side in 1974. These bands included the Ramones, Patti Smith, Television, the Heartbreakers, Suicide, Richard Hell, the Voidoids, and many others mentioned in this book. From this scene, the punk movement was born as an artistic and often romantic way to rebel against the corporate conformity that had been foisted upon U.S. consumers by record labels obsessed with musical proficiency and self-indulgent soloing. The movement was given a name and focus by John Holmstrom and Legs McNeil of *Punk* magazine and given a fashion sense and romantic vision by Richard Hell. This movement inspired punk in other countries and led to punk becoming a worldwide and largely reviled form of music and a lifestyle that almost guaranteed that those identifying as punk would be mocked or verbally abused. To those who subscribe to this scenario, punk was co-opted by record labels, which marketed the more accessible bands such as Blondie and others as New Wave and ignored the others, leading to the movement's eventual demise and mutation into the much more underground hardcore scene.

Those who subscribe to a second scenario, including almost every English academic that ever wrote on the subject, believe punk was a British working-class movement that was inspired by the political and subversive reactions of the situationists and the rebellion of the 1960s and was fired and inspired by British class discontent. In this scenario, wily older anarchists such as Malcolm McLaren and Bernie Rhodes acted as Svengali's to young disaffected British kids such as Joe Strummer and Johnny Rotten, who formed bands that articulated the revolutionary politics of their mentors in the Clash and the Sex Pistols. To those who believe in this scenario, punk rock was uniquely British and inspired U.S. punk rock, which did not get the unique nature of the British movement, which burned out circa 1980 due to a lack of concern with black music and mutated into the much more adventurous postpunk.

The Clash, pictured here in 1977, was often known as "the only band that matters." *Photo by Ray Stevenson/Rex Features.*

The difficulty with both of these scenarios is that they not only locate punk in a specific time and place, but they don't seem to explain adequately why punk was so dynamic and attractive to the marginalized of society in the first place. Nor do they explain why in almost every small town in the United States today one can still see groups of young kids creating bands, xeroxing zines and flyers, and creating Web sites and blogs devoted to the subject of punk rock. Are these kids merely nostalgic, simply living in the past, devoted to an old movement, and as anachronistic as British Teddy Boys of the 1970s? I do not think the answer is so simple. To me and to others who try to theorize and document punk rock, this does not explain the attraction of punk and how it connected to people. Punk is a subculture, and although subcultures have founders and some codes, established fashions, signifiers, and very often rules, this does not mean that those rules remain static or that a movement is over after the founders have left the scene. In his book on Rastafarian culture (1988), Leonard Barrett correctly points out that even though the founders of the Rastafarian movement are long gone, Rasta ideology is an evolving culture and one that has an evolving dogma that takes into account the passage of time. The same thing is true of punk rock. Punk did not end at any specific time; punk changed, evolved, mutated, and changed in viral ways. New punks constantly reinvigorated the scene, creating new rules, new fashions, and new signifiers of identity that many of the originators would not recognize but that are still arguably and demonstrably punk. This book does not put dates on punk or even consider punk one unified subculture. Punk is inclusive enough to include both Queercore and straight edge and skinheads, some of which may be hostile to each other but can still be examined under the wider label of punk rock. Even though many critics were saying punk was dead in 1979, to a small-town teen in the rural United States, punk is as much a way of constructing identity as it was in 1976, 1984, or 1991. Punk may be dead for those who no longer choose to identify as punks, but for those who still use the loose precepts of punk (the DIY aesthetic, the general disregard for authority, and the overall resistance to the co-option of subculture) to create and maintain a coherent identity, punk is best seen as a virus, one that mutates constantly and resists efforts at understanding or codification.

A typical mosh pit at a punk concert. *Photo by Chris Moorhouse/Stringer/Hutton Archive/Getty Images.*

THE CRITERIA FOR INCLUSION IN THIS ENCYCLOPEDIA

The debate of what can be labeled as punk rock is ongoing and made the criteria for inclusion in this book somewhat problematic. Many early punks would argue that punk did not exist after a certain time period and that musical and cultural movements such as hardcore are not true punk. Some in the hardcore scene make a similar argument about other forms of music. Blush (2001) argues that hardcore, the successor to punk rock, died out circa 1986. I feel strongly, however, that restricting punk to a specific period of time and place (New York, Los Angeles, London, etc.) limits punk and tries to pin down and define a movement that has always resisted easy categorization. To put a date on punk or offer a strict definition of that is punk and what is not is best argued (often eloquently and with good cause) in the pages of *Maximum Rock 'n' Roll* and other worthy zines. As I have stated previously and as I argue in other entries in this work, however, I consider punk an overlapping and expanding subculture—one that is not bound by the rigid categorizations offered by many early in the movement—but an evolving subculture with common symbols and a common canon of music that can be considered punk. Nonetheless, in this encyclopedia, I do not pretend to be canonizing specific bands and movements as being the true face or standard-bearers for punk music, fashion, style, or politics. Although Craig O'Hara in his book *The Philosophy of Punk* (1999) makes a compelling argument about common punk ideals, it can also be argued that punk is open and constantly evolving. In fact, even trying to carbon-date or create a family tree for punk is problematic as well. John Holmstrom, creator of *Punk* magazine (and a man who more than most would be well qualified to offer a definition of punk), mentioned to me that he thought the idea of punk predated his magazine naming the movement, not just in the sense of how rockabilly and garage and protopunk predated punk, but that works such as Jarry's *Ubu Roi*, the quintessential scandalous play of its day, could also be considered punk. Although this could open the debate so wide that it would be impossible to ever define punk (a friend asked, "Why isn't Mozart punk?"), it led me to be as inclusive as possible in this work. Obviously, I have tried to include every major band that has been labeled punk over the years, but it would be impossible to list every punk band from around the world. As a necessity, this book has several limitations. It necessarily confines itself to mostly bands from the United States and England, not only because that is where the movement started but because even a cursory examination of worldwide punk rock over the last several decades would require several additional volumes. Punk bands from other countries such as Japan, France, Ireland, Belgium, the Netherlands, and Canada are covered, but they are included usually because the bands are acknowledged as being influential on the overall movement or because they have influenced the scene in the United States. Another limiting criterion is that the scenes in large cities were the best known and best documented of the punk movement, and therefore this book is forced by necessity to omit bands that might have been enormously influential locally but never achieved recognition and adequate documentation outside their region. Yet another limitation is that many punk bands provided little documentation (other than records and other musical archival material) about their existence and often worked under assumed names, listed only first names, or changed members so rapidly that accurate documentation is difficult at best. Nonetheless, my research team and I made every effort to be as accurate as possible, and any inadvertent inaccuracies or full or real names we could not discover will be corrected in later editions of this work if such corrections are brought to the author's attention.

In terms of what *is* included, I have tried to include every major punk band and many minor ones that were and are enormously influential on the scene. Although some bands have exhaustive musical outputs that are difficult to catalog accurately (for the band the Fall, for example, a large catalog of releases does not necessarily mean the band is influential), conversely, a small output, such as the one real album of music by the Sex Pistols, also should not indicate that the band is not enormously influential. I have also tried to be as recent as possible and have included many bands that critics and punk zines have regarded as keeping the spirit of punk alive—not as a museum piece or as a style to be slavishly imitated but as a constantly evolving musical form. New bands such as the Ergs, SmokeWagon, and others are putting out music in the context of punk that is as fresh and punk in its own way as any band in the punk canon. I have also included entries on other music genres, such as reggae, ska, and rockabilly, and they are discussed as to how they relate to punk and how punk has incorporated the other genres into the music. Likewise, musicians as diverse as Frank Zappa, Captain Beefheart, and even Napalm Death are included as well due to their influence on punk rock. I err on the side of including movements some would disassociate from punk rock, such as hardcore, postpunk, Queercore, emo, and others that are the objects of much debate within punk. While I err on the side of including larger movements, I have taken great pains *not* to include many bands that merely wear punk outfits and fashion and pay lip service to punk. For that reason, many modern emo bands (although most of these bands dislike being called emo bands) are not included, nor are those that use punk as a marketing tool, such as Avril Lavigne, Blink 182, and Sum 41. Numerous other works are available on the many modern bands that use punk as a fashion statement, and the reader looking for discussions of those bands is advised to consult the many other sources available.

Finally, this book is by its nature incomplete. It is simply impossible to include every punk band that ever put out a record or gigged. It is also impossible for me to provide a punk litmus test, such as whether a band recorded on a major label or ever had their music used in an advertisement. Although I have much more personal respect and admiration for those bands and record labels that eschew such marketing (such as Dischord Records and Fugazi), I am not the punk police. Hit singles are not an indicator of whether a band should or should not be in this book. Although some bands in this book had top-10 singles (Blondie and Talking Heads, for example), that does not mean they should be excluded or included; it only means that they chose for whatever reason to operate in a different way. Early punk bands, especially bands such as the Clash, Sex Pistols, and Ramones, did not have the enormous underground networks created by the relentless touring across the country and world by bands such as Black Flag and the Minutemen. Although it can be argued that modern bands on major labels are more suspect than earlier punk bands thanks to the opportunities provided by a world much more friendly to DIY endeavor, I also am not using this as the ultimate criteria for inclusion in this volume. If the reader dislikes or disagrees with the inclusion of a specific band in this book, they are invited to scribble over the offending entry or put a sticker from a band they like better over the entry (that is, if they own a copy; please respect library copies). To me, punk is an ever growing, mutating, and expanding movement, and this book is ultimately an attempt to provide an introduction to both scholars and novices. Although this work may be consulted by academics interested in the field of subcultural studies or punk ethnography, it is also accessible to upper-level students in both high school and college. This book is designed to try to give the reader a sense of the urgency and importance of punk rock and how utterly raw and revolutionary it was when it first came out and also to indicate how vital and extremely necessary punk is to the present day. In a world of bland corporate music and conformity, punk is as essential now as a corrective to the uninspired as it was 30 years ago. Despite what the graffiti on the wall says, punk is not dead. As long as bored teenagers get together and work on zines, start their own bands, and try to live by their own artistic and aesthetic code, as opposed those imposed by society, punk is very much alive.

ABC NO RIO

Independent club and social center located at 156 Rivington Street on the lower East Side in New York City, owned and operated by a punk collective. Bands that play at ABC No Rio range from national acts to local punk bands to those without reputation that have been touring on the grassroots level. Bands that play at ABC No Rio are asked to submit lyrics or recordings of songs beforehand so that they can be screened for potentially racist, sexist, or homophobic content. The club faced numerous financial difficulties over the years due to rising rents and the gentrification of the Lower East Side during the 1990s and the early years of the twenty-first century. The social center was largely the result of the Real Estate Show of 1979, during which a radical artists' collective occupied 123 Delancy Street and turned it into a gallery that was shut done by New York City's Housing Preservation and Development Agency, which subsequently granted use of the Rivington Street building. Although the city later agreed to sell the building to the collective, the status of ABC No Rio is still in legal limbo. In addition to the punk/**hardcore** collective that hosts the weekly punk/hardcore matinees on Saturday afternoons, the building also holds an extensive **zine** library, a computer lab, a darkroom collective, and numerous other community-oriented groups and projects.

ACCUSED

The Accused was one of the more popular and influential of the early grindcore bands (bands that played at the speed of light and mixed extreme heavy metal with science fiction and horror film lyrics with punk) from Seattle, Washington. The band started in 1984 and originally featured John Dahlin on lead vocals (later replaced by Blaine Cook, from the Fartz), Tom Niemeyer on guitar, Chibon Batterman on bass (later replaced by Alex "Maggot Brain" Sibbald), and Dana Collins on drums (later replaced by Steve Nelson). The band broke up in the early 1990s.

Discography: *Return of Martha Splatterhead* (Combat, 1986); *More Fun than an Open Casket Funeral* (Combat, 1987; Relativity, 1991); *Grinning Like an Undertaker* (Nastymix, 1990); *Hymns for the Deranged* (Musical Tragedies/Empty, 1990); *Martha Splatterhead's Maddest Stories Ever Told* (Combat, 1991); *Straight Razor* (Nastymix, 1991); *Splatter Rock* (Nastymix, 1992).

ACME ATTRACTIONS

The second most influential fashion shop in London during the early days of British punk. The store was located at 135 King's Road in Chelsea and employed **Don Letts** (punk film-maker and future member of Big Audio Dynamite) as a DJ and his then girlfriend Jeanette Lee, who later went on to join **Public Image Limited** and manage the British band Pulp. The store sold punk clothing but also mod 1960s suits and retro and soul clothing. It had numerous punk customers, such as **Johnny Rotten,** Billy Idol, Tony James, **Sid Vicious,** and Bob Marley. Along with **Malcolm McLaren** and **Vivienne Westwood**'s Let It Rock and **Sex** stores, Acme Attractions was the key store involved in **punk fashion** during the mid-1970s.

ADICTS

British punk rock group founded in Ipswich, Suffolk, England, in the mid-1970s by Singer Monkey (Keith Warren), guitarist Pete Davidson, Mel Ellis on bass, and Kid Dee (Michael Davidson) on drums. The Adicts are known for their colorful clown makeup and top hats, eerily reminiscent of *A Clockwork Orange*'s gang of Alex and his Droogs. The band continues to tour and record to this day.

Discography: *Songs of Praise* (Dwed, 1981); *Sounds of Music* (Cleopatra, 1982); *Bar Room Bop* (Fall Out, 1985); *Smart Alex* (Cleopatra, 1985); *This is your Life* (Fall Out, 1985); *Fifth Overture* (Fall Out, 1987); *Live and Loud* (Cleopatra, 1993); *Twenty-Seven* (Cleopatra, 1993); *Joker in the Pack* (Harry May); *Rise and Shine* (Captain Oi); *Rockets into Orbit* (Fallout/Jungle); *Mae in England* (SOS, 2005); *Rollercoaster* (SOS, 2005).

ADOLESCENTS

Poppy and melodic Southern California punk band known for songs such as "Amoeba." The original lineup consisted of Tony (Brandenburg) Cadena on vocals, Rikk Agnew on guitar, Frank Agnew on guitar, Steve Soto on bass, and Casey Royer on drums. After an early rough start, scenester **Rodney Bingenheimer** played their first single, "Amoeba," on his influential *Rodney on the Rock* radio program and championed the Adolescents. The band released their self-titled debut record in 1981 to critical acclaim and healthy sales. Rikk Agnew soon departed, however, to record a solo record and play with goth band Christian Death. Steve Roberts replaced Agnew, but the band broke up in 1982. Royer went on to front **DI.** The Adolescents reunited in 1986 for a series of shows, but Frank Agnew left soon after, as did Royer, and the two were replaced by Alfie Agnew and Sandy Hansen, and that lineup recorded the *Brats in Battalions* album. After that album, Alfie Agnew and Tony Cadena quit the band, and Rikk Agnew and Soto took over lead vocals for the *Balboa Fun Zone* record before splintering again in 1989. Cadena toured with Adz and for a while. Rikk Agnew returned to Christian Death. The band sporadically reunites for tours and in 2005 released a new album with the lineup of Tony Cadena on lead vocals, Frank Agnew on guitar, Frank Agnew Jr. on guitar, Steve Soto on bass, and Derek O'Brien (formerly of **Social Distortion**) on drums. Lead singer Tony Cadena/Montana teaches third grade in California. The Adolescents are among the key early **hardcore** bands from California and are an important part of punk history, despite the almost *Spinal Tap*-like nature of their ever-changing lineup.

Discography: *Adolescents* (Frontier, 1981; Epitaph, 1997); *Brats in Battalions* (Triple X, 1987, 1994); *Balboa Fun Zone* (Triple X, 1988, 1994); *Live 1981 and 1986* (Triple X, 1989, 1994); *Return to the Black*

Hole (live; Triple X, 1997); *Live at the House of Blues* (Kung Fu, 2004); *The Complete Demos 1980–1986* (Frontier, 2005); *O.C. Confidential* (Finger Records, 2005). **Rikk Agnew:** *All by Myself* (Frontier, 1982, 2003); *Emotional Vomit* (Triple X, 1990, 1994); *Turtle* (Triple X, 1994).

ADVERTISING, USE OF PUNK IN

Even though it seems that punk and mass culture were naturally in opposition and that many punks regarded punk as naturally oppositional to mainstream culture, punk rock was eventually used in many mainstream television commercials and other kinds of advertisements. Starting in the mid-1990s, many punk songs were used in advertising, such as **"Search and Destroy"** by **Iggy and the Stooges,** "London Calling" by the **Clash,** and **"Blitzkrieg Bop"** by the **Ramones.** A long-standing argument in the punk community was whether punk rock could be used in advertising or whether this was an act of selling out. Some bands such as the Ramones saw no problem in selling their songs to advertisers, and "Blitzkrieg Bop" is almost as ubiquitous today at baseball stadiums as peanuts and Cracker Jack. Other uses of punk songs in advertisements were initially more surprising, such as the many **Iggy Pop** songs that were used to sell products as diverse as cars and cameras. The **Buzzcocks** and even **Black Flag** have allowed their songs to be used in commercials, and in 1991 Subaru famously tried to sell a car as being "like punk rock."

A secondary issue regarding punk and advertising is how much advertising was generally accepted by punk bands outside of mainstream culture. Although many in the punk scene relied on **flyers** and mentions in **zines** to get recognition, others advertised more aggressively and accepted promotional opportunities from different products, such as alliances with the **Vans Warped tour,** or placement of their songs in movies and video games. The Vans Warped tour is particularly controversial, but many punks accept this kind of corporate sponsorship as a necessary evil, tolerated in order to finance large-scale punk tours and, as in the case of **Punkvoter.com,** to raise political awareness. This also brings up larger issues discussed in other entries, such as the relationship of punk and major labels and what kinds of advertisements were acceptable for certain zines. Many zines would not accept ads from major labels or would have a different pay scale for major label advertisements and independent label advertisements; some zines would not review major label releases on the logic that they had enough promotion without the additional support a zine could provide. Despite the seeming ubiquity of punk in advertising and mainstream culture, this is still a contentious issue for many in the disparate punk communities around the world, and the overall attitude toward the relationship between punk and advertising (and, indeed, between punk and commercial culture) has much to do with standards in individual scenes and the conscience of the individual within that community. It is also strange and somewhat puzzling that songs that have completely contradictory messages, such as Iggy Pop's "Lust for Life," which is primarily about injecting heroin, can be used to advertise the good life as epitomized by a cruise line or that the Buzzcocks' songs about repressed homosexual longing and rejection can be used to sell cars to (presumably) straight consumers. At advertising agencies to this day, many younger workers who grew up listening to punk rock and **hardcore** have no problem using punk music to sell products such as cars, despite the apparent contradictions. Ultimately, it is still too early to tell if the inadvertent exposure to punk rock on unwitting consumers, which may lead to more fans for punk rock bands and the punk notions of authenticity, or whether the use of pun songs in advertisements will just turn into another commodity to be used to sell soap.

ADVERTS

Early English punk band from the first wave of punk, lead by front man T. V. Smith and bassist Gaye Advert. The band, which was originally going to be called One Chord Wonders (the title of the first Adverts single), was best known for their single "Gary Gilmore's Eyes." The Adverts released their first album, *Crossing the Red Sea with the Adverts*, in February 1978. It featured T. V. Smith on vocals, Gaye Advert on bass, Laurie Driver on drums (later replaced by Rod Latter and later Rick Martinez), Howard Pickup on guitar (later replaced by Paul Martinez), and latter-day keyboard player Tim Cross. The band endured unfair criticism about having a woman in the band, and Gaye Advert was used as a reluctant sex symbol in advertising and in music magazines. The Adverts were one of the first bands to criticize the growing conformity within the British punk scene and had already made considerable musical strides by the time of their demise. The band called it quits by 1980, and T. V. Smith went on to a sporadic and lengthy solo career.

Discography: *Crossing the Red Sea with the Adverts* (UK Bright, 1978; UK Butt, 1982; UK Link Classics, 1990; Phantom, 1997; Fire Records UK, 2002); *Cast of Thousands* (Anagram Punk, 1980; Anagram Punk UK, 1999; Fire Records UK, 2005); *The Peel Sessions* EP (UK Strange Fruit, 1987); *Live at the Roxy* (UK Receiver, 1990, 1999); *Radio 1 Sessions* (Pilot, 1997); *The Best of the Adverts* (Anagram Punk UK, 1999); *The Wonders Don't Care* (Pilot, 2001); *Live and Loud* (Step 1, 2002; Harry May, 2005); *Anthology* (Fire Records UK, 2003); *The Punk Singles Collection* (Anagram Punk UK, 2004).

AFRO-PUNK

A film by James Spooner, with the full title *Afro-Punk: The Rock and Roll Nigger Experience*, details the tribulations and prejudice suffered by black and other minorities within the punk community. Although the film largely follows four underground punks, there are also interviews with members of Fishbone and the **Dead Kennedys.** The film has a Web site at http://www.afropunk.com.

AGENT ORANGE

Surf guitar punk band from Placentia, California, formed in 1979 and led by longtime scene stalwart Mike Palm. Best know for its electrifying first album, *Living in Darkness*, and the surf-punk classic "Bloodstains" (years later, the **Offspring** in their hit song "Keep 'em Separated" paid tribute to the distinctive riff in "Bloodstains"). Original bassist Steve Soto went on to form the **Adolescents.** Although the band was influential in Californian **hardcore,** they never capitalized on their success. The band has reunited in recent years and was touring as of 2005.

Essential Discography: *Living in Darkness* (Restless, 1992); *Real Live Sound* (Restless, 1997); *This is the Voice* (Restless, 1997); *When You Least Expect It* (Restless, 1997); *Sonic Snake Session* (Restless Records, 2003).

AGNOSTIC FRONT

New York City's seminal activist, skinhead, **hardcore** band fronted by Roger Miret and featuring longtime guitarist Vinnie Stigma, bassist Rob Kabula, and drummer Rob Cryptcrash (later replaced by Ray "Raybeez" Barberi, later of **Warzone,** and then by a variety of others) that performed regularly at the **CBGB's** hardcore matinees during the mid- to late 1980s. In the mid-1980s, with the addition of a second guitar player, Stigma stopped actually playing guitar, and the band became more metallic, writing songs with guitarist Pete Steele of Carnivore. The band had a resurgence on the **Epitaph** label in the late 1990s and continues today with various shifts in personnel. Their classic first album, *Victim in Pain*, contained numerous skinhead anthems. By the second album, *Cause for Alarm*, the band had moved in a more metallic direction that reflected the band's internal turmoil at the time. The next album, *Liberty & Justice . . .* , was a return to form, but Miret went to jail for two years following the completion of the album, derailing the band's momentum at a crucial point. The latest lineup of the band that recorded for Epitaph records was Miret, Stigma, Jimmy Colettei on drums,

Agnostic Front was the prototypical New York City hardcore band. *Photofest.*

and Mike Gallo on bass. The band performs sporadically, and lead singer Roger Miret performs with his new band, Roger Miret and the Disasters.

Discography: *Live in New York* (Combat, 1983); *Victim in Pain* (Relativity, 1984; Combat Core, 1986); *Cause for Alarm* (Relativity, 1986); *Liberty & Justice For . . .* (Combat, 1987; Relativity, 1991); *Live at CBGB* (Combat, 1989; Relativity, 1990); *Cause for Alarm/Victim in Pain* (Relativity, 1991); *One Voice* (Relativity, 1992, 1999); *To Be Continued: The Best of Agnostic Front* (Relativity, 1992); *Last Warning* (Relativity, 1993); *Raw Unleashed* (Grand Theft Auto, 1995); *Raw* (Grand Theft Auto, 1996); *Something's Gotta Give* (Epitaph, 1998); *Riot, Riot, Upstart* (Epitaph, 1999); *Dead Yuppies* (Epitaph, 2001); *Do or Die! Rage and Live Tracks* (Dk, 2002); *Working Class Heroes* (Knockout, 2003); *Another Voice* (Nuclear Blast, 2005). **Madball:** *Ball of Destruction* EP (In Effect/Relativity, 1989).

AKRON, OHIO

Many smaller cities across the United States were fertile homes for music scenes that one would not necessarily expect from their geographic locations. Akron, Ohio, was home to two bands that created early permutations of punk rock and experimental music: the Bizaros and the later, much more popular **Devo.**

ALBINI, STEVE

Controversial producer, musician, and punk and indie theorist as well known for his production techniques (low-fi and low involvement by the producer) as for his clients (everyone from **Nirvana** to Robert Plant) and his bands (**Big Black,** Rapeman, Shellac) and his feuds (almost anyone he has come in contact with over the last two decades). Albini is a polarizing and often obnoxious punk foil but also an important figure on the punk and indie scenes and would have been regarded as such if his career had simply ended after fronting the seminal noise band Big Black. Albini continued as a producer and musician, however, and after forming the short-lived (and controversial) band Rapeman, he returned to form with the more adventurous Shellac.

ALL

Experimental, musically bewildering, and jazz-inflected group formed by the remaining members of the **Descendents** when Milo Auckerman left to return to graduate school. Perhaps the tightest and most musically adept group outside of the **Bad Brains,** despite a rotating cast of lead singers (Dave Smalley followed by Scott Reynolds and Chad Price). The band was also inspired by the philosophy of life developed by Bill Stevenson and friend Pat McCuistion after a revelation from the basemaster general. The band, led by master drummer Stevenson and including guitarist Stephan Egerton and bassist Karl Alvarez, took its name from the title of the last Descendents record and Bill Stevenson's motto (borrowed from Bill's fisherman friend Pat McCuistion) about always going for "ALL." The original singer was Dave Smalley of **DYS, Down by Law,** and the first incarnation of **Dag Nasty,** who had left Dag Nasty to take a graduate fellowship in Israel. Smalley the left the band after *Allroy for President* EP to form his own band, Down by Law. The band also recorded an album as TonyAll with ex-Descendent Tony Lombardo and Reynolds and bassist songwriter Karl Alvarez singing songs Lombardo had recorded about girls and breakups. Stevenson, Alvarez, and Egerton moonlight in numerous other bands (including the Lemonheads) and continue to be in high demand as producers of other bands from their Fort Collins, Colorado, base. The three core members also periodically reunite with Descendents singer Milo Auckerman for Descendents projects and tours. The All family grew to an extended family with the additions of key roadies Bug and Gooch. All is apparently on extended hiatus while the members pursue other projects.
Discography: *Allroy Sez . . .* (Cruz, 1988); *Allroy for Prez . . .* (Cruz, 1988); *Allroy's Revenge* (Cruz, 1989); *Trailblazer* (Cruz, 1990); *Allroy Saves* (Cruz, 1990); *Percolater* (Cruz, 1992); *Breaking Things* (Cruz, 1993); *Pummel* (Interscope/Atlantic, 1995); *Mass Nerder* (Epitaph, 1998); *Greatest Hits* (Owned & Operated, 1999); *Problematic* (Epitaph, 2000); *Live Plus One* (Epitaph, 2001). **TonyAll:** *New Girl, Old Story* (Cruz, 1991).

ALLIN, G.G.

Legendary and notorious for his drug and alcohol fueled escapades and so-called performances in which few songs where played, G.G. Allin chased audience members with sanitary napkins and human feces. He put out numerous recordings with his band the Murder Junkies but is far better known for his life and early death. G.G. started off as a fairly pedestrian version of **Iggy Pop,** confronting the audience and breaking glasses, but soon his antics increased until he was rarely completing an entire set. Usually after two or three songs, G.G. Allin would defecate on stage and chase audience members around with clumps of his own feces in each hand. Occasionally, he would eat or throw women's used sanitary napkins as well. G.G. promised to kill himself onstage on October 31, 1987, but after a women in the crowd alleged that G.G. Allin had assaulted and burned her, G.G. was arrested and eventually served three years in prison, where the date of his promised suicide came and went without incident. After his release, G.G. resumed touring with his band the Murder Junkies featuring his brother Merle and played in any club foolish or naive enough to book him. After returning to New York City at the commencement of their tour, Allin played a show at the Gas Station Club in Alphabet City in New York and subsequently overdosed on a combination of drugs. The film *Hated: G. G. Allin and the Murder Junkies* was made about G.G., and includes his notorious performance at New York University. After G.G. Allin's demise, his former roadie Evan Cohen wrote a book, *I Was a Murder Junkie,* detailing his work on G.G. Allin's last tour across the United States. G.G. Allin's brother

Merle continues to tour with the Murder Junkies and keep the legacy of G. G. Allin alive by selling assorted G. G. merchandise and memorabilia to fans who can't get enough of the legend.
Discography: G. G. Allin and the Jabbers: *Always Was, Is and Always Shall Be* (Orange, 1980; Black & Blue, 1988; Halycon, 1998); *Public Animal #1* EP (Orange, 1982; Black & Blue, 1998); *No Rules* EP (Orange, 1983); *Banned in Boston, Vols. 1 & 2* (Black & Blue, 1989, 1998). **G. G. Allin and the Scumfucs:** *Eat My Fuc* (Blood, 1984; Black & Blue, 1988, 1998); *Hard Candy Cock* EP (Blood, 1984); *I Wanna Fuck Your Brains Out* EP (Blood, 1985). **G. G. Allin and the Scumfucs/Artless:** *G. G. Allin and the Scumfucs/Artless* (Ger. Starving Missle/Holy War, 1985). **G. G. Allin:** *Live Fast, Die Fast* EP (Black & Blue, 1984, 1998); *Hated in the Nation* (ROIR, 1987, 1992, 1994, 1998); *Freaks, Faggots, Drunks & Junkies* (Homestead, 1988; Aware One, 1994); *Suicide Sessions* (Awareness, 1989; Aware One, 1998); *Doctrine of Mayhem* (Black & Blue, 1990); *Anti-Social Personality Disorder: Live* (Evergreen, 1993); *Brutality and Bloodshed for All* (Alive, 1993); *Dirty Love Songs* (New Rose Blues, 1994); *War in My Head* (Aware One, 1995); *Aloha from Dallas* (Roir, 1995; Last Call, 2002); *Hated* (soundtrack; Aware One, 1995);*Carnival of Excess* (Rockside Media, 1996); *Terror in America* (live; Alive, 1996); *Boozin' & Pranks* (live; Black & Blue, 1998); *Res-Erected* (live; Roir, 1999); *Singles Collection, Vol. 1* (Temperance, 1999); *Troubled Troubadour* (Aware One, 2000); *Rock 'n' Roll Terrorist* (Last Call, 2003); *Expose Yourself: The Singles Collection 1977–1991* (Aware One, 2004). **G. G. Allin and the Holy Men:** *You Give Love a Bad Name* (Homestead, 1987; Aware One, 1995). **G. G. Allin & Antiseen:** *Murder Junkies* (New Rose Blues, 1994; Last Call, 2002; TKO Round 2004).

ALTERNATIVE TENTACLES

San Francisco independent record label operated by **Jello Biafra,** lead singer of the **Dead Kennedys.** The label was started in June 1979 and released not only the Dead Kennedys' catalog but also records by NoMeansNo, **Butthole Surfers,** Neurosis, Leftover Crack, and the long-lost Los Angeles space alien band **Zolar X** as well as more political work such as the spoken-word recordings of founder Jello Biafra and radical historian Howard Zinn. Jello Biafra remains the owner, even though he lost the rights to the name Dead Kennedys in a bitter lawsuit with his ex-bandmates. The label relocated to Emeryville, California, in 2002 and continues to release music by a variety of bands as well as books, T-shirts, and other punk and underground products.

ALTERNATIVE TV

Experimental punk and **postpunk** band led by Mark Perry, former editor of the influential **zine** *Sniffin' Glue,* on vocals, guitar, and tapes; Alex Fergussen on guitar; Tyrone Thomas on bass; Chris Bennett on drums; and a contribution from youthful Jools Holland on keyboards. Alternative TV was an experimental and Frank Zappa–influenced band that tried to make punk live up to its promise to actually break rules as opposed to making them. Their poppiest and best-known song was the classic "Action Time Vision." The band went through various personnel changes and eventually called it quits in March 1979.
Discography: *The Image Has Cracked* (UK Deptford Fun City, 1978); *Vibing up the Senile Man (Part One)* (UK Deptford Fun City, 1979); *Live at the Rat Club '77* (UK Crystal/Red, 1979); *Action Time Vision* (UK Deptford Fun City, 1980); *Strange Kicks* (IRS, 1981); *Peep Show* (UK Anagram, 1987); *Splitting in 2* (UK Anagram, 1989); *Sol* EP (UK Chapter 22, 1990); *Dragon Love* (UK Chapter 22, 1990). **Here & Now/Alternative TV:** *What You See . . . Is What You Are* (UK Deptford Fun City, 1978). **Good Missionaries:** *Fire from Heaven* (UK Deptford Fun City, 1989). **Mark Perry:** *Snappy Turns* (UK Deptford Fun City, 1981).

AMATEUR PRESS ASSOCIATION

Nonprofit organization of independent journals, **zines,** and amateur journalists founded in 1936 to promote the circulation of low-budget and underground journals and zines to a wider audience. Several zines are jointly written by members and traded and shared using a central mailer to get the finished product out to group members. The original organization was a prototype of the zine revolution of the 1970s and a precursor to online discussion lists and Listservs. Many of these zines were originally generated by fans of science fiction, movies, and comic books, which were the subjects of many of the original zines from the 1930s onward. The roots of the organization go back to the 1890s in the United States and Britain, although a U.S. association may have been active in Philadelphia several decades earlier. The Amateur Press Association is important because it provides an outlet for sharing and creative expression and demonstrates that the punk **DIY** aesthetic predated punk by decades in many respects and that many punks are unaware of the legacy of early zine publishers and independent writers.

ANARCHY

In the political sense, anarchy is a concept relating to individual human freedom from government control. Many punks were attracted to the concept of anarchy, even if their knowledge of the political ramifications of the philosophy were vague. The ubiquitous *A* for anarchy symbol could be found in numerous punk logos, on T-shirts, and spray painted on walls throughout England and the United States during the late 1970s and early 1980s. Numerous artists openly espoused anarchy in their music, including the **Sex Pistols** with **"Anarchy in the UK"** and the **Exploited** with "I Believe in Anarchy." Their actual commitment to anarchy is questionable, however, especially in the case of the Sex Pistols, who signed to a major label. Some bands such as **Crass** and **Rudimentary Peni** were also involved in anarchist organizations and promoted the concept consistently in their music and lifestyle.

"ANARCHY IN THE UK"

One of the key punk singles by the **Sex Pistols** and one that epitomized the nature of punk and some of its constructive **nihilism.** The single was originally released in December 1976 on EMI (before EMI subsequently dropped the band). Although many complained that it did not capture the raw fury of the Sex Pistols' live performances, the debut single rose to number 38 on the British charts, which demonstrates how difficult it was for punk rock to break out at that time; in England, at least, that would change within several months. The song went on to become one of the most famous songs in punk history and has been covered by thousands of bands, including Megadeth and Mötley Crüe.

ANGELIC UPSTARTS

English punk band mentored by Jimmy Pursey of **Sham 69** and influenced by the political punk of the **Sex Pistols** and **Clash** with an emphasis on working-class issues. They released their debut record in July 1979, and the original lineup featured Mensi (Tommy Mensforth) on vocals, Mond on guitar, Steve Forsten on bass, and Decca Wade on drums. They also were prone to invasions from members of the British Fascist movement the **National Front,** who disrupted sets and shouted Nazi slogans. The band was also a proponent of the **DIY** aesthetic and released their first independent single, "The Murder of Liddle Towers," in 1978. The band was signed by Warner Brothers, and key supporter Pursey produced their first record, *Teenage Warning* in 1979. The band played many gigs and fought against racism until finally breaking up in 1983. The Angelic Upstarts have reformed many times and have gone through countless bass players and drummers. The band records and tours to this day with a new lineup.
Discography: *Teenage Warning* (UK Warner Bros., 1979; Captain Oi!, 2003); *We Gotta Get out of This Place* (UK WEA, 1980; Phantom, 2003); *2,000,000 Voices* (UK EMI, 1981; Captain Oi!, 2002); *Live*

(UK EMI, 1981); *Still from the Heart* (UK EMI, 1982; Castle Music UK, 1994; Import, 2003); *Reason Why?* (UK Anagram, 1983; Import, 2001); *Angel Dust (The Collected Highs 1978–1983)* (UK Anagram, 1983, 1999); *Last Tango in Moscow* (UK Picasso, 1984; UK Razor 1988; Captain Oi!, 2000); *Live in Yugoslavia* (Picasso, 1985; Griffin, 1995); *Power of the Press* (UK Gas, 1986; UK Link Classics, 1990; Step 1, 2001); *Bootlegs and Rarities* (UK Dojo, 1986); *Blood on the Terraces* (UK Link, 1987; Captain Oi!, 2000); *Brighton Bomb* (Chameleon, 1987); *Live and Loud!!* (UK Link, 1988; Harry May, 2005); *England's Alive* EP (UK Skunx, 1988); *Bombed Out* (Dojo, 1995); *Kids on the Street: Best Of* (Cleopatra, 1998); *Who Killed Liddle?* (Recall, 1999); *Independent Punk Singles Collection* (Anagram, 1999); *BBC Punk Sessions* (Captain Oi!, 2000); *Never Ad Nothing* (Harry May, 2000); *Lost and Found* (Harry May, 2000, 2002); *Rarities* (Captain Oi!, 2000); *EMI Punk Years* (Captain Oi!, 2000); *Live from the Justice League* (TKO, 2001); *Greatest Hits Live* (Harry May, 2002); *Collection* (EMI, 2002); *Sons of Spartacus* (Captain Oi!, 2002); *Anthems against Scum* (Import, 2002).

ANGRY SAMOANS

Los Angeles joke punk band led by "Metal" Mike Saunders (who claims to have coined the term *metal*) and guitarist Gregg Turner, best known for short, jokey, **hardcore** songs such as "My Old Man's a Fatso," "They Saved Hitler's Cock" (possibly an answer song to **Unnatural Axe**'s "They Saved Hitler's Brain"), and the ode to compulsory blindness "Light's Out" (later covered by Boston **ska** band the Mighty Mighty Bosstones). The band sporadically gets back together and records to this day.
Discography: *Inside My Brain* EP (Bad Trip, 1980; PVC, 1987; Triple X, 1994); *Back from Samoa* (Bad Trip, 1982; PVC, 1987; Triple X, 1992); *Yesterday Started Tomorrow* EP (PVC, 1987; Triple X, 1992); *Gimme Samoa: 31 Garbage-Pit Hits* (CD; PVC, 1987); *STP Not LSD* (PVC, 1988; Triple X, 1992); *Live at Rhino Records* (Triple X, 1992); *Return to Samoa* (UK Shakin' Street, 1990); *The Unboxed Set* (Triple X, 1995); *The '90s Suck & So Do You* (Triple X, 1999). **Metal Mike:** *Plays the Hits of the 90's* EP (Triple X, 1991).

ANOTHER STATE OF MIND

Documentary film that chronicles the ill-fated tour by **Social Distortion** and **Youth Brigade** as they played, squabbled, and stayed in various punk **squats.** Although some (including **Mike Watt** of the **Minutemen** and Firehose) have criticized the movie for portraying an unrealistic portrayal of touring during the "econo-tour" days of punk rock, the film is a good historical look at some of the reality of touring when punk was not a major commodity and did not have tour support from record labels. The film is now available on DVD.

ANTHRAX

Popular Connecticut club known for allowing **hardcore** and **straight-edge** shows when many clubs would not allow them. Run by brothers Brian and Sean Sheridan, the Anthrax was located first in Stamford but eventually moved to Norwalk, where it hosted numerous shows featuring local bands like **76% Uncertain, Vatican Commandoes** (featuring a pre-techno Moby on guitar), and **Youth of Today,** before it moved to New York City. The Anthrax was a popular place for many in the punk scene who did not have the money or the time to journey all the way to New York City in order to see their favorite bands play and was one of a string of clubs across the United States that helped support touring punk in an age long before the Internet.

ANTI-CLUB

Los Angeles club where numerous punk bands played during the heyday of 1970s punk in Los Angeles.

ANTI-FLAG

Antiauthority, antireligion, and anticorporate culture band from Pittsburgh, Pennsylvania. They are among the most politically active bands in the current punk scene, and their constant desecration of the U.S. flag as a logo marks their stance outside mainstream U.S. society. The band was formed in the early 1990s by Justin Sane on guitar and vocals, Andy Flag on bass and vocals (later replaced by various bassists and later number two on bass and vocals), Pat Thetic on drums, and later Chris Head on guitar and vocals. The band remains resolutely anticapitalist and is one of the most politically active and consistent bands in modern punk rock.

Discography: *Die for the Government* (New Red Archives, 1996); *Their System Doesn't Work for You* (A-F, 1998); *A New Kind of Army* (Go-Kart, 1999); *Underground Network* (Fat Wreck Chords, 2001); *The Terror State* (Fat Wreck Chords, 2003); *Live at Fireside Bowl* EP (Liberation, 2003).

ANTI-NOWHERE LEAGUE

Notorious British punk band from the early 1980s formed by Animal and Magoo, two former motorcycle gang members, with Winston Blake on bass and PJ on drums joining early on. The band toured with the **Exploited** and other bands early on but is perhaps best known for an incident that occurred on tour with the **Damned** in 1981 in which in order to shock the room, Winston put a mayonnaise-covered carrot up his rectum and then proceeded to eat the carrot. The band's early records were banned for their lyrical content, and the Anti-Nowhere League survived by touring, as they were banned from *Top of the Pops*, and then went though various personnel changes due to internal and substance-abuse problems. The band changed into a new romantic direction for subsequent albums. The band disbanded in 1987, but after Metallica invited Animal onstage to sing the Anti-Nowhere League song "So What" with them, the band reunited in the early 1990s and currently tours with Animal, PJ, and Jez on guitar and Shady on bass. Although the band is an important early punk band, they will probably be best remembered for their antics.

Discography: *We Are . . . The League* (WXYZ, 1982); *Live in Yugoslavia* (ID, 1983); *Long live the League* (ABC, 1985); *RIP* (Dojo, 1985); *Perfect Crime* (GWR, 1987); *Live and Loud!* (Link, 1990); *The Horse is Dead* (Receiver, 1996); *Scum* (Pavement, 1998); *Out of Control* (Receiver, 2000); *So What* (Harry May, 2000); *Return to Yugoslavia* (Knock Out, 2001); *Live Animals* (Step 1, 2002); *I Hate People . . . Long Live the League* (Hary May, 2002).

ANTI-PASTI

British punk band from the early 1980s that released only a few albums of punk protest before breaking up. The self-titled third album is a singles collection. The band regained prominence when a member of a British boy band was seen wearing an Anti-Pasti t-shirt in a video.

Discography: *Four Sore Points* EP (UK Rondelet, 1980); *The Last Call . . .* (Shatter, 1981); *Caution in the Wind* (UK Rondelet, 1982); *Anti-Pasti* (UK Rondelet, 1983).

AOD

New Jersey **hardcore** punk band, also known as Adrenalin OverDrive, largely active in the mid- to late 1980s and known for its humor, hyperfast music, and garish outfits. They gradually evolved into a more melodic band as they progressed and experimented with metal, pop, and psychedelic music. The band was started in the early 1980s by vocalist Paul Richards, bassist Jack Steeples, Jim Foster on guitar (Foster was later replaced by guitarist and vocalist Bruce Wingate for the final record), and Dave Scott on drums.

Discography: *The Wacky Hijinks of . . .* (Buy Our Records, 1984); *Humungousfungousamongus* (Buy Our Records, 1986); *Cruising with Elvis in Bigfoots UFO* (Buy Our Records, 1988); *Ishtar* (Restless, 1989); *Sittin' Pretty* (Grand Theft Audio, 1995).

A7

New York City club where bands such as **Bad Brains** played many of their early New York shows. During the early days of **hardcore** in New York City, the club played host to numerous bands and was a frequent gathering place for many of the often underage punks who populated New York's East Village and Lower East Side during the early 1980s. The club was also occasionally known for drug use and **violence** due to the large population of homeless punks who lived in nearby Tompkins Square Park. The club closed for good during the mid-1980s, and the neighborhood has changed so drastically that the punk community has almost completely left the area (except for Tompkins Square Park).

AVAIL

Ferocious hardcore band headquartered in Richmond, Virginia. Avail is known for having one of the most energetic and ferocious live shows in U.S. post-**hardcore,** augmented by "Cheerleader" Beau Beau, who dances manically on stage as the band performs, and was one of the most popular bands of the late 1990s. The band was originally formed in Washington, D.C., in the late 1980s with Joe Banks on guitar, Tim Barry on drums, and several other members who quickly quit. After a band reconfiguration and a move to a new headquarters in Richmond, Virginia (which figures prominently in the bands' lyrics), Tim Barry took over lead vocal duties, Ed Trask was added on drums, and the enigmatic Gwomper was added on bass. Avail straddled the line between the more experimental bands and the straight-out harder punk bands in the **Washington, D.C.,** scene during the late 1980s and played gigs with almost every luminary of the scene. The band is also known for its intensely personal lyrics.
Discography: *Satiate* (Lookout, 1992); *Dixie* (Lookout, 1994); *4 AM Friday* (Lookout, 1996); *The Fall of Richmond* EP (Lookout, 1997); *Over the James* (Lookout, 1998); *V.M. Live* (Liberation, 1999); *One Wrench* (Fat Wreck Chords, 2000); *Front Porch Stories* (Fat Wreck Chords, 2002); *Live at the Kings Head Inn* (Old Glory, 1999).

AVENGERS

Early U.S. punk band led by singer Penelope Houston, who opened for the **Sex Pistols** during their U.S. tour stop at Winterland in San Francisco along with another female-led punk band, the **Nuns.** The original band consisted of Penelope Houston on vocals, Danny Furious on drums, Greg Ingraham on guitar, and Jonathan Postal (replaced by Jimmy Wisley) on bass. The band parlayed the androgynous look and a particularly U.S. brand of punk that was not always well received during the Avengers time period due to the resistance to punk in general as well as inherent sexism within the U.S. punk rock scene. The band released little legitimate material during its lifetime, and various releases of their album, usually poor-quality bootlegs, had been floating around for years until the official release on **Lookout Records** years after the fact. After the dissolution of the Avengers, Penelope Houston became a prolific solo artist and toured sporadically with various incarnations of the Avengers and her own band.
Discography: *Avengers* EP (White Noise, 1978,+ 1981); *Avengers* (CD Presents, 1983); *The Avengers Died for Your Sins* (Lookout!, 2000). **Penelope Houston:** *Birdboys* (Subterranean, 1988).

BACK DOOR MAN

Influential early punk **zine** from **Los Angeles** started by Phast Phreddie (Fred Patterson) that covered the locals scene in Hollywood as well as wrote about influential early punk and garage music and bands such as **Iggy Pop, Pere Ubu,** Roxy Music, and Brian Eno. The magazine provided valuable information to the first generation of Los Angles punks who could rely on no real radio or mainstream coverage of music for information on the new scene. Phast Phreddie was also a popular DJ and emcee and was a key player in the early Los Angeles punk scene.

BAD BRAINS

Incendiary but internally troubled Rastafarian-**hardcore** band that was extremely influential on both the **New York** and **Washington, D.C.,** scenes. The band was formed in Maryland by a group of jazz-fusion-loving African Americans with no Caribbean influences. They took their name from a **Ramones** song, and soon Darryl Jennifer (bass), Gary "Dr. Know" Miller (guitar), Earl Hudson (drums), and Paul "H.R." Hudson (vocals) had left jazz fusion behind for what would become the ultimate hybrid of hardcore's acceleration with metallic crunch and spacey **dub reggae.** The band released as many groundbreaking works as duds and is especially known for the members' unmatched virtuosity and the electrifying performances of lead singer H.R. The band released the groundbreaking "Pay to Cum" single in 1980 and the Roir cassette *Bad Brains* in 1982, which influenced a generation of hardcore kids musically as well as spiritually.

Although Bad Brains started out as typical American middle-class suburbanites, they became Rastafarians (followers of a Jamaican religion that venerated Haile Selassie, the former emperor of Ethiopia, as God) after seeing the movie *Rockers* and a double bill of Stanley Clarke and Bob Marley, and they grew their hair out into dreadlocks and began speaking in Jamaican patois and eating according to Rastafarian dietary restrictions. In 1980, the band stayed in New York City (a move that was inspired by the book *Think and Grow Rich* by Napoleon Hill) and gigged, eventually becoming the tightest band in hardcore. They were invited by the **Damned** to tour England with them but were not allowed into that country and returned to the United States.

Bad Brains went back to Washington, D.C., to regroup but quickly returned to New York City, where they recorded the "Pay to Cum" single and opened for the **Clash** at the legendary Bond's Casino. The band went on a national tour to promote the Roir cassette but effectively ruined their career though erratic and intolerant behavior. In April 1982 in Texas, the Bad Brains had a problem when H. R. got into an altercation with singer Biscuit of the **Big Boys** over Biscuit's open homosexuality, and the band later stiffed the band in a marijuana deal. **MDC,** friends of the Big Boys, spread the word via **flyers** and newsletters warning the punk scenes of the Bad Brains' intolerance, and the Bad Brains became persona non grata to many punks. In 1982, however, the band met fan Ric Ocasek (from the **New Wave** band the Cars), who produced the album *Rock for Light* in 1982 for the Gem label, which quickly folded. After a brief breakup over whether to sign to Elektra records, the Bad Brains regrouped in 1986 for the powerful *I against I* on **SST** records. Although H. R. had been arrested for selling pot (he recorded the vocals for the song "Sacred Love" over the phone from jail), the record was a huge success in underground circles and best established the Bad Brains as musically light years ahead of their peers and many imitators. H. R. quit again, and the band continued without him, but he retuned in time to record vocals for the *Quickness* album in 1989 (Mackie from the **Cro-Mags** played drums, although Earl is featured on the cover). H. R. quit again, and the band recorded *Rise* with Israel Joseph I (Dexter Pinto) on lead vocals, although H. R. returned in time to record the *God of Love* album for Madonna's Maverick label. The band subsequently broke up, toured, and re-formed, this time as Soul Brains because they no longer had the right to use the name Bad Brains.

Although the Bad Brains are musically and perhaps ideologically one of the most important U.S. punk bands, they will probably also be remembered for their internal turmoil and emotional and philosophical problems that doomed the band to years of struggle. The band went through several lineup changes involving the Hudson brothers at various points. H. R. struggled for several years with questions of whether his Rastafarian beliefs fit in with the commercial nature of rock and roll or whether his beliefs even allowed the rhythms used in rock and roll. (Many Rastafarians believe that only a pure form of reggae music is spiritually acceptable, and there are many in the movement who feel that even Bob Marley went too far in the direction of secular, nonreggae music. *See also* Reggae.) According to other sources, H. R. also struggled with overuse of drugs and perhaps emotional or psychological problems that led to arrest and arguments and physical altercations with everyone from fellow bandmates, to members of other groups, and even to record executives. Although Bad Brains never achieved their true potential, they remain one of the most influential bands in punk, hardcore, heavy metal, and hard rock, and new bands are influenced by the work of these seminal hardcore icons.

Select Discography: *Bad Brains* (tape; Roir, 1982; Dutch East India Trading, 1991; Roir, 1996); *Bad Brains* EP (UK Alternative Tentacles, 1982); *I and I Survive* EP (Important, 1982); *Rock for Light* (PVC, 1983; Caroline, 1991); *I against I* (SST, 1986); *Live* (SST, 1988); *Attitude: The Roir Sessions* (In-Effect/ Relativity, 1989); *Quickness* (Caroline, 1989); *The Youth Are Getting Restless* (Caroline, 1990); *Spirit Electricity* (SST, 1991); *Rise* (Epic, 1993); *God of Love* (Maverick/Warner Bros., 1995); *Black Dots* (Caroline, 1996); *Omega Sessions* (Victory Records, 1997); *Banned in D.C.: Bad Brains Greatest Riffs* (Caroline, 2003). **H. R.:** *Its About Luv* (Olive Tree, 1985; SST, 1988); *Human Rights* (SST, 1987); *H. R. Tapes '84–'86* (SST, 1988); *Singin' in the Heart* (SST, 1989); *Charge* (SST, 1990).

BAD RELIGION

Bad Religion has long been one of the most politically active, lyrically dense, and melodically driven bands in the history of punk rock and **hardcore** music and is also one of the most prolific. The band is well known for the multisyllabic lyrics of guitarist Mr. Brett and lead singer (and Ph.D. candidate) Greg Graffin and their classic albums that maintained a melodic but still musically ferocious edge to punk rock, such as *No Control, Suffer,* and *Stranger than Fiction.* The band

Bad Religion, one of the most politically active punk bands, helped keep punk alive during the mid-1980s. *Photofest.*

had several radio and **MTV** charting songs such as "21st Century (Digital Boy)," "Infected," and "Stranger than Fiction." For some time during the 1990s, while the band was signed to a major label, Bad Religion was considered to be one of the more apparent breakthrough punk bands. Bad Religion was originally formed in 1980 in Southern California in the San Fernando Valley by students Greg Graffin and "Mr." Brett Gurewitz (who also founded and runs **Epitaph,** one of the most successful and profitable independent record labels in punk history), along with Jay Bentley on bass and Pete Finestone on drums. The band started to get noticed when a 15-year-old Graffin gave Greg Hetson from the **Circle Jerks** a demo tape that indicated how much raw talent could be found in Bad Religion. The band released its first EP, the eponymous *Bad Religion*, in 1981, followed by the somewhat more melodic *How Could Hell Be Any Worse?*, which was released later that year. After touring Southern California and becoming one of the more popular live acts of the early 1980s, the band evidently became disillusioned with the limitations inherent in the punk scene, and with Graffin away at college at the University of Wisconsin in 1983, Bad Religion went though a radical change of musical direction, releasing the keyboard driven and confusing (at least to punk fans of the time) *Into the Unknown*. That album may have been a daring move for any punk band, and many in the punk and **hardcore** scenes at the time were convinced that the for-mulaic nature of punk was holding back any real innovation, but for fans who had become accus-tomed to the Bad Religion sound, the release of the album was tantamount to heresy. The album, which closely follows the template created by **New Wave** bands such as **Devo,** is not as much of a departure as one would expect today, but at the time it was almost unthinkable for a hardcore band. Sad truisms about punk and hardcore are that too often the music becomes calcified and fans generally disapprove of experimentation. Bentley briefly left the band during this period, and the band went on hiatus following the critical pans given to *Into the Unknown*. (*Into the Unknown* was eventually deleted by Epitaph and is still not available legally.) In 1984, the band was re-formed at the suggestion of Circle Jerks guitarist Greg Hetson (who had previously provided a guitar solo to the song "Part III" on the first album), with Hetson on second guitar, and released the far more orthodox punk *Back to the Known* EP, which was partially made to demonstrate to their fans that Bad Religion was now back and ready to resume in the same style they had left off earlier. After another hiatus during which Graffin acquired a master's degree and started work on a Ph.D. at Cornell, the full quintet lineup of Graffin, Gurewitz, Hetson, Bentley, and Finestone was finally reestablished in 1988 for *Suffer*, the first release in a string of remarkable albums. In the 1980s and early 1990s, when most punk and hardcore acts had broken up, Bad Religion continued to tour and release records that were some of the most interesting and vital of the time. After punk rock was back on the radar of mass media in the early 1990s, Bad Religion was signed as of the *Recipe for Hate* album and debuted with the album *Stranger than Fiction*, which led to MTV videos for "Infected" and the remake of the earlier "Twenty-First Century (Digital Boy)."

After *Stranger than Fiction*, however, founder Mr. Brett left to work on running Epitaph full time and to deal with a drug problem. Mr. Brett was replaced by Brian Baker (of **Minor Threat, Dag Nasty,** and the embarrassing metal band Junkyard, which also featured Chris Gates of the **Big Boys**). With Baker in the mix, the band recorded several records and toured extensively, including several times on the **Vans Warped tour.** The band left Atlantic records in 2001 and re-signed with indie powerhouse Epitaph. Drummer Bobby Schayer also retired from the band that year and was replaced by Brooks Wackerman, formerly of **Suicidal Tendencies.** Bad Religion continued to record and perform and were one of the most lyrically challenging and consistently entertaining bands in punk history. They were major contributors to keeping the punk aesthetic alive during the lean years of the mid- to late 1980s.

Discography: *Bad Religion* EP (Epitaph, 1981); *How Could Hell Be Any Worse?* (Epitaph, 1982; remastered, Epitaph, 2004); *Into the Unknown* (Epitaph, 1983); *Back to the Known* EP (Epitaph, 1984); *Suffer* (Epitaph, 1988; remastered, Epitaph, 2004); *No Control* (Epitaph, 1989; remastered, Epitaph, 2004); *Against the Grain* (Epitaph, 1990; remastered, Epitaph, 2004); *80–85* (Epitaph, 1991); *Generator* (Epitaph, 1992; extra tracks and remastered, Epitaph, 2004); *Recipe for Hate* (Epitaph, 1993; Atlantic, 1993); *Stranger than Fiction* (Atlantic, 1994); *All Ages* (Epitaph, 1995); *The Gray Race* (Atlantic, 1996); *Tested* (live; Epic, 1997); *No Substance* (Atlantic, 1998); *The New America* (Atlantic, 2000); *The Process of Belief* (Epitaph, 2002); *The Empire Strikes First* (Epitaph, 2004).

BAGS

Early **Los Angeles** punk group formed in 1977 and led by Alice Bag on lead vocals, Crag Bag (Craig Lee, later of Catholic Discipline) and Rob Ritter (later of 45. Grave) on guitars, Terry "Dad" Bag (Terry Graham) on drums, and Pat Bag (Patricia Morrison, later of the **Gun Club,** the Sisters of Mercy, and the **Damned**) on bass. Later members included D.J. Bonebrake of **X** on drums, Geza X on guitar, and Jane Koontz on guitar .The band formed when Alice and Patricia met at an audition for **Kim Fowley**'s next project after the demise of the **Runaways** and decided they were better off forming a band on their own. The Bags were originally supposed to perform with bags over their heads in a bid for anonymity, but the plan was foiled when Darby Crash took the bag off of Alice Bag's head. The Bags appeared in Penelope Spheeris's *Decline of Western Civilization* before breaking up in 1980.

Discography: *Survive* 7" (Dangerhouse, 1978); *Disco's Dead* (Artifix, 2003).

BANGS, LESTER

Influential and often-imitated critic who wrote for *Creem Magazine* and many other publications. He had a love-hate relationship with punk rock and especially with Ur-punk **Lou Reed,** about whom Bangs often wrote. He was especially well known for his early interest in the English band the **Clash** and his disdain for the traces of racism and white supremacy that he saw in the nascent scene. Bangs was also a musician and wrote and played in Birdland with Mickey Leigh, **Joey Ramone**'s younger brother. Bangs died of an overdose of prescription drugs in 1981, and his work has been anthologized in two volumes, *Psychotic Reactions and Carburetor Dung* and *Mainlines, Bloodfeasts, and Bad Taste.* After Bangs's death, Leigh continued to perform in the band the Rattlers, performing some songs cowritten with Bangs. Bangs is as well known for his visionary, often surrealistic rants in his rock criticism as for his espousal of the rock-and-roll lifestyle, including the prerequisite substance abuse and fast living. His writing style is often imitated but rarely equaled, as was his lifestyle.

BATTALION OF SAINTS

U.S. **hardcore** band from San Diego, California, formed in the early 1980s that played in a style that emulated British bands such as **Discharge.** The band originally featured James Cooper on bass (later replaced by Dennis Frame, then Captain Scarlet, then Gregor Kramer, who left to rejoin the **UK Subs,** and was replaced by Ken Ortman), Chris Smith on guitar, Ted Olsen on drums (later replaced by Joey Maya, then by Mathew McCoy, and then by Mark Bender after McCoy left to rejoin UK Subs), and George Anthony on vocals. The band was originally founded by Anthony and Smith as the Nutrons in 1978 and then changed the name after a few lineup changes to Battalion of Saints in the early 1980s. The band broke up in 1984 when Smith left to join **Kraut;** he subsequently died of an overdose. The band went through numerous lineup changes and later re-formed in the late 1990s with only Anthony left from the original lineup. The band was briefly known as Battalion of Saints A.D. and featured a mostly British lineup of Anthony, Terry "Tezz" Bones (of Discharge and **Broken Bones**) on guitar, plus UK Subs members Kramer and McCoy. The band re-formed in 2004 with new members.

Discography: *Fighting Boys* EP (Nutrons, 1982); *Second Coming* (Nutrons/Enigma, 1984, 1995); *Rock in Peace: The Best of the Battalion of Saints* (Mystic, 1988, 1995); *Death-R-Us* (Taang!, 1995); *Best Of* (Mystic, 2003). **Battalion of Saints A.D.:** *Cuts* (Taang!, 1996).

BEAHM, PAUL

Original name of **Darby Crash,** lead singer of Los Angeles punk band the **Germs,** who is well known for his manipulative powers of persuasion, introspective lyrics, and often romanticized early death. Even before changing his name first to Bobby Pyn and then to Darby Crash, Beahm had been a powerful and influential student at the IPS program, a special program for gifted students at University High School, where he learned brainwashing techniques and talked very early of his eventual suicide. Beahm learned techniques of manipulation from his study of Friedrich Nietzsche and **nihilism.** The legacy of Paul Beahm's life is a tragically wasted musical talent cut short by drugs and mental illness. Several books have been published about Darby Crash and his life and times, including one novel and the book *Lexicon Devil* by **Brendan Mullen** and Don Bolles.

BEAT HAPPENING

Minimalist and intentionally amateurish band led by indie rock giant and **K Records** mastermind Calvin Johnson. The band is certainly punk occasionally but can be considered punk more by the **DIY** aesthetic of Johnson and collaborators Heather Lewis and Brett Lunsford played in a bassless trio (echoing a more childlike version of the **Cramps** on their early records). Several of the earliest releases are on cassette and difficult to find, but the band's essential material has been repackaged for CD in a variety of formats.

Select Discography: *Beat Happening* EP (tape; K, 1984); *1983–1985* (K/Feel Good All Over, 1990); *Beat Happening* (K, 1996).

BEEFEATER

Washington, D.C., political punk band that recorded for **Dischord Records** during the 1980s and were active in various Washington, D.C., political movements such as **Revolution Summer** in 1985. The band was started by singer Tomas Squib in 1984 with guitarist Fred Smith, bassist Doug Birdzell, and drummer Bruce Atchely. Beefeater, despite its name, was dedicated to vegetarianism and radical politics played in a punk-funk style that was quite rare in punk rock at the time. Squib was known for his energetic but pacifist shows, including one notorious show during which he stripped off all his clothes in an effort to quell an extraordinarily violent **pit.** The band was also dedicated to examining spirituality and living an honest punk life as opposed to simply talking and dressing like a punk.

Discography: *Plays for Lovers* (Dischord, 1985, 1995); *House Burning Down* (Dischord, 1986, 1995); *Need a Job* (Olive Tree, 1988).

BELUSHI, JOHN

Comedic actor and member of the original cast of NBC's *Saturday Night Live*. Belushi was a punk aficionado who championed punk bands such as **Black Flag** and **Fear** and was instrumental in getting Fear to appear on *Saturday Night Live* in 1981. The gig ended in a near riot when invited guest punks **Ian MacKaye** and John Joseph of the **Cro-Mags** led a group of **skinheads** and punks in a raucous pit that almost broke a camera and ended with MacKaye grabbing the microphone and shouting "New York sucks." Belushi was often seen sporting punk buttons on his jacket, and aside from the blues (which he parlayed into a secondary musical career with the band the Blues Brothers with Dan Aykroyd), he was one of the first mainstream champions of punk rock. He died of an overdose of cocaine and **heroin** (also known as a speedball).

BETTER YOUTH ORGANIZATION

Movement and record label started by the Stern brothers (Shawn, Mark, and Adam) of the band **Youth Brigade** in 1979. The Stern brothers tried to create a positive space where members of the punk rock community could release albums and play (the band also occasionally ran a club) outside of the corporate structure of the regular recording industry. The label released its first album, the compilation *Someone's Got Their Head Kicked In*, in 1982. The band then organized the Someone Got Their Head Kicked In tour with **Social Distortion**, which was later made into the notorious punk documentary *Another State of Mind.*

BIAFRA, JELLO

Lead singer (real name Eric Boucher) for the **Dead Kennedys**, author, activist, former mayoral candidate in San Francisco, and frequent collaborator with other musicians. When his career with the Dead Kennedys came to an end in the late 1980s, Biafra reinvented himself as a political activist and provocateur, sort of a punk rock storyteller, political comedian, and musician, who went on numerous tours of clubs and college campuses, spreading mischief and agitating against conformist and establishment politics. Biafra was also busy creating music with disparate collaborators, such as Al Jourgenson from Ministry (under the moniker Lard) and **Ian MacKaye** from **Fugazi,** as well as more straight-ahead punk material with **DOA,** NOMEANSNO, and Mojo Nixon on his Alternative Records label. Biafra was the target of a savage beating at the **Gilman Street** club in 1994 by young street punks who doubted his punk authenticity, but he did not let that stop his activism. In the late 1990s, Biafra was the subject of a contentious lawsuit filed against him by East Bay Ray, D.H. Pellilgro, and Klaus

Flouride, the other former members of the Dead Kennedys. He ultimately lost the case and the rights to the name Dead Kennedys, leading the rest of the band to re-form and tour without him. Biafra is a punk icon not only for his groundbreaking work with the Dead Kennedys, but also for his relentless activism and refusal to compromise his principles.

Select Solo Discography: *No More Cocoons* (Alternative Tentacles, 1987); *High Priest of Harmful Matter—Tales from the Trial* (Alternative Tentacles, 1989); *I Blow Minds for a Living* (Alternative Tentacles, 1991); *Beyond the Valley of the Gift Police* (Alternative Tentacles, 1994); *If Evolution is Outlawed, Only Outlaws Will Evolve* (Alternative Tentacles, 1998); *Become the Media* (Alternative Tentacles, 2001); *Machine Gun in the Clown's Hand* (Alternative Tentacles, 2002); *The Big Ka-Boom Part One* (Alternative Tentacles, 2002). **Witch Trials:** *The Witch Trials* EP (Subterranean/Alternative Tentacles, 1981). **Lard:** *The Power of Lard* EP (Alternative Tentacles, 1988); *The Last Temptation of Reid* (Alternative Tentacles, 1990); *Pure Chewing Satisfaction* (Alternative Tentacles, 1997). **Jello Biafra with D.O.A.:** *Last Scream of the Missing Neighbors* (Alternative Tentacles, 1990). **Jello Biafra with NOMEANSNO:** *The Sky Is Falling and I Want My Mommy* (Alternative Tentacles, 1991). **Tumor Circus:** *Tumor Circus* (Alternative Tentacles, 1991). **Jello Biafra with Plainfield:** *Jello Biafra with Plainfield* EP (Alternative Tentacles, 1993). **Jello Biafra with Mojo Nixon:** *Will the Fetus Be Aborted?* EP (Alternative Tentacles, 1993).

BIG BLACK

Confrontational and aggressively noisy band from Chicago led by the mercurial **Steve Albini** and considered one of the key bands in establishing the indie rock touring and musical blueprints of the 1980s. Big Black was started in 1982 with Albini and a drum machine, but after the *Lungs* EP, Jeff Pezzati came aboard on bass and Santiago Durango on guitar (who both played in the band Naked Raygun). After recording two EPs, Pezzati was replaced by Dave Riley. Big Black is perhaps best known not only for its aggressive and harsh music but also for the confrontational lyrics of provocateur Steve Albini, who turned a penchant for black humor into a career, and which led to accusations of racism and sexism against the band. In 1987, Durango left to go to law school, and the band decided to retire after releasing the *Songs about Fucking* album. Albini later formed the short-lived Rapeman and the longer-lasting Shellac after Big Black's demise. Today, Albini is one of the most sought-after engineers in music (technically, Albini is a producer but refuses to use the title in his recording), working on albums by **Nirvana,** Jesus Lizard, the **Pixies,** and even Robert Plant. Albini also remains a controversial figure because of his feuds with bands such as Urge Overkill and his adherence and love of all things analog, which have become almost as well known as his musical endeavors.

Discography: *Lungs* EP (Ruthless, 1982); *Bulldozer* (Ruthless, 1983); *Racer X* (Homestead, 1984); *Atomizer* (Homestead, 1986); *The Hammer Party* (Homestead, 1986); *Headache* (Touch & Go, 1987); *Atomizer* (Touch & Go, 1986); *Songs about Fucking* (Touch & Go, 1987); *Pigpile* (Touch & Go, 1992).

BIG BOYS

One of the first and most successful groups to merge funk rhythms with **hardcore** punk and a clear influence on many more successful bands such as the Red Hot Chili Peppers. This Austin, Texas, band was also notable for having openly gay members at a time when many in the punk community did not tolerate open homosexuality. The Big Boys redefined punk as more inclusive in terms of musicality and sexuality. The Big Boys first formed in Austin in 1978 with vocalist Biscuit (Randy Turner), guitarist Tim Kerr, bassist Chris Gates, and drummer Steve Colier (who was later replaced by Greg Murray, followed by Fred Schultz, and Rey Washam). The band gigged mostly in Texas, and although they released only on minor labels, their influence was felt around the country. In 1983, they were the opening band on the legendary Washington, D.C., Punk Funk Spectacular, which featured local go-go band Trouble Funk and **Minor Threat** in their last performance. The Big Boys were also known for the incident in which **Bad Brains** front man H. R. got into an altercation with Biscuit because of H. R.'s intolerance of homosexuality, leading to accusations and counteraccusations that effectively ruined Bad Brains' career in the punk underground. The band broke up in the mid-1980s, and guitarist Tim Kerr went on to form Poison 13 and remains a part of the Austin scene, mentoring younger bands. Bassist Gates went on to form the Los Angeles glam metal band Junkyard with Brian Baker of Minor Threat. Biscuit remained a popular artist in Austin until his untimely death on August 17, 2005.

Discography: *Recorded Live at Raul's Club* (split LP with the Dicks; Rat Race, 1980); *Where's My Towel* (Wasted Talent, 1981); *Fun, Fun, Fun ...* EP (Moment, 1982); *Lullabies Help the Brain Grow* (Moment/Enigma, 1983); *No Matter How Long the Line Is at the Cafeteria, There's Always a Seat* (Enigma, 1985); *Wreck Collection* (Unseen Hand, 1989; Gern Blandsten, 2002); *The Skinny Elvis* (Touch & Go, 1993); *The Fat Elvis* (Touch & Go, 1993).

BIG DRILL CAR

Loud and poppy punk band from Orange County, California, that recorded during the late 1980s to mid-1990s, mostly on Bill Stevenson's Cruz label. The band featured vocalist Frank Daly and guitarist Mark Arnold with a revolving rhythm section. The band broke up in the mid-1990s, and several members joined with John Kastner of the **Doughboys** to form the punk supergroup All Systems Go.

Discography: *Small Block* EP (Variant, 1988); *Album Type Thing* (also known as *Tape* or *CD Type Thing*; Cruz, 1989); *Batch* (Cruz, 1991); *Toured (A Live Album)* (Headhunter/Cargo, 1992); *No Worse for Wear* (Headhunter/Cargo, 1994).

BIGGS, RONNIE

Ronald Arthur Biggs (born August 8, 1928 [?]), usually called Ronnie Biggs, is best known as a participant in the Great Train Robbery in 1963 and as, briefly, a member of the disintegrating **Sex Pistols.** After escaping from a British prison and first fleeing to France and then to Australia and getting plastic surgery, he was forced to go into exile in Brazil in 1965, where England could not extradite him because his girlfriend was pregnant. After **Johnny Rotten** quit the Sex Pistols in 1978, the remaining members, Paul Cook and Steve Jones (minus a dope-sick **Sid Vicious**), flew down to Rio de Janeiro at the request of manager and provocateur **Malcolm McLaren** to record two songs and make a video with Biggs. The two resulting songs, "A Punk Prayer" and "No One Is Innocent," were released as an EP and also were included on the soundtrack of the Sex Pistols' posthumous film, *The Great Rock 'n' Roll Swindle,* in which the video with Biggs appears. The recordings with Biggs, who may well be guilty of murder, appeared to be another cheap publicity stunt by the publicity-savvy McLaren or can be seen as a true punk statement of rebellion against authority, depending on one's viewpoint. Biggs spent his years after the Sex Pistols as a fugitive celebrity, charging curious tourists money to meet him or have his picture taken with him. Biggs later recorded a song, "Carnival in Rio (Punk Was)," with Germany's **Die Toten Hosen** on their 1991 album *Learning English, Lesson One.* Biggs tired of life in exile in 2001 and returned to face charges England, where he was returned to prison. He is best known as a footnote to the Sex Pistols' career and another example of McLaren's attempts to milk the dying cow for all it was worth.

BIKINI KILL

Perhaps the best known and most dynamic of the so-called **Riot Grrrl movement** of the early to mid-1990s, Bikini Kill featured the sometimes screaming, sometimes cooing vocals of lead

singer **Kathleen Hanna** and extremely emotional and sometimes outright confrontational songs about gender, identity, and violence. Many of the songs were influenced by the degradation Hanna experienced as a stripper and her later work as a founder (along with Molly Neumann, Erin Smith, Allison Wolfe [later of **Bratmobile**] and Jen Smith) of *Riot Grrrl* zine, which published the first writings on Riot Grrrl and started a movement. The band also featured Kathi Wilcox on various instruments, drummer and sometime singer Tobi Vail, and guitarist Billy Karren. The band relocated from Olympia, Washington, to **Washington, D.C.,** in 1991 to take advantage of the far more hospitable D.C. scene. During their prime, Bikini Kill was one of the more important Riot Grrrl bands and worked to create a safe environment for women to actually participate in shows without being attacked or groped. Numerous Bikini Kill shows allowed "safe" places for women to dance creatively during the sets. The band recorded their first cassette by themselves but were soon signed to the progressive **Kill Rock Stars** label that was ideal for the confrontational punk rock that Bikini Kill was producing. Bikini Kill remained one of the most politically engaged bands of the 1990s. After the band's demise, Hanna went on to form the equally confrontational gender-questioning **Le Tigre.**
Discography: *Revolution Girl Style Now* (cassette; no label, 1991); *Bikini Kill EP* (Kill Rock Stars, 1992); *New Radion EP* (Kill Rock Stars, 1993); *Pussy Whipped* (Kill Rock Stars, 1994); *The C.D. Version of the First Two Records* (Kill Rock Stars, 1995); *Reject All American* (Kill Rock Stars, 1996).

BINGENHEIMER, RODNEY

Los Angeles scenemaker and DJ on L.A.'s influential **KROQ** radio station. Bingenheimer was an early proponent of both glam and punk rock and played numerous punk bands on his radio show before the styles were popular or had any mainstream exposure. Early in the 1970s, he ran a club called the English Disco, and he started playing punk music on KROQ in August 1976. Bingenheimer's life was analyzed in the documentary, *Mayor of the Sunset Strip*, released in 2004.

BLACK FLAG

Tremendously influential **Los Angeles hardcore** band, founded by guitarist **Greg Ginn** in 1979, that went through many lineup changes and is best known for both slowing down hardcore and combining it with the sludgy riffs of Black Sabbath and for the lyrics and unmatchable stage presence of latter-day lead singer **Henry Rollins.** The band is also largely responsible for establishing the ethos of touring regularly across the United States and contributed almost more than any other band to establishing a network of regionally connected scenes and **squats,** touring without major label promotion or tour support, and blazing the way for subsequent bands to follow the trail that Black Flag had helped to blaze across the country. The band's label, **SST,** was also one of the most influential punk labels of the early 1980s, and had numerous key bands signed at one point or another, including **Sonic Youth, Bad Brains,** the **Minutemen, Hüsker Dü,** and the **Meat Puppets.** Members of Black Flag, particularly Ginn, were keen on improvisation and jamming, and Ginn formed combos such as October Faction (a loose aggregation of players who could not hear each other) and a collaboration between Black Flag and the Minutemen called Minuteflag.

Black Flag, the band that probably best articulated the early hardcore sound, was founded as Panic by guitarist Greg Ginn in Hermosa Beach, California, after Ginn had become excited by the first **Ramones** album. Panic included **Keith Morris** (later to found the **Circle Jerks**) on vocals and Greg's brother, the artist **Raymond Pettibon,** on bass, and drummer Brian Migdol. Pettibon soon left the band and was replaced by Gary McDaniel, who changed his name to Chuck Dukowski in a thinly veiled tribute to the drunken writer Charles Bukowski. Robo, an illegal

Black Flag were the undisputed kings of Southern California hardcore and the hardest touring band in punk. © *Erica Echenberg/Redferns/Retna Ltd.*

alien from Colombia, replaced Migdol soon after, and the band jelled in its first lineup, and they recorded the *Nervous Breakdown* EP. After learning of a British band of the same name, the band changed its name to Black Flag at Pettibon's suggestion, named after the Black Flag, a symbol of anarchy. (Pettibon designed the band's logo, the waving black flag often referred to as "the bars," as well as numerous band **flyers** and album covers.) After an unsuccessful attempt to released the first record on pop label Bomp, Ginn formed SST records (out of a business he owned that sold radio and electronics parts) to release the *Nervous Breakdown* EP. Black Flag made its official public debut at an outdoor Parks Department concert at Hollywood Park, where the band was met by a hostile, food-throwing crowd that did not get Black Flag (to the crowd's credit, Ginn had booked the band there claiming that they were a Fleetwood Mac cover band). The band soon started playing with like-minded bands and released the Minutemen's *Paranoid Time* EP, cementing a long partnership between the two bands. The band had a setback when Morris departed the band in August 1979, but the members recruited Ron Reyes (Chavo Pederast), the drummer from teen punk rock band **Red Kross (Red Cross),** to record the *Jealous Again* EP. During a show at the Fleetwood in Los Angeles, Reyes quit midset, and the band went into an epic version of "Louie Louie" to pacify the crowd. Yet another former member of Red Kross, guitarist Dez Cadena, took over on vocals, and Black Flag began to play much more frequently. The band soon gained a reputation as a violent band when police and punks clashed outside a show at the Whiskey on Sunset Boulevard in Los Angeles, which led to even more police surveillance and harassment and eventually to Black Flag's name becoming synonymous with "punk violence" at Los Angles punk shows. The band recorded several singles with Dez before he decided to move to guitar in July 1981, and the band recruited superfan Henry Garfield (who later adopted the name Rollins, who along with friend **Ian MacKaye** had often driven from Washington, D.C., to New York City to catch Black Flag whenever they were in the area) as their new vocalist after an audition in New York. Rollins then toured with the band, learning the new songs under Dez's tutelage. Black Flag toured relentlessly, and Rollins soon gained a reputation for confronting the crowds, which heaped abuse on him. In 1981, the band recorded the album *Damaged*, a punk classic, with SST house producer Spot, which featured the famous cover image of Rollins smashing his fist into a mirror, with blood apparently dripping from his hand. Greg Ginn had made a deal with a small label, Unicorn, to distribute the album, but the parent label, MCA, objected and declared the album "antifamily," which the band promptly made into a sticker and placed it on the album. After a disastrous tour of England that found the band almost starving, the now-departed Robo was replaced briefly by Bill Stevenson, then by Emil, who lasted for one or two recording sessions, and then Chuck Biscuits of **DOA,** who stayed in the band for six months before being fired by the workaholic Ginn. Because **Descendents** singer Milo Auckerman was in college and the Descendents in limbo, Bill Stevenson rejoined the group, just in time for legal wrangling with Unicorn that put the band in recording limbo. Aside from the nonlabeled *Everything Went Black* compilation of early material (which led to brief incarceration for Ginn and Dukowski), the band was unable to record till 1984. In the meantime, the band went through stylistic and musical changes, with Rollins and Ginn growing their hair and the band starting to move in a slower, more metallic direction, as evidenced by the next release, *My War*, which demonstrated the band at its most experimental, especially on side two, with three grindingly slow songs that may have been too much for fans to process. Kira Roessler eventually replaced Dukowski (who had been replaced briefly by Dale Nixon, a pseudonym for guitarist Greg Ginn, who played bass on the *My War* album) on the next several records and added some adventurous bass lines that complemented and grounded Ginn's radical experimentation. The band at first lived on starvation wages, eating paste sometimes and stealing food other times, along with most of the SST staff and their faithful roadie Mugger (Steve Corbin), who also played in the frequent Black Flag opening band Nig Heist (with Ginn, Dukowski, and Stevenson). Rollins continued with his bodybuilding, and his lyrics became both more convoluted and more personal as time went on, and his stage presence became more aggressive and confrontational. The band released two more increasingly metallic and complex records, *Loose Nut* and *In My Head*. Drummer Bill Stevenson left the band in summer 1985, and Kira was dismissed from the band after the live recording *Who's Got the 10 1/2?* in late 1985. The new lineup featured Anthony Martinez on drums and C'el on bass, and after a final tour that had several instrumental Black Flag shows, Rollins was sacked and Ginn broke up the band. Ginn then went on to tour and record with his instrumental power trio Gone, playing many shows (once they played six times in one day in New York City) before concentrating more on running SST records into the ground and losing all of the acts that had made SST so special. Kira went on to play in the dual bass band Dos with her then husband Mike Watt of the Minutemen. Bill Stevenson rejoined the Descendents and, after that band folded, continued as **All** and later juggled both All and the Descendents. Rollins went on to form the **Rollins Band** with Sim Cain and Andrew Weiss from Gone and Washington, D.C., guitarist Christ Haskett and toured to much success on **MTV** with his band and spoken word throughout the 1990s. Ginn continued to put out numerous solo records and other projects under a variety of names, including Gone, but without any other original members. In 2004, he organized a Black Flag reunion show in Los Angeles without any of the key members of the band and with a bass machine labeled "Dale Nixon" on bass. Even though Black Flag ended ignobly, they remain one of the most popular and influential hardcore punk bands of all time, and both Ginn's guitar playing and Rollins's vocals inspired an entire generation of punks and the grunge scene that followed them. *See also* Circle Jerks; Descendents; Ginn, Greg; Minutemen; Morris, Keith; Rollins, Henry; SST; SWA.

Discography: *Nervous Breakdown* EP (SST, 1978, 1992); *Jealous Again* EP (SST, 1980, 1991); *Damaged* (SST, 1981, 1990); *Everything Went Black* (SST, 1983, 1990); *The First Four Years* (SST, 1984, 1990); *My War* (SST, 1984, 1990); *Family Man* (SST, 1984, 1990); *Slip It In* (SST, 1984, 1990); *Live '84* (SST, 1984, 1998); *Loose Nut* (SST, 1985, 1990); *The Process of Weeding Out* EP (SST, 1985, 1990); *In My Head*

(SST, 1985, 1990); *Who's Got the 10 1/2?* (SST, 1986, 1990); *Wasted . . . Again* (SST, 1987, 1990); *I Can See You* EP (SST, 1989); *Six Pack* EP (SST, 1992); *TV Party* EP (SST, 1992).

BLACK RANDY AND THE METROSQUAD

Chaotic band led by the incredibly charismatic Black Randy (John Morris), a diabetic alcoholic street hustler. The Metrosquad usually consisted of members of other **Los Angeles** bands such as K. K. Garrett from the **Screamers** on guitar, Pat Garrett from the **Dils** on bass, Bob Dead on guitar, and Dan Brown on piano. The band was one of the first bands to use shocking imagery, and Black Randy used blaxpolitation humor and sort of an early version of rap to convey his songs about subjects such as African dictator Idi Amin and cannibalism, which he knew would annoy and hopefully provoke his audience. Black Randy died of AIDS after years of drug abuse.

BLACK TRAIN JACK

New York hardcore band from the 1990s formed by former **Token Entry** drummer Ernie Parada. The band featured Parada on guitar, and the lyrics mostly concerned **straight edge** topics and remaining true to one's core values.
Discography: *No Reward* (Roadrunner, 1993); *You're Not Alone* (Roadrunner, 1994).

BLACK VELVET FLAG

Parody band that performed lounge versions of punk songs such as "Amoebae" by the **Adolescents.** The band was essentially a lounge version of punk rock.

BLANK GENERATION

There were two movies with the title *Blank Generation*, both involving **Richard Hell,** one a documentary and one a fiction film. The documentary by Amos Poe and Ivan Kral was made in 1976 and includes performances at **CBGB's** by **Television, Talking Heads, Blondie,** the Shirts, Tuff Darts, **Patti Smith,** and the **Ramones.** The second film with the title was made in 1980 by Uli Lommel and involves a French journalist's quest to find Andy Warhol.

"BLANK GENERATION"

One of the key early punk songs written by **Richard Hell** for his original band the **Neon Boys** (which later evolved into **Television**), which is reminiscent of both the Stray Cats' "Stray Cat Strut" (which is clearly inspired by "Blank Generation") and the song "Beat Generation" by Bob McFadden (actually Rod McKuen, who wrote the song for a exploitation film), which is clearly a precursor of "Blank Generation." Although "Blank Generation" is one of the earliest punk songs, it was not released until years after the fact because Hell had first performed the song with Television and later with the **Heartbreakers** with **Johnny Thunders,** before he was asked to leave both bands and had to eventually found his own band, Richard Hell and the **Voidoids.** The song represents the poetic and romantic influences on early U.S. punk and also reflects the alienation felt by many in the early punk communities.

BL'AST!

California **hardcore** band signed to **Black Flag's SST** label and very similar in sound to early Black Flag. The band started as M.A.D. in 1982 but changed its name to Bl'ast! in 1984. The original lineup included Clifford Dinsmore on vocals, Mike Neider on guitar, and Dave

Cooper on bass. Most of the songs were about surfing, including their anthem "Surf and Destroy." Dinsmore left in the early 1990s, and the band broke up shortly thereafter but reunited in 2001 for several reunion shows. Dinsmore later went on to form Space Boy, and Neider formed the similarly named Ghetto-Blast.

Discography: *The Power of Expression* (Wishing Well, 1984; SST, 1987, 1990); *It's in My Blood* (SST, 1987, 1990); *Take the Manic Ride* (SST, 1989, 1991).

BLASTING CONCEPT

Compilation of numerous **SST** bands, including **Hüsker Dü, Meat Puppets, Black Flag,** the **Minutemen,** and many others. Several volumes were released.

BLISTERS

New Jersey pop-punk band of the early 1990s that played an earnest variety of speeded up odes to the problems inherent in leaving adolescence behind and joining the race. It was originally formed by bassist and singer Steve Bahr with guitarist Dennis Marmon and drummer Bill Kleemeyer. The band went through numerous personnel changes, at one point adding second guitarist Steve Shiffman and a variety of new drummers. The second album, *Pissed to Meet Me*, playfully acknowledged the band's debt to the **Replacements** as well as the **Ramones.**

Discography: *Off My Back* (Albertine, 1991); *Pissed to Meet Me* (Ger. Incognito, 1992).

"BLITZKRIEG BOP"

Key song in punk history and one of the most used in movies, commercials, and on television. The song appears on the **Ramones** first album and establishes the band's connection to pop music almost right off the bat with its anthemic "Hey Ho, Lets Go!" chant. Although the Ramones were the band that established most of the idioms of the punk movement in the United Stated and abroad, "Blitzkrieg Bop" demonstrated that one of the band's goals was to write catchy songs that could be played on the radio. (The song was written by drummer Tommy Ramone as a Bay City Rollers imitation.) Although not a hit when the Ramones first record was released, the song is now well known outside the punk community for the countless number of times it has been used in movies, commercials, and sports stadiums across the United States. Sadly, the song's popularity came too late to help most of the Ramones because the band retired in 1996 and key members Johnny, Joey, and Dee Dee passed away before the Ramones' inevitable acceptance by mainstream culture.

BLONDIE

Although it was not a punk band as many would define the term, Blondie was one of the most successful bands to evolve from the fertile **CBGB's** scene of the mid-1970s. The band was led by the dynamic and charismatic Debbie Harry, guitarist and Harry's former boyfriend Chris Stein, keyboard player Jimmy Destri, drummer Clem Burke, and original bassist Gary Valentine (later replaced by Frank Infante and, after Infante switched to guitar on *Parallel Lines*, by Nigel Harrison). Blondie was one of the few bands to break out almost immediately. Led by the arresting stage presence and beauty of Harry (controversy over her being the public face of Blondie led to a campaign by the record company to promote the slogan "Blondie Is a Group" on T-shirts and stickers), Blondie scored numerous chart hits, such as "Heart of Glass" and "Call Me." Later singles such as the "Tide Is High" and "Rapture" saw the band dabbling in, and helping to popularize, **reggae** and rap, respectively. The band disbanded in

Blondie took the trappings of punk and turned them into mainstream gold. © *Robert Barry Francos.*

the early 1980s (due as much to lack of inspiration after the lackluster album *The Hunter* as to Stein's lengthy illness) but regrouped in the late 1990s with several core members, released several well-received records, and continued to tour sporadically. Many punks were annoyed by Blondie's popularity and saw them as selling out the promise of early punk by adopting disco rhythms and even rap in their quest for commercial success. Blondie was not the punk sellout that many thought; their experimentation and use of different rhythms and musical styles actually locates them more firmly in punk's **DIY** aesthetic than many bands that stuck to the traditional beat and guitar sound.

Discography: *Blondie* (Private Stock, 1976; Chrysalis, 1977); *Plastic Letters* (Chrysalis, 1977); *Parallel Lines* (Chrysalis, 1978); *Eat to the Beat* (Chrysalis, 1979); *Autoamerican* (Chrysalis, 1980); *The Best of Blondie* (Chrysalis, 1981); *The Hunter* (Chrysalis, 1982); *Blonde and Beyond* (Chrysalis/ERG, 1993); *The Platinum Collection* (Chrysalis/EMI, 1994); *Remixed Remade Remodeled: The Remix Project* (Chrysalis/EMI, 1995); *Picture This Live* (Chrysalis/EMI-Capitol, 1997); *No Exit* (Beyond/BMG, 1999); *Blondie Live* (Beyond/BMG, 1999); *Greatest Hits* (Chrysalis/Capitol, 2002); *The Curse of Blondie* (UK Epic, 2003; Sanctuary, 2004). **Debbie Harry/Blondie:** *Once More into the Bleach* (Chrysalis, 1988); *The Complete Picture: The Very Best of Deborah Harry and Blondie* (UK Chrysalis, 1991). **Debbie Harry:** *KooKoo* (Chrysalis, 1981); *Rockbird* (Geffen, 1986; Geffen Goldmine, 1997); *Def, Dumb & Blonde* (Sire/Reprise, 1989); *Debravation* (Sire/Reprise, 1993). **Jimmy Destri:** *Heart on a Wall* (Chrysalis, 1982).

BODY ART

Although most of the original punks did not have tattoos or piercings, the practice of body modification became prevalent among street punks. Early New York City punks such as Harley Flannagan and John Joseph of the **Cro-Mags** were largely responsible for introducing tattoos to the **New York** scene in the early 1980s, as was **Henry Rollins** of **Black Flag,** who tattooed images from his favorite bands on his body along with quotes and other designs. Although earrings were fairly common in the early U.S. and British scenes, more radical types of piercing did not become prevalent until the early 1980s, when tattoos were no longer seen as being predominantly worn by military personnel and bikers. For many punks, there was no better way to indicate allegiance to one's favorite band then by wearing the band's logo, permanently inscribed on an arm, leg, or the torso. Many bands highlighted the body art of their fans and displayed it in album inserts, as if to demonstrate the extreme loyalty of their fans. Piercings were also relatively uncommon during the early days of punk, except for earrings on men and the occasional safety pin though the nose. Pioneers such as Genesis P-Orridge of **Throbbing Gristle,** however, started ritual scarification, outlandish and ritualistic tattoos, and elaborate piercings and weights, including his notoriously pierced genitals. Although most punks did not take piercing or body art to the extreme that P-Orridge did, he did inspire many punks to get piercing in places that had previously been considered taboo.

BOLD

Straight edge band featuring Matt Warnke on lead vocals, Tim on bass, Tom Capone on guitar, and Drew Thomas (also of **Youth of Today** and later of Into Another) on drums. The band originally performed as **Crippled Youth** when the members were in the seventh grade and were mentored by **Youth of Today.** In 1986, the band changed its name to Bold. The band played primarily in the Connecticut and **New York** scenes. The band was known for its straight-edge militancy with a sense of humor.

BORIS THE SPRINKLER

Green Bay, Wisconsin, band formed in 1992 led by brilliant and deranged zine writer and lead singer Rev. Norb. The band originally featured Paul Schroder on guitar, Erik Lee on bass (replaced by Eric James, then Ric 6), and Ronny Johnny Kispert on drums (replaced by Paul 2). The band released numerous singles and several albums in a whimsical **Ramones**-influenced style highlighted by Rev. Norb's lyrics, which were honed by his years of writing for **zines** such as *Maximum Rock 'n' Roll* and *Go Metric.* Rev. Norb started out with the zine *SicTeen* and formed Boris the Sprinkler circa 1992 to provide an outlet for his love of pop culture and topics such as Star Trek and comic books. Rev. Norb is also known for writing the world's longest song ("R' rilly Gonna Mess U Up," which clocks in at 13,000 words and 74 minutes) and is working on a collection of Bob Dylan covers to be released on **Alternative Tentacles.**
Discography: *Drugs and Masturbation* (Mutant Pop, 1995); *End of the Century* (Clear View, 1998); *Suck* (Go Kart, 1999); *Gay* (Go Kart, 2000); *Mega Anal* (Bulge Records, 2000).

BOSTON

Boston had two particularly fertile periods of punk rock. In the late 1970s, the city had a thriving punk scene with bands like **Unnatural Axe,** the Neighborhoods, **Mission of Burma,** the Lyres, as well as Jonathan Richman and the **Modern Lovers.** Although most of the early Boston scene centered around these bands and more pop-oriented acts such as the Cars and Human Sexual Response, Boston had a thriving early scene that petered out when **New Wave** and major labels diluted the early punk energy that had been maintained at shows at the **Rat,** Cantone's, and the Underground.

   In the early 1980s, a **hardcore** scene around clubs like Gallery East led to numerous influential bands, a compilation that helped define punk and the Boston scene (the *This Is Boston, Not LA* compilation), as well as numerous bands that helped punk and the **straight edge** movements develop. Particularly important was the contribution of Al Barile, a hockey player and beer drinker who transformed his life after seeing **Minor Threat** and became one of the biggest, most violent proponents of the straight edge movement through his band SS Decontrol. A typically intimidating part of the Boston hardcore show rituals was the notorious "pig-piles," in which numerous members of the clique would pile upon newer punks who dared to join the pit. Another Boston straight edge tradition included some of the more militant members knocking beers out of the hands of people who dared to drink at straight edge shows. Other bands loosely associated with SS Decontrol in the Boston crew were the metal-tinged **DYS,** featuring Dave Smalley (later of **Dag Nasty, All,** and **Down by Law**), and Jack "Choke" Kelly's bands **Negative FX,** Last Rites, and überstraight edge band **Slapshot.**

Not all of Boston's bands were straight edge or part of a particular scene, however. Other Boston bands included **Gang Green** (known for its excessive partying and devotion to beer), **Jerry's Kids,** the F.U.'s (which later changed its name to Straw Dogs in an attempt to become more commercial), as well as the **Freeze** (who were somewhat ostracized by the other bands because of their poppier sounds and roots in Cape Cod). The Proletariat was led by Richard Brown, who walked as well as talked the Marxist walk. Most of these bands were showcased on the influential *This Is Boston, Not LA* compilation and the *Unsafe at Any Speed* EP that demonstrated the diversity of the Boston sound (except for **SSD** and DYS, who considered themselves a separate scene). By the mid-1980s, SSD, DYS, and Gang Green were turning in a more metal direction, and by the late 1980s the scene had become less vital, although many of the classic Boston bands still re-formed for occasional tours. (*This Is Boston, Not LA* is available on CD, packaged with the *Unsafe at Any Speed* EP.) Other band such as the Johnnies kept the Boston torch burning in the meantime, and there is still a small and dedicated Boston scene today, although it is not as vital as it was during punk's heyday at clubs such a the Abbey, where local bands and touring punk bands play on a regular basis.

BOUNCING SOULS

One of New Jersey's longest lasting and most popular punk bands, formed in 1987. The band released its early material on its own Chunksaah label. The band featured Greg Attonito on vocals, Michael McDermott on drums, Bryan Papillion (Kienlen) on bass, and Pete "the Pete" Steinkept on guitar. The band recorded several albums for **Epitaph** and toured extensively and is still a very popular act, particularly in the New York, New Jersey, and Connecticut tristate area.

Discography: *Argyle* EP (Chunksaah, 1993); *Neurotic* EP (Chunksaah, 1993); *The Greenball Crew* (Chunksaah, 1993); *The Good, the Bad, and the Argyle* (Chunksaah, 1994; BYO, 1995); *Maniacal Laughter* (BYO, 1995); *The Bouncing Souls* (Epitaph, 1997); *Tie One On* EP (live; Epitaph, 1998); *Hopeless Romantic* (Epitaph, 1999); *The Bad, the Worse and the Out of Print* (Chunksaah, 2000); *How I Spent My Summer Vacation* (Epitaph, 2001); *Anchors Aweigh* (Epitaph, 2003); *Do You Remember* (Chunksaah, 2003).

BOWIE, DAVID

British megastar David Bowie was a huge influence on punk, particularly in his Ziggy Stardust and Berlin periods. He also helped promote the careers of **Lou Reed** and **Iggy Pop.** Bowie was perhaps most influential to the earlier, more frenetic, "louder and faster" version of punk that had its roots in glam and pub rock. His Berlin-based collaborations with musical soundscaper Brian Eno during his three-record experiment in mood and dynamics became a key influence on **postpunk** bands such as **Joy Division** (which may have taken its original name, Warsaw, from the song "Warszawa" on the *Low* record). Bowie also produced Lou Reed's *Transformer* album, and his company **MainMan** provided the finances for the recording of **Iggy and the Stooges'** *Raw Power*. Although many punks were disappointed by Bowie's later stylistic changes, many of the younger generation were clearly inspired by his music and fluidity in changing identity. **Johnny Rotten** of the **Sex Pistols** was clearly a fan, bringing in a Bowie record (alongside numerous **reggae** records) to play on the air during his famous radio interview on the Tommy Vance show on Capital Radio, London (July 16, 1977).

Select Discography: *The Rise and Fall of Ziggy Stardust and the Spiders from Mars* (RCA, 1972); *Aladdin Sane* (RCA, 1973); *Pin-Ups* (RCA, 1973); *Diamond Dogs* (RCA, 1974); *Low* (RCA, 1977); *Heroes* (RCA, 1977); *Lodger* (RCA, 1979); *Scary Monsters* (RCA, 1980).

BOYS

Minor punk band from London best known for the single "Brickfield Nights," an engaging slice of pop-punk later covered by **Die Toten Hosen** on their album *Learning English, Lesson One*. The band featured the youthful Duncan "Kid" Reid on vocals and bass, Casino Steel on keyboards, "Honest" John Plain on guitar, and Jack Black (not the actor) on drums. The band broke up in 1981 but gets together for periodic reunions. The Boys also released a Christmas album as the Yobs.

Discography: *The Boys* (UK NEMS, 1977; UK Link Classics, 1990; ,Captain Oi!, 2000); *Alternative Chartbusters* (UK NEMS, 1978; UK Link Classics, 1990; Captain Oi!, 2001); *To Hell with the Boys* (UK Safari, 1979; Captain Oi!, 2002); *Boys Only* (UK Safari, 1980; Captain Oi!, 2003); *Power Cut* (Anagram, 1999); *Live at the Roxy Club* (Receiver, 1999); *BBC Sessions* (live; Vinyl Japan, 1999, 2003); *Sick on You* (Harry May, 2000); *Complete Punk Singles Collection* (Anagram, 2000); *Punk Rock Rarities* (Captain Oi!, 2000); *Svengerland* (Captain Oi!, 2002); *Very Best of the Boys* (Anagram, 2002). **Yobs:** *The Yobs Christmas Album* (UK Safari, 1980; UK Great Expectations, 1989).

BRACKET

Pop-punk band from Forestville, California, that initially followed the same musical template for pop punk in the early to mid-1990s. They were signed during the fury when record companies wanted to capitalize on **Green Day's** million-selling popularity. The band maintained a relentlessly charming pop sound with some metallic edges.

Discography: *924 Forestville* (Caroline, 1994); *4-Wheel Vibe* (Caroline, 1995).

BRATMOBILE

Next to **Bikini Kill,** the most influential and respected band of the **Riot Grrrl movement** of the late 1980s and early 1990s. The band consisted of the geographically far-flung singer Allison Wolfe, guitarist Erin Smith, and drummer Molly Neumann (although the band frequently switched instruments), who originally formed on a dare in 1991 to play at the **K Record's** International Pop Underground convention in Olympia, Washington. The band released several singles, followed by the brilliant, blink-and-you'll-miss-it *Pottymouth* in 1993. The band broke-up in 1994 but re-formed in 1998 to tour and release new records. Wolfe and Neumann also worked in the zine *Girl Germs* as well as the *Riot Grrrl* zine and movement. Drummer Molly Neumann played in the band Peeches in the mid-1990s.

Discography: *Pottymouth* (Kill Rock Stars, 1993); *The Real Janelle EP* (Kill Rock Stars, 1994); *The Peel Session EP* (Strange Fruit/Dutch East India Trading, 1994); *Ladies, Women and Girls* (Lookout, 2000); *Girls Get Busy* (Lookout, 2002). **Peeches:** *Scented Gum EP7* (Lookout, 1995); *Do the Math* (Kill Rock Stars, 1996); *Games People Play* (Kill Rock Stars, 1997); *Life* (Kill Rock Stars, 1999).

BROKEN BONES

English **hardcore** band along the lines of **Discharge,** formed by former Discharge guitarist Bones, Nobby on bass (later replaced by Tezz) and vocals, Oddy on bass, and Baz on drums. *Dem Bones* is a punk-metal hybrid, and subsequent records are more standard metal.

Discography: *Dem Bones* (UK Fall Out, 1984); *Seeing thru My Eyes* EP (UK Fall Out, 1985); *Live at the 100 Club* (UK Subversive Sounds, 1985); *Bonecrusher* (Combat Core, 1986); *F.O.A.D.* (Combat Core, 1987); *Decapitated* (UK Fall Out, 1987); *Losing Control* (Heavy Metal, 1989).

BROMLEY CONTINGENT

Loose-knit group of early punks and **Sex Pistols** fans that followed the group around from gig to gig and spread the word about the band early on. Some of the original members were William Broad (who changed his name to Billy Idol), Steve Bailey, (later Steve Severin of **Siouxsie and the Banshees**), and Sue Catwoman (Sue Lucas). They first saw the Sex Pistols at Ravensbourne art college outside London and followed the band around, at one point even renting a van in order to drive to Paris for a gig. Eventually, many of the members went on to found bands of their own, to varying degrees of success.

BUTCHIES, THE

Queer female band from Durham, North Carolina, started by former members of **Team Dresh** after the demise of that band, featuring vocalist and guitarist Kaia Wilson, drummer Melissa York, along with bassist Alison Martlew. The band recorded for indie label **Mr. Lady Records** (founded by Kaia Wilson and Tammy Rae Carlson) before moving to slightly larger indie Yep Roc in 2004. The Butchies worked to increase awareness of queer social issues and the permeability of gender while rocking with a gleeful sense of humor. (The first album, *Are We Not Femme?*, with a front cover picture of the Butchies in skirts and wigs, plays not only on the title of the first **Devo** album but also on the idea that butch lesbians can play with predominant notions of gender and femininity.) The band remained one of the most inherently politically playful queer bands on the scene.
Discography: *Are We Not Femme?* (Mr. Lady, 1998); *Population 1975* (Mr. Lady, 1999); *Three* (Mr. Lady, 2001); *Make Yr Life* (Yep Roc, 2004).

BUTTHOLE SURFERS

Almost uncategorizable noise-punk band from Texas led by the dynamic Gibby Haynes, who often sang through a megaphone. In the early 1990s, they scored a minor U.S. hit with "Pepper." The band was well known for its bizarre permutations of existing song structures and nonsensical lyrics about how the shah of Iran slept in Lee Harvey Oswald's grave and Negro Observers. One early song was composed almost entirely of snorting and spitting. The Butthole Surfers also stood apart with their original dual drummers, Teresa and King Koffee, who would play without a bass drum and standing up. The band was started in San Antonio, Texas, in the early 1980s by Gibson "Gibby" Haynes (the son of a local children's TV show host, Mr. Peppermint), guitarist Paul Lear, Quinn Mathews on bass, and Scott Mathews on drums (Scot Mathews was replaced first by King Koffee (Paul Coffey) and was later joined by Teresa on second drums). The Butthole Surfers released increasingly uncategorizable music that challenged and often offended audiences. The Butthole Surfers toured relentlessly more as a circus sideshow than as a band, sometimes blinding the audience with strobe lights, showing films of medical experiments in the background, or throwing thousands of photocopies of roaches into the audience during gigs. The band eventually signed to a major label, and although they had a surprise hit with the relatively tame song "Pepper," they were eventually dropped by a record label that had difficulty promoting a band that many radio stations refused to play based solely on the bands name. A particularly interesting harmonic convergence occurred when former Led Zeppelin bass

The Buzzcocks were perhaps the most emotionally realistic band in British punk. *Photo by Andre Csillag/Rex Features.*

player John Paul Jones produced *Independent Worm Saloon.* Gibby and Jeff Pinkus also moonlighted as the dance band Jackofficers. The band dissolved in the late 1990s, and Gibby toured with his own band.

Discography: *Butthole Surfers* (Alternative Tentacles, 1983); *Live PCPEP* (Alternative Tentacles, 1984); *Psychic . . . Powerless . . . Another Man's Sac* (Touch and Go, 1985); *Cream Corn from the Socket of Davis* EP (Touch and Go, 1985); *Rembrandt Pussyhorse* (Touch and Go, 1986); *Locust Abortion Technician* (Touch and Go, 1987); *Hairway to Steven* (Touch and Go, 1988); *Double Live* (Buggerveil, 1989); *Widowmaker* EP (Touch and Go, 1989); *Pioghd* (Rough Trade, 1992); *Independent Worm Saloon* (Capitol, 1994); *The Hole Truth . . . and Nothing Butt* (Trance Syndicate, 1995); *Electriclarryland* (Capitol, 1996).

BUZZCOCKS

Seminal punk band whose insightful love songs by second front man Pete Shelley and poppy harmonies helped to bridge the gap between punk rock and power pop. Formed by Howard Devoto (Howard Trafford) and Pete Shelley (Peter McNeish), with Steve Diggle originally on bass and John Maher on drums, the band was one of the first to release an independent seven-inch in Britain, the seminal *Spiral Scratch EP,* released in January 1977. Devoto quit the band in February 1977 to pursue other projects, including Magazine, which was best known for its song "Shot by Both Sides," and Luxuria. The band continued without him, to great success and acclaim, during a long and productive career. The Buzzcocks first formed in Manchester, England, in 1976, inspired by the punk energy of the **Sex Pistols,** whom they had seen playing at the Manchester Lesser Free Trade Hall. They debuted, opening for the Sex Pistols at the Manchester Lesser Free Trade Hall, on July 20, 1976. After *Spiral Scratch,* the band became a major draw, and even Devoto's departure did not slow the Buzzcocks' meteoric rise. New bassist Garth Davies, who had taken over when Diggle moved to guitar, proved to be unreliable, but he was quickly replaced by Steve Garvey, who remained with the band till their dissolution. They were initially known as a singles band and released seminal early punk singles such as "Ever Fallen in Love" and "What Do I Get?," with most songs written primarily by key songwriter Shelley. After the release of several pivotal singles such as "Orgasm Addict" and "What Do I Get?," the Buzzcocks released their first album, *Another Music in a Different Kitchen*, to critical acclaim and reasonable sales. The Buzzcocks soon settled into a schedule of touring and recording that would eventually tear the band apart. Their second album, *Love Bites*, was quickly rushed out seven months later to capitalize on the first album's success. The band continued to experiment musically with their third album, *A Different Kind of Tension*, which featured the epic philosophical essay "I Believe," in which Shelley gloomily lists a contradictory set of beliefs before proclaiming "There is no love in this world anymore" over and over to end the song. The band toured the United States in 1979 and courted controversy at a gig at Club 57 in New York City, where drummer John Maher tore down a banner for the sponsoring station WPIX-FM, and the band was forced to flee the venue. The band attempted to regroup when they returned to England, recording the EPs *Parts One, Two, and Three* with drug-crazed producer Martin Hannet (who had previously produced **Joy Division** as well as the *Spiral Scratch* EP), but the sessions turned into chaos. After some halfhearted attempts to record a fourth album, Shelley and regular producer Martin Rushent recorded the song "Homosapien," which became Shelley's debut solo single. Shelley dissolved the band via letters to the other members and embarked on a solo tour. Maher and Diggle briefly formed Flag of Convenience, and Garvey played on Shelley's first tour before moving to New York and retiring. The original Buzzcocks (although without Garvey and Maher, who retired and were replaced by bassist Tony Barber and drummer Phil Barker) reunited in the late 1980s for a still-continuing reunion tour. With this lineup, the Buzzcocks continued to record and tour. They cemented their place as punk's romantic conscience, consistently released new material that evoked their old songs, but examined the same themes of alienation and loneliness they dealt with on their first three albums. Shelley also recorded some electronic material with former lead singer Howard Devoto in 2002 as the Buzzkunts. The full version of the sessions recorded for the *Spiral Scratch* EP were eventually released on the Mute label in 2000 after years of bad bootleg copies had circulated.

Discography: *Spiral Scratch* EP (UK New Hormones, 1977+ 1981); *Another Music in a Different Kitchen* (UK UA, 1978); *Love Bites* (UK UA, 1978); *A Different Kind of Tension* (UK UA, 1979; IRS, 1989); *Singles Going Steady* (IRS, 1979); *Parts One, Two, Three* EP (IRS, 1984); *Total Pop 1977–1980* (Ger. Weird Systems, 1987); *The Peel Sessions* EP (UK Strange Fruit, 1988); *Lest We Forget* (Roir, 1988); *Live at the Roxy Club April '77* (UK Absolutely Free, 1989; UK Receiver, 1990); *Product* (Restless Retro, 1989); The Peel Sessions Album (UK Strange Fruit, 1989; Strange Fruit/Dutch East India Trading, 1991); *Time's Up* (UK Receiver, 1991); *Operators Manual: Buzzcocks Best* (IRS, 1991); *Alive Tonight* EP (UK Planet Pacific, 1991); *Entertaining Friends: Live at the Hammersmith Odeon March 1979* (IRS, 1992); *Trade Test Transmissions* (Caroline, 1993); *French* (IRS, 1996); *All Set* (IRS, 1996); *Modern* (Go-Kart, 1999). **Steve Diggle:** *Heated and Rising* EP (UK Three Thirty, 1993). **Various Artists:** *Something's Gone Wrong Again: The Buzzcocks' Covers Compilation* (C/Z, 1992).

CAN

Experimental German band, very influential on **postpunk** in general and **John Lydon** and **Public Image Limited** in particular. Can usually was lumped under the term *Krautrock* and experimented with different approaches to music in which the vocal was simply another instrument that would often complement or comment on the music being played. The band started when Holger Czukay and Irmin Schmidt met as classmates under the tutelage of Karlheinz Stockhausen. The original musical lineup of Can consisted of Holger Czukay on bass and vocals, Michael Karoli on guitar and vocals, Jaki Liebezeit on drums and vocals, Irmin Schmidt on keyboards and vocals, and U.S. expatriate Malcolm Mooney on vocals (later replaced by Damo Suzuki from Japan). In 1969, the band released its first album, *Monster Movie*, which included the epic funk/drone "You Doo Right," which demonstrated the potential of Can's approach. Later with Suzuki, Can became even more experimental with Czukay's tape experiments combined with tight and focused songwriting. Suzuki left in 1973, and the band continued until 1979 and reunited with Mooney for a short-lived reunion in 1989. The various members continued with solo careers, Czukay's being the most prolific. Guitarist Karoli died in 2001. The postpunk sounds of bands, particularly Public Image Limited, are particularly indebted to Can.

Discography: *Monster Movie* (UK UA, 1969; Spoon/Mute/Restless Retro, 1990; Mute, 1998; remastered, Mute, 2004); *Soundtracks* (UK UA, 1970; Spoon/Mute/Restless Retro, 1990; Mute, 1998); *Tago Mago* (UK UA, 1971; Spoon/Mute/Restless Retro, 1990; remastered, Mute, 2004); *Ege Bamyasi* (UA, 1972; Spoon/Mute/Restless Retro, 1990; remastered, Mute, 2004); *Future Days* (UA, 1973; Spoon/Mute/Restless Retro, 1990; Mute, 2005); *Limited Edition* (UK UA, 1974); *Soon over Babaluma* (UA, 1974; Spoon/Mute/Restless Retro, 1990; Mute, 2005); *Landed* (UK Virgin, 1975; Spoon/Mute/Restless Retro, 1990; remastered, Mute, 2005); *Unlimited Edition* (UK Caroline, 1976; Spoon/Mute/Restless Retro, 1990; remastered, Mute, 2005); *Opener 1971–1974* (UK Sunset, 1976); *Flow Motion* (UK Virgin, 1976; Spoon/Mute/Restless Retro, 1990; Mute, 1993); *Saw Delight* (UK Virgin, 1976; Spoon/Mute/Restless Retro, 1990; Mute, 1993); *Out of Reach* (Peters Int'l, 1978; Tko Magnum Midline, 1999); *Cannibalism* (UK UA, 1978); *Can* (UK Laser, 1979; Spoon/Mute/Restless Retro, 1990; Mute, 1993); *Cannibalism 1* (Ger. Spoon, 1980; Spoon/Mute/Restless Retro, 1990; Mute, 1998); *Delay 1968* (Ger. Spoon, 1980; Spoon/

Mute/Restless Retro, 1990; Mute, 1998); *Incandescence 1969–1977* (UK Virgin, 1981); *Onlyou* (tape; Ger. Pure Freude, 1982); *Prehistoric Future—June, 1968* (tape; Fr. Tago Mago, 1984); *Rite Time* (UK Mercury, 1989; Mute, 1997); *Cannibalism 2* (Spoon/Mute/Restless Retro, 1990; Mute, 1998); *Cannibalism 3* (Spoon/Mute/Restless Retro, 1990; Mute, 1998); *Radio Waves* (Sonic Platten, 1997); *Sacrilege: The Remixes* (Mute, 1997); *Inner Space* (Tko Magnum Midline, 1998); *Anthology 1968–1993* (Mute, 1998); *Can Box Music (Live 1971–1977)* (Mute, 1999); *Box* (boxed set; Mute, 1999); *Can & Out of Reach* (Audelic, 2003). **Holger Czukay:** *Movies* (UK EMI, 1980); *On the Way to the Peak of Normal* (UK EMI, 1982); *Der Osten Ist Rot* (UK Virgin, 1984); *Rome Remains Rome* (UK Virgin, 1987); *Radio Wave Surfer* (UK Virgin, 1991); *Good Morning Story* (Tone Casualties, 1999). **Holger Czukay/Rolf Dammers:** *Canaxis* (Ger. Spoon, 1982).

CANADIAN PUNK

Like its neighbor to the south, Canada also has had a rich and varied **punk** scene that included stalwarts such as **DOA** and the **Doughboys.** Two of the earliest Canadian punk bands were the Diodes, which released one record, *The Diodes,* in 1977, and the Viletones, led by the confrontational Nazi Dog (Stephen Leckie). Although most Americans were not exposed to Canadian punk rock bands, many, such as the **Subhumans** (not to be confused with the identically named English band) and DOA, toured relentlessly and made inroads into the U.S. marketplace. In the mid-1980s, bands such as the Doughboys often toured the United States, but most Americans remained unaware of the rich and varied Canadian scene. The Canadian government also provides funding for some bands to tour, something unheard of in the United States.

CANDY ASS RECORDS

Independent record label from Portland, Oregon, that lasted from 1992 to 1999 and was run by influential **queercore** rocker Jody Bleyle (formerly of **Team Dresch** and later of Family Outing). Candy Ass Records released albums by bands such as Team Dresch, Heavens to Betsey, and **Sleater-Kinney** (in partnership with Chainsaw Records). The 1995 double album *Free to Fight* featured all-female bands such as Fifth Column, Excuse 17, Cheesecake, and Lois, all of which dealt with safety issues. The album included a 75-page illustrated booklet about self-defense against harassment and rape and also featured practical advice, stories, and poems. The label released the first two Team Dresch albums in conjunction with Chainsaw. Other artist released by Candy Ass include Containe, Cypher in the Snow, Hazel, the Third Sex, New Bad Things, and Vegas Beat. Candy Ass Records was another example of how a politicized **DIY** company can make a difference.

CANTERBURY APARTMENTS

Los Angeles apartment building where many punks lived or squatted during the late 1970s and early 1980s. The Canterbury Apartments were one of the most famous U.S. **squats,** and **Darby Crash** as well as other famous and notorious Los Angeles punks lived or crashed there at one point or another. The most useful thing about the Canterbury Apartments was its close proximity to the **Masque.**

CAPTAIN BEEFHEART

Experimental U.S. singer and songwriter (born Don Van Vliet) who recorded with the Magic Band primarily in the 1960s. His work influenced numerous avant-garde and **post-punk** bands, and **Johnny Rotten** cited him as an influence and played his song "The Blimp (Mousetrapreplica)" while deejaying on London's Capital Radio on the Tommy Vance show in

1977. Van Vliet had worked with **Frank Zappa** early on and developed an ear for the esoteric and the strange, forming the original Magic Band as a rhythm-and-blues band. The Magic Band soon evolved into a more eccentric group, and after signing to Frank Zappa's Straight Records, Beefheart recorded *Trout Mask Replica*, considered by many to be his masterpiece. In the late 1970s, Beefheart returned to his off-kilter roots after several fairly (by his standards) pedestrian albums and put out the album *Shiny Beast*, which anticipated the rhythmic experimentations of postpunk. Van Vliet retired from music in 1982 to become a painter in the Mojave Desert. His influence can be seen in the rhythmic jerkiness of bands such as **Gang of Four, Public Image Limited,** the **Minutemen,** and **Talking Heads.**

CAPTAIN OI!

British **punk** label devoted to reissuing out-of-print punk and **oi** records as well as new releases from **UK Subs, Cockney Rejects, Angelic Upstarts,** and Argy Bargy. The label also acts as a distributor for smaller punk labels and supports teams from the Premier Division of the Ryman Football League.

CARROLL, JIM

Punk poet and author of numerous books of poetry and short stories. Jim Carroll was a junkie and drug abuser for many years before cleaning up his act and performing more on a regular basis. He produced several records during the late 1970s and early 1980s and was best known musically for the epic song "People Who Died" and the album *Catholic Boy*. The 1995 film *The Basketball Diaries* was based on one of Carroll's autobiographical books and starred Leonardo DiCaprio. Carroll concentrated on his writing and recorded sporadically.
Discography: Music: *Catholic Boy* (Atco, 1980, 1989); *Dry Dreams* (Atco, 1982); *I Write Your Name* (Atlantic, 1983, 1991); *A World without Gravity: The Best of the Jim Carroll Band* (Rhino, 1993); *Pools of Mercury* (Polygram, 1998); *Runaway EP* (Kill Rock Stars, 2000). **Spoken Word:** *Rimbaud Lectures* (The American Poetry Archive, 1978); *Naropa Institute* (Naropa Institute Archives Project, 1986); *Praying Mantis* (Giant, 1991); *The Basketball Diaries* (Audio Literature, 1994); *Curtis's Charm* (Rabid Dog Productions, 1996); *Pools of Mercury* (Mercury, 1998).

CATHAY DE GRANDE

Los Angeles Chinese club turned **punk** club. Along with **Madame Wong's** and Hong Kong Garden, Cathay de Grande was a place for punks to play when most clubs would not allow them.

CAUSE FOR ALARM

New York hardcore band from the mid-1980s that played extensively in the city scene area and toured.
Discography: *Beyond Birth and Death* (Victory, 1995); *Cheaters and the Cheated* (Victory, 1997); *Birth after Birth* (Victory, 1997); *Beneath the Wheel* (Victory, 1998); *Nothing Ever Dies* (Victory, 2000).

CBGB'S

Seminal Bowery club run by **Hilly Kristal** where the early **punk** scene in New York City was born. Located at the corner of Bowery and Bleeker, the club still serves as a stage for new bands via its Audition Showcase on Monday nights and provides a platform for aging punk bands. The club was founded in the early 1970s as a biker bar by Hilly Kristal, who named the club CBGB & OMFUG, which stands for "Country, Bluegrass, Blues and Other Music for Uplifting Gourmandizers," at 315 Bowery in the heart of the then-decrepit Bowery area of New York City. CBGS' hosted the first real performances of the **Ramones, Television, Talking Heads, Blondie, Richard Hell,** and countless others. Kristal was unable to make ends meet until Television and other bands started playing there in March 1974. Soon, bands such as Talking Heads, Blondie, the Ramones, and the **Dead Boys** dominated the scene that was dubbed punk rock. By the time the club decided to release an album documenting the scene, most of the original bands had moved on, and mostly minor bands filled the record. As the 1970s ended, more of the original bands had either broken up or moved to the national stage, and a new scene coalesced around CBGB's: the **New York hardcore** scene. In the early to mid-1980s, bands such as **Youth of Today, Bold, Judge, Warzone, Agnostic Front,** and **Murphy's Law** played the fabled and often violent hardcore matinees on Sunday afternoons. The club ended the matinees because of violence, and the CBGB's scene quieted down when fewer national bands played the club. Unknowns could be found at the club most nights, although national acts such as **Green Day** would stop by for surprise visits. The club became part of the punk legend, and the CBGB's T-shirt was seen all over the world. Over time, various other ventures were tried, including a pizzeria, which closed, and the much more successful CB's 313 Gallery, which show-cases art and quieter music. In 2005, the existence of CBGB's came under attack by the Bowery Residents Committee, which tried to have the club evicted due to issues with back rent. Kristal, who maintained that most of the estimated $2 million CB's received each year from merchan-dising simply went back into the business, organized several benefit concerts to save the club in August 2005. The club justifiably can be called the birthplace of U.S. punk rock, and new bands can still be seen there, especially at the Monday night Audition Showcase that debuted bands such as the Dead Boys. This club is scheduled to close on October 31, 2006.

CELIBATE RIFLES

Australian **punk** band inspired by the **Sex Pistols** and the **Ramones.** Celibate Rifles featured Damien Lovelock on vocals, Kent Steedman on guitars, Dave Morris on guitars, Mikey Couvert on bass, and Paul Larsen on drums. The band was formed by high school friends in 1978 and was influenced by **Radio Birdman, Iggy and the Stooges,** and especially the Ramones. The Celibate Rifles briefly disbanded but reportedly reunited. Lovelock released a solo record, Steed-man released a record as Crent, and former member James Darroch recorded as Eastern Dark. **Discography:** *But Jacques, the Fish?* EP (Aus. no label, 1982); *Sideroxylon* (Aus. Hot, 1983); *The Celibate Rifles* (Aus. Hot, 1984); *Quintessentially Yours* (What Goes On, 1985); *The Turgid Miasma of Existence* (Hot/Rough Trade, 1986); *Mina Mina Mina* (What Goes On, 1986); *Kiss Kiss Bang Bang* (What Goes On, 1986); *Roman Beach Party* (What Goes On, 1987); *Dancing Barefoot* EP (What Goes On, 1988); *Blind Ear* (Aus. True Tone/EMI, 1989); *Platters du Jour* (Ger. Hot/Rattlesnake/Normal, 1990); *Heaven on a Stick* (Hot, 1992); *Yizgarnnoff* (Hot, 1993); *Sofa* (Hot, 1993); *Spaceman in a Satin Suit* (Hot, 1994); *On the Quiet* (Hot, 1996); *Wonderful Life* (Tronador, 1997); *Mid-Stream of Consciousness* (Real-O-Mind, 2002). **Eastern Dark:** *Long Live the New Flesh!* EP (What Goes On, 1986); *Girls on the Beach (With Cars)* (Aus. Waterfront, 1990). **Damien Lovelock:** *It's A Wig, Wig, Wig, Wig World* (Aus. Hot/Survival, 1988). **Crent:** *Crent* (Aus. Waterfront, 1990).

CHALK CIRCLE

The first all-female band from the **Washington, D.C., hardcore** scene. Chalk Circle formed in the early 1980s and featured Sharon Cheslow on guitar and vocals, Mary Green on bass and vocals, and Anne Bonafede on drums. The band was relatively popular on the Washington, D.C., scene but still had to face the usual sexism and allegations that female bands could not play or rock as male bands rocked.

CHELSEA

British **punk** band best known for the classic punk single "Right to Work" and for birthing the original lineup of **Generation X.** The original lineup included Gene October on vocals, Billy Idol on guitar, Tony James on bass, and drummer John Towe. When the instrumentalists in the band left to form Generation X, vocalist Gene October regrouped the band with Dave Marin on guitar and vocals, James Stevenson on guitar, Geoff Myles on bass, and Chris Bashford on drums. The band released its debut album, *Chelsea,* in 1979. Chelsea was also known for combining the art world and punk rock when the band opened for the first **Throbbing Gristle** show at a gallery in London. October continued to record and tour with new lineups of Chelsea when not working as a garbage man in London.

Discography: *Chelsea* (UK Step Forward, 1979; Captain Oi!, 2000); *No Damage* (IRS, 1980); *Alternative Hits* (UK Step Forward, 1980; Weser, 1996; Captain Oi!, 2000); *No Escape* (IRS, 1980); *Evacuate* (IRS, 1982; Captain Oi!, 2005); *Live and Well* (Punx, 1984; Rhythm Vicar, 2003); *Just for the Record* (UK Step Forward, 1985); *Original Sinners* (UK Communique, 1985); *Rocks Off* (UK Jungle, 1986); *Backtrax* (UK Illegal, 1988); *Ultra Prophets* (IRS, 1989); *Underwraps* (UK IRS, 1989); *Unreleased Stuff* (UK Clay, 1989); *Traitors Gate* (Weser, 1996); *Fools and Soldiers* (Receiver, 1997); *Punk Singles* (Captain Oi!, 2000); *Punk Rock Rarities* (Captain Oi!, 2000); *BBC Punk Sessions* (live; Captain Oi!, 2001); *Metallic F.O.: Live at CBGB's* (Captain Oi!, 2002); *Urban Kids: A Punk Anthology* (Castle Us/Ryko, 2005); *Live & Loud* (Harry May, 2005).

CHILDERS, LEEE BLACK

Manager, scenester, and photographer who worked with **David Bowie** at **MainMan** management and at points had the unenviable task of keeping **Iggy Pop** from overindulging. Childers was present from the early days of **punk** and later managed the **Heartbreakers** on their drug-fueled tour of Europe. Childers is regarded as one of the best photographers of the early punk era who benefited from his ready access to members of the scene.

CH3

Punk band from Cerritos, California, also known as Channel Three. The original lineup consisted of Mike Magrann and Kimm Gardener on guitars and vocals, Larry Kelley on bass, and Mike Burton on drums. The band went though numerous rhythm sections and stylistic changes in the mid-1980s and alienated many fans with the experimentation of albums such as *Airborne.*

Discography: *CH3 EP* (Posh Boy, 1981); *I Got a Gun* (Posh Boy, 1983); *After the Lights Go Out* (Posh Boy, 1984); *Airborne* (Enigma, 1984); *Last Time I Drank* (Enigma, 1985); *Rejected* (Lone Wolf, 1989); *How Do You Open the Damn Thing* (Lost and Found, 1996); *Channel Three* (Dr. Strange, 2002).

CHUMBAWUMBA

British **punk** collective started in Leeds in 1984, best known for the anthemic song "Tubthumping." An unlikely radio and **MTV** hit in 1997, the song is now ubiquitous at sports arenas. The band actually had a long and politically active career and, before they became ever-present at sporting arenas, originally started out as an anarchist collective that was notorious for playing anti–Margaret Thatcher protests and leftists benefits that were often the target of raids by British police. The band was an independent stalwart for ideological reasons for most of its early career and caused a bit of controversy among anarchist punks when it signed to EMI. When Chumbawumba decided to sign to a major label, the members took a preemptive strike by sending letters to **zines** claiming that they could have more success bringing about social change by working with the system. The song "Tubthumping" off the *Tubthumper* record turned out to be a major hit, and the follow-up single "Amnesia" cemented the success of the band worldwide. The band immediately caused controversy with subversive actions, such as playing the song in a country-and-western style when promoting the record or advocating on national television that punks had a right to shoplift from major record stores. Subsequent albums were just as politically abrasive, and EMI dropped the band in 2000, much later than anyone really had a right to expect, considering the lyrical content of most of Chumbawumba's songs. After being dropped by EMI, Chumbawumba returned to independent recording, and the message remained as consistent and anticapitalist as it was when the band started. Chumbawumba is the most unlikely anarchist collective to ever score a major hit single. Although their sound has little to do with the bombast that most people associate with punk, the band's consistency and ideological stance locates them squarely in the punk camp.

Discography: *Pictures of Starving Children Sell Records* (Agit Prop, 1986); *Slap!* (Agit Prop, 1990); *Homophobia* (Import, 1994); *Showbusiness (Live)* (One Little Indian, 1995); *Swinging with Raymond* (One Little Indian, 1996); *Tubthumper* (Republic/Universal, 1997); *Shhh* (Agit Prop, 1997); *Anarchy* (EMI, 1998); *English Rebel Songs 1381–1984* (Import, 1998); *What You See Is What You Get* (Republic/ Universal, 2000); *Readymates* (Republic/Universal, 2002); *Shhlap!* (Mutt, 2003); *UN* (Koch, 2004).

CIRCLE JERKS

Southern California **punk** band associated with the **hardcore** movement that featured former **Black Flag** singer Keith Morris on vocals (he appeared only on the first seven-inch single) and Greg Hetson, who also played in the early **Red Kross (Red Cross), Bad Religion,** and Black Flag. The Circle Jerks were one of the most popular punk bands of the early 1980s, equally adept at party anthems, biting social commentary, and speeded-up covers of 1970s kitsch songs. The band feuded briefly with Black Flag and Red Kross over ownership of songs brought to the band by Morris and Hetson but quickly became one of the most popular bands on the **Los Angeles** scene. The best-remembered lineup of the band appeared on the *Golden Shower of Hits* album and subsequent tour and featured Earl Liberty (formerly of Saccharine Trust) on bass and Chuck Biscuits (formerly of Black Flag and **DOA**) on drums. The band also appeared in the film *Repo Man,* parodying themselves as cheesy lounge singers laconically covering their classic "When the Shit Hits the Fan." Keith Morris was involved in one of the most famous **pit**-related accidents when he broke his back diving into a pit in 1984. The Circle Jerks released several influential albums, including *Group Sex, Wild in the Streets,* and *Golden Shower of Hits,* and although bass players (such as Ron Reyes) and drummers (such as powerhouse Chuck Biscuits) came and went, the core songwriting group remained. The band gained a more stable lineup and veered into more metallic territory with the release of *Wonderful* in 1985 and went almost full-out slowed-down metal with *VI* in 1987. The Circle Jerks became less visible in the late 1980s and early 1990s as Hetson began to concentrate more on Bad Religion and Morris began to take more of an interest in artist representation for record companies (A&R) and production. Between the 1980s and 1990s, the band occasionally re-formed with key members Morris and Hetson, with the addition of Zander Schloss from the **Weirdos** (and the movie *Repo Man* as well as numerous other bands and projects) on bass. The band reunited for the record *Oddities, Abnormalities and Curiosities* in 1995, which featured a puzzling cameo by Debby Gibson on a cover of "I Want to Destroy You" by the Soft Boys (Robyn Hitchcock's original band). Today, Hetson mostly tours with Bad Religion, Schloss tours with the reunited Weirdos, and Morris is an A&R man for a record label, although the band occasionally re-forms with at least Morris and Hetson for sporadic tours. Morris has one of the truly original voices in hardcore and will be equally be remembered for his work with Black Flag as well as the Circle Jerks.

Discography: *Group Sex* (Frontier, 1980); *Wild in the Streets* (Faulty Products, 1982); *Golden Shower of Hits* (LAX, 1983); *Wonderful* (Combat Core, 1985); *VI* (Relativity, 1987); *Gig* (Relativity, 1992); *Oddities, Abnormalities and Curiosities* (Mercury, 1995).

CIV

Melodic **punk** band led by charismatic bald singer Civ (Anthony Civocelli) that featured former members of **Gorilla Biscuits** (Civocelli, bassist Arthur Smilios, and drummer Sammy Siegler) and was produced by former Gorilla Biscuits and current **Quicksand** guitarist Walter Schreifels. Civ scored a minor radio and video hit with the catchy song "Can't Wait One Minute More" off the hit record *Set Your Goals*, which melded various aspects of punk rock to commercial production during the period when it looked as though punk would indeed rule the airwaves. A follow-up album was less successful, and the band called it quits in 1998. "Can't Wait One Minute More" was used in a car commercial.

Discography: *Set Your Goals* (Revelation/Lava/Atlantic, 1995); *Thirteen Day Getaway* (Atlantic, 1998).

CLAMOR

Zine started in February 2000 by Jen Angel, formerly of the **zines** *Fucktooth* and **Maximum Rock 'n' Roll,** who also published the zine yearbook. *Clamor* is also run by Jason Kucsma, who cofounded the zine when Angel left *Maximum Rock 'n' Roll* and who founded and runs the zine conference, the Allied Media Conference. *Clamor* works toward progressive social change by showcasing writing that challenges mainstream consumer culture. The zine was a quick success, and *Utne* magazine named *Clamor* the best new title in 2000.

CLASH

One of the most famous, critically acclaimed, and commercially successful **punk** bands in both England and the United States and among the few punk bands that nonpunks can name. Although the Clash had several successful tours and record sales in the United States and abroad, this British band ultimately will be best known for its commitment to politics (although it is a somewhat haphazard ideology to actually pin down) and its experimental approach to punk rock. Ultimately, the Clash was the band that for most of its brief career was (after the demise of the **Sex Pistols**) the public face of punk rock as far as mass media was concerned. Very much like the Sex Pistols, the Clash was more or less the idea of a Svengali, in this case Bernie Rhodes, a **situationist** and friend of **Malcolm McLaren** who wanted to form a band to rival the Sex Pistols. The band formed in London in June 1976 out of the ashes of the **London SS** (featuring Mick Jones, future **Generation X** bassist Tony James, as well as future PIL member Keith Levene) and the **101ers, Joe Strummer's** pub rock band. Strummer had been convinced to quit the 101ers by Rhodes, who simply introduced him to the others and announced that Strummer would be working with them. A search for a drummer eventually found Terry Chimes (sometimes known as Tory Crimes), who supported the band until its first record. After fighting over musical direction, Levene was forced out, and the lineup solidified with Strummer on lead vocals and guitar, Mick Jones on guitar and vocals, and Paul Simonon on bass (which he did not play as such but learned his parts). Simonon provided much of the artistic direction and look, aided by Rhodes, and Strummer and Jones soon formed a musical partnership that would rival John Lennon and Paul McCartney for sheer output and musical breadth. A major turning point for the band musically and politically was the Notting Hill riot of August 1976 in which the police clashed with young black men. The subsequent violence inspired two of the Clash's best early songs, "White Riot" and "White Man in

For a while it seemed as though the Clash would single-handedly make radio relevant again. *Photofest.*

Hammersmith Palais," which demonstrated the Clash's commitment to social change as opposed to mere **nihilism.** The Clash then joined the notorious Anarchy tour of December 1976, with the Sex Pistols, the **Damned,** and the **Heartbreakers,** but the initial 19 dates were marked by chaos, confrontation, cancellations, and the removal of the Damned from the tour. The Clash stunned the punk community by signing to CBS Records in January 1977, which many, including the zine *Sniffin' Glue,* saw as a sellout. The band began recording its first record in early 1977, and the album, *The Clash,* was released in England in November 1977 but was not released at that time in the United States due to record company concerns about the quality of the production. In October 1978, the Clash released its second record produced by Blue Oyster Cult producer Sandy Pearlman, *Give 'Em Enough Rope,* which was, due to contractual disputes, the band's first release in the United States. (The first Clash album was not considered commercial enough, and when it was finally released in the United States, several of the "less commercial" tracks had been substituted by other songs.) After the first record, the apolitical Chimes left the band and was replaced by the musically adventurous Topper Headon, who would stay with the band until the last record. Although *Give 'Em Enough Rope* was a worthy follow-up, the band felt constrained by the sound of punk, and Strummer and Simonon were in particular fascinated by the **reggae** sounds of Britain's Caribbean subculture. In 1979, the band followed with the double record **London Calling,** which contained 19 new songs. The album's unlisted final track on side four, "Train in Vain" (often mistakenly called "Stand by Me"), which had been left off the original track listings because it was intended to be included as a flexi-disc, became a hit for the band when it was released as a single. The cover of *London Calling* was a parody/homage to the first Elvis Presley album, and some ads promoting the album featured a young Elvis holding the album aloft while sneering. The album was an instant classic that mixed funk, reggae, punk, **rockabilly,** and jazz over ambitious riffs and critiques of capitalism and consumer culture. The Clash tasted success through experimentation and became a formidable live band. In 1980, they played a legendary extended stay at New York City's Bond's Casino in Times Square, where they allowed bands as diverse **Kraut** to the **Bad Brains** to early rap stars to support them, much to the dismay of many of the more parochial punk fans. If many fans were disappointed by the Clash's embrace of world music, the next album, the politically charged and musically all-over-the-map *Sandinista!,* was the nail in the coffin. The record company at first balked at the unwieldy three-record set but later relented when the Clash agreed to lose money by selling the album at a single-album price. *Sandinista!* was much more musically diverse and politically ambitious, but the quality suffered. After the Clash lost money on the record and touring, the band regrouped to record the much more accessible (at least on side one) *Combat Rock* album, which spawned the hit singles "Should I Stay or Should I go" and "Rock the Casbah." The Clash had its highest profile tour, with drummer Terry Chimes returning to replace the drug-addicted Topper Headon, and opened for the Who in a stadium tour. Tensions between Strummer and Jones reached a peak, however, and the band subsequently booted Jones. Drummer Chimes left quickly, and Strummer and Simonon recruited two guitarists and a new drummer to record the much-maligned *Cut the Crap* album. After the Clash finally called it quits following the tours that supported *Cut the Crap,* Strummer took a brief hiatus before releasing the solo record *Earthquake Weather* and doing soundtrack work for Alex Cox and took a substantial hiatus from music before returning to rock with the Mescaleros in the 1990s. The Mescaleros released two albums before Strummer's untimely death of a heart attack in December 2002, and a posthumous album was released that contained 10 songs the band had been working on at the time of Strummer's death. Mick Jones formed the adventurous Big Audio Dynamite after leaving the Clash and produced several hits in the United States and Europe before ending the second version of Big Audio Dynamite in the 1990s. Jones turned to producing band such as the Libertines and formed the group Carbon/Silicon with Tony James of Generation X. Paul Simonon worked briefly for the band Havana 3 a.m. before concentrating on his painting. The Clash were inducted into the Rock and Roll Hall of Fame in 2003, although long-time drummer Topper Headon was not able to attend due to problems with his visa, thanks to prior drug-related convictions.

The legacy of the Clash is impossible to underestimate, and the members' commitment to their ideals, no matter how tenuous some of the those ideals may have been, has been extremely inspirational to legions of punks who idolized the Clash when they were around (calling them the "only band that matters") and, in particular, idolized lead singer Joe Strummer for his consistency, dedication to his own vision, and as a spiritual godfather to the British and U.S. scenes. The Clash are also famous for expanding punk's sonic palette to include rap, reggae, funk, **dub,** and world music and for educating numerous young punks to the fact that punk was not just three chords and a speeded-up beat.

Discography: *The Clash* (UK CBS, 1977,+ 1999); *Give 'Em Enough Rope* (Epic, 1978,+ 1999); *The Cost of Living* EP (UK CBS, 1979); *The Clash* (Epic, 1979,+ 1999); *London Calling* (Epic, 1979,+ 1999,+ 2004); *Black Market Clash* (Epic, 1980); *Sandinista!* (Epic, 1980,+ 1999); *Combat Rock* (Epic, 1982,+ 1999); *Cut the Crap* (Epic, 1985); *I Fought the Law* EP (UK CBS, 1988); *The Story of the Clash Volume 1* (Epic,

1988); *Crucial Music: The Clash Collection* (CBS Special Products/Relativity, 1989); *Crucial Music: 1977 Revisited* (CBS Special Products/Relativity, 1990); *Return to Brixton* EP (Epic, 1990); *Clash on Broadway* (Epic/Legacy, 1991); *The Singles* (Epic, 1999); *Super Black Market Clash* (Epic, 1999); *From Here to Eternity* (Epic, 1999). **Joe Strummer:** *Walker* (Virgin Movie Music, 1987); *Earthquake Weather* (Epic, 1989); *Gangsterville* EP (UK Epic, 1989); *Island Hopping* EP (UK Epic, 1989). **Joe Strummer and the Mescaleros:** *Rock Art and the X-Ray Style* (Mercury, 1999); *Global a Go-Go* (Hellcat, 2001); *Streetcore* (Hellcat, 2003). **Havana 3 A.M.:** *Havana 3 A.M.* (IRS, 1991).

CLEVELAND

The fertile Cleveland, Ohio, music scene of the early 1970s was the home of classic punk forefathers, such as **Rocket from the Tombs** (featuring future members of the **Dead Boys** and **Pere Ubu** and legendary songwriter Pete Laughner); the band that anticipated much of punk's fashion sense and style, the **Electric Eels;** early punk rock legend the **Pagans;** as well as other bands that coalesced around the scene, such as Pere Ubu, the **Cramps,** and **Devo.** Cleveland was perhaps as good a birthplace for punk as anywhere else, but the low rents and general insolvency of the city (it went bankrupt in 1978) encouraged bands first to be creative and later to move away in search of a more creative outlet for their music.

COCKNEY REJECTS

English **punk** band associated with the **oi** movement both because of its working-class lyrics and for the 1980 song "Oi! Oi! Oi!" The Cockney Rejects were followed by **National Front** members, who did not get the band's working-class message of solidarity.
Discography: *Greatest Hits Volume 1* (EMI, 1980); *Greatest Hits Volume 2* (EMI, 1980); *Greatest Hits Volume 3* (EMI, 1981); *The Power and the Glory* (Zonophone, 1981); *The Wild Ones* (AKA, 1982); *Quiet Storm* (Heavy Metal Records, 1984); *Unheard Rejects* (Wonderful World Records, 1985); *Lethal* (Neat Records, 1990); *The Punk Singles Collection* (Dojo, 1997); *Greatest Hits Volume 4* (Rhythm Vicar, 1997); *Out of the Gutter* (Captain Oi!, 2003).

CONFLICT

British **hardcore punk** band started in 1981 by vocalist Colin Jerwood that espoused causes such as vegetarianism and animal rights. Other members included Paco Correnon (drums) and Kerry Bavell (vocals). The increasingly political nature of the band caused controversy in the British press and clashes with the increasingly nervous British police force. Conflict, like **Crass** before it, was extremely vocal in its opposition to the dominant political structure of Great Britain and advocated real political action as opposed to simply singing about anarchy. The band demanded that its followers also be dedicated to fighting against injustice. Steve Ignorant from Crass joined the band in the late 1980s as a co-lead vocalist and contributed songs from the Crass repertoire to the band's live shows. After Ignorant departed in 1989, the band released the album *The Final Conflict*, supposedly announcing their demise, but the band re-formed in the early 1990s and continued to record and tour sporadically.
Discography: *It's Time to See Who's Who* (Corpus Christi, 1983); *Increase the Pressure* (Motorhate, 1984); *Only Stupid Bastards Help EMI* (Model Army, 1986); *The Ungovernable Force* (Motorhate, 1987); *Turning Rebellion into Money* (Motorhate, 1987); *From Protest to Resistance* (Motorhate, 1988); *Against All Odds* (Motorhate, 1989); *The Final Conflict* (Motorhate, 1989); *Conclusion* (Cleopatra, 1994); *We Won't Take No More* (Conflict, 1995); *Deploying All Means Necessary* (Cleopatra, 1997); *In the Venue* (Motorhate, 2000); *In America* (Go Kart, 2001); *Carlo Giuliani* (Jungle, 2003); *There's No Power without Control* (Motorhate, 2003); *Rebellion Sucks* (Motorhate, 2004).

COOPER-CLARKE, JOHN

English **punk** poet who opened for many prominent punk acts and released several records of spoken-word social commentary. John Cooper-Clarke battled a **heroin** problem for several years but returned to touring and performing live. He appeared as a commentator in **Don Letts**'s movie *Punk Attitude* in 2005.

Discography: *Disguise in Love* (CBS, 1978); *Ou Est la Maison de Frommage* (Epic, 1978); *Walking Back to Happiness* (Epic, 1979); *Snap, Crackle and Bop* (Epic, 1980); *Me & My Big Mouth* (Epic, 1981); *Zip Style Method* (Epic, 1982).

CORROSION OF CONFORMITY

Punk band from North Carolina that helped pioneer the crossover between punk rock and heavy metal during the mid-1980s. Corrosion of Conformity's debut album, *Eye for an Eye*, was standard thrash, but *Animosity* in 1985 helped pave the way for the punk-metal crossover, as done by punk bands such as **Suicidal Tendencies, DRI,** and **TSOL.** The band continued to make music well into the 1990s with numerous personnel changes. The original band consisted of Reed Mullins on drums, Mike Dean (who left for Blind and was replaced by Phil Swisher but returned for the *Deliverance* album) on bass, Woody Weatherman on guitar, and vocalist Benji Shelton. Numerous singers came and left, including Eric Eycke, Simon Bob, Karl Agell, and Pepper Keenan (and Dean sang as well as played bass for a while). Corrosion of Conformity is best known for taking punk's energy and adding metal influences, spearheading both the punk-metal crossover and the introduction of many metal fans to punk rock and many punk rock fans to speed metal. The band broke up in 2001 but re-formed in 2005 for touring and recording.

Discography: *Eye for an Eye* (Caroline, 1983, 1990); *Animosity* (Combat, 1985; Metal Blade, 1994); *Technocracy* (Combat, 1987; remastered, Sony, 1995); *Blind* (Combat, 1991; extra tracks and remastered, Sony 1995); *Vote with a Bullet* (Relativity, 1992); *Deliverance* (Sony, 1994); *Wiseblood* (Sony, 1996); *America's Volume Dealer* (Sanctuary, 2000); *Live Volume* (Sanctuary, 2001); *In the Arms of God* (Sanctuary, 2005).

COUNTY, WAYNE/JAYNE

Campy, preoperative, budding transsexual Wayne/Jayne County was a key influence on the early days of **punk** and was a key scenemaker at **Max's Kansas City** during its heyday. First as a DJ and later as the leader of Wayne County and the Electric Chairs, Wayne County pioneered a raunchy, glam-influenced version of punk that dealt with gender issues in songs such as "Man Enough to Be a Woman" and "Wonder Woman."

Wayne County was born in Dallas, Texas, and grew up feeling as though he should have been born a woman. He gained notoriety performing at drag show in the gay bars of Atlanta before moving to New York City and joining the downtown theater and gay club scene, taking part in the Stonewall riots. At Stonewall, County became roommates with **Leee Black Childers** as well as Andy Warhol associates Holly Woodlawn and Jackie Curtis and soon was performing in the Warhol play *Pork* in England. There, Wayne became a local celebrity and encountered **David Bowie,** who signed her to his MainMan management company, but Bowie never got around to producing a record for Wayne's first band, Queen Elizabeth, which also featured Jerry Nolan, later of the **New York Dolls.** After the breakup of Queen Elizabeth, Wayne continued deejaying at Max's (allegedly the first U.S. DJ to play "Anarchy in the UK" by the **Sex Pistols)** and formed a second band, Wayne County and the Backstreet Boys. Wayne relocated to England and solidified the band (now called the Electric Chairs) with guitarist Greg Van Cook, bassist Val Haller, and eventually J.J. Johnson on drums. While in England, the band appeared in the Derek Jarman film *Jubilee* and put out a single on Miles Copeland's illegal label but did not find much success until Safari Records, under a pseudonym, released the seminal punk single "Fuck Off" (featuring piano by Jools Holland from Squeeze). The song solidified Wayne's reputation for provocation, which was furthered by the release of the band's first album, *The Electric Chairs*, with member Henry Padvoni (formerly of the Police). After the record's release, Van Cook left and was replaced by former Backstreet Boy Elliot Michaels for the second record, *Storm the Gates of Heaven*. By the time of the album *Things Your Mother Never Told You*, Wayne had begun having surgeries in his quest to change his identity to Jayne County. At that point, the Electric Chairs and Jayne split amicably, and Jayne moved to Berlin.

County was also the focus of a famous incident at **CBGB's** in which, after enduring heckling by Handsome Dick Manitoba of the **Dictators,** she attacked him with a microphone stand, sending Manitoba to the hospital with a broken collarbone. The local scene divided over who to support, with some punks siding with Manitoba and some punks siding with County and playing a benefit for her. County continued to record and tour, sometimes sharing a stage with old nemesis Handsome Dick Manitoba, old wounds seemingly forgotten. The legacy of Wayne/Jayne County can be seen in the gender-bending experiment s of David Bowie and others of the glam movement, who, if not directly influenced by County, were certainly aware of her work before they began their own experimentations.

Discography: *The Electric Chairs* (Safari, 1978); *Storm the Gates of Heaven* (Safari, 1978); *Blatantly Offensive* (Safari, 1978); *Man Enough to Be a Woman* (Safari, 1978); *Things Your Mother Never Told You* (Safari, 1979); *Rock n' Roll Resurrection* (live; Safari, 1980); *The Best of Jayne/Wayne County and the Electric Chairs* (Safari, 1981); *Private Oyster* (Revolver, 1986); *Amerikan Cleopatra* (Konnexion, 1987); *Betty Grable's Legs* EP (Jungle, 1989); *Goddess of Wet Dreams* (ESP, 1993); *Rock n' Roll Cleopatra* (RPM, 1993); *Let Your Backbone Slip* (RPM, 1995, 2000); *Deviation* (Royalty, 1996); *Wash Me in the Blood of Rock and Roll* (Fang, 2002); *So New York* (Ratcage, 2003).

CRAMPS

Enormously influential band that crossed **punk** rock with U.S. roots music, **rockabilly,** blues, and country to form a unique hybrid that was later adapted by numerous underground bands across the United States and particularly in Europe and Japan. The band has existed (with various personnel changes) for almost 30 years and continues to tour. The nucleus of the band met in California in 1972 when Lux Interior picked up a hitchhiker who turned out to be Poison Ivy Rorschach and briefly relocated to Akron, Ohio, before going to New York City. They debuted at an audition night at **Max's Kansas City** in New York City in 1976 and first released a record in March 1978, a cover of "Surfing Bird" with "The Way I Walk" in a style that subsequently became known as **psychobilly,** a cross between frenetic, raved-out rockabilly and either psychedelic or psychotic music, depending upon who is telling the tale. The band featured Lux Interior (Erick Purkhiser) on vocals, Poison Ivy Rorschach (Kristy Wallace) on guitar, Bryan Gregory on guitar, and Nick Knox on drums. For many of the first records, the band had no bass player and originally saw no need for one due to the members' devotion to the sound of early rockabilly and science fiction based music. The Cramps proved immensely influential, although they received almost no mainstream recognition. Various guitar players came and went, although the band has remained stable for years, with new musicians backing up the ever-agile Interior and the ever-vamping Ivy. The influence of the Cramps can be found in acts as diverse as the Reverend Horton Heat and White Zombie.

Discography: *Hot Club* (bootleg; CRA, 1977); *Lucky 13* (Drug Fiend, 1978); *Tales from the Cramps* (bootleg; Cave, 1979); *This is Pop* (bootleg; Wolf, 1979); *Same As the Caveman* (bootleg; So What, 1979); *Gravest Hits* EP (Illegal, 1979); *Nazibilly Werwoelfen N'ont Pas De Bausparvertrag* (bootleg; Democrazy, 1979); *Songs the Lord Taught Us* (Illegal/IRS, 1980; A&M, 1990); *Rock n' Roll Monster Bash* (bootleg; Turn Blue Records, 1980); *Psychedelic Jungle* (IRS, 1981); *Human Fly* (bootleg; CPS, 1981); *Psychedelic*

With lead singer Steve Ignorant, Crass was a band that made the Sex Pistols seem like the Bay City Rollers. © *Retna Ltd.*

Safari (bootleg; Creepy) 1982*Spank 'n' Roll* (bootleg; Non Profit, 1982); *Total Destroy Seattle!!* (bootleg; Prairie Dog, 1982); *Live at Larry's* (bootleg; Vengeance, 1982); *Fetishism* (bootleg; Ghoul-Ash, 1982); *Live At Harry's* (bootleg; Vengeance, 1982); *Beyond the Valley of the Cramps* (bootleg; LUX, 1983); *Voodoo Rhythm* (OK, 1983); … *Off the Bone* (UK Illegal, 1983); *Smell of Female* (Enigma, 1983, 1990; Restless, 1994; Vengeance, 2001); *Werewolf in My Pocket* (bootleg; Tel International, 1983); *Teenage Drug Idol* (bootleg; Tel International, 1983); *Bad Music for Bad People* (IRS, 1984; A&M, 1990); *Faster Pussycat* (bootleg; CRA, 1984); *Sex & Cramps & Rock 'n' Roll!* (bootleg; The Swingin' Pig, 1986); *These Pussies Can Do the Dog* (bootleg; Good Taste, 1986); *A Date with Elvis* (UK Big Beat 1986; Enigma, 1990; Restless, 1994; Vengeance, 2001); *Kizmiaz* (bootleg; Lounging, 1986); *Rockinnreelininaucklandnewzealandxxx* (live; UK Vengeance, 1987; Vengeance/Restless, 1994, 2001); *What's Inside a Ghoul* (Pow Wow, 1988); *Gravest Hits/Psychedelic Jungle* (IRS, 1989); *Booze Party* (bootleg; LUX, 1989); *Electric Cheese* (bootleg; Alien, 1990); *Stay Sick!* (Enigma, 1990; Dutch East Wax, 1991; Vengeance, 2001); *All Women Are Bad EP* (UK Enigma, 1990); *Songs the Cramps Taught Us!* (bootleg; Brace, 1990); *Bikini Girls with Machine Guns Are Searching the Creature from the Black Leather Lagoon* (bootleg; SP, 1990); *Eyeball in My Martini* (Big Beat, 1991); *Look Mom No Head!* (Restless, 1991, 1993); *FlameJob* (Medicine, 1994; Epitaph, 1994); *Big Beat from Badsville* (Epitaph, 1997); *Off the Bone* (Phantom, 1998); *Fiends of Dope Island* (Vengeance, 2003); *Off the Bone/Songs the Lord Taught Us* (Empire, 2003); *How to Make a Monster* (Vengeance, 2004).

CRASS

Crass is probably the best known and most consistent early British **punk** band to espouse **anarchy** and the communal life as well as the **DIY** aesthetic. Led by drummer and songwriter Penny Rimbaud (Jeremy John Ratter) and singer Steve Ignorant, the group began as a radical collective (who lived together in a farmhouse that Rimbaud had long rented and established a commune) and rejected the empty sloganeering of much of English punk rock of the late 1970s for an anarchic sound and ideology dedicated to radical ideals and a radical anticapitalist lifestyle. The band was often controversial and firm in its ideological stance, and in 1978 the original pressing of their first record, *The Feeding of the 5000*, was notable for the refusal of the Irish pressing plant to press the record unless the original opening track, "Asylum," an antireligious rant, was deleted. The original versions were released without the song, which was replaced by two minutes of silence called "Free Speech." The original band was formed as a so-called art collective and lasted for only a few performances before calling it quits. The second version of the band, which called itself Crass (after a line in **David Bowie's** "Ziggy Stardust" that "the kids was just Crass"), supplanting Rimbaud's original choice of Storm-trooper, featured Penny Rimbaud on drums, Pete Wright on bass, Andy Palmer (who apparently never learned a single chord but played by open-tuning and sliding his hand on the guitar neck) and Phil Free on guitars, and Steve Ignorant (Oscar Thompson), Eve Libertine, and Joy De Vivre on vocals. In the spirit of the commune and the band's artistic philosophy, the band also featured Gee, who did art and graphic design, and Mick, who did the disturbing experimental films that were projected behind the band as they played onstage. The band worked as a true collective, and each member had veto power over band decisions, guaranteeing that any band product, lyrics, or statements represented the entire band, not just a particular member. Accordingly, **flyers** were produced and handed out at every show that explained the band's philosophical approach and vegetarian beliefs. True to form, Crass's first gig was a benefit concert for a group of squatters held in a children's playground in London. After gigging for a while, the band released its first record, *The Feeding of the 5000* (named for the 5,000 copies originally pressed), which was reissued when the initial pressing on the Small Wonder label sold out. This time, however (as with all future releases), it was released on the band's own **Crass Records** label, which eventually also released numerous other records by like-minded bands such as the **Poison Girls.** The next record, *Stations of the Crass*, celebrated the anticapitalism graffiti campaign on the London Underground pioneered by Rimbaud and Libertine. The third Crass record was a remarkable feminist statement called *Penis Envy*, on which all vocals were sung by the band's two female vocalists, Eve Libertine and Joy De Vivre. The album was controversial, but even more controversial was a prank the band played in conjunction with the album's release. Under the pseudonym Creative Recordings and Sound Services, the band offered the schmaltzy track "Our Wedding" as a free flexi-disc to a British teen magazine called *Loving*, which, unaware of the band, accepted the flexi-disc and made it a part of their special brides issue. Controversy erupted when it was discovered that the song was a parody. Subsequent recordings such as *Christ—The Album* reiterated the band's philosophy, but when Great Britain declared war against Argentina over the Falkland Islands, Crass was reenergized and released an extremely polarizing attack on Margaret Thatcher; "How Does It Feel to Be the Mother of a Thousand Dead" led to controversy in the British media as well as discussion in Parliament. In 1982, in response to government pressure and facing possible obscenity charges, Crass engaged in civil disobedience, culminating in several "Stop the City" protests designed to grind London's business district to a halt. Thousands of protesters participated, which led to greater inspiration for worldwide days of civil disobedience.

Crass was dedicated to getting out the members' anarchistic, antireligion, anticapitalist views rather than making money as a band and felt that bands such as the **Clash** and the **Sex Pistols** had betrayed the original promise of punk rock by signing to major labels. The assumption of the band was that simply singing about anarchy was not enough and that the band's political and social statements had to be backed up by action and consistency. Former communard (of the commune, not the **New Wave** band) Dave King designed the ambiguous Crass logo, which combined elements of the swastika, the Christian cross, and two serpents' heads, that was also later used by many anarchist punks as a symbol of rebellion to the dominant power structure, along with the anarchy *A* symbol, which the band also quickly adopted for its stage shows. Most of Crass's shows were benefits for various causes, including the Campaign for Nuclear Disarmament (CND) and squatters' rights. The band was also notorious for the so-called Thatchergate tapes, which were doctored by band member Pete to mimic a phone call between Prime Minister Margaret Thatcher and U.S. President

Ronald Reagan in which Thatcher indicated her responsibility for the sinking of a British warship. The band's prank led to a statement from the U.S. State Department denouncing the tape as a KGB forgery and considerable media outcry until the hoax was discovered by the British newspaper *The Observer*. The band eventually succumbed to internal strife and police harassment and broke up in 1984 after playing a final benefit performance for striking miners in southern Wales.

Crass is still regarded as one of the most influential punk bands and certainly one of the most consistent successful punk bands to kept true to the punk DIY aesthetic. Various members went on to other projects, most notably Steve Ignorant, who worked with British punk band **Conflict,** and Penny Rimbaud, who wrote several books on his life and philosophy. Out of the entire dispute over what constitutes punk rock, Crass made the most compelling argument that the loud-and-fast sound is not necessarily the benchmark of what punk rock is. Rather, the essence of punk rock is in attitude, authenticity, and keeping to a consistent personal ethic. A really cool punk name does not hurt either. Although the legacy of Crass lives on, some do not seem to get the band, and soccer superstar David Beckham was photographed in 2005 talking to Elton John while wearing a Crass T-shirt.

Discography: *Reality Asylum 7″* (Crass, 1978); *The Feeding of the 5000* (Small Wonder, 1978; second sitting, Crass, 1980, 1995); *Stations of the Crass* (UK Crass, 1979, 1995); *Penis Envy* (UK Crass, 1981, 1995); *Christ—The Album* (UK Crass, 1982, 1995); *Yes Sir, I Will* (UK Crass, 1983, 1995); *10 Notes on a Summer's Day* (UK Crass, 1986, 1998); *Best Before 1984* (Crass, 1995); *Christ: The Bootleg* (live; Allied, 1996; No Idea, 1999); *You'll Ruin It for Everyone* (Import, 2001). **Penny Rimbaud & Eve Libertine:** *Acts of Love* (UK Crass, 1985).

CRASS RECORDS

Independent record label formed by anarchist collective and band **Crass** to promote its own music and that of similar bands that also wished to work outside of the capitalist music industry. Bands on Crass records at one point or another included **Poison Girls,** Donna and the Kebobs, **Zounds,** Snipers, Dirt, **Rudimentary Peni, Conflict, Flux of Pink Indians,** and like-minded U.S. band **MDC.**

CRIME

San Francisco area **punk** band that released the classic single "Hot Wire My Heart," which was later covered by **Sonic Youth.** Crime was started in 1976 by Johnny Strike on guitar and vocals, Frankie Fix on guitar and vocals, Ron the Ripper on bass (replaced by Elton in 1986 and Ron Greco for the 2004 reunion), and Chris Cat on drums (replaced by Ricky Tractor, Brittely Black, and Hank Rank). The band released primarily singles on the Crime Records label and regarded itself as "San Francisco's first Rock and Roll band." The best compilation of Crime's recordings was rereleased in 2004 as *San Francisco's Still Doomed*. The band reunited with Johnny Strike, Hank Rank, Michael Lucas on bass, and guitarist Pat "Monsignor" Ryan. Crime was notorious for sometimes performing in police uniforms and played San Quentin Prison. The band broke up in 1981, re-formed in 1986 and again in 2004.

Discography: *All the Stuff, Vols. I–III* (unknown label, 1990s); *San Francisco's Doomed* (Solar Lodge, 1992); *Terminal Boredom* (Out of Darkness, 1992); *Hate Us or Love Us, We Don't Give a Fuck* (live; Planet Pimp/ Repent, 1994); *San Francisco's First and Only Rock 'n' Roll Band* (Criminal, 1999); *Piss on Your Turntable* (Lady Butcher, 2001); *Cadillac Faggot* (live; Red Legacy, 2003); *San Francisco's Still Doomed* (Swami, 2004).

CRIPPLED YOUTH

Early name of the group that evolved into **straight edge hardcore** band **Bold.** The band reportedly realized that too many other bands already had the word *Youth* in their names. *See also* Bold.

CRO-MAGS

One of the hardest and heaviest bands in **New York hardcore,** led by Harley Flanagan (of the **Stimulators**) and influenced heavily by **Bad Brains.** The original band featured Harley Flanagan on bass, John Joseph McGeown on lead vocals, Parris Mitchell Mayhew and Doug Holland (formerly of **Kraut**) on guitar, and Mackie Jayson (who later played with Bad Brains) on drums. One of the key bands of the mid-1980s hardcore matinee scene at **CBGB's** and also politically outspoken, the band sang about Krishna Consciousness, courtesy of lead singer John Joseph, alongside brutal riffs that attracted both hardcore punks and metalheads to the scene. John Joseph left the band after the first record, and Harley took over on lead vocals for the next two albums. Although the group disbanded acrimoniously and lead singer John Joseph later served time in a naval brig for desertion, the band continued to reunite sporadically.
Discography: *The Age of Quarrel* (Rock Hotel/Profile, 1986, 1994); *Best Wishes* (Profile, 1989); *Alpha-Omega* (Century Media, 1992); *Near Death Experience* (Century Media, 1993); *Age of Quarrel/Best Wishes* (Another Planet, 1994); *Hard Times in an Age of Quarrel* (live; Century Media, 1994; Import, 2000); *Before the Quarrel* (Cro Mag, 2000); *Revenge* (Cro Mag, 2000).

CRUCIAL YOUTH

Goofy punk band that satirized the **straight edge** movement by taking it to its ridiculous extreme. Members included Joe Crucial (vocals), Ollie Grind (guitar), Maynard Krebs (guitar), Melvin Berkley (bass), and Gentleman Jim (drums).
Discography: *Straight and Loud* (Faith, 1987); *A Gig Too Far* (live; b-core, 1991); *Posi Machine* (New Red Archives, 1995); *Singles Going Straight* (New Red Archives, 2001).

CRUCIFUCKS

Cheerfully blasphemous **punk** band from Lansing, Michigan, that formed in 1982 with vocalist Doc Corbin Dart, guitarist Gus Varner, and drummer Steve Shelley (who later joined **Sonic Youth**). The band broke up but re-formed to play the **Alternative Tentacles** 20th anniversary party in 1998. The band was particularly offensive and tried to provoke whenever possible. An album cover for the record *Our Will Be Done* featured a dead police officer and caused the band to be sued by the Philadelphia Fraternal Order of Police in 1992. The latest lineup featured Dart, Steve Merchant on drums, Dave Breher on bass, and Nat Warren on guitar.
Discography: *The Crucifucks* (Alternative Tentacles, 1985); *Wisconsin* (Alternative Tentacles, 1987); *Our Will Be Done* (Alternative Tentacles, 1992); *L. D. Eye* (Alternative Tentacles, 1996). **Doc Corbin Dart:** *Patricia* (Alternative Tentacles, 1990).

CRUST PUNK

Term used to denote an abrasive offshoot of anarcho-**punk** that dealt with political topics such as the abolition of capitalism, animal rights, and veganism. Some key crust bands include Amebix, Deviated Instinct and **Nausea.**

DAG NASTY

Melodic **punk** band from **Washington, D.C.,** that originally featured Dave Smalley on vocals and Brian Baker of **Minor Threat** on guitar. The band is credited as one of the first bands (along with Rites of Spring) to pioneer the emotional brand of pop punk later called **emo.** Dag Nasty was started by Brian Baker, fresh from the demise of Minor Threat in Washington, D.C., after he was inspired by the crop of new bands that sprang in up in the mid-1980s. The band originally featured vocalist Shawn Brown, who was replaced by Dave Smalley on vocals for the *Can I Say* album. Smalley left after the first album to accept a graduate studies scholarship at New York University that allowed him to live in Israel for a year and was replaced by Pete Courtner, who played in the *Wig Out at Denkos* and *Field Day* albums, which saw the band become less emo and more commercial in sound. After losing the original rhythm section, Dag Nasty split in 1988, and Baker resurfaced in the glam metal band Junkyard with Chris Gates of the **Big Boys.** After the demise of Junkyard, Baker returned to sanity and joined **Bad Religion** after Mr. Brett left the band. Dag Nasty reunited with singer Smalley for several reunions over the next two decades and toured sporadically. Smalley sang in the post-**Descendents** band **All** and formed his own band, **Down by Law.**
Discography: *Can I Say* (Dischord, 1986; remastered, 2002); *Wig Out at Denkos* (Dischord, 1987; remastered, 2002); *Field Day* (Giant, 1988; Positive, 1995); *Trouble Is* (Giant, 1988); *85–86* (Selfless, 1991); *Four on the Floor* (Epitaph, 1992); *Can I Say/Wig Out at Denkos* (Dischord, 1995); *Minority of One* (Revelation, 2002). **Junkyard:** *Junkyard* (Geffen, 1989); *Sixes, Sevens & Nines* (Geffen, 1991).

DAMNED

One of the first wave of English **punk** bands and one of the most important and long lasting. The Damned was the first punk band to release a punk single: their debut single "New Rose" (the B-side was a cover of the Beatles song "Help") in October 1976 on **Stiff Records.** The Damned was also the first British punk band to play in the United States when they played **CBGB's** in April 1977.

The Damned was formed by Brian James, who wrote all of the band's original material, along with drummer Rat Scabies (Chris Millar), bassist Captain Sensible (Ray Burns), and singer Dave Vanian, a former grave digger who slicked his hair back and dressed entirely in black. The band began in 1975 and quickly became one of the most important punk bands as well as one of the most volatile; the Damned endured numerous breakups over its 30-year career. After the success of its first album, *Damned Damned Damned*, the band released a second record, *Music for Pleasure*, in November 1977 with second guitarist Lu (Robert Edmunds). The Damned demonstrated early that it was an extremely volatile band by breaking up shortly thereafter for the first of many times. After a few months (of presumably boredom), the Captain, Rat, and Dave Vanian began to reunite and play gigs as a three-piece as the Doomed. The Damned reunited in December 1978 without guitarist Brian James but with Captain Sensible on guitar and assuming most of the writing, which had primarily been done by James in the band's first incarnation. The Damned briefly went through several bass players, including Henry Badowski and Lemmy Kilmeister from Motörhead, before settling on Alsdair "Algy" Ward. With a stable lineup in place, the band recorded their most popular album, *Machine Gun Etiquette*. The album featured the U.K. hits "Love Song" and "Smash It Up," parts one and two (part one was an instrumental written by Captain Sensible for the late Marc Bolan of T-Rex, who had championed the Damned by having them open for him on his last tour), which established a new and experimental direction for the Damned. At the same time, the extremely prolific Captain Sensible had also been working on a solo project and had the first of

The Damned was the first British band to release a punk single and tour the United States. *Photo by Richard Young/Rex Features.*

several U.K. hits with a cover of the show tune "Happy Talk" from the musical *South Pacific.* Tensions over Captain Sensible's solo success led to his departure from the band in the early 1980s. During the mid-1980s, the band shifted in a more gothic direction with the release of the album *Phantasmagoria.* Even without the help of the departed Captain Sensible, the band was able to score several U.S. and U.K. hits with "The Shadow of Love." The original Damned reunited in the late 1980s for a tour, but that lineup did not last because of mounting tensions between Scabies and James. Eventually, the Captain agreed to rejoin only if Scabies was asked to leave.

The most current lineup of the band is Vanian, Captain Sensible, and Patricia Morrison (formerly of Los Angeles's the **Bags** and the Sisters of Mercy), who is also Vanian's wife and the mother of their child. Rat Scabies coauthored the book *Rat Scabies and the Holy Grail.*

Discography: *Damned Damned Damned* (UK Stiff, 1977; UK Demon, 1986; Frontier, 1989); *Music for Pleasure* (UK Stiff, 1977; UK Demon, 1986); *Machine Gun Etiquette* (UK Chiswick, 1979; Big Beat, 1982; Emergo, 1991); *The Black Album* (IRS, 1980); *Friday the 13th* EP (UK NEMS, 1981); *The Best of the Damned* (UK Big Beat, 1981; Emergo, 1991); *Strawberries* (UK Bronze, 1982; Dojo, 1986); *Live at Shepperton 1980* (UK Big Beat, 1982); *Live in Newcastle* (Damned, 1983); *Damned EP* (UK Stiff, 1985); *Damned but Not Forgotten* (UK Dojo, 1985); *Phantasmagoria* (MCA, 1985); *Is It a Dream?* EP (MCA, 1985); *Damned Damned Damned/Music for Pleasure* (UK Stiff, 1986); *The Captain's Birthday Party* (UK Stiff, 1986); *The Peel Sessions* EP (UK Strange Fruit, 1986); *Not the Captain's Birthday Party?* (UK Demon, 1986); *Anything* (MCA, 1986); *The Peel Sessions* EP (UK Strange Fruit, 1987); *Mindless, Directionless, Energy. Live at the Lyceum 1981* (ID/Revolver, 1987); *The Light at the End of the Tunnel* (MCA, 1987); *The Long Lost Weekend: Best of Volume 1 1/2* (UK Big Beat, 1988); *Final Damnation* (Restless, 1989); *The Peel Sessions Album* (UK Strange Fruit, 1990; Strange Fruit/Dutch East India, 1991); *EP* (UK Deltic, 1990). **Naz Nomad & the Nightmares:** *Give Daddy the Knife Cindy* (UK Big Beat, 1984).

DANCE OF DAYS

Key punk book (full title *Dance of Days: Two Decades of Punk in the Nation's Capital*) published in 2001 that analyzes the **Washington, D.C., hardcore** and political movements from the 1980s to the 1990s. The book contains numerous interviews with key players from **Minor Threat, Bad Brains, Fugazi,** Rites of Spring, and **Bikini Kill** as well as obscure bands such as Urban Verbs. It is also packed with invaluable information on the origins of **straight edge,** the rise of **Dischord Records,** and the politicization of much of punk rock. Authors Mark Jenkins, a journalist who covered many of the bands in the book, and Mark Anderson, who provides an insider's account of the role of **Positive Force** D.C. on the politicization of the punk scene, cover all the bases regarding the important players in the Washington, D.C., scene.

DANGERHOUSE RECORDS

Los Angeles record label started by Dan Brown, Pat Garrett, and Black Randy to give a voice to the artistic and political ambitions of Los Angeles's **punk** bands. The label released compilations and singles featuring many in the early punk scene during the late 1970s and early 1980s. Some of the bands that released singles on Dangerhouse included seminal Los Angeles punk bands the **Weirdos, X,** the **Dils,** the Alley Cats, the **Avengers,** and the **Bags** as well as lesser known bands such as the Randoms (led by Pat Garrett, with their controversial "Let's Get Rid of NY"), **Black Randy and the Metrosquad,** the Deadbeats, the Eyes, and Rhino 39. Dangerhouse released music primarily between 1977 and 1979 in a true **DIY** style with clear plastic sleeves and occasionally on four-track recording equipment.

DARBY CRASH

Lead singer for seminal **Los Angeles punk** band the **Germs** and as well known for his complex lyrics as his debauched life and early death. By all accounts, Darby Crash was a master

The late Stiv Bators of the Dead Boys was one of the most electrifying performers in punk rock. © *Robert Barry Francos*.

manipulator and creator of the infamous "Germs Burn" cigarette burn on the arms of Germs fans. Also known as Bobby Pyn, the former Jan Paul Beahm was revered by many as the U.S version of **Sid Vicious,** a punk with a romanticized life and an equally glamorized death. There are several books that detail his tormented life and death (Kief Hillsbery's *What We Do Is Secret* and Brendan Mullen and Don Bolles's *Lexicon Devil*).

DEAD BOYS

Key early U.S. **punk** band from Ohio best known for the punk anthem "Sonic Reducer." One of the first wave of U.S. bands grew out of the ashes of classic **Cleveland** punk bands **Rocket from the Tombs** and **Frankenstein.** The early incarnation featured lead singer Stiv Bators, guitarist Cheetah Chrome (Gene O'Conner), guitarist Jimmy Zero (William Wilder), and drummer Johnny Blitz (John Madansky) and at first played without a bass player. The band Frankenstein had been playing around Cleveland without much success when the members met the **Ramones,** who were playing a gig in the city. **Joey Ramone** was instrumental in getting the Dead Boys a Monday-night audition at **CBGB's,** and after their second gig **Hilly Kristal,** the owner of CBGB's, signed on as their manager, and within a few weeks they were singed to the Sire label and recorded their first album. The Dead Boys soon gained a following for their onstage antics, which included Stiv hanging himself with a belt, Nazi paraphernalia, and sometimes onstage fellatio from a helpful CBGB's waitress. After the first album was released (on which Bob Clearmountian played bass), the band added bassist Jeff Magnum and record their second album with Felix Pappalardi (who had worked with Cream in the 1960s). The record captured none of the live Dead Boys sound, however, and failed to make an impact on the U.S. charts. Johnny Blitz was also injured badly in a fight in which some thugs stabbed him with his own knife, and the band organized a series of benefit concerts at CBGB's that saw many bands play and guest such as Divine (the drag performer who starred in many of John Water's films) and **John Belushi,** who briefly played drums with the Dead Boys. The benefits got Blitz back on his feet (although they also caused some controversy because **Blondie** roadie Michael Sticca, who had been in the fight alongside Blitz, was arrested for his role in the fracas and spent time in jail before the charges were dismissed). The band began to argue more after this, and Sire owner Seymour Stein decided that punk was dead and that the Dead Boys should change their name, look, and image. (Stein had also sent radio stations letters asking them to refer to the music coming out of New York City as New Wave as opposed to punk; Stein largely attributed the unpleasant connotations and seemingly poor sales of punk music to the notoriety of the **Sex Pistols.**) The band decided to break up after several more concerts and after Chrome had a drug-fueled nervous breakdown and had to be dragged away by the police. Bators recorded s solo record and several singles for Greg Shaw's Bomb label and later formed the band Lords of the New Church, a sort of punk supergroup with bassist Dave Tregunna from **Sham 69** and guitarist Brian James from the **Damned.** The band became concerned with Bators's back problems and eventually put an add in the papers looking for a new lead singer, leading to Bators's departure from the group. While in Paris after the demise of the Lords of the New Church, Bators also attempted to form a supergroup with **Dee Dee Ramone** and **Johnny Thunders,** but tensions split that band before it could record. Bators was hit by an automobile and died of internal injuries on June 4, 1990. The Dead Boys without Bators reunited for a concert to save CBGB's in August 2005.

Discography: *Young Loud and Snotty* (Sire, 1977, 1992); *We Have Come for Your Children* (Sire, 1978; Wea International, 2001); *Night of the Living Dead Boys* (live; Bomp!, 1981, 1998); *The Return of the Living Dead Boys* (Revenge, 1987); *Liver Than You'll Ever Be* (live; Pilot, 1988, 2002); *Younger, Louder and Snottier (The Rough Mixes)* (UK Necrophilia, 1989; Bomp!, 1997); *Twistin' on the Devil's Fork: Live at CBGB's* (Bacchus, 1997); *Down in Flames* (Bomp!, 1998); *Magnificent Chaos* (Bomp!, 1998); *All This & More* (Bomp!, 1998); *3rd Generation Nation* (Msi, 1999).

DEAD KENNEDYS

Extremely influential **punk** band from San Francisco that featured the politicized and satirically biting lyrics of lead singer **Jello Biafra** (Eric Boucher, who took the name Jello Biafra as a way of juxtaposing U.S. consumer culture and a region of Africa with much internal strife). The classic version of the band consisted of guitarist East Bay Ray (Ray Pepperel), bassist Klaus Flouride (Jeff Lyle), and drummer Darren "D.H." Peligro. They quickly gained popularity and notoriety with their early singles "Holiday in Cambodia" and "California, Uber Alles" and the album *Fresh Fruit for Rotting Vegetables.* The Dead Kennedys made it a point to play all-age shows to inculcate younger fans into the mysteries of **hardcore** and political activism. To promote their vision and release records outside of the mainstream, Biafra formed **Alternative Tentacles** records with Bill Gilliam. The Dead Kennedys were one of the two or three most influential punk bands, and they were perhaps one of the most politically active bands that stuck to the **DIY** aesthetic, released their own records, and kept control of their own production. Biafra also ran for mayor of San Francisco, ranking a respectable fourth out of 10 candidates. Aside from being remembered for several musically adventurous albums that helped set the sonic template for hardcore punk, the Dead Kennedys were embroiled in a lengthy lawsuit about the insert poster of their last album, *Frankenchrist,* which featured drawings of penises by artist H.R. Giger (who conceptualized the alien in the *Alien* films). In 1986, the Dead Kennedys retired after releasing the *Bedtime for Democracy* record. The other members of the band later reunited without Biafra after wresting control of the Dead Kennedys' catalogs on Alternative Tentacles from Biafra in a lawsuit over unpaid royalties. The band continued to tour the United States with new lead singer and former child actor Brandon Cruz, formerly of the band **Dr. Know.** Jello Biafra continued his spoken-word performances, recorded, and collaborated with bands such as **DOA.**

Discography: *Fresh Fruit for Rotting Vegetables* (IRS, 1980; Alternative Tentacles, 1993; Manifesto/Cleopatra, 2002; with extra tracks, Cherry Red, 1999); *In God We Trust, Inc.* EP (Alternative Tentacles/Faulty Products, 1981; Manifesto, 2001); *Plastic Surgery Disasters/In God We Trust, Inc.* (Alternative Tentacles, 1982; Manifesto, 2001); *Frankenchrist* (Alternative Tentacles, 1985; Manifesto, 2001); *Bedtime for Democracy* (Alternative Tentacles, 1986; Manifesto, 2001); *Give Me Convenience or Give Me Death* (Alternative Tentacles, 1987, 1990; Manifesto, 2001); *Mutiny on the Bay* (live; Manifesto, 2001); *Live at the Deaf Club 1979* (Manifesto, 2004). **Klaus Flouride:** *Cha Cha Cha with Mr. Flouride* (Alternative Tentacles, 1985); *Because I Say So* (Alternative Tentacles, 1988); *The Light Is Flickering* (Alternative Tentacles, 1991).

DEAD MILKMEN

Humorous **punk** band from Philadelphia that scored minor chart hits with "Punk Rock Girl" and "Bitchin' Camaro." The band was part of a less violent reaction to the reactionary movements prevalent in **hardcore** during the early to mid-1980s and was also known for the members' keen social satire. The band consisted of singer Rodney Anonymous (sometimes under a variety of different last names, including Mellencamp at one point), Joe Jack Talcum on guitar (and occasionally lead vocals, especially on the hit "Punk Rock Girl"), Dean Clean on drums, and Dave Blood on bass. The band started out as a fairly straightforward but melodic punk band (highlighted by Talcum's almost jangly guitar) with roots in hardcore that celebrated the absurd. Songs parodied everything from Charles Nelson Reilly to goth wannabes to the punk rock scene itself. *Beelzebubba* was probably the artistic and commercial highlight, but things started to go downhill the more Talcum shared the vocal duties with Rodney. After the band broke up, the members formed various side projects and, tragically, Blood committed suicide in 2003. As an interesting side note, former Detroit Tigers infielder Jim Walewander was ostracized by fans and team management when he outed himself as a Dead Milkmen fan and the local media portrayed him, essentially, as a crazed lunatic for liking punk rock.
Discography: *Big Lizard in my Back Yard* (Fever/Enigma, 1985); *Eat Your Paisley!* (Fever/Restless, 1986); *Bucky Fellini* (Fever/Enigma, 1987); *Beelzebubba* (Fever/Enigma, 1988); *Metaphysical Graffiti* (Enigma, 1990); *Soul Rotation* (Hollywood, 1992); *Not Richard, but Dick* (Hollywood, 1993); *Chaos Rules: Live at the Trocadero* (Restless, 1994); *Stoney's Extra Stout (Pig)* (Restless, 1995).

DECLINE OF WESTERN CIVILIZATION

Movie by filmmaker Penelope Spheeris (who later directed *Wayne's World* and many other mainstream films) released in 1981 that detailed the early days of the **Los Angeles punk** scene. The film featured performances by **Black Flag,** the **Germs,** and **X,** which helped both to popularize and to sensationalize the scene. It was a priceless historical document of how certain punks looked at the scene and themselves during that time period and of the media's desire to somehow explain and codify the punk movement as something understandable for audiences that were not certain about what being a punk entailed.

DECLINE OF WESTERN CIVILIZATION PART III

Movie released in 1998 by filmmaker Penelope Spheeris, who also directed parts I and II (part II had the subtitle *Metal Years* and had nothing to do with punk rock), that concentrated on **Los Angeles** street punks.

DEEP WOUND

Early **hardcore** band from Massachusetts that featured a young J. Mascis on drums, Lou Barlow on guitar, Scott Helland on bass, and vocalist Charlie Nakajima. Barlow and Mascis formed the much more successful band Dinosaur Jr.

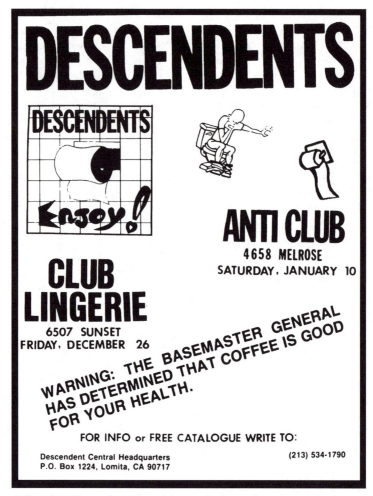

A flyer for a Descendents show. Homemade flyers often advertised upcoming gigs. *Collection of the author.*

DESCENDENTS

Enormously influential pop **punk** band from California. Almost every current pop punk band owed the Descendents royalties of some sort or at least an acknowledgment of from whom they were stealing. The band was founded in 1979 by Bill Stevenson as a three-piece with bassist Tony Lombardo, and guitarist Frank Navetta for the *Ride the Wild* EP7 but became better known with the addition of vocalist Milo Auckerman, who recorded the classic *Fat* EP, which included the song "Weinerschnitzel" (later featured in the Film *Pump up the Volume*). Stevenson and Auckerman were the mainstays of the band, which went through numerous personnel changes before finally solidifying in the late 1980s with the additions of Stephen Egerton on guitar and Karl Alvarez on bass. A typical Descendents song was a glorification of coffee, girls, being a geek, or a combination of all of the above. (A key part of the Descendents mythology was their love of caffeine, as epitomized by the legendary "Bonus Cup," which featured one-third cup of instant coffee and five spoonfuls of sugar.) The Descendents quickly became a popular and influential band, largely thanks to their talent for writing a poppy **hardcore** song, the less gruff (than usual in punk or hardcore) vocals of Auckerman, and the inventive drumming of Stevenson. The band had several lengthy hiatuses, the first when Milo Auckerman left for college (to pursue a career as a scientist, as immortalized in the classic album *Milo Goes to College*) and another when he pursued a Ph.D. in biochemistry. Stevenson played on several **Black Flag** records and toured with the band for several years, leaving acrimoniously in 1985 to re-form the Descendents (minus Frank Navetta, who had moved to Oregon and was replaced by Ray Cooper) for the *I Don't Want to Grow Up* album, which continued the melodic trend of its predecessor. The band continued in the same vein for the *Enjoy!* album (which contained the title song, an ode to the joys of releasing gas) with new bassist Doug Carrion, who had previously toured with the band, and then the experimental and almost jazzlike *All* record, featuring new guitarist Stephen Eggerton and bassist Karl Alvarez, who joined after the departure of Carrion and Cooper. *All* contained the brief title song and an almost as short "No! All!," which introduced the philosophy of all (a philosophy of going for all, as revealed to Stevenson and friend Pat McCuistion by the basemaster general himself) to the general public. After *All*, Auckerman left the band again to concentrate on science and finishing his Ph.D. Rather than continue the band without him, Stevenson later formed the band **All** with Alvarez, Eggerton, and singer Dave Smalley from **Dag Nasty.** Auckerman returned to the new lineup to record two albums, *Everything Sucks* and *Cool to Be You*, that continued in the vein of earlier records and showed increasingly subtlety in songwriting, although the topics of coffee, food, and girls continued to be an obsession with the Descendents. Longtime friend and inspiration McCuistion died in a fishing accident in 1987, and All released a record as *TonyALL*, featuring Tony Lombardo for the original lineup on bass and vocals). *See also* All; Black Flag.

Discography: *Fat* EP (New Alliance, 1981; SST, 1988); *Milo Goes to College* (New Alliance, 1982; SST, 1988, 1991); *Bonus Fat* (New Alliance, 1985; SST, 1988, 1991); *I Don't Want to Grow Up* (New Alliance, 1985; SST, 1988, 1990); *Enjoy!* (New Alliance/Restless, 1986, 1991); *All* (SST, 1987, 1990); *Liveage!* (SST, 1987, 1990); *Two Things at Once (Milo Goes to College/Bonus Fat)* (SST, 1988, 1991); *Hellraker* (live; SST, 1989, 1990); *Somery* (SST, 1991); *Everything Sucks* (Epitaph, 1996); *Live Plus One* (Epitaph, 2001); *Cool to Be You* (Fat Wreck Chords, 2004).

DEVIL DOGS

Long-running **New York punk** band with connections to Billy Childish and the Raunch Hands. Obviously influenced by the **Ramones** and **Dictators** (both of which the band covered on its first album), the Devil Dogs played a skuzzy, extremely New York–centric brand of old-school punk rock led by guitarist and singer Andy Gortler, bassist and singer Steve Baise, and a rotating cast of drummers. The band broke up in 1994, and Baise formed the more melodic Vikings.

Discography: *Devil Dogs* (Crypt, 1989); *Big Beef Bonanza* (Crypt, 1990); *The Devil Dogs Live in Tokyo* EP (Japan 1+2, 1991); *We Three Kings* (Crypt, 1992); *30 Sizzling Slabs* (Crypt, 1992); *Saturday Night Fever* (Crypt, 1993); *Stereodrive!* (Japan 1+2, 1994); *Laid Back Motherfuckers* EP (Headache, 1994); *(With the Raunch Hands) Sink or Swim* (Fin. GaGa Goodies, 1990).

DEVO

Cryptic, hit-making, bizarrely costumed, anarchist spuds from Akron, Ohio, who critiqued consumer culture and somehow made a lengthy career out of it. Devo is best known for the catchy 1980s hits "Whip It," "Working in a Coal Mine," and "Beautiful World." The band gelled into its most serious form around 1975, and the original lineup featured the brothers Mark, John, and Bob Mothersbaugh and Gerald Casale. The band released several singles on its own Booji Boy label in 1977, which led to their signing with Warner Brothers in 1978, and put out *Mongoloid/Jocko Homo* and a full-length album, with Brian Eno producing, that showcased their wry commentary on consumer culture. The second album demonstrated more of the band's philosophy, but without as many hooks, so Devo seemed to be just as unmarketable as Warner Brothers had feared, but the band had long been pioneers of the short-form video, and combined with their pop hooks the band had a major hit in 1980 with the song and video for "Whip It," off the self-produced *Freedom of Choice* album, which also showcased some of the band's best material, such as "Girl U Want" and "Gates of Steel." The following records showed less astute social commentary—"Beautiful World" aside—and moved in a more dance-oriented direction. After *Shout*, the band took a prolonged hiatus to regroup and try to figure out what Devo stood for in the postmodern world they had been predicting for years. Devo was perhaps one the most commercially successful bands that started in the artistic wing of the **punk** underground, and Mark Mothersbaugh had a lucrative career scoring TV shows such as *Rugrats*. Devo reunited occasionally after the 1990s, toured to numerous fans who had not been born when the band first released material, and once again spread the cryptic message of devolution. Devo was also an unofficial insult hurled at punks by passersby in the 1980s in **Los Angeles.**

Discography: *Q: Are We Not Men? A: We Are Devo* (Warner Bros., 1978); *Be Stiff* EP (UK Stiff, 1978); *Duty Now for the Future* (Warner Bros., 1979); *Freedom of Choice* (Warner Bros., 1980); *Dev-o Live* EP (Warner Bros., 1981); *New Traditionalists* (Warner Bros., 1981); *Oh No! It's Devo* (Warner Bros., 1982); *Shout* (Warner Bros., 1984); *E-Z Listening Disc* (Rykodisc, 1987); *Total Devo* (Enigma, 1988); *Now It Can Be Told* (Enigma, 1989); *Smooth Noodle Maps* (Enigma, 1990; Dutch East Wax, 1991); *Hardcore Vol. 1, 74–77* (Rykodisc, 1990); *Devo Greatest Hits* (Warner Bros., 1990); *Devo Greatest Misses* (Warner Bros., 1990). **Mark Mothersbaugh:** *Muzik for Insomniaks Volume 1* (Enigma, 1988); *Muzik for Insomniaks Volume 2* (Enigma, 1988).

D GENERATION

New York City **punk** band led by longtime scene members Jesse Malin (formerly of Heart Attack) and bassist Howie Pyro of the Blessed along with guitarists Danny Sage and Richard Bacchus and drummer Belvy K, who do an earnest distillation of **New York** punk and rock and roll. The band was signed to a major label but was dropped when it turned out that punk was not the next big thing after all. Bassist Howie Pyro had been an early part of the New York scene along with singer Jesse Malin and along with Jerry Only of the **Misfits** had been present at the dinner party the night that **Sid Vicious** overdosed and died in New York City. D Generation is another example of a band signed during the post–**Green Day** feeding frenzy when major labels had no idea how to market punk to a mass audience. The band is fondly remembered from the New York City 1990s scene, and Jesse Malin performs as a solo act and with alt-country rocker Ryan Adams.

Discography: *D Generation* (Chrysalis, 1994); *No Lunch* (Columbia, 1996).

DHARMA PUNX

Memoir by former addict and petty criminal Noah Levine, who reformed into a **straight edge punk** and eventually embraced spirituality to become a Buddhist teacher in training. Levine now leads meditation retreats and groups in juvenile detention halls and prisons.

Levine's rejection of violence and **nihilism** goes against the media image of many punks as inherently antisocial, and he to provide a positive counterpoint to the mainstream image of punks as criminals. Levine's commitment to understanding and appreciation of other religions as compatible with punk's **DIY** ethos also goes against the grain. *Dharma Punx* fits squarely with the tradition of punks seeking spirituality, as epitomized by **Bad Brains'** embrace of Rastafari and members of **Youth of Today, Shelter,** and the **Cro-Mags** embrace of Krishna Consciousness. The book is primarily of interest to punks in recovery (**Social Distortion's** Mike Ness, an ex-junkie, provides a cover blurb) or to students of spirituality. *Dharma Punx's* main drawback is that Levine never really takes the time to explain the various branches of Buddhism he frequently and casually mentions, much less what the word *dharma* means.

DI

DI (Drug Ideology) featured numerous members of **Los Angeles hardcore** bands. The classic lineup included vocalist Casy Royer and guitarists Rick and Alfie Agnew, all from the **Adolescents.** The band also appeared in the movie *Suburbia* by director Penelope Spheeris. A version of DI reunited for the benefits to save **CBGB's** in August 2005.
Discography: *Ancient Artifacts* (Reject, 1987); *Horse Bites Dog Cries* (Reject, 1987); *Team Goon* (Reject, 19987); *What Good Is Grief to a God?* (Triple X, 1988); *Tragedy Again* (Triple X, 1989); *Live at the Dive* (Triple X, 1993); *State of Shock* (Doctor Dream, 1994); *Caseyology* (Cleopatra, 2002).

DICKIES

Goofier **Los Angeles** version of the early **Ramones** that featured Leonard Graves Phillips on vocals and Mellotron, Stan Lee on guitar, Chuck Wagon on keyboards, Billy Club on bass, and Karlos Kabellero on drums. The Dickies was essentially a silly band with tongue stuck firmly in cheek on classic tracks such as "You Drive Me Ape (You Big Gorilla)" and "If Stewart Could Talk" (an ode to the perceived wisdom of lead singer Phillips's penis; in the live show Phillips donned a large penis puppet and channeled Stewart). Although the Dickies were among Los Angeles's longer-lasting **punk** bands, they also were regarded as more of a parody of punk's conventions than actual punks themselves. Although **heroin** abuse limited the band's success, the Dickies were still one of the best-known U.S. punk bands from that time period. The band had a long and semisuccessful career and still toured in a revised configuration that featured original members Stan Lee and Leonard Graves Phillips. The Dickies remained famous for being the first Los Angeles band to be signed to a major label and for successfully integrating humor into punk rock in what sometimes could be a relatively bleak and humorless scene.
Discography: *Incredible Shrinking Dickies* (A&M, 1979); *Dawn of the Dickies* (A&M, 1979); *Stukas over Disneyland* (PVC, 1983); *We Aren't the World* (Roir, 1986); *Killer Klowns from Outer Space* EP (Enigma, 1988); *Great Dictations* (A&M, 1989); *Second Coming* (Enigma, 1989); *Live in London—Locked and Loaded* (Taang!, 1991); *Idjit Savant* (Triple X, 1995).

DICKS

The Dicks were a **hardcore** band from Austin, Texas, that helped develop the early hardcore sound. The band was also known for having one of the few openly gay front men in punk, Gary Floyd. (It is interesting to note that the two bands with which the Dicks were most associated, the **Big Boys** and **MDC,** also had openly gay front men.) The original lineup featured Floyd on vocals, Buxf Parrot on guitar, Pat Deason on drums, and bassist Glen Taylor and released the early hardcore classic single "Dicks Hate the Police," which demonstrated the Dicks' disdain for authority and Floyd's commitment to smashing capitalism. The Dicks released several singles and albums as well as a split album with the Big Boys. The band relocated to San Francisco to find a more hospitable home base where their pro-Communist, prohomosexuality songs would be more accepted, but the band did not gel in its new surroundings. Floyd later dissolved the first version and formed a new version of the Dicks in 1983. After the band split again, Floyd formed Sister Double Happiness in San Francisco and continued to record under his own name. Floyd and the Dicks were influential musically, for bringing a queer perspective to a formerly closed (and closeted) punk scene, and for promoting a radical perspective to the punk communities of Austin and San Francisco. The 1990s alternative band Imperial Teen was cofounded by drummer and pianist Lynn Perko, a later member of the Dicks.

Discography: *Kill from the Heart* (SST, 1983); *These People* (Alternative Tentacles, 1985); *Dicks: 1980–1986* (Alternative Tentacles, 1997). **Dicks/Big Boys:** *Recorded Live at Raul's Club* (Rat Race, 1980). **Sister Double Happiness:** *Sister Double Happiness* (SST, 1988); *Heart and Mind* (Reprise, 1991); *Uncut* (Dutch East India Trading, 1992); *Horsey Water* (Ger. Sub Pop/EFA, 1994); *A Stone's Throw from Happiness: Live & Acoustic at the Great American Music Hall 6/17/92* (Innerstate, 1999). **Gary Floyd Band:** *Broken Angels* (Ger. Glitterhouse, 1995). **Gary Floyd:** *Back Door Preacher Man* (Innerstate, 1999). **El Destroyo:** *The Latest Drag* (Innerstate, 1999). **Black Kali Ma:** *You Ride the Pony (I'll Be the Bunny)* (Alternative Tentacles, 2000). **Imperial Teen:** *Seasick* (Slash/London, 1996); *What Is Not to Love* (Slash/London, 1999); *On* (Merge, 2002); *Live at Maxwell's* (DCN, 2002).

DICTATORS

One of the key early **New York** (originally from the Bronx) bands that bridged the gap between the garage rock of the 1960s, the legacy of **Iggy and the Stooges,** and the **punk** of the early to mid-1970s. The band started out as a straight-ahead melodic New York band led by bassist and multi-instrumentalist Adny (Andy) Schernoff before "secret weapon" Handsome Dick Manitoba (who had previously sung the encores, usually "Wild Thing" by the Troggs) took center stage and became the de facto lead vocalist. The Dictators had an album out well before most of the early punk bands: *The Dictators Go Girl Crazy!* in 1975. This album (along with **John Holmstrom's** illustration teachers at the School of Visual Arts [SVA] in New York and Harvey Kurtzman of *Mad* magazine) inspired Holmstrom and **Legs McNeil** to found **Punk** magazine, in part to meet and hang out with the Dictators. The Dictators courted controversy in the mid-1970s when Handsome Dick Manitoba was hit on the shoulder with a microphone stand by **Wayne/Jayne County,** whom Manitoba had heckled mercilessly during the concert. This led to a wild melee at **CBGB's** and ended with Manitoba thrown out and a blood-soaked Jayne County continuing the set. Handsome Dick sued, and several bands, including **Patti Smith, Blondie,** and **Suicide,** played a benefit gig for County, further alienating the Dictators from much of the New York City scene. The Dictators bounced back, however, and signed to Elektra Records and put out several more records before finally calling it quits. Members formed bands such as Manowar and the Del Lords and Handsome Dick's Wild Kingdom. The Dictators reformed in the 1990s and released several compelling comeback records and toured sporadically. Lead singer Handsome Dick Manitoba opened a bar called Manitoba's on Avenue B in New York City. Schernoff is a respected wine connoisseur.

Discography: *The Dictators Go Girl Crazy!* (Epic, 1975; Sony, 1990); *Manifest Destiny* (Asylum, 1977; Wounded Bird, 2004); *Bloodbrothers* (Asylum, 1978; Dictators Multi/Media, 1998, 2002); *Fuck 'Em if They Can't Take a Joke* (tape, Roir, 1981, 1995; Fr. Danceteria, 1991); *The Dictators Live: New York New York* (Roir, 1998); *D.F.F.D.* (Dictators Multi/Media, 2001); *Viva Dictators* (live; Escapi Music/New Media Studio, 2005). **Manitoba's Wild Kingdom:** *And You?* (Popular Metaphysics/MCA, 1990).

Handsome Dick Manitoba of the Dictators performs live at the Bottom Line in New York City in 1978. © *Robert Barry Francos.*

DIE TOTEN HOSEN

Long-running **punk** band (the name translates alternately as "the Dead Trousers" or "the Dead Boring") from Düsseldorf, Germany. Die Toten Hosen put out a fairly substantial body of work in its native Germany but is best known in the United States for the 1992 album *Learning English, Lesson One,* which teamed the band with a variety of classic punk vocalists such as **Joey Ramone, Johnny Thunders,** and even **Ronnie Biggs,** the Great Train robber.
Select Discography: *Learning English, Lesson One* (Charisma, 1992); *Love, Peace and Money* (Atlantic, 1995).

DILS

One of the most political bands of the original **Los Angeles punk** scene of the mid- to late 1970s, the Dils were led by brothers Maoist Chip Kinman on guitar and vocals and Tony Kinman on lead vocals and bass with, originally, Pat Garett on drums. The Kinman brothers formed the much less political band Rank and File in the 1980s with Alejandro Escovedo from the **Nuns.** When Rank and File did not have the commercial success that the brothers and the record company had expected, the brothers formed the more experimental BlackBird.
Discography: *Live!* (Iloki-Triple X, 1987); *The Dils* (Lost, 1990). **Rank and File:** *Sundown* (Slash/Warner Bros., 1982); *Long Gone Dead* (Slash/Warner Bros., 1984); *Rank and File* (Rhino) 1987.

DIM STARS

New York punk supergroup that featured **Richard Hell** and **Sonic Youth** members Thurston Moore and drummer Steve Shelley as well as producer Don Fleming from Gumball. The Dim Stars released one CD and a few singles before calling it quits in the early 1990s. **Voidoids** guitarist Robert Quine played on five tracks on the album, and Hell resumed his career writing and performing poetry and working on novels.

Discography: *Dim Stars* EP7 (Ecstatic Peace, 1991); *Dim Stars* (Caroline, 1992).

DISCHARGE

British **hardcore punk** band often associated with **crust punk** or the anarchist movement and very influential in the heavy metal hardcore crossover of the 1980s. The band formed in 1977 and broke up for the first time in 1991 and then again in 1997. The original lineup included Terry "Tezz" Roberts on vocals (replaced by Cal in 1979), Tony "Bones" Roberts on guitar (replaced by Peter Pyrtle, Les Hunt, then Stephen Brooks; Bones returned for the 1997 reunion), Roy "Rainy" Wainwright on bass, and Hacko on drums (replaced by Terry Roberts, Gary Maloney, then Nick Haymaker; Roberts returned for the 1997 reunion). Discharge was among the many punk bands that flirted with heavy metal and influenced the crossover of the 1980s.

Discography: *Realities of War* EP (Clay, 1980); *Fight Back* EP (Clay, 1981); *Decontrol* EP (Clay, 1981); *Why* (Clay, 1981; Castle, 2003); *Hear Nothing, See Nothing, Say Nothing* (Clay, 1982; Castle, 2003); *Never Again* (Clay, 1984; Castle, 2003); *Grave New World* (Profile, 1986); *Massacre Divine* (Clay, 1991, 1995); *Shooting Up the World* (Clay, 1991, 1995); *Live at City Gardens, NJ* (Clay, 1995); *Clay Punk Singles Collection* (Clay, 1995); *Live Nightmare Continues* (Clay, 1996); *Protest & Survive 1980–1984* (Clay, 1996); *Vision of War* (Recall, 1998); *Hardcore Hits* (Cleopatra, 1999); *Discharge* (Sanctuary, 2002); *Decontrol: The Singles* (Castle, 2002); *Society's Victims* (boxed set; Castle, 2004); *Anthology Free Speech* (Castle, 2004); *Born Immortal* (Rebellion, 2005).

DISCHORD RECORDS

Key U.S. independent label located in **Washington, D.C.,** and founded and run by **Ian MacKaye** and Jeff Nelson from **Minor Threat.** Perhaps one of the most influential independent labels in the United States, if not the world, Dischord has stayed true to its mission since it was founded in 1980. The label releases only bands from the Washington, D.C., area and sells records for much less (including postage-paid records) than any other label, major or independent. Major bands on the label over the years include Minor Threat, **SOA (Henry Rollins's** first band), Rites of Spring, **Fugazi, Jawbox, Beefeater,** Shudder to Think, **Dag Nasty,** Embrace, Faith, Fidelity Jones, **Government Issue,** the **Nation of Ulysses,** and Q and Not U., to mention but a few.

Dischord was founded when Ian MacKaye's original band, the **Teen Idles,** had money left over upon breaking up and decided to release a record with the funds. After releasing the Teen Idles' *Minor Disturbance* EP in 1980, Ian MacKaye was inspired by independent record labels such as Los Angeles's **Dangerhouse Records** and the vitality of the local scene, which included new bands such as SOA featuring Henry Garfield (later Henry Rollins), John Stabb's Government Issue, Ian's brothers' band the Untouchables (not to be confused with the later **ska punk** band), as well as **Youth Brigade,** started by Nathan Strejeck, the former lead singer of the Teen Idles (not to be confused with the **Youth Brigade** that founded the **Better Youth Organization**). The label then released records by SOA, Minor Threat, Youth Brigade, and

Government Issue. By the end of 1981, Dischord expanded into a larger operation and moved into the Dischord House in Arlington, Virginia (whereupon original third founder Nathan Strejeck ceased to be involved in the label). In 1982, Dischord released the classic *Flex Your Head* compilation of 32 songs by a variety of Washington, D.C., bands. Records by Void, Marginal Man, and Minor Threat followed, but the label almost went under due to a precarious cash flow. This problem was solved through a partnership with John Loder of Southern Studios in London, who had released records by the like-minded band **Crass,** who helped arrange European distribution. By the mid-1980s, Dischord had become busier, releasing new records by bands such as Gray Matter and Ignition. Dischord worked closely with the political activists in **Positive Force** D.C. to stage benefit concerts, protests (especially during **Revolution Summer**), and the compilation album *The State of the Union*, which benefited Positive Force. During the late 1980s, the company grew larger and formed Discord Direct to help in the distribution process.

The 1990s saw a sea change in the popularity of punk and indie rock bands, and the label had numerous offers during the feeding frenzy by major labels to buy either portions of the company or the entire company, but these offers were never considered and were rejected out of hand. Jawbox and Shudder to Think did sign to major labels, but they were never as successful or popular as when they were signed to Dischord, and the bands broke up not long after joining the majors. Fugazi, however, which had quickly became the flagship band of Dischord, rejected all offers by major labels and continued to be a major seller and substantial concert draw until its apparent hiatus after the *Argument* album. Because Dischord sees itself not as a record company (as the Web site indicates) but as a way to document the music being made by a relatively small geographic community, it is not beholden to standard industry practices and still operates only on handshake deals to release and distribute records. Dischord is a business, however, and maintains a small and devoted staff that earns a living wage and receives health benefits, far from the norm of most independent labels. Dischord is a true example of the undiluted and uncompromising **DIY** spirit that epitomizes punk rock, and even when not every band on the label can be categorized musically as punk rock, the bands still must fit the Dischord mission of documenting local artistic endeavors. *See also* MacKaye, Ian; Minor Threat; Positive Force; Washington, D.C.

DIY

DIY is short for "do it yourself," and this aesthetic has long been a key component of the loose aggregation of ideas and ideologies that passes for a coherent philosophy of what it means to be a true punk. An example of the DIY movement includes independent record labels established to bypass the corporate control of the record industry, such as the Buzzcocks' seminal *Spiral Scratch* EP and the numerous U.S. independent labels such as **SST, Epitaph,** and **Fat Wreck Chords.** In recording, if a band did have to sign with a major label, the philosophy was extended to control over the selection of producer, songs, and single releases. (A song that epitomizes the difficulties in reconciling the DIY philosophy with corporate culture is the **Clash** song "Complete Control," which details the band's frustration at the record company's insisting on the release of "Remote Control" as a single from their first album.) DIY also applies to fashion, such as how a band's members clothe and adorn themselves outside of mainstream fashion outlets. The early punk looks of ripped or altered clothes, such as **Johnny Rotten's** homemade "I Hate Pink Floyd" T-shirt, and the safety pins and ripped clothing worn by the **Electric Eels, Weirdos,** and **Richard Hell** are also key examples of this trend. The use of alternative or homemade media such as **zines** is also a key component in DIY, and there have been literally thousands of zines produced in the punk community, some of which had little to do with music but covered numerous other subjects from sports to animal rights to feminist topics. Zines, often self-produced and printed on copiers at work and distributed at shows, sold at independent record stores or given out for free on the street are a way to bypass the monolithic media outlets that many punks feel stifle creativity. **Flyers** are also a key part of the DIY aesthetic, and because most punk shows cannot rely on traditional means of advertising (due either to police regulations, lack of money, or simply because the show is in someone's basement or in a VFW hall), they are either posted on telephone poles or given out at shows. Although there is no one complete and easy definition of the DIY aesthetic and many punks disagree among themselves as to what truly constitutes a true DIY initiative, it can be sufficient to summarize the DIY ethos as one of independence from corporate control with an emphasis on individual creativity and self-expression. The DIY aesthetic is controversial to this day as to the extent one can work within the system and how much an individual can have control over his or her work and means of production.

DOA

Long-running and extremely influential Canadian **punk** band led by Joey Shithead Keithley (sometimes spelled Keighley) of British Columbia. Like DOA's U.S. compatriots the **Ramones,** the band survived a rigorous schedule of touring and churning out records to limited financial success, but it developed an international reputation as one of the most consistent (except for lineup) punk bands of the last 30 years. The band went through more lineup changes than most people have had hot meals. The original lineup formed in 1977 as the Skulls and consisted of Joey "Shithead" Keithley, Ken "Dimwit" Montgomery, Gerry "Useless" Hannah, and Brad "Kunt" Kent. After replacing Hannah and Kent with Brian Goble and Simon Werner, the Skulls toured Canada and moved briefly to **London** to try to find success in the British punk scene. The band moved back to Canada and broke up. Hannah, Mike Graham Montgomery, and Wimpy formed the rival band **Subhumans,** and Shithead formed DOA with bassist Randy Rampage, drummer Chuck "Biscuits" Montgomery (Ken Montgomery's younger brother), and Brad Kent and late adding second guitarist Dave Gregg. Shithead, along with manager and political activist Ken Lester, wrote numerous songs that openly challenged the political system. The band toured extensively and released one of the earliest **hardcore** records, *Hardcore 81*, in 1981 but achieved more recognition with the **Alternative Tentacles** release *War on 45* in 1982. The next two decades saw relentless touring and numerous personnel changes. Tragedy struck the band in 1995 when longtime drummer Ken Jensen was killed in a house fire. The band responded with the album *The Black Spot* dedicated to his memory. Keithley ran for parliament in the 2001 British Columbia election for the Green Party and received an impressive number of votes. Keithley also runs the Sudden Death label. The band also collaborated with other punks such as **Jello Biafra.** Joey Shithead also released the autobiographical *I, Shithead: A Life in Punk,* which detailed the problems inherent in living (and touring) the punk life for 30 years.

Discography: *Disco Sucks* EP7 (Can. Sudden Death, 1978; Can. Quintessence, 1978); *Triumph of the Ignoroids* EP (Can. Friend's, 1979); *Something Better Change* (Can. Friend's, 1980; Sudden Death, 2000); *Hardcore 81* (Can. Friend's, 1981; Sudden Death, 2002); *War on 45* (Alternative Tentacles, 1982); *Bloodied but Unbowed* (Alternative Tentacles, 1984; Restless, 1992); *Don't Turn Yer Back (on Desperate Times)* EP (Alternative Tentacles, 1985); *Let's Wreck the Party* (Alternative Tentacles, 1985); *The Dawning of a New Error* (Virus, 1985; Alternative Tentacles, 1992); *True (North) Strong & Free* (Rock Hotel/Profile, 1987, 1990); *Ready to Explode* (Profile, 1987); *Ancient Beauty* (Philo, 1988); *Ornament of Hope* (Philo, 1988); Talk – Action = Zero (Restless, 1988, 1990, 1993); *Murder* (Restless, 1990, 1993); *Last Scream of Missing Neighbors* (Alternative Tentacles, 1990); *The Dawning of a New Error* (Alternative Tentacles, 1991); *Great-*

John Doe, the charismatic leader of the punk band X, is also known for his movie roles. *Photofest.*

est Shits (QQRYQ, 1991); *13 Flavours of Doom* (Alternative Tentacles, 1992); *It's Not Unusual … but It Sure Is Ugly!* EP (Alternative Tentacles, 1993); *Loggerheads* (Alternative Tentacles, 1993); *Moose Droppings* (Nightmare Music, 1993); *The Black Spot* (Can. Essential Noise/Virgin, 1995); *Festival of Atheists* (Sudden Death, 2000); *Lost Tapes* (Orchard, 2000); *Alive & Kickin'* (Orchard, 2001); *Win the Battle* (Sudden Death, 2002); *Are U Ready* (Sudden Death, 2003); *Live Free or Die* (Sudden Death, 2004); *From Out of Nowhere* (New World, 2004). **Randy Rampage:** *Randy Rampage* EP (Can. Friend's, 1982).

DOC MARTENS

Boot of choice for many in the **punk** community and especially many **skinheads.** Doc Martens were first worn by British skinheads in emulation of working-class style during the 1960s, and soon a codified style was established for how to wear the boots and what the particular styles meant to different punk subcultures.

DOE, JOHN

Leader of **Los Angeles punk** band **X** and prolific actor and solo artist. John Doe was Married for several years to X singer Exene Cervenka. He was one of the founders and key players in the Los Angeles punk scene of the late 1970s and early 1980s and, due to his songwriting savvy and vision, helped propel his band X to become one of the key long-running bands to survive the notorious excesses of the Los Angeles scene. Doe also toured on his own and released several roots-rock records. He also infrequently appeared as an actor in films, such as *Great Balls of Fire*, the Jerry Lee Lewis biopic. Doe also reunited with his other band, the country-based side project the Knitters (along with D.J. Bonebrake, Exene Cervenka, and Dave Alvin), for an album and tour in 2005.

DONNAS

All-female band clearly influenced by the sound and look of the **Ramones.** The members of the band all went by the first name Donna and had an identifying initial at the end of their names to identify them. The band formed while the members were in high school, and early efforts were poorly produced and showed a welcome lack of professionalism. Subsequent efforts on **Lookout Records** showed a gradual maturity and the introduction of some metallic crunch. The band signed to a major label and made several highly regarded records and soon appeared in numerous advertisements and on **MTV.** The women in the band subsequently dropped the common Donna first name, the source of much of their initial innocent charm.

DOUGHBOYS

Energetic Canadian band from Montreal that toured relentlessly and released several highly regarded records. Key members of the group came and left, but the classic lineup featured John Kastner on lead vocals, Brock Pytel on drums and vocals, John Bonehead on bass, and Jon Cummings on guitar. Kastner later founded All Systems Go with members of **Big Drill Car.**
Discography: *Whatever* (Pipeline, 1987; Cargo, 1995); *Home Again* (Restless, 1989, 1993); *Happy Accidents* (Restless, 1991, 1993); *When Up Turns to Down* (Restless, 1992); *Something's Gone Wrong—The Buzzcock Covers* (C/Z, 1992); *Crush* (A&M, 1993); *Fix Me* (Cargo, 1995); *Turn Me On* (Universal/Polygram, 1992; A&M, 1996).

DOWN BY LAW

Punk band led by vocalist Dave Smalley after he left **Dag Nasty** and **All.** The band went through frequent lineup changes, and Smalley was the only constant. Several releases were put out by major indie labels **Epitaph** and Go Kart Records. Smalley later toured as a solo artist and posted political commentary from a slightly right of center perspective that was surprising to many of his early fans.
Discography: *Down by Law* (Epitaph, 1991); *Blue* (Epitaph, 1992); *Punkrockacademyfightsong* (Epitaph, 1994); *Down by Law & Gigantor* (Lost & Found, 1995); *All Scratched Up!* (Epitaph, 1996); *Last of the Sharpshooters* (Epitaph, 1997); *Fly the Flag* (Go Kart, 1999); *Split* (with Pseudo Heroes; Theologian, 2000); *PunkRockDays: The Best of DBL* (Epitaph, 2002); *Windwardtidesandwaywardsails* (Union Local 2112, 2003).

DRAMARAMA

Long-running New Jersey band led by Jon Easdale and bassist popmeister Chris Carter along with guitarists Peter Wood and Mark "Mr. E Boy" Englert and several drummers, including Clem Burke before the reunion of **Blondie.** Dramarama best demonstrated the benefits and perils of the commercial record industry. The band started in the early 1980s and combined **punk**'s energy and the pop of the Beatles with glam and traditional rock and roll influences (Mott the Hoople is an obvious reference point, and the band covered Mott the Hoople's "I Wish I Was Your Mother" on one album). Despite plugging away for years and several minor and perennial radio hits such as "Anything, Anything (I'll Give You)," "Last Cigarette," and "Work for Food," Dramarama was forced to call it quits. To sum up the career of Dramarama would be to say that a worthy band never got a break. In particular, the song "Work for Food" chronicled the band's efforts to get a hit by telling the story of how having talent is not enough to make a living. The lyrics portrayed the lead singer as a has-been homeless man, wandering the streets and bemoaning the fact that "I wasn't always paranoid / I sang a song on Uncle Floyd / but the records never sold and that was bad." In a sign that some major-league corporations give when others take (an example of this would be the band Wilco being dropped from one label in the Warner Brothers' empire only to be picked up by another one), VH1's *Band's Reunited* brought Dramarama back together in 2004 for a reunion special (which featured a particularly poignant moment when the host found guitarist Peter Wood driving heavy equipment on a construction site) and for live concert. Subsequently, several members of the band revived the Dramarama name and toured.

Discography: *Comedy* EP (Questionmark, 1984); *Cinema Verite* (Fr. New Rose, 1984); *Box Office Bomb* (Questionmark, 1987); *Stuck in Wonderamaland* (Chameleon, 1990); *Live at the China Club* EP (Chameleon, 1990); *Vinyl* (Chameleon/Elektra, 1991); *The Days of Wayne and Roses* (*The Trash Tapes*) (No Label, 1992); *Hi-Fi Sci-fi* (Chameleon/Elektra, 1993); *18 Big Ones: The Best Of* (Elektra/Rhino, 1996).

DRI

Abbreviated name for the Houston **hardcore** band known as Dirty Rotten Imbeciles. DRI was one of the fastest of the early hardcore bands, and on the first album few of its songs clocked in at more than one minute. Subsequent albums saw a tendency toward a **punk** rock and heavy metal crossover that was a dominant trend in the mid-1980s and was influential on numerous speed metal and hardcore bands in the late 1980s. DRI also was well known for its iconic logo that featured a figure skanking, presumably to the music of DRI. The band consisted of Kurt Brecht on vocals, Spike Cassidy on guitar, bassist Dennis Johnson (later replaced by Josh Pappe, John Menor, then Chumly Porter), and drummer Eric Brecht (later replaced by Felix Griffin then Rom Rampy). The band went though many lineup changes but helped pioneer a style of crossover heavy metal and punk that remained popular. The band continued to record and tour.

Discography: *Dirty Rotten* (Rotten, 1982); *Violent Pacification* EP (Rotten, 1984); *Dealing with It!* (Death/Metal Blade/Enigma, 1985; Rotten, 1991); *Crossover* (Metal Blade/Enigma, 1987; Rotten, 1995); *4 of a Kind* (Metal Blade/Enigma, 1988; Restless, 1993); *Thrash Zone* (Metal Blade/Enigma, 1989); *Dirty Rotten LP/Violent Pacification* (Rotten, 1991); *Definition* (Rotten, 1992); *DRI Live* (Rotten, 1995); *Full Speed Ahead* (Rotten, 1995); *Dirty Rotten Imbeciles* (Cleopatra, 2001).

DR. KNOW

Los Angeles hardcore band of the early 1980s to 1990s that featured Brandon Cruz, a former child actor on the 1960s television show *The Courtship of Eddie's Father*, on lead vocals. Cruz later joined the reunited **Dead Kennedys** in the early twenty-first century as a replacement vocalist for **Jello Biafra.** (The band Dr. Know bore no relation to the guitarist Dr. Know from **Bad Brains**).

Discography: *This Island* (Death/Restless, 1986, 1993); *Wreckage in Flesh* (Restless, 1988, 1993); *The Original Group* (Mystic, 1995); *Island-Wreckage* (Enigma, 1995); *Valu Pak* (Mystic, 1995); *Habily: What Was Old Is New* (Cleopatra, 2001); *Best of Dr. Know* (Mystic, 2003).

DROPKICK MURPHYS

Boston band that fused **hardcore punk** with traditional Irish music. The band was formed in 1995 by vocalist Mike McColgan (later replaced by Al Barr), guitarist Rick Barton (later replaced by Mark Orrell), leader and most constant member bassist Ken Casey, and the usual revolving cast of drummers until the lineup stabilized with the addition of Matt Kelly. The Dropkick Murphys changed again in 1999 and added James Lynch on guitar, Spicy McHaggis on bagpipes, and Ryan Foltz on mandolin. The band was considered a more raucous U.S. hardcore version of the **Pogues** that had pride in the members' Irish and Bostonian heritage.

Discography: *Do or Die* (Epitaph, 1998); *The Gangs All Here* (Epitaph, 1999); *Mob Mentality* (Taang, 2000); *Sing Loud, Sing Proud* (Epitaph, 2001); *Live on St. Patrick's Day from Boston, MA* (Epitaph, 2002); *Blackout* (Hellcat, 2003); *The Warriors Code* (Hellcat, 2005).

DRUGS

Drug use was practiced to one degree or another in almost every **punk** scene, although the chemical of choice varied from scene to scene and country to country. Among the most prevalent drugs used were amphetamines and **heroin.** Numerous instances of fatalities were linked to drugs, including **Sid Vicious, Dee Dee Ramone, Darby Crash,** and **Johnny Thunders.** Different scenes indulged in different drugs, and if alcohol were included on the list, it would appear that much of early punk was influenced chemically in one way or another. Although many punks did not use drugs and some rejected them from a moral and political standpoint (such as the **straight edge** movement), many punks were inspired by the lives of excess led by many of the founders of punk rock. Johnny Thunders, in particular, discovered heroin as a member of the **New York Dolls** and was considered most responsible for spreading the drug to England when he toured with his band the **Heartbreakers** and for introducing the drug to Sid Vicious (who idolized Thunders) and Dee Dee Ramone. It seems an apparent contradiction that bands such as the **Sex Pistols** made public comments disparaging hippies yet also indulged in drug use themselves. As punk evolved and the **hardcore** movement took over, many younger punks, alarmed by the prevalence of drugs and alcohol in the punk scene, created straight edge, inspired by the **Minor Threat** song of the same name, and bands such as **SSD** decided to celebrate the energy provided through clean living. It is unclear to what extent drugs are still used in the punk rock community, and it seems reasonable to assume that drug use is more tolerated in some scenes (members of the English punk scene, led by the **Clash** and other bands that had an affinity for **reggae,** were probably more likely to smoke marijuana than others) but differs from scene to scene and city to city.

DUB

A less commercial, spacey version of **reggae** in which instruments drop in and out and echo and reverb are used extensively, pioneered by Jamaican innovators such as King Tubby, Scientist, and Lee Scratch Perry. Many of the early British **punk** bands, such as the **Clash,** the **Ruts, Generation X,** and the **Slits,** were inspired by early reggae and used dub; and producers such as Lee Perry and Mikey Dread pioneered the use of dub. Seminal early tracks such as "Wild Dub" by Generation X and "Bankrobber Dub" by the Clash illustrated how an exotic production sound could appeal to the general public, although reggae and dub were certainly much more popular in the 1970s and early 1980s in England than in the United States and there was no seemingly political alliance between Rastafarians and punk rockers. Later on in the 1980s, some U.S. bands such as **Bad Brains** also used dub in their ritualistic praise of Jah Rastafari, the Rastafarian deity. The Bad Brains were an exception to the rule, however, and their use was largely inspired by the political beliefs of the band members. U.S. punk bands do very little dub, with the exception of **NOFX,** which uses reggae and dub in some of its music. Although **ska** music was quite popular on and off in the U.S. punk scene, there was no widespread effort to use reggae rhythms or production styles in U.S. punk. *See also* Bad Brains; Clash; Punk and Race; Reggae.

DWARVES

U.S. scuzz **punk** band from San Francisco (after Chicago) known for their outrageous shows that resemble GWAR's shows to a certain degree. The Dwarves' album covers featured copious nudity, but the records did not feature much actual music. The band is known for the outrage that erupted when the members faked the death of guitarist He Who Cannot Be Named, who allegedly was stabbed to death in Philadelphia in 1993. The controversy led the label Sub Pop to drop them. The Dwarves could always be counted on to court controversy.
Discography: *Horror Stories* (Voxx, 1986); *Toolin' for a Warm Teabag* (Nasty Gash, 1988); *Astro Boy* EP7 (Sub Pop, 1990); *Blood, Guts & Pussy* (Sub Pop, 1990); *Lucifer's Crank* EP7 (No.6, 1991); *Thanks Heaven for Little Girls* (Sub Pop, 1991); *Sugarfix* (Sub Pop, 1993).

DYS

Punk and metal band that featured future **Dag Nasty** and **Down by Law** singer Dave Smalley. The band took its name from the Massachusetts Department of Youth Services, the bureaucracy in charge of juvenile detention. The band formed in **Boston** and was inspired by **SSD** (originally SS Decontrol) and the budding Boston **hardcore** scene. The original lineup included Jon Anasta (later of **Slapshot**) on bass, Dave Smalley on lead vocals, Andy Strahan on guitar, and drummer Dave Collins. DYS promoted the **straight edge** movement to ridiculous extremes and confronted audience members about their behavior. The band released one significant album and moved in a more metallic direction, performing heavy metalesque power ballads. DYS almost signed to major label Elektra before breaking up in 1985. Smalley later joined Dag Nasty for its first album, then joined the post-Descendents band **All,** and finally started his own band, Down by Law, and toured solo and blogged on punk and political issues.
Discography: *Brotherhood* (x-Claim!, 1983); *D.Y.S.* (Modern Method, 1986).

EATER

First-generation British punk band best known for the relative youth of the members (who considered the **Sex Pistols** to be "too old." The original lineup included 15-year-old Andy Blade (Ashie Radwan) on lead vocals, 15-year-old Brian Chevette (Brian Haddock) on guitar, 15-year-old Ian Woodcock on bass, and Social Demise on drums (later replaced by 13-year-old Dee Generate [Roger Bullen], later replaced by Phil Rowland). The band played often after opening for the **Buzzcocks** in 1976 and notably appeared in **Don Letts'** *Punk Rock Movie* (1978). After numerous personnel changes the band finally called it quits at the end of 1978. Drummer Rowland later played with **Slaughter and the Dogs.**

Discography: *The Album* (UK The Label, 1977); *Get Your Yo Yos Out* EP (UK The Label, 1978); *The History of Eater Vol. 1* (UK DeLorean, 1985); *All of Eater* (Cargo, 1995, 1997); *The Compleat Eater* (Anagram Punk, 1999); *Eater Chronicles 1976–2003* (Anagram Punk, 2003); *Live at Barbarella's 1977* (Anagram Punk, 2004).

EFFIGIES

Skinhead hardcore band form Evanston, Illinois, influenced by the British sound and image of the early 1980s. Led by John Kezdy on lead vocals, Earl Oil Letiecq (replaced by Robert O'Conner, Letiecq rejoined for the reunion then was replaced by Robert McNaughton) on guitar, Paul Zamost on bass, and Steve Economou on drums. The band went through acrimonious deals with various labels and was falsely accused of being Nazis and racists because of their look. The band disbanded in 1987 but got back together for sporadic reunions.

Discography: *Haunted Town* EP (Autumn, 1981; Ruthless, 1984); *We're da Machine* EP (Ruthless/Enigma, 1983); *The Effigies* EP (Ruthless/Enigma, 1984); *For Ever Grounded* (Ruthless/Enigma, 1984); *Fly on a Wire* (Fever/Enigma, 1985); *Ink* (Fever/Restless, 1986); *Remains Nonviewable* (Roadkill, 1989; Touch & Go, 1995); *V.M.L. Live Presents the Effigies 12/16/95* (V.M.L., 1996).

EGG HUNT

Side project of **Ian MacKaye** and Jeff Nelson after the break up of **Minor Threat.** The project released one single containing the song "We All Fall Down," recorded in England in 1986. The song had originally been written for Embrace, MacKaye's post–Minor Threat band, but was rejected by the other members of the band. The Egg Hunt project marked the last time that MacKaye and Nelson would work together musically.

ELECTRIC EELS

One of the few bands that both predated punk(circa 1972) and anticipated most of the innovations of the early scenes musically, socially, and through the use of fashion and style. Although not well known outside of their home base in Ohio, the band played music identifiable as punk years before the **Ramones** or **Sex Pistols** and dressed in ripped clothing and outlandish outfits before **Richard Hell** pioneered the punk look in New York City. The band included Nick Knox on drums (later to join the **Cramps**), David "E" McManus on vocals and percussion, John Morton on guitar and vocals, and Brian McMahon on guitar. The band put out the protopunk single "Cyclotron" in May 1975, described their music as "art terrorism," wore safety pins, and used rude slogans and had noisy, often violent shows. Although the band existed early on in the punk scene, their seminal single that established them as a major force in the United States and abroad, "Agitated," was only finally released by **Rough Trade** in 1979 at the urging of journalist Jon Savage. The Electric Eels in their original lineup played few shows but were a punk legend before punk had solidified into any kind of coherent form.

Discography: *Having a Philosophical Investigation with the Electric Eels* (Tinnitus, 1989); *God Says Fuck You* (Homestead, 1992, 1995); *Beast 999 Presents the Electric Eels in Their Organic Majesty's Request* (Overground, 1998); *The Eyeball of Hell* (Scat, 2001).

EMBARRASSMENT

Midwestern art punk band from Kansas that was influential on the artier punk and alternative American bands in the 1980s and 1990s. The band consisted of John Nicols on lead vocals, Bill Goffrier on guitar, Brent Gieessman on drums (who were all **Sex Pistols** fans from Wichita), along with bassist Ron Klaus. The band toured extensively and played the major clubs in Kansas and New York City but never became well known. The band called it quits in 1983 and is today best remembered for their epic song "Sex Drive."

EMO

Emotional style of punk developed in the 1980s by bands such as **Dag Nasty** and Rites of Spring (there are many reports of both men and women weeping openly at overtly emotional shows by Rites of Spring). *Emo* primarily means "emotional" (although the term was also used for bands who played in a certain style and tempo) and generally refers to bands with confessional lyrics that deal with difficulties in relationships, fitting in, and being honest in a world that is difficult to navigate. Bands such as Jimmy Eat World, Dashboard Confessional, and Weezer (based largely on their second album, the underselling, but critically acclaimed, *Pinkerton*) were often described as emo. There was even an unofficial emo uniform that involved baggy clothing, rumpled hair, and large nerdy glasses. Many modern bands resent the term and refuse to be labeled emo bands, considering the term to be essentially meaningless and more of a corporate attempt to label music than an honest reaction to a musical style. Other offshoots created by rock critics include screamo and extremo, which are more raucous versions of the same style, as epitomized by bands such as the Used and others who screamed their confessional lyrics as opposed to singing them melodically.

END OF THE CENTURY

Documentary about the **Ramones** released in 2004 that detailed the long and tumultuous career of the four "brudders" from Forest Hills, who in reality could barely get along and often did not speak to each other for years at a time. The documentary explores such issues as lead singer **Joey Ramone**'s obsessive-compulsive disorder and his terminally romantic view of love and loyalty, **Dee Dee Ramone** as a hopeless junkie and brilliant songwriter trying to express his troubled psyche, and guitarist Johnny Ramone as the true leader of the band who kept the band to a rigorous touring and rehearsal schedule, often at he expense of the band actually getting along. The most interesting thing about the film is the absolute candor with which they get Dee Dee, Johnny, and Marky (once a self-destructive alcoholic) to discuss the complex and extremely dysfunctional way in which the Ramones operated for more than 20 years. *End of the Century* is one of the best and most instructive of all punk documentaries that helps to establish the Ramones' place in the pantheon of both punk rock and rock and roll in general.

ENGINE KID

Seattle punk band influenced by indie rock as well as **hardcore.** The band included Greg Anderson on guitar and vocals, Brain Kraft on bass, and Chris Vanderbrooke on drums (Jade Devitt replaced Vanderbrooke in 1995). The band broke up in 1995 after the *Angel Wings* record.
Discography: *Astronaut* EP (C/Z, 1993); *Bear Catching Fish* (C/Z, 1993); *Iceburn/Engine Kid* EP (Revelation, 1994); *Angel Wings* (Revelation, 1995).

EPITAPH

Enormously successful independent punk label started by Mr. Brett, guitarist for **Bad Religion.** Epitaph released some of the most influential punk records of the 1980s and 1990s. Epitaph floundered for some time as Mr. Brett struggled with his addiction to **heroin.** The **Offspring** released one of the highest selling records every released on an independent record label with their record *Smash.* Bad Religion was initially one of the key groups on Epitaph but left for a major label after the release of *Stranger than Fiction*; they returned after several years of diminishing sales. The Epitaph roster includes or has included bands such as Bad Religion, **NOFX, Pennywise, Agnostic Front, Descendents, All, Rancid,** and others.

EQUAL VISION RECORDS

Independent U.S. record label that released records by Saves the Day, Fivespeed, Seemless, Bane, Converge, and **Serpico.** Equal Vision Records was founded by Ray Cappo (**Youth of Today, Shelter**) in the early 1990s and started out releasing material by Cappo's band Shelter but soon branched out to become one of the key hardcore labels of the 1990s. The label has a Web site at http://www.equalvision.com/.

EX

Long-running Dutch anarchist punk band with jazz and improvisational tendencies that consistently rejected major labels to produce their own product in their own idiosyncratic way. The band has been through numerous lineup changes but still tours today.
Discography: *Disturbing Domestic Peace* (Hol Verrecords, 1980); *History Is What's Happening* (Hol. More DPM, 1982); *Blueprints for a Blackout* (Hol. Pig Brother Productions, 1983); *Dignity of Labor* (Hol. VGZ, 1983); *Gonna Rob the Sperbank* EP (Hol. Sneeelleeer, 1983); *Tumult* (Hol. FAI, 1983); *1936 (The Spanish Revolution)* EP (Hol. Ron Johnson, 1985); *Pokkeherrie* (Hol. Pockabilly, 1985); *Live in Wroclaw* (Hol. Red, 1987); *Too Many Cowboys* (Mordam, 1987); *Hands Up! Your Free* (Hol.Ex, 1988); *Joggers and Smoggers* (Hol. Ex, 1989); *Dead Fish* EP (Hol.Ex, 1990); *Mudbird Shivers* (Hol. Ex/RecRec, 1995). **With Tom Cora:** *Scrabbling at the Lock* (Hol. Ex, 1991); *And the Weathermen Shrug Their Shoulders* (Fist Puppet, 1993). **Ex and Guests:** *Instant* (Hol. Ex, 1995).

EXPLOITED

Seminal Scottish **hardcore** punk band led by punk provocateur Wattie Buchanan that has toured and released ultrafast political hardcore for three decades and counting. The band was founded in Edinburgh, Scotland, in 1979 by Wattie Buchanan, and early members included the aptly named Big John on guitar for the first record, *Punks Not Dead*, and the *Troops of Tomorrow*. By the time of the third album, the lineup had changed with the addition of Karl, Willie, and Billie; *Let's Start a War* was a vicious attack on Margaret Thatcher and the Falklands War. By the time of *Horror Epics*, the exploited were becoming more metallic and experimental but still included sing-along choruses and socially conscious epics such as the title track, which asserts that compared to the horrors of global starvation, "Real Life is much more horrible than fiction." The band continues to record and tour, often with completely new lineups on each record, and performs to large audiences in some countries but smaller crowds in other countries. The Exploited's lengthy career is owed largely to the persistence and vision of lead singer Wattie Buchanan.

Discography: *Punks Not Dead* (Grand Slamm, 1981); *Troops of Tomorrow* (Grand Slamm, 1982); *Let's Start A War . . . Said Maggie One Day* (Combat, 1983); *Horror Epics* (Combat, 1985); *Live at the Whitehouse* (Combat, 1985); *Jesus is Dead* (Combat, 1986); *Totally Exploited* (Dojo, 1986); *Death before Dishonor* (Combat, 1987); *Live and Loud* (Link, 1987); *Punks Alive* (Skunx, 1988); *Massacre* (Rough Justice, 1990); *War Now* (Combat, 1990); *Live in Japan* (Dojo, 1994); *Beat the Bastards* (Relativity, 1996); *Fuck the System* (Import, 2002); *Punk* (Cargo Music, 2002).

FACE TO FACE

Victorville, California, **punk** rock band best known for its anthem "Disconnected" and the gruff but immensely appealing voice of guitarist Trevor Keith. The band also featured guitarist Chad Yarro, bassist Matt Riddle, and drummer Rob Kurth. Face to Face played the punk circuit for several years and was subsequently signed and dropped by A&M, which could not figure out how to market the band's intricate and hook-driven punk anthems, even when the band rerecorded "Disconnected" a second time. Face to Face also showed its commitment to the members' punk roots with excellent choices in covers (the **Descendents** "Bikeage," which they retired from the live set when the Descendents reformed) and a split EP with **Dropkick Murphys'** "The Dirty Glass," "Fortunate Son," and "21 Guitar Salute." Riddle later joined No Use for a Name.
Discography: *Face to Face* (Dr. Strange, 1991; Fat Wreck Chords, 1992; A&M, 1996); *Don't Turn Away* (Dr. Strange, 1991; Fat Wreck Chords, 1992, 1994); *Over It* (Victory, 1994); *Big Choice* (Victory, 1995); *Face to Face* (A&M, 1996; Vagrant, 2000); *Econolive* EP (Lady Luck/Victory, 1996); *Live* (Lady Luck/Victory, 1998); *Standards and Practices* (Lady Luck/Victory, 1999; Vagrant, 2001); *Ignorance Is Bliss* (Beyond, 1999); *So Why Aren't You Happy* EP (Atomic Pop, 1999); *Reactionary* (Beyond, 2000); *We Love Gas* (Musea, 2001); *How to Ruin Everything* (Vagrant, 2002).

FALL

Long-running **punk** and **postpunk** provocateurs led by the dour and reclusive Mark E. Smith, which retained the name despite what seemed like several hundred personnel changes. The Fall can be a maddening band to follow because of its long and intricate history of personnel and stylistic changes that make even the most ardent fan confused as to whether to enjoy this week's new direction or simply relax and wait for the next about-face. The Fall's early songs were somewhat straight-ahead, repetitious punk songs (including the extremely repetitious "Repetition") but soon became much more complex. There are far too many Fall CDs to list in a discography, and an entire book could be written about the band's ridiculously prolific output (sometimes as many as five different records coming out each year, many of them pointless live exercises and compilations), but they are, and were, one of the most important of the postpunk bands that influenced a generation of U.S. bands, most notably Pavement and possibly **Sonic Youth.** (Smith noted that he felt that Stephen Malkmus of Pavement stole the Fall's sound.) The Fall continued to record and tour, although their glory days are as long gone as singer Mark E. Smith's original teeth. Beginners are recommended to buy the compilation *50,000 Fall Fans Can't Be Wrong,* which examined the Fall's career from the beginning until about 2004 (which means that by the time this encyclopedia is printed, there will be approximately another 25 Fall CDs available). **Extremely Select Discography:** *Live at the Witch Trials* (StepForward/IRS, 1979); *50,000 Fall Fans Can't Be Wrong* (Beggars Banquet, 2004).

FASTBACKS

Extremely long-running (they were founded in 1979) Seattle **punk** band led by the versatile songwriting of Kurt Bloch, also a member of the Young Fresh Fellows, and featuring the vocals of guitarist Lulu Gargiulo and bassist Kim Warnick and a cast of seemingly thousands of drummers (an early version of the band featured Duff McKagen on drums, but for 11 years the drummer was Mike Musberger). The band first began recording in 1982 with *Play Five of Their Favorites* EP but did not release a full-length album until 1987. The Fastbacks played a mixture of punk and pop, mostly written by Bloch and sang by Warnick, who left the band in 2002 to form a band called Visqueen. The Fastbacks called it quits after her departure. The band was one of the longest-running independent punk bands with a female vocalist in the United States.
Discography: *Play Five of Their Favorites* EP (No Threes, 1982); *Every Day Is Saturday* EP (No Threes, 1984); *. . . and His Orchestra* (PopLlama Products, 1987); *Bike-Toy-Clock-Gift* (Bus Stop, 1988); *Very, Very Powerful Motor* (PopLlama Products, 1990); *In America, Live in Seattle* (Ger. Lost and Found, 1991); *Never Fails, Never Works* (UK Blaster, 1991); *The Question Is No* (Sub Pop, 1992); *Zucker* (Sub Pop, 1993); *Gone to the Moon* EP (Ger. Sub Pop, 1993); *Answer the Phone, Dummy* (Sub Pop, 1994); *New Mansions in Sound* (Sub Pop, 1996).

FAT WRECK CHORDS

Popular and successful independent **punk** label run by Fat Mike, leader of **NOFX,** that put out many influential punk records by bands such as No Use for a Name, **Lagwagon,** and **Avail.** The company remained one of the largest indie punk labels in the United States.

FEAR

Early **Los Angeles punk** band led by aggressive and abrasive singer **Lee Ving,** better known for his outrageous stage persona in which he taunted, berated, and castigated members of the audience. Fear was known for the aggression and violence of its shows and its satirical songs, such as "Lets Start a War" and "New York's All Right if You Like Saxophones," which put down everyone who was not a current member of Fear. The original band consisted of Lee Ving on vocals, Philo Cramer on guitar, Derf Scratch on bass, and Spit Stix and was a favorite of actor **John Belushi,** who famously got them a gig on *Saturday Night Live,* which caused a near riot. **Ian MacKaye** and John Joseph of the **Cro-Mags** led a slam **pit** of ferocious intensity that led the *Saturday Night Live* crew to claim (falsely) that $100,000 in damage had been done to the studio. This episode only helped to advance the notoriety that surrounded Fear. Ving was known for trying to provoke the crowds, often by using antigay epithets and general misogyny, but it is unclear where the joke ended or if most people were aware that Ving was trying to get a rise out of them and not simply attacking them. The band was inactive for most of the 1980s, due partly to Ving's acting career (which included a role in the movie *Clue* and many other mostly forgettable parts) as well as to various internal squabbles. After a near 10-year hiatus, Ving re-formed Fear with no original members for the heavily beer-centric

Have Another Beer with Fear in 1995. Fear was also known for its appearance in the original *Decline of Western Civilization* film directed by Penelope Spheeris, which helped to highlight the band's reputation for outrageous stage behavior.

Discography: *The Record* (Slash, 1982); *More Beer* (Restless, 1985); *Live . . . for the Record* (Restless, 1991); *Have Another Beer with Fear* (Sector 12, 1995).

FIELDS, DANNY

Talent scout and artist representative (A&R) man for several major labels who worked with **Iggy and the Stooges,** the **MC5,** and the **Ramones.** Fields started out as the "company freak" at Elektra records and, while working there, introduced Nico to Jim Morrison of the Doors while acting as Morrison's unofficial caretaker. While at Elektra, Fields was also responsible for signing the MC5 and Iggy and the Stooges on the same day. In the 1970s, Fields went on to manage the Ramones.

FILTH AND THE FURY, THE

A movie made in 2000 as a direct challenge to the assertions of *The Great Rock 'n' Roll Swindle* and **Malcolm McLaren's** assertions that he was the true genius behind **the Sex Pistols.** The movie featured rare footage and interviews with the surviving members of the Sex Pistols filmed in silhouette. Through the use of lengthy interviews and discussions of how much the band contributed to lyrics and songwriting (essentially everything) and how much Malcolm McLaren contributed to hype and promoting the band in often detrimental ways to the band's progress and commercial success (essentially everything), *The Filth and the Fury* was a welcome corrective to the hype machine and boasting that was evident in *The Great Rock 'n' Roll Swindle.* Even more astounding is the fact that both films were made by director Julien Temple only two decades apart.

FLESH EATERS

Flesh Eaters was a California band founded by Chris D. (Chris Desjardins) that featured a veritable who's who of the cream of **Los Angeles punk** musicians. Among those who played in the band over the years include John Doe and D.J. Bonebrake from **X,** Stan Ridgeway of Wall of Voodoo, Tito Larriva of the Plugz, and Dave Alvin of the Blasters. Chris D. remained the band's only constant member during the band's existence from 1977 to 1983. The Flesh Eaters released new material and toured from 1989 to 1994 and then returned with a new lineup in 1998. The band continued to record and tour. Chris D. also played in the band Divine Horsemen.

Discography: *EP* (Upsetter, 1979); *No Questions Asked* (Upsetter, 1980; with bonus tracks, Atavistic, 2004); *A Minute to Pray, a Second to Die* (Ruby, 1981; Slash, 1993); *Forever Came Today* (Ruby, 1982); *A Hard Road to Follow* (Upsetter, 1983); *Greatest Hits—Destroyed by Fire* (SST, 1986); *Live* (Homestead, 1988); *Prehistoric Fits, Vol. 2* (SST, 1990); *Dragstrip Riot* (SST, 1991); *The Sex Diary of Mr. Vampire* (SST, 1992); *Crucified Lovers in Woman Hell EP* (SST, 1992); *Ashes of Time* (Upsetter, 1999, 2001); *Miss Muerte* (Atavistic, 2004); *The Complete Hard Road to Follow Sessions* (remastered; Atavistic, 2004).

FLEX YOUR HEAD

Influential compilation of early **Washington, D.C., hardcore** bands. The title of the compilation was a play on the phrase *flexing your muscles,* in this case, flexing one's mind.

FLIPPER

Incredibly noisy and bombastic **hardcore** sludge band from San Francisco with a chaotic and somewhat sporadic touring and recording career. Flipper was led by singers and bassists Will

Shatter and Bruce Lose, with Ted Falconi on guitar and Steve DePace on drums. The band was best known for its signature song "Sex Bomb" and was championed by **Jello Biafra** from the **Dead Kennedys.** Flipper would have been more successful (Rick Rubin was a fan and later signed the band to his Def American label), but Shatter died of a **heroin** overdose in 1987. The band soldiered on after a brief hiatus with new bassist John Dougherty for the Def American release *American Grafishy.* A reunited Flipper toured in 2005 with various bands and played at the benefit concerts to save **CBGB's** in August 2005.

Discography: *Generic Flipper* (Subterranean, 1982); *Blow'n Chunks* (Roir, 1984); *Gone Fishin'* (Subterranean, 1984); *Public Flipper Limited Live 1980–1985* (Subterranean, 1986); *Sex Bomb Baby!* (Subterranean, 1988); *American Grafishy* (Def American, 1992).

FLIPSIDE

Long-running and influential punk zine that helped set the standards for California **punk** and **hardcore,** now defunct. *Flipside* was started in 1977 by writers such as Pooch and X-8 and was originally designed to cover only the **Los Angeles** area but quickly grew to include featured reviews, scene reports, and information of the regional and international punk scenes during its existence. *Flipside* also released record compilations, such as the *Rodney on the Roq* compilation that came with issue number 21 by bands such as Doggy Style to Beck, and a series of videos of punk bands in the mid-1980s. The zine finally folded in 2001. Todd Taylor, who had worked on the later version of the zine, went on to found *Razorcake* and publish some of the most acclaimed zine writing in the United States.

FLOWERS OF ROMANCE

Early British **punk** supergroup featuring Viv Albertine, **Sid Vicious** on vocals, Steve Walsh, and Keith Levine. Naturally, the band was too much a clash of divergent personalities to last long, but it did provide the impetus for Sid Vicious to become a charismatic, if almost completely untalented, stage performer. The use of casual blasphemy, attack on formal religion, and holocaust references became a fairly well-established part of punk rock during that time period.

FLUX OF PINK INDIANS

British **hardcore punk** band formed in 1980 with a distinct anarchist slant that recorded social-protest songs on the **Crass** record label and later on their own Spiderleg label. The band comprised vocalist Colin Birkett, Derek Birkett on bass, Kevin Hunter on guitar, and Martin Wilson on drums. Many outlets banned one of their records, the provocatively named *The Fucking Cunts Treat Us Like Pricks*, and a store was prosecuted for carrying the record. After recording one more record simply as Flux in 1986, the band broke up, and Derek Birkett went on to found the One Little Indian record label, which released albums by **Chumbawumba** and other bands. Flux of Pink Indians will also be remembered as one of the more consistently political British bands of the 1980s.

Discography: *Strive to Survive Causing Least Suffering* (Spiderleg, 1982); *The Fucking Cunts Treat Us Like Pricks* (One Little Indian, 1984); *Treat* (One Little Indian, 1986); *Uncarved Block* (One Little Indian, 1986); *Not So Brave* (Overground, 1997); *Live Statement* (Voiceprint, 2000); *Fits and Starts* (Dr. Strange, 2003).

FLYERS

Because mainstream advertising was almost nonexistent for **punk** rock shows in the early days of the U.S. and British scenes, many bands had to resort to homemade flyers that they produced themselves and pasted on telephone poles, traffic lights, walls, and wherever else they could before the police came and told them to cease and desist. Some flyers were relatively crude in execution and concept, often giving only the name of the band and the place in which the concert was going to take place, but many flyers were considered artwork in their own right. (For example, the art of **Raymond Pettibon,** the "house artist" for the **SST** label and brother of **Greg Ginn,** is now nationally known and has been the subject of different exhibitions.) It is unclear if many punks who created flyers were inspired by the **situationist** art and politics of **Jamie Reid,** who did much of the artwork for the **Sex Pistols,** nonetheless, there are numerous similarities between the **DIY** aesthetics of both English and U.S. flyers. Within a few years, a distinct style was developed. In **Los Angeles,** many punks who designed flyers were clearly influenced by Pettibon's juxtaposition of surreal imagery and text, and many early flyers look like Pettibon imitations. As the 1980s commenced, however, many different styles and traits were seen in various scenes. Many flyers can be regarded as experiments in cut and paste and are often works of art that resemble either situationist or postmodern collage styles, sometimes intentionally and sometimes just due to the sheer luck or cleverness of the artist assembling the flyer. Bryan Ray Turcotte and Christopher Miller's book *Fucked up and Photocopied,* released by Ginkgo Press in 1999, also provides a lucid and well-documented look at how flyers have evolved over since the 1970s.

"FORMING"

One of the earliest U.S. **punk** rock singles from the **Los Angeles** band the **Germs** on What? Records in July 1977. Although the lyrics are quite literate, they are almost incomprehensible, and the rhythm differs from the usual blitzkrieg speed of punk of that time. "Forming" was a key early U.S. independent release that also inspired many other bands to release their records independently and gave the impetus for many in the early Los Angeles scene to either record or release their own records. The record received extensive airplay from DJ **Rodney Bingenheimer** on his **KROQ** show.

4-SKINS

British skinhead band connected to the **oi** scene of the early 1980s that went though numerous personnel changes (bassist Hoxton Tom being the most stable member of the band). The band released several **ska**-tinged oi songs about the plight of the British working class. The band broke up in the early 1980s.
Discography: *The Good, the Bad & the 4 Skins* (Secret, 1982); *A Fistful of 4 Skins* (Syndicate, 1983); *From Chaos to 1984* (Syndicate, 1984); *Live and Loud!* (Link, 1989); *Clockwork Skinhead* (Harry May, 1999); *One Law for Them* (Cancan, 2000); *Low Life* (Get Back, 2000); *The Secret Life of the 4-Skins* (Captain Oi, 2001).

FOWLEY, KIM

Among the most controversial and reviled figures in early U.S. punk, Fowley is best known for masterminding the **Los Angeles** band the **Runaways** (featuring Joan Jett and Lita Ford among others) and putting out the 1960s novelty single "They're Coming to Take Me Away Ha-Ha" as Napoleon XIV. It was the Runaways that cemented Fowley's claim to fame—or infamy—when he bullied the teenage girls in the Runaways and practiced mental-intimidation techniques on them until most of the band quit and it eventually fell apart.

FRANKENSTEIN

Early version of the **Dead Boys,** following the demise of **Rocket from the Tombs.** Frankenstein featured Gene O'Conner (Cheetah Chrome), John Madansky (Johnny Blitz), with friend Stiv

A typical punk flyer by artist Thomas King. During the early days of punk, bands used their own flyers to advertise shows. *Collection of the Author.*

Bators. After a while, the band evolved into the Dead Boys and moved to **New York** to join the scene that was becoming more solidified in the late 1970s.

FREEZE

Boston hardcore band from the early 1980s that appeared on the *This Is Boston, Not LA* compilation. The Freeze was known for being more melodic than most of the Boston hardcore bands, which did not endear them to some of the more aggressive bands in the Boston scene.

FROM THE VELVETS TO THE VOIDOIDS

Book published in 1993 that details the early origins of **punk** rock by Clint Heylin (full title *From the Velvets to the Voidoids: A Pre-Punk History for a Post-Punk World*). The book relates in exhaustive and meticulous detail how the punk scene coalesced in various cities across the United States from the mid-1960s to the mid-1970s. The book was recently reissued and in the new introduction takes issue with other punk history books such as **Legs McNeil**'s *Please Kill Me* as being inadequate and insufficiently rigorous.

FUGAZI

Perhaps the most respected **punk** band in terms of integrity and consistency in U.S. punk history. Fugazi was the brainchild of **Ian MacKaye** (of punk legend **Minor Threat** as well as **Teen Idles,** Embrace, and **Egg Hunt** and founder and proprietor of **Dischord Records**) and Guy Picciotto of **Rites of Spring,** along with Brendan Canty (guitar) and Joe Lally (drums). Fugazi was a consistently experimental band that served as a moral benchmark for other punk bands by the members taking control of their careers in almost unprecedented ways. The band was legendary for keeping door prices at shows at a reasonable level (usually no more than $5 or $6), not selling merchandise (although there are many bootleg T-shirts available with the logo "This is not a Fugazi T-shirt"), touring econo-style, and refusing to be interviewed by magazines that accepted cigarette or alcohol advertisements. Fugazi started out with just MacKaye on guitar, and the early songs were more straightforward, but soon the band began incorporating shredding blasts of guitar noise and **reggae** and **dub** rhythms that marked them as musically more akin to British **postpunk** than to U.S. **hardcore.** Hardcore punks flocked to Fugazi shows, however, and a visibly annoyed MacKaye often asked for calm or admonished the audience that the **pit** had gotten out of control or was hostile to female participants. As Fugazi grew as a band, the members became more political, and eventually all of the other members adopted MacKaye's dedication to vegetarianism and a substance-free lifestyle and agreed on the policies not to sell merchandise and to keep gig prices as low as $5. The band also began to incorporate a more politicized stamp to their music, singing about a woman's right to cross the street free of lascivious suggestions and catcalls and bemoaning the loss of Justice William Brennan from the Supreme Court. Although some of the later albums were hit and miss, Fugazi was a relentlessly aggressive live band, as documented in the Gem Cohen documentary *Instrument*, whose members were unable to compromise their musical or political vision for mainstream success. Although Fugazi may have broken up or gone on hiatus after the *Argument* record, the legacy of the band as the one true uncompromising U.S. punk band that stuck to its principles and ideals cannot be underestimated.

Discography: *Fugazi* EP (Dischord, 1988); *Margin Walker* EP (Dischord, 1989); *13 Songs* (Dischord, 1990); *Repeater* (Dischord, 1990; plus three songs, 2004); *Steady Diet of Nothing* (Dischord, 1991); *In on the Kill Taker* (Dischord, 1993); *Red Medicine* (Dischord, 1995); *End Hits* (Dischord, 1998); *Instrument* (Dischord, 1999); *Argument* (Dischord, 2001); *Fugazi Live Series, Vols. 1–20* (Fugazi Live Series, 2004).

FUGS

Band of pranksters and musicians led by Tuli Kufenberg and Ed Sanders, who were seen by many as lost influences on the **New York punk** scene during their tenure as kings of New York protest music during the 1960s. The Fugs were considered by many to be a forerunner of the punk style adopted by many in the New York punk scene in the early 1970s, as epitomized by bands such as **Patti Smith** and others who mixed the personal and the political. The Fugs went on several lengthy hiatuses and re-formed sporadically for benefits and protest concerts.

FURIOUS GEORGE

Punk band led by prolific writer and musician **George Tabb,** who was known as well for his books *Playing Right Field, A Jew Grows in Greenwich,* and *Surfing Armageddon: A Memoir.* Furious George was also (sadly) known for the litigation brought against the band by lawyers representing the children's book character Curious George, who challenged the depiction of the Curious George character used in the band's logo. Tabb was one of the best known and most respected musicians and writers on the contemporary **New York** scene.

FURY, DON

Punk producer who ran his own studio and produced records such as **Agnostic Front's** *Victim in Pain* album. That success led to Fury becoming sort of a house producer for **New York hardcore** bands such as **Gorilla Biscuits** and **Youth of Today**. Fury continued to record bands to this day

F.U.'S

Boston hardcore band from the early 1980s that eventually went in a more metallic direction and changed its name to the more commercially palatable Straw Dogs. The band included Steve Grimes on guitar and vocals, Steve Martin on guitar, and Chris "Bones" Jones on drums. Brian "Pushead" Schroeder did the cover art for the *Kill for Christ* album.

Discography: *Kill for Christ* (X-Claim, 1982; Taang!, 2002); *My America* (X-Claim, 1983; Taang!, 2002); *Do We Really Want to Hurt You?* (Gasatanka, 1983; Taang!, 2002). **Straw Dogs:** *Straw Dogs* EP (Restless, 1986); *We Are Not Amused* (Restless, 1986); *Yellow and Blue Attack* (Enigma, 1988); *Your Own Worst Nightmare* (Lone Wolf, 1990).

GANG GREEN

Hard-drinking **Boston skate punk** band led by Chris Doherty and fueled by a constant diet of beer and illicit substances. The band was founded by Chris Doherty after he left **Jerry's Kids,** with original members Mike Dean on drums and Bill Manley on bass, but it shifted to its classic lineup with the additions of the Stilphen brothers, Chuck and Glen, on guitar and bass and Brian Betzger (also from Jerry's Kids) on drums. After several successful releases that celebrated the joys of alcohol, the Stilphens left to form the metallic band Mallet-Head, and Gang Green soldiered on for a few years with new bassist Joe Gittleman (who later left the band to join the Mighty Might Bosstones and was replaced by Josh Pappe) and Fritz Erickson on guitar (later replaced by Bob Cenci, another alumnus of Jerry's Kids). The band went on hiatus in the 1990s as Doherty and Betzger played in the major label punk band **Klover** and then re-formed in 1996 with a new lineup featuring Doherty, Cenci, Walter Gustafson on drums, and Matt Sandonato on bass.

Gang Green was best known for being a welcome antidote to the solemnity of the Boston **straight edge** scene and being a consistently fun band, even going so far as to cover the 'Til Tuesday classic "Voices Carry."

Discography: *Drunk and Disorderly, Boston, MA* EP (Deluxe, 1986); *Another Wasted Night* (Taang!, 1986, 1991); *P.M.R.C. Sucks* 12" EP (Taang!, 1987); *You Got It* (Roadrunner, 1987, 1992); *I81B4U* EP (Roadrunner, 1988, 1990); *Older . . . Budweiser* (Roadrunner, 1989); *Can't Live without It* (live; Roadrunner, 1990); *King of Bands* (Roadrunner, 1991); *Another Case of Brewtality* (Taang, 1997); *Preschool* (Taang, 1997); *Back and Gacked* EP (Taang, 1998); *You Got It/Older . . . Budweiser* (Roadrunner, 2003). **Mallet-Head:** *Mallet-Head* (Old Nick/Frontier, 1988); *Yeah Yeah Yeah* (Frontier/BMG, 1990).

GANG OF FOUR

One of the key bands in **postpunk** rock, Gang of Four combined leftist politics with spastic funk rhythms that were influential on many bands in the postpunk revival in **New York** during the early part of the twenty-first century. The band featured Dave Allen on bass, Hugo Burnham on drums, John King on vocals, and Andy Gill on guitar. Gang of Four was one of the quintessential postpunk bands, known for herky-jerky, almost **reggae** rhythms and strongly socialistic lyrics by singer John King. The band's first single was "Damaged Goods" in October 1978. The first album and EP established them as key innovators in British postpunk.

The last several records without the rhythm section followed the law of diminishing returns and called into question the band's ideology and contemporary relevance, but later tours with the original band members were reminders of why Gang of Four were regarded as extremely influential.

Discography: *Entertainment* (Warner Bros., 1979); *Gang of Four* EP (Warner Bros., 1980); *Solid Gold* (Warner Bros., 1981); *Songs of the Free* (Warner Bros., 1982); *Hard* (Warner Bros., 1983); *The Peel Sessions* (UK Strange Fruit, 1986); *A Brief History of the Twentieth Century* (Warner Bros., 1990); *Mall* (Polydor, 1991); *Shrinkwrapped* (Castle, 1995).

GAS HUFFER

Seattle **punk** band that dabbled with different styles and genres, from psychobilly to straight-out punk rock. The band was formed in the late 1980s by Tom Price on guitar, who had previously been in the influential U-Men, singer Matt Wright, and drummer Joe Newton. The album *The Inhuman Ordeal of Special Agent Gas Huffer* was accompanied by a comic book that fans could receive by mail.

Discography: *Ethyl* EP7 (Black, 1991); *Janitors of Tomorrow* (eMpTy, 1991); *Integrity, Technology and Service* (eMpTy, 1992); *One Inch Masters* (Epitaph, 1994); *The Inhuman Ordeal of Special Agent Gas Huffer* (Epitaph, 1996).

GAUNT

Columbus, Ohio, punk band with a raved-up sound courtesy of vocalist Jerry Wick and Jovan Karcic's country-punk guitar. The band ranged all over the map from straight-ahead shouted rock and roll to occasional country twang. The band was formed by Jerry Wick on vocals and guitar, Jovan Karcic on guitar, Eric Barth on bass (who left in 1991, was replaced briefly by Jim Motherfucker, who left the band in 1992 when Barth returned, and Brett Falcon, who joined the band when Barth left again in 1996), and Jeff Regensburger on drums (who was replaced by Sam Brown in 1996). Lead singer Wick was killed in January 2001 when a car stuck him while he was riding a bike.

Discography: *Whitey the Man* EP (Thrill Jockey, 1993); *Sob Story* (Thrill Jockey, 1994); *I Can See Your Mom from Here* (Thrill Jockey, 1995); *Yeah, Me Too* (Amphetamine Reptile, 1995); *Kryptonite* (Thrill Jockey, 1996); *Bricks and Blackouts* (Warner Bros., 1998). **Wick under a Pseudonym:** *Cocaine Sniffing* (Triumph, 1996).

GBH

Long-running British **punk** band started in Birmingham in 1979 (the name comes from the British police term *grievous bodily harm*) and known for its anthemic albums, such as *City Baby Attacked by Rats*, and for the gravity-defying haircuts the band sported. The band was initially known as Charged GBH but shortened the name in 1982 to GBH. The band featured Colin Abrahall on lead vocals, Colin "Jock" Blyth on guitar, Ross Lomas on bass, and Kai on drums. The band remained active and recorded and toured.

Discography: *Leather, Bristles, Studs and Acne* EP (UK Clay, 1981, 1990, 1995); *Leather, Bristles, No Survivors and Sick Boys . . .* (Clay/Combat, 1982); *City Baby's Revenge* (Relativity, 1984; Captain Oi!, 2002); *Midnight Madness and Beyond . . .* (Combat Core, 1986); *Oh No It's G.B.H. Again!* EP (Combat Core, 1986); *Clay Years: 1981–1984* (Clay, 1986, 1995); *No Need to Panic!* (Combat, 1987); *City Baby Attacked by Rats* (UK Clay, 1982; Clay/Combat, 1987; Captain Oi!, 2004); *Wot a Bargin'* EP (Combat,

1988); *No Survivors* (UK Clay, 1989); *A Fridge Too Far* (UK Rough Justice, 1989; Triple X, 1999); *From Here to Reality* (Restless, 1990, 1993); *Diplomatic Immunity* (UK Clay, 1990, 1995); *Clay Punk Singles Collections* (Clay, 1995); *Charged GBH: Clay Records* (Clay, 1996); *Celebrity Live Style* (Cleopatra, 1996); *Punk Junkies* (Triple X, 1997); *Live in Japan* (Creative Man, 1998); *Church of the Truly Warped* (Triple X, 1999); *Punk Rock Hits* (Cleopatra, 1999); *The Punk Singles 1981–1984* (Castle, 2002); *Dead on Arrival: A Punk Rock Anthology* (Castle, 2005).

GENDER AND PUNK

There is a complex and often contradictory relationship between **punk** and gender. On one hand, punk rock seemed to promise that there would be a revision of the traditional gender roles in rock both onstage and offstage. In reality, although many women were pioneers in the punk movement, many were marginalized, depending on where the scene was located and at what time the women were active. (An example of this is the frequent complaints of Exene Cervenka and others in the **Los Angeles** punk scene about the exclusion of women from the scene and from the **pit** as **hardcore** grew in Los Angeles and eventually became the dominant musical style.) The role of women was often very formalized according to mainstream conventions. In particular, the hardcore punk scene, although sometimes more original than the original punk scene, was sometimes even more rigid and inflexible in regard to what role women could play than earlier forms of punk rock. Although many women played a key part in early punk, overt displays of sexism (as well as displays of antihomosexual behavior, even in the gay-friendly New York and Los Angeles scenes) were often the norm. When the British punk band the **Adverts** featured a woman considered attractive by the media of the time, she was held up as a sex symbol rather then taken seriously as a musician.

In the United States, punk has always been dominated by men. Men outnumber women in the audience and onstage by a sizable majority, and women are often made to feel distinctly unwelcome at many hardcore and punk shows, where groping and outright sexual abuse are sometimes the norm. In his book *American Hardcore*, Steven Blush observed, "Hardcore boys saw girls as outsiders, even distractions" (34). Many of the first-generation punk scenes in the United States, such as Exene Cervenka of **X**, found the new hardcore scenes to be intimidating to women. Later bands from the **queercore** movement challenged the dominant notions of gender, and **Team Dresh** and others denounced the rigidity of the norms accepted in most punk scenes.

GENERATION X

Early punk band best known for its poppy hits (including the original version of "Dancing with Myself" on their third record) and as the embryonic spawning ground of future 1980s megastar Billy Idol. Generation X took its name from a 1964 book about teenage mods. The band has a surprisingly deep catalog, even though it was often dismissed by many punk purists. Formed in late 1976 after Tony James and Billy Idol (William Broad), chafing under the leadership of Chelsea singer Gene October, left to form their own group, taking short-lived drummer John Towe with them. They quickly recruited guitarist Bob "Derwood" Andrews and new drummer Mark Laff (Mark Laffoley). The band signed to Chrysalis records in July 1977 and in March 1978 released its first record, which contained numerous pop-punk classics such as "Ready Steady Go" and "Your Generation" and was one of the first punk attempts at a **reggae** and **dub** crossover with the remix of the song "Wild Youth" into "Wild Dub." A second less successful album, *Valley of the Dolls*, produced by Ian Hunter (of Mott the Hoople), marked the end of the original lineup, and by the third record they were joined by, among others, Terry Chimes from the **Clash** and Steve Jones, late of the **Sex Pistols.** Although the band is still perhaps best known as launching pad for Billy Idol's later solo career, the band's first album, *Generation X*, was one of the lesser-known punk gems and also included one of the earliest punk dub experiments, "Wild Dub." Tony James later went on to form the late 1980s hit makers Sigue Sigue Sputnik, perhaps one of the most ridiculous bands in the history of **New Wave.** Andrews and Laff formed the more standard rock-oriented Empire in 1981 for one album. In 2005, Tony James announced that he had formed the band Carbon/Silicon with Mick Jones from the Clash.

Discography: *Generation X* (Chrysalis, 1978; remastered, EMI International, 2002); *Valley of the Dolls* (Chrysalis, 1979; EMI International, 2002); *Kiss Me Deadly* (Chrysalis, 1981; Capitol, 1990; EMI International, 2005); *Dancing with Myself* EP (Chrysalis, 1981); *The Best of Generation X* (Chrysalis, 1985); *Live* (MBC, 1988); *Perfect Hits 1975–1981* (Capitol, 1991); *The Gold Collection* (EMI, 2000); *Live at the Paris Theatre, 1978 & 1981* (EMI International, 2000); *Perfect Hits* (EMI Gold, 2002); *Radio One Sessions* (Strange Fruit, 2002); *BBC Live—One Hundred Punks* (Strange Fruit, 2003); *Anthology* (Capitol, 2003); *Sweet Revenge Xtra* (Vivid Sound, 2003; Revel Yell, 2004); *Live at Hatfield Poly 1980* (EMI International, 2005). **Empire:** *Empire* (UK Dinosaur, 1981).

GERMS

Short-lived but enormously influential punk band from **Los Angeles** led by the charismatic and twisted **Darby Crash** (Jan Paul Beahm), equally well known for its music as well as the myths that surrounded the band and Crash's early and ugly death from a planned **heroin** overdose. The band was initially started by longtime Queen fan Jan Paul Bheam (who also went by the name Bobby Pyn), who, along with long time friend Pat Smear, met future Go-Go's member Belinda Carlisle and friend Terri Ryan outside the Beverly Hills Hilton waiting to meet the band Queen. The four decided to form a band with Carlisle on drums and Ryan (now Lorna Doom) on bass, but Carlisle was sidelined with mononucleosis and was replaced by Becky Barton (Donna Rhia, who was later replaced by Don Bolles and then Rob Henley) for the embryonic version of the Germs. Led by the charismatic and dangerous Crash, the Germs initially could not play their instruments, but became almost a cult, with the protofascist Darby Crash practicing mind-control techniques and initiating people into his circle through the "Germs Burn," a cigarette burn on the arm that followers were then allowed to give others to initiate them into the mysteries of the Germs. The Germs started playing around Los Angeles with other bands and played the famous Kim Fowley Presents New Wave Nights at the Whiskey in summer 1977, where Fowley got on the radio and asked bands from the new scene to show up and play. When the Germs released their single "Forming" on What? Records in 1977, it marked a new moment in Los Angles punk and clearly foreshadowed the **hardcore** explosion that would take over Los Angles music in a few short years. The Germs signed to Slash, and although the ever-contrary Darby Crash wanted Mark Lindsey of Paul Revere and the Raiders to produce their first record, the more sympathetic Joan Jett from the **Runaways** was brought in to produce what was quickly hailed as a punk classic. As Darby's behavior became more erratic, and his drug usage more prominent, more and more Los Angeles punks decided to emulate him, and Crash, unsure of what to write next, embarked on a disastrous project to try to come up with new Germs material to be used in the Al Pacino film *Cruising*. After the sessions proved particularly uninspired, Crash relocated briefly to England, where he returned with a **Mohawk** and a newfound fascination for Adam and the Ants. Crash then re-formed the Germs, for a show at the Starwood in December 1980, which was an unqualified success, but by then Crash's mood had become darker and his friendship with Casey Cola, a member of the local scene and Darby's heroin enabler, became destructive. On December 8, 1980, Darby Crash and Casey Cola overdosed. Cola survived, but Crash died, ending one of the most fascinating careers in punk rock. The remaining Germs disbanded, and Pat Smear later went on to join **Nirvana** and the Foo Fighters. The Germs' material is available on a CD anthology, and the legend of Darby Crash, who can also be seen at his chaotic best in the film *The Decline of Western Civilization*, lives on as the U.S. version of Sid Vicious.

Discography: *Germicide—Live at the Whisky* (Mohawk, 1977; tape, Roir, 1982; Bomp, 1998); *Live from the Masque 1978, Vol. 1* (House of Punk, 1978); *Tooth and Nail* (Upsetter, 1979); *Yes LA* (Dangerhouse, 1979); *(GI)* (Slash, 1979); *What We Do Is Secret* (Slash, 1981); *What?* (What, 1982); *Life Is Boring So Why Not Steal This Record?* (New Underground, 1983); *Let the Circle Be Unbroken* (Gasatanka, 1985); *Lion's Share* (Aus. Ghost o' Darb, 1985); *Rock n' Rule* (XES, 1986); *Media Blitz* (live; Cleopatra, 1993); *Cat's Clause* (Munster/Casatanka, 1993); *Germs (Tribute)—A Small C* (Sony, 1996); *Real Punk! The Nasty Years* (Cleopatra, 1996); *MIA: The Complete Anthology* (Rhino/Wea, 2000); *Media Blitz: The Germs Story* (Cleopatra, 2004).

GET IN THE VAN

In 1994, poet, singer, and former **Black Flag** front man **Henry Rollins** published his tour diaries from his days in Black Flag in a book titled *Get in the Van: On the Road with Black Flag.* The book documented the squalid lifestyle and police harassment that the band endured on its frequent journeys via van across the United Stated during the early to mid-1980s and featured a realistic and gritty look at the extremely unglamorous life of early **DIY** bands on the road, the abuse from audiences, and the lack of food that bands of that period often had to endure on a regular basis. Rollins became especially well known as a writer with his **2.13.61** publishing company (which published Nick Cave and others as well as Rollins's own material), and this diary is a good way to analyze how difficult it was for early punks such as Black Flag to establish themselves in an often hostile environment and to watch the evolution of Rollins as a writer. *Get in the Van* documents a lifestyle that, although strenuous and difficult, became the template for how punk bands would tour and produce music on a DIY basis. The book is also available in a CD version read by Rollins.

GI

The first and only record by the **Germs** and one of the key early punk records from the **Los Angeles punk** scene with numerous classic punk songs, such as "What We Do Is Secret," "Communist Eyes," "Media Blitz," and "Lexicon Devil." Although *GI* is not particularly well recorded (Joan Jett is listed as the producer), it nonetheless reveals the raw and remarkable talent of the Germs in their prime. Shortly after the record, the band tried to record more songs for the soundtrack of the movie *Cruising*, but **Darby Crash's** erratic lifestyle made it clear that the band was not meant to survive long, and Crash killed himself with a **heroin** overdose in December 1980.

GILMAN STREET

924 Gilman Street, also known as the Alternative Music Foundation, is an all-age, collective music club in North Berkeley, California. It is one of the key U.S. punk clubs run by and for genuine punks who want to see a show without interference from the authorities, drunks, or stoners. Gilman Street was the breeding ground for numerous well-known punk bands, such as **Operation Ivy** and **Green Day.** The club was formed along the same lines as other punk clubs, such as New York's **ABC No Rio,** and did not allow alcohol or visibly intoxicated or stoned punks on the premises because they distracted from the idea of a showcase for punk bands where the police would not be allowed to hassle or shut down shows due to rowdiness.

 Jello Biafra was beaten up there by young people who considered him to have sold out. The club continues to showcase new punk and hardcore bands.

GINN, GREG

Guitarist and founder of seminal **punk** band **Black Flag** and creator of **SST** record label, one of the most successful indie punk labels during the 1980s. Ginn led Black Flag through numerous personnel changes, especially in the lead singer department, finally solidifying with the most famous lineup that featured **Henry Rollins** on lead vocals, Bill Stevenson on drums, and Kira Roessler on bass. Although Black Flag is regarded by many as the premier Californian **hardcore** punk band, in reality it also pioneered a mixture of hardcore's energy combined with the sludgy riffs of heavy metal bands such as Black Sabbath to create its own unique, but much imitated, sound that would influence grunge in the 1990s. The Ginn guitar style can be described as a mixture of shrieking feedback and dissonance that sometimes sounds as though several people are playing guitar at the same time. After he ended Black Flag in 1986, he played in numerous bands, such as Gone and Confront James, and released several solo projects. Ginn played benefit shows in 2003 as Black Flag, but without Henry Rollins and with a computerized bass machine. Ginn also recorded under the name Dale Nixon (which was also used by Brian Baker on a **Dag Nasty** album when he could not perform due to contractual obligations). Ginn was one of the most influential guitar players in the punk scene, known for his wildly experimental guitar playing that expanded the parameters of the punk guitar vocabulary beyond the palette developed by Johnny Ramone and Steve Jones. *See also* Black Flag; Rollins, Henry; SST.

GLUE

Popular drug used by some punks in the 1970s (although this has been the subject of some dispute) due to its relative cheapness and ubiquity. The **Ramones** immortalized its use in their songs "Now I Wanna Sniff Some Glue" and the banned "Carbona, Not Glue" on their first and second records, respectively. Glue sniffing was certainly passé by the 1980s, replaced by gas huffing, crack, pot, alcohol, and perennial favorite **heroin.**

GOBBING

The often-criticized practice of spitting at band members in order to show appreciation or, sometimes, contempt for the music or the performers. The trend started in England in the late 1970s and was not as much of a factor in the U.S. version of punk. Many punk bands, including the **Sex Pistols** frowned on gobbing, and **Johnny Rotten** of the Sex Pistols and Siouxsie of **Siouxsie and the Banshees** blamed it for some of the diseases that they and others contracted during the period when gobbing was at its most prevalent. Gobbing and spitting are relatively unknown at punk shows today, although throwing things such as beer and other liquids remains inexplicably popular.

GODFATHERS

Punk band that formed in London in 1985 with garage overtones, best known for the song "Birth, School, Work, Death" and the members' sartorial style. The original lineup included Peter Coyne on lead vocals, his brother Chris Coyne on bass and vocals, Mike Gibson on guitar, Kris Dollimore on guitar (later replaced by Chris Burrows), and George Mazur on drums. The Godfathers were originally known as the Syd Presley Experience before they wisely changed their name. The band released several records and had some college radio and **MTV** exposure but ended up calling it quits in the mid-1990s.
Discography: *Hit by Hit* (UK Link, 1986; Link, 1996); *Birth, School, Work, Death* (Epic, 1988; Sony, 1990); *Cause I Said So* EP (Epic, 1988); *More Songs about Love and Hate* (Epic, 1989); *BBC Radio 1 Live* (Dutch East India, 1989); *Out on the Floor* EP (Epic, 1990); *Unreal World* (Epic, 1991); *Afterlife* (Intercord, 1996); *Birth, School, Work, Death: The Best of the Godfathers* (Sony, 1996).

"GOD SAVE THE QUEEN"

One of the key early British punk singles by the **Sex Pistols** and notoriously released in time for the Queen Elizabeth II's jubilee (her 25th anniversary of ascending to the throne and the cause of much national celebration in Great Britain). The song was originally written in 1976 as "No Future," but in 1977 it evolved into "God Save the Queen," which was the first Sex Pistols single on A&M records, and most of the copies were destroyed when A&M dropped the band. After signing to Virgin, the single was finally released in June 1977 and was quickly banned by the BBC and most commercial airwaves. The single became an instant hit but was not listed as one on the charts in an effort not to embarrass the queen on the occasion of her jubilee. The song remains one of the pivotal punk songs of all time, helped make the reputation of the Sex Pistols, and established the power of punk in social protest and attacking the government.

GOGOL BORDELLO

Gypsy **punk** band led by musician, writer, actor, and DJ Eugene Hutz that blended the thrash of punk to gypsy music in a sound reminiscent of the **Pogues** first few records. Hutz was the mastermind of the explosion of gypsy music and a key player in the amalgamation of world music and punk rock. Hutz also costarred in the movie adaptation of *Everything is Illuminated*.
Discography: *Voi-la Intruder* (Rubric, 2002); *Multi Kontra Kulti vs. Irony* (Rubric/Stinky, 2002); *East Infection* (Rubric, 2005).

GOLDFINGER

Los Angeles ska-influenced punk band that scored a radio hit with "Here in Your Bedroom" in the mid-1990s. Goldfinger featured John Feldmann on guitar and lead vocals, Charlie Paulson on guitar (replaced by Brain Arthur in 2002), "Dangerous" Darrin Pfeiffer on drums, and Simon Williams on bass (replaced by Kelly LeMieux in 2000). The band toured extensively and played the **Vans Warped tour.**
Discography: *Richter* EP (Mojo, 1995); *Goldfinger* (Mojo, 1996); *Hang-Ups* (Mojo, 1997); *Darrin's Coconut Ass* (Mojo, 1999); *Stomping Ground* (Mojo, 2000); *Open Your Eyes* (Mojo/Jive, 2002); *Live at the House of Blues* (Kung Fu, 2004); *The Best of Goldfinger* (Mojo/Jive/Legacy, 2005); *Disconnection Notice* (Maverick, 2005).

GOOD CHARLOTTE

Commercially successful pop punk band popular on radio and **MTV** during the early part of the twenty-first century. They were best known for their best-selling record *Lifestyles of the Rich and Famous* and singles such as that record's title song. The band was seen as the epitome of the state of punk in which bands that dressed in punk styles and played a catchy, faster version of power pop were considered punk rock. Equally suspect was the band's close association with MTV, which featured many of the band's songs (including the inevitable power ballads) and had the Madden brothers work as hosts for several MTV events. Good Charlotte worked the punk tour circuit and played on the **Vans Warped tour,** but ultimately the band demonstrated the uneasy way in which many people in the punk community viewed the relationship between punk and commerce. Was Good Charlotte still a punk band if they slowed down their style and commercialized their image and music? This was a tricky question, and the level of authenticity attributable to the band was questionable. This relationship between art and commerce was under discussion by punks.

GOOD VIBRATIONS

Northern Irish **punk** pop record label led by Terry Hooley. The label released singles by bands such as Rudi, Protex, Outcasts, and, most notably, the **Undertones.** Good vibrations allowed many young Irish bands to release material early on and helped establish the Undertones as a band to watch.

GORILLA BISCUITS

Melodic New York City **straight edge punk** band active during the 1980s that played in the style of pop punk bands such as the **Descendents.** The original lineup included Civ on lead vocals, Walter Schreifels (who also occasionally played bass for **Youth of Today** and later founded the art-punk band Quicksand) on guitar, Arthur Smilios on bass, Ernie on drums, and eventually Sam Siegler on drums (who also played with Youth of Today, **Shelter, Judge, Bold,** and **Side by Side**). The band was signed to **Revelation Records** and first put out a song on the *New York Hardcore—The Way It Is* compilation. The band released *Start Today*, a poppy hardcore classic, in 1989. Gorilla Biscuits ended around 1992, and Civ went on to start a tattoo shop before regrouping most of the members and later forming the commercially successful **Civ,** which had two successful records before disbanding in the mid-1990s.
Discography: *Gorilla Biscuits* EP (Revelation, 1988); *Start Today* (Revelation, 1989). **Civ:** *Set Your Goals* (Revelation/Lava/Atlantic, 1995).

GOVERNMENT ISSUE

Washington, D.C., punk hardcore band led by the gruff-voiced John Stabb along with numerous other members, including former **Minor Threat** member Brian Baker. The band was one of the more influential bands of the Washington, D.C., scene during the 1980s. The original lineup featured John Stabb on vocals, John Barry on guitar (replaced by Brian Baker of Minor Threat, followed by Tom Lyle), Brian Gay on bass (replaced by Tom Lyle, who switched to guitar when Brian Baker left, then Michael Fellows, and then John Leonard), and stalwart Mark Alberstadt on drums. The band started out playing straight-ahead hardcore, but by the *Government Issue* record it began to experiment with different sounds and became noticeably poppier and more melodic. By the 1990s, frequent lineup changes and diminishing returns caused Stabb to break up the band, although he continued to play music under a variety of names.
Discography: *Legless Bull* EP (Dischord, 1981); *Make an Effort* EP (Fountain of Youth, 1982); *Boycott Stabb* (Dischord/Fountain of Youth, 1983; Giant, 1988); *Joyride* (Fountain of Youth, 1984); *The Fun Just Never Ends* (Fountain of Youth, 1985); *Give Us Stabb or Give Us Death* EP (Mystic, 1985); *Live on Mystic* (Mystic, 1985); *Government Issue* (Fountain of Youth, 1986; Giant, 1986); *You* (Giant, 1987); *Crash* (Giant, 1988); *Strange Wine* EP (Giant, 1988); *Joyride/The Fun Just Never Ends* (Giant, 1990); *Beyond* (Rockville, 1991). **Various Artists:** *Four Old 7"s on a 12"* (Dischord, 1985).

GREAT ROCK 'N' ROLL SWINDLE, THE

Controversial, and ostensibly "true," movie story of the **Sex Pistols** as seen through the eyes of manager and Svengali **Malcolm McLaren,** who casts himself as a master manipulator of the naive musicians whom he shaped and molded into manufactured controversy. An answer film, *The Filth and the Fury*, was made by the members of the Sex Pistols in the late 1990s to counter the most bizarre of McLaren's assertions. *The Great Rock 'n' Roll Swindle* was also rushed into production and completed prematurely in order to pay off McLaren's sizable legal bills after **John Lydon** and others successfully sued his company, Glitterbeast, to recoup royalties and other fees not paid by McLaren. After years of wrangling and legal troubles, the DVD of the film was released in 2005.

GREEN DAY

One of the most popular and most wrongly maligned bands of the late 1980s and early 1990s, Green Day is best known for helping to break **punk** rock in the United States and indirectly making the music more accessible to those unaware of punk's rich history. In reality, singer and guitarist Billy Joe Armstrong was one of the most interesting and varied songwriters of the U.S. punk rock scene, despite never finishing high school, and also recorded sporadically with his other band, Pinhead Gunpowder. The other members of the band, bassist Mike Drint (Mike Pritchard) and longtime drummer Tre Cool (Frank Wright), provided proof that a consistent and tight rhythm section was half of the formula for mass acceptance in the mainstream market. The band originally started out as Sweet Children when the members were 15, but switched to Green Day and recorded some early material for **Lookout Records** with drummer Al Sobrante. Although Green Day was a considerable underground success story on Lookout Records, particularly with its ultra-pop punk record *Kerplunk*, it was the album *Dookie*, released in 1994, that made the band platinum superstars and the first real punk crossover band to sell millions of albums. The album also inspired the major-label feeding frenzy that led to so many of the major indie and punk bands of the 1990s getting signed by, and subsequently dropped from, major labels. The band's telegenic looks, expressive use of videos, and high-profile touring also helped to get the message out. A particularly notorious performance that made the band's reputation as band to watch was at the 1994 Woodstock Festival reunion, where the audience complied with a request to shower the band with mud and dirt to hilarious effect.

After a few years' layoff and some controversy (including the arrest of Armstrong for drunk driving in Los Angeles), the newly politicized Green Day returned with its most audacious concept yet, the 2004 rock opera *American Idiot*, which skewered U.S. voter apathy, media culpability in the dumbing down of the United States, and corporate culture, just in time for the 2004 presidential election. The newly politicized Green Day seemed back and more energized and vital than ever.

Discography: *1,000 Hours* EP (Lookout, 1989); *39/Smooth* (Lookout, 1990); *Slappy* EP (Lookout, 1990); *Sweet Children* EP7 (Skene!, 1990); *1,039 Smoothed out Slappy Hours* (Lookout, 1991); *Kerplunk* (Lookout, 1992); *Dookie* (Reprise, 1994); *Insomniac* (Reprise, 1995); *Nimrod* (Reprise, 1997); *Warning* (Reprise, 2000); *International Super Hits!* (Reprise, 2001); *Shenanigans* (Reprise, 2002); *American Idiot* (Reprise, 2004).

GROOVIE GHOULIES

Pop punk band from Sacramento, California, influenced by the **Ramones** as well as comic books and science fiction and horror films. The lineup changed many times but the main lineup was Kepi on bass and vocals, his wife Roach on guitar, and Wendy/Powell on drums (later replaced by Scampi). The band played poppy punk with a ghoulish twist and released an album of Chuck Berry songs on the Green Door label.

Discography: *Appetite for Adrenochrome* (Crimson Corpse, 1989; Lookout!, 1996); *Born in the Basement* (Green Door, 1994; Lookout!, 1996); *World Contact Day* (Lookout!, 1996); *Running with Bigfoot* EP (Lookout!, 1997); *Re-Animation Festival* (Lookout!, 1997); *Fun in the Dark* (Lookout!, 1999); *Travels with My Amp* (Lookout!, 2000); *Freaks on Parade* (Hol. Stardumb, 2001); *Go! Stories* (Hol. Stardumb, 2002); *Monster Club* (Springman, 2003); *Berry'd Alive* EP (Green Door, 2005).

GUN CLUB

Blues- and gospel-influenced **punk** band led by Jeffrey Lee Pierce, who started out as a Los Angeles punk and ended up as a latter-day bluesman trying to find something primal in U.S. roots music that resembled the fierce energy and integrity of punk rock. Pierce had a notoriously troubled life and had substance-abuse problems that strained his relationship with collaborators such as Kid Congo Powers (Brian Tristan), formerly of the **Cramps** and future member of the Bad Seeds, as well a former **Bags** member Patricia Morrison and Dee Pop from the Bush Tetras, to name but a few. Pierce continued the Gun Club for many years with a variety of lineups that usually contained Kid Congo and seemed to have gained a handle on the worst of his problems when he died of a cerebral blood clot in March 1996. Numerous Gun Club albums are spotty, and several live records do not show the band off to the best of the members' abilities, but on *Miami* and particularly *The Las Vegas Story*, the band demonstrates why Pierce's channeling of long-gone bluesmen and the primal swamp of U.S. roots music were such a compelling idea in the first place.

Discography: *Fire of Love* (Ruby, 1981); *Miami* (Animal, 1982); *Death Party* EP (UK Animal, 1983); *The Las Vegas Story* (Animal, 1984); *The Birth the Death the Ghost* (UK ABC, 1984); *Sex Beat 81* (Fr. Lolita, 1984); *Two Sides of the Beast* (UK Dojo, 1985); *A Love Supreme* (UK Offense, 1985); *Danse Kallinda Boom: Live in Pandora's Box* (UK Dojo, 1985); *Mother Juno* (Fundamental, 1987); *Pastoral Hide and Seek* (UK Fire, 1990); *Divinity* (Fr. New Rose, 1991); *In Exile* (Triple X, 1992); *The Gun Club Live in Europe* (Triple X, 1992); *Lucky Jim* (Triple X, 1993).

HANNA, KATHLEEN

Influential musician, writer, and theorist who sang in the band **Bikini Kill** and currently works in Le Tigre, well known for her political stances on issues relating to women and ideas about gender. Hanna started out in Olympia, Washington, running an art gallery, Reko Muse, that featured art by women. She realized there how insular and sexist the art and **punk** scenes were and was inspired to create her own music and art that had a distinctly women-centered focus. In her first band, Bikini Kill, Hanna pioneered an extremely confrontational and confessional style in which she sung and sometimes screamed intensely personal and political lyrics that decried inequality and sexism. After the demise of Bikini Kill, Hanna moved to Portland, Oregon, and worked on her solo project, Julie Ruin. In Portland, she roomed with zine writer and artist Johanna Fateman, and they worked as a group called the Troublemakers. After a brief hiatus, Hanna moved to New York, where she again teamed with Fateman along with Sadie Benning, a musician and video artist, and the three started the Le Tigre project, a queer and feminist-friendly band that pushed the boundaries of gender norms while cranking out incredibly dancy songs. After Benning left the band in 2000, J.D. Sampson, a film-maker and choreographer, took over and solidified the band's collaborative approach to making music and political statements. Hanna remained one of the most polarizing and politically active members of the punk scene.

HARDCORE

Harder and much faster variation of the original **punk** style, largely attributed to **New York** and **Los Angeles** bands from the late 1970s to the end of its original heyday in the mid- to late 1980s. Bands identified as members of the hardcore movement included **Minor Threat, Black Flag, TSOL, the Circle Jerks, JFA, SSD, Bad Religion, Youth of Today, Agnostic Front, Youth Brigade, Seven Seconds, Bad Brains,** and countless others from the early 1980s to the present day. (Although hardcore continued as a style, many critics and members of the punk scene regard it as becoming less of a dominant force in the punk scene by the time **CBGB's** ended its hardcore matinee at the end of the 1980s.)

Bikini Kill's Kathleen Hanna, one of the founders of the Riot Grrrl movement, demanded that women's voices be heard. © *Larry Busacca/Retna
Ltd.*

It is a matter of speculation when hardcore began, although many critics trace it back to
the **Ramones** (although the Ramones were certainly fast, they did not begin to play hardcore
rhythms until the mid-1980s, on songs such as "Warthog" and "Endless Vacation," in which they
attempted to play catch-up to the many bands inspired by them). Steven Blush, in his book
American Hardcore: A Tribal History, suggests that the first true hardcore punk record might
have been the "Our Out of Vogue" single by Middle Class from Santa Ana, California, or perhaps the "Pay to Cum" single by the Bad Brains. The first use of the term *hardcore* in a record was
DOA's *Hardcore 81* album, but the term predates the album and had become a frequently used
phrase by 1980 or so.

Hardcore can be regarded as a rethinking of punk that was in many ways a rejection of some
of the excesses and stylistic dead ends in which the first wave of U.S. punk had seemingly ended
up. Hardcore, especially U.S. hardcore, can also be seen as the start of a youth movement that
regarded older punk as having become codified and insular. The movement also saw a shift in
punk demographics from the larger cities, such as **Boston,** Los Angles, and New York City,
where movements began, to the suburbs, where bored suburban kids found an outlet for their
aggressions and suspicions about the future in the speeded-up rhythms and harsh stylistic

differences in hardcore punk. Hardcore, like punk rock itself, should also be analyzed not simply as one movement but as a series of overlapping movements that both politicized U.S. punk rock and also brought out a sense of resentment and anger that had lurked below the surface for many years, especially among younger punks from the suburbs. There was also an element of violence involved for many in the hardcore scene as slam dancing became more speeded up and tribalized and many **skinhead** bands became leaders in the movement. Although hardcore bands still tour (especially on larger tours like the **Vans Warped tour,** which often features bands such as **Pennywise, NOFX, No Use for a Name,** and **Lagwagon**) and record today, and new hardcore bands form almost every day, it seems as though the heyday of hardcore is over. Author Steven Blush identified the end of true hardcore around 1986, when many of the higher profile bands in the movement had either disbanded (such as Minor Threat) or had become heavy metal bands (as in the case of TSOL) and many of the fans began to turn to other interests and musical styles. A major problem with hardcore punk rock may be that musically it is a fairly limited genre. Especially during the 1980s, many in the hardcore audience could not accept any kind of stylistic innovation, and many of hardcore's pioneers were quick to leave it behind for other forms of music. As Steven Blush quotes Grant Hart (from hardcore pioneers Hüsker Dü), "I got bored with Hardcore very fast. Over time a lot of people started doing what we were doing—it lost its uniqueness" (43).

The violence that surrounded hardcore shows may also have been a reason for hardcore's demise because, increasingly, promoters like **Hilly Kristal** of CBGB's refused to book hardcore bands due to insurance and liability issues. *See also* Gender and Punk; Violence.

HATED: G. G. ALLIN AND THE MURDER JUNKIES

Documentary film released in 1994 about the sordid life and times of **punk** legend **G. G. Allin** by Todd Phillips (then at New York University), who later directed the mainstream movie *Road Trip* with Tom Green among many others. The film documented the debased life and disturbingly compelling (at least from the safe distance afforded by film) stage antics and slow downward spiral of G. G. Allin's life in one of his final tours. G. G. Allin had a burst of popularity for his "shows" (to call it a show would indicate that G. G. had actually played more than a song or two and then debased himself and chased the remaining audience around the room with handfuls of excrement or blood), although he soon died of an accidental overdose. The documentary revealed the more outrageous and dangerous aspects of punk rock as well as some of the sadder and more pathetic moments in punk history. *See also* Allin, G.G.; *I Was a Murder Junkie: The Last Days of G. G. Allin.*

HEARTBREAKERS

New York punk band from the 1970s led by former **New York Doll Johnny Thunders** and Jerry Nolan, known for punk anthems such as "Born to Lose" and "Chinese Rocks" as well as their seemingly unlimited appetite for drugs and self-destruction. Thunders and Nolan formed the band after they became dissatisfied with the way the New York Dolls were going under new manager **Malcolm McLaren.** The original band featured Johnny Thunders on guitar and vocals, Walter Lure on guitar and vocals, Jerry Nolan on drums, and **Richard Hell** on bass. After infighting between Hell and Thunders, Billy Rath replaced Hell on bass. The band split for the first time in late 1977 after touring England with the **Sex Pistols,** the **Clash,** and the Damned on the Anarchy tour and releasing classic punk record *L.A.M.F.* The band reunited without drummer Nolan for a live album recorded at **Max's Kansas City.** Although it would have been commercially more successful to get the original Heartbreakers back together, Thunders proved too erratic or unmotivated to do so and worked on various projects by himself, as did the other members. After years of touring g as a solo artist, Thunders died of a **heroin** overdose in 1991. Nolan died of meningitis a few months later, weakened by years of drug and alcohol abuse. Walter Lure became a success on Wall Street and still toured with his band the Waldos. The Heartbreakers must not be confused with the identically named backup band for Tom Petty, which, needless to say, is a radically different band.

Discography: L.A.M.F. (Track, 1977; Jungle, 1984); *Live at Max's Kansas City* (Max's Kansas City, 1979); *D.T.K.—Live at the Speakeasy* (UK Jungle, 1982). **Johnny Thunders & the Heartbreakers:** *L.A.M.F. Revisited* (UK Jungle, 1984); *D.T.K. L.A.M.F.* (UK Jungle, 1984); *Live at the Lyceum Ballroom 1984* (ABC, 1984; Receiver, 1990).

HELLCAT RECORDS

Offshoot label of **Epitaph** run by Tim Armstrong from **Rancid** dedicated to putting out **ska**- and **reggae**-influenced **punk** bands.

HELL, RICHARD

One of the key players stylistically and musically in the formation of **New York punk** rock during the 1970s. Richard Hell played in the embryonic versions of two famous bands, the **Heartbreakers** and **Television,** before going out on his own with the **Voidoids.** He released several records with the Voidoids, including the classic album *Blank Generation*, which featured punk classics such as the title song, "Love Comes in Spurts" and "Betrayal Takes Two." Richard Hell (born Richard Meyers) brought a sense of the poetic to punk along with fellow poets and musicians **Patti Smith** and Tom Verlaine. He also created the punk look of short, spiked hair, ripped clothing, and safety pins as fashion accessories. **Malcolm McLaren** was particularly taken by Hell's style and tried his best to import first Hell and then Hell's stylistic contributions to the early British punk scene. Hell and Tom Verlaine (born Tom Miller) had been schoolmates in Delaware (Hell preceded Verlaine by two years) before moving to New York City and working as poets, trying to reinvent themselves in the image of their Parisian poet idols who had helped start the Romantic movement in poetry. In much the same way, Hell hoped to start a sort of romanticized version of the Romantic movement in New York City. His aim was to take the machismo out of rock and roll and restore its roots in poetry (they published the book of poems *Wanna Go Out* under the name of a fictitious prostitute poet, Theresa Stern), and they (mostly Hell) worked as poets before forming the band the **Neon Boys.** When they added guitarist Richard Lloyd and drummer Billy Ficca, the band evolved into Television. A power struggle ensued when Verlaine began to cut Hell's material from the set, eventually causing Hell to leave Television for the Heartbreakers of his own volition with guitarist **Johnny Thunders.** After the same problem happened with Thunders, Hell at last went solo, forming his own group, the Voidoids, and releasing the seminal first album *Blank Generation* in 1977, although much of the material on the album had been played with Television or the Heartbreakers. The addition of master guitarist and jazz aficionado Robert Quine led to a new more improvisational complexity to the songs that had been lacking in previous versions. Second guitarist Ivan Julien and drummer Marc Bell (later of the **Ramones**) rounded out the Voidoids. The band put out two more records with only Hell and Quine before calling it quits in the early 1980s, partly due to Hell's frustrations with rock and roll. Hell worked on his poetry and fiction for the next two decades and appeared in several films, most notably *Smithereens* by Susan Seidelman. Drummer Marc Bell went on to greater success as Marky Ramone. Guitarist Quine committed suicide in 2004. Hell continued to record sporadically, including the Dim Stars project with Thurston Moore and Don Fleming and continued to write poetry and novels, including the novel *Go Now* in 1997 and *Godlike* in 2005.

Richard Hell in a still from the movie *Smithereens*. Hell of the Voidoids was one of the founding fathers of punk. *Photofest*.

Discography: *R.I.P.* (tape, Roir, 1984; Roir/Important, 1990); *Go Now* (Tim/Kerr, 1995); *Another World* (Overground, 1998); *Time* (Matador, 2002); *Spurts: The Richard Hell Story* (Sire/Rhino, 2005). **Richard Hell & the Voidoids:** *Richard Hell* EP (Ork, 1976); *Blank Generation* (Sire, 1977; Sire/Warner Bros., 1990); *Richard Hell/Neon Boys* EP (Shake, 1980); *Destiny Street* (Red Star, 1982; UK ID, 1988; Razor & Tie, 1995); *Funhunt: Live at the CBGB's & Max's* (tape, Roir, 1990; Roir/Important, 1990, 1995). **The Heartbreakers:** *What Goes Around . . .* (Bomp, 1991); *Live at Mothers* (Fan Club, 1991). **Dim Stars:** *Dim Stars* EP (Ecstatic Peace!, 1991; Caroline, 1992); *Dim Stars* (Caroline, 1992). **Bibliography:** *Artifact* (New York: Hanuman, 1990); *The Voidoid* (Hove, U.K.: Codex, 1996); *Go Now* (New York: Scribner Paperback, 1997); *Weather* (New York: CUZ Editions, 1998); *Hot and Cold: Essays, Poems, Lyrics, Notebooks, Pictures, Fiction* (New York: powerHouse, 2001); *Godlike* (New York: Little House on the Bowery, 2005).

HEROIN

Heroin, an extremely addictive opiate, was prevalent on the early **punk** scene, and **Iggy Pop,** long a junkie after the breakup of the **Stooges,** was blamed for hooking numerous other musicians, most notably **Johnny Thunders** of the **Heartbreakers** and **New York Dolls.** Thunders died of a heroin overdose under mysterious circumstances in New Orleans in 1991. Another notable junkie was **Sid Vicious** of the **Sex Pistols,** who died of a heroin overdose in New York City in 1979. Many in punk (and, of course, in heavy metal) romanticized the figure of the junkie as analogous to that of the doomed poet, which might explain why heroin was as popular as it was, despite the numerous punk casualties of heroin overdoses and the lengthy rehabs, such as Brett Guerewitz from **Bad Religion** and **Epitaph.** The relative cheapness of heroin in various U.S. cities during the late 1960s and early 1970s may also have had something to do with its early popularity, but once the price of opiates increased as the decades wore on, it was more likely the glamorization of the drug that led to its prevalence. Despite the obvious dangers of heroin, the use of the drug in punk is still prevalent in many scenes, particularly in New York.

HIT LIST

Berkeley, California, magazine edited by Jeff Bale that extensively covered underground music and what it considered "real rock and Roll" music. *Hit List* was one of the more influential sources on new music.

HIVES

Swedish punk-garage **punk** revivalists known for their outlandish sense of style, their grandiose sense of self, and their place in the worlds of music and popular culture. The Hives were a consistently amusing and musically intense band that, despite frequent airplay on **MTV,** carved their own niche in the world punk scene. The Hives harken back to the early days of punk when bands wore distinctive group uniforms, such as the **Ramones,** and to the suit-and-tie look of 1960s bands, such as the Beatles. The Hives' next release in the United States was less successful, but the band continued to record and tour, only without the promised (at least by the band during their numerous stage pronouncements and in press releases touting the invincibility of the Hives) and expected commercial success.
Discography: *Barely Legal* (Burning Heart, 1997); Veni, Vedi, *Vicious* (Epitaph, 2000); *Tyrannosaurus Hives* (Interscrope, 2004); *Your New Favorite Band* (Telstar, 2004).

HOLMSTROM, JOHN

Artist, writer, designer, visionary, and founder and editor of *Punk* magazine during the late 1970s. John Holmstrom was closely associated with the **Ramones** and present at many of the pivotal events in early **punk** history at **CBGB's** in New York City. *Punk* gave a name to the new movement in **New York** in the 1970s, and his magazine became legendary for its groundbreaking work in journalism and design that influenced countless magazines and **zines** in the punk movement. According to Holmstrom, he "didn't want to create a magazine about rock and roll, he wanted to do a magazine that *was* rock and roll." Although Holmstrom made no money from *Punk* magazine and helped to finance it through his work as a freelance illustrator, *Punk* was a success in terms of sales and influence. Holmstrom's magazine was a key source of publicity for early punk rock and had contributions from Mary Harron, **Richard Hell,** Roberta Bayley, Bob Gruen, and others who established the **DIY** aesthetic for punk. He also drew the front cover of the album *Road to Ruin* and the back cover for the Ramones record *Rocket to Russia.* Holmstrom also was a prolific editor and publisher and was the publisher of *High Times* magazine for many years. *Punk* magazine was immediately hailed by newspapers such as *The Village Voice* as a major new magazine and was recognized by some as the next logical step in popular-culture journalism. Holmstrom also created the comic strip *Joe* for Scholastic publications and worked there for many years. He, along with **Legs McNeil** and Gedd (George Edgar) Dunn, changed the face of independent publishing and also named and championed the new movement of punk rock in New York City. Holmstrom published a new version of *Punk* magazine with several new writers in 2001 and continued to champion New York City bands. Currently, he is working on several new projects, including a new version of *Punk* magazine. Holmstrom studied under legendary artist Will Eisner at the School of Visual Arts (SVA), where he developed his acclaimed artistic style so closely associated with the Ramones and the punk movement. Holmstrom also created cover art and illustrations for the Kowalskis and **Murphy's Law.**

HOMOSEXUALITY

Punk, especially **hardcore** punk, had a long and troubled relationship with homosexuality. Although many of the founders of the various punk scenes were either gay or bisexual, or at least experimented with the fluidity of gender roles (such as the transsexual **Wayne/Jayne County,** Lance Loud of the Mumps—who came out as gay on national television on the PBS documentary series *An American Family*—Patrick Mack of the **Stimulators,** Bob Mould and Grant Hart of **Hüsker Dü, Darby Crash** of the **Germs,** the **Screamers** in Los Angeles, and even the **New York Dolls** dressing in pseudodrag or the glitter rock and glam connections to punk rock), many in the hardcore community were intolerant of open displays of homosexuality. There are numerous recorded instances of gay bashing and other hate crimes, even though many young street punks sometimes resorted to male prostitution to get money for drugs or just to survive (as epitomized by the Ramones song "53rd and 3rd," in which **Dee Dee Ramone** related how he stabbed a prospective john in order to prove that he was "no sissy"). The **Bad Brains,** whose members had converted to the Rastafarian creed, embraced the religion's intolerance to homosexuality. Lead singer H.R. once got into an ugly confrontation with Randy "Biscuit" Turner from the **Big Boys** over Turner's openness about his sexuality that ended with H.R. screaming that he was in "Babylon!" Although most early hardcore bands with gay or lesbian members were largely closeted, some early hardcore punk bands such as the Big Boys and the **Dicks** had openly gay members, and many members of the early **Los Angeles** and **New York** scenes were openly gay or experimental in terms of sexuality (Darby Crash of the Germs being a prominent example of this sort of punk). Others in the punk community (most notoriously the Bad Brains) were vocally intolerant and expressed their discomfort in no uncertain terms. Other prominent, nearly out members of the punk community included Gary Floyd from the Dicks and Dan Dictor from the political band **MDC.** A fluidity in gender was not acknowledged in many scenes, and not-straight (presumably) punk singers Tesco Vee of the **Meatmen** and **Henry Rollins** of **Black Flag** were featured in the gay porn magazine *In Touch* (Vee's photo shows him with a Milkbone in his rectum). The 1990s also saw the rise of **queercore** punk and bands such as Sta-Prest, **Team Dresh, Tribe 8,** and **Pansy Division,** particularly on **Outpunk Records,** the first record label devoted exclusively to queer punk bands. (Outpunk Records had risen from an influential zine, also called *Outpunk,* published by Matt Wobensmith.) Many of the bands on Outpunk and other labels were much more outspoken than the earlier generation of punks who were largely closeted, and bands such as Tribe 8 openly questioned traditional ideas of gender by performing sex acts onstage using strap-ons and experimental straight boys. Other bands openly celebrated gay male sexuality with anthems such as Pansy Division's "Smells Like Queer Spirit." Many openly gay punks also rejected traditional labels, such as gay or lesbian, as too confining and politically charged and preferred the term *queer* as being more inclusive. This is not to say that all of the punk scenes are equally open about their sexuality or that all scenes are equally inclusive (it is doubtful that a skinhead scene would be welcoming to queer punks, although there certainly are subdivisions within skinhead culture that are identified as queer) or that gay, lesbian, and transgender punks are accepted. Based upon the openness not expressed during the early days of punk rock, however, there are certainly signs that the punk community is far more accepting of differences in gender and sexuality than it had been in the past.

Bob Mould of Hüsker Dü performs a sound check at the Peppermint Lounge. © *Robert Barry Francos.*

HOMOSEXUALS

Obscure British art **punk** band dedicated to the **DIY** aesthetic. The Homosexuals recorded sporadically during their brief existence but are counted as influential to postpunk and 1990s indie rock. The original lineup consisted of Bruno "Wizard" McQuillon on vocals, Anton Hayman (George Harassment) on guitar, and Jim "L. Voag" Welton on bass. They released numerous singles during their existence from 1978 to 1981 and originally started out as the Rejects, which had a small measure of fame and opened up for **the Jam** and the **Damned** but eventually evolved into a band that incorporated styles as diverse as funk, punk, **dub,** and abrasive antipop into a DIY stew. The band never went for glossy production values but maintained their DIY stance throughout its brief existence. Their entire recorded output was rereleased on a compilation CD by Morphius.
Discography: *The Homosexuals' Record* (UK Recommended, 1984; Morphius, 2004); *Astral Glamour* (Morphius, 2004).

HOOLEY, TERRI

Proprietor of the Northern Irish record label **Good Vibrations,** best known for releasing early works by the **Undertones** and others. Terri Hooley was instrumental in recording many early **punk** bands from Ireland.

HUGGY BEAR

Mostly female band associated with the **Riot Grrrl movement** led by an anonymous male vocalist. The band toured extensively and played numerous shows with other bands associated with the Riot Grrrl movement.
Discography: *Rubbing the Impossible to Burst* EP7 (UK Wiiija, 1992); *Kiss Curl for the Kid's Lib Guerrillas* EP7 (UK Wiiija, 1992); *Her Jazz* EP (UK Catcall/Wiiija, 1993); *Don't Die* EP (UK Wiiija, 1993); *Taking the Rough with the Smooch* (Kill Rock Stars, 1993); *Long Distance Lovers* EP7 (Gravity, 1994); *Main Squeeze* EP7 (UK Famous Monsters of Filmland/Rugger Bugger, 1994); *Weaponry Listens to Love* (Kill

Rock Stars, 1995). **Huggy Bear/Bikini Kill:** *Our Troubled Youth/Yeah Yeah Yeah Yeah* (Catcall/Kill Rock Stars, 1993). **Various Artists:** *Shimmies in Super-8* EP7 (UK Duophonic, 1993).

HÜSKER DÜ

Commercially successful but artistically adventurous band that challenged the orthodoxy of mid-1980s **punk** by incorporating elements of pure power pop and psychedelia in their music. Hüsker Dü had numerous minor hits and **MTV** videos before various addictions and tensions between lead singers Grant Hart and Bob Mould boiled over, destroying the band. Hüsker Dü was formed by singer and guitarist Bob Mould, drummer and singer Grant Hart, and bassist Greg Norton in Minneapolis in 1979 and released their first single, the hyper-speeded-up "Statues" EP7, in January 1981. The band toured constantly and became friends with the **Minutemen** (who released the first two Hüsker Dü albums on their New Alliance imprint) and **Black Flag** (who released most of the quintessential Hüsker Dü albums of the mid-1980s). The first **SST** release, the *Metal Circus* EP, contained several brilliant poppy songs that showed the band's annoyance at the limitations of **hardcore** they had found on the previous live *Land Speed Record* and the follow-up *Everything Falls Apart*. Following the success of the *Metal Circus* EP, the group embarked on its most ambitious project, a concept double album, *Zen Arcade*, that covers the musical gamut from Hart's psychedelic pop masterpiece "Pink Turns to Blue" to Mould's subtle hardcore take on relationships on "Pride" to the monumental instrumentals of "Reoccurring Dreams" and "Dreams Reoccurring." The next record, *New Day Rising*, was a less experimental version of some of the themes that showed Hüsker Dü moving in a more pop direction, culminating in their last record for SST, *Flip Your Wig*. After quarreling with SST house producer Spot over sound (the Hüskers found that their increasingly ambitious pop sensibilities clashed with SST's dynamic and recording ideas), the ambitious Hüskers signed to a major label, Warner Brothers, and put out their debut *Candy Apple Grey* in 1986, which benefited from better production values and showed off the band members' skill at pop music. A second album, the ambitious but flawed *Warehouse: Songs and Stories*, followed the next year. After the suicide of their manager David Savoy and amid growing tensions between key songwriters Mould and Hart, the band decided to split in 1987. Grant Hart released the autobiographical *2541* record, formed the band Nova Mob, and toured under that name and as a solo artist before taking time off from his musical career to deal with various addictions. Mould found more success with his new band Sugar and several solo records and also recorded and wrote music for wrestling programs and video games before returning to recording and touring on his own. Norton became a chef and started his own restaurant. Hüsker Dü remained one of the most important bands of the indie and punk scenes of the mid-1980s and demonstrated that the rigid formula embraced by many in the hardcore scene could be transcended and that there was no one acceptable formula for making punk rock.

Discography: *Land Speed Record* (New Alliance, 1981; SST, 1987); *Everything Falls Apart* (Reflex, 1982); *Metal Circus* (Reflex/SST, 1983); *Zen Arcade* (SST, 1984); *New Day Rising* (SST, 1985); *Flip Your Wig* (SST, 1985); *Candy Apple Grey* (Warner Bros., 1986); *Sorry Somehow* EP (Warner Bros., 1986); *Warehouse: Songs and Stories* (Warner Bros., 1987).

ICEBURN

Intricate "Math Rock" band from Salt Lake City that melded elements of punk and the intricacies of jazz into a unique style. The band included Gentry Densley on guitar and vocals, Doug Wright on bass, Dan Thomas on drums, and James Holder on guitar and saxophone.

Discography: *Hephaestus* (Revelation, 1994); *Poetry of Fire* (Revelation, 1994); *Split* (with Engine Kid; Revelation, 1994); *Firon* (Caroline, 1995); *Meditavolutions* (Revelation, 1996); *Power of the Lion* (Iceburn, 1998); *Polar Bear Suite* (Iceburn, 2000).

IGGY POP

Iggy Pop (James Osterberg) along with his 1960s band the Stooges is considered by most to be the godfather of punk rock. He is well known for such iconic songs as "Search and Destroy," "Now I Wanna Be Your Dog," "Loose," and "Lust for Life." Since his start as a drummer in the mid-1960s, Iggy Pop has remained a true original, influencing generations of punks and countless front men who usually emulate his earlier excessive behavior (rolling in glass and peanut butter, fighting with the audience) as opposed to his creativity and electric dynamism as a front man. *See also* Stooges, Iggy and the.

Discography: *The Idiot* (RCA, 1977; Virgin, 1990); *Lust for Life* (RCA, 1977; Virgin, 1990); *TV Eye Live* (RCA, 1978; Virgin, 1994); *New Values* (Arista, 1979; Buddah, 2000); *Soldier* (Arista, 1980; Buddah, 2000); *Party* (Arista, 1981; Buddah, 2000); *Zombie Birdhouse* (Animal, 1982; IRS, 1991); *I Got a Right* (Invasion, 1983; Enigma, 1985; Fr. Revenge, 1987); *Choice Cuts* (RCA, 1984); *Blah-Blah-Blah* (A&M, 1986); *Compact Hits* EP (UK A&M, 1988); *Instinct* (A&M, 1988); *Brick by Brick* (Virgin, 1990); *Livin' on the Edge of the Night* EP (UK Virgin, 1990); *American Caesar* (Virgin, 1993); *Naughty Little Doggie* (Virgin, 1996); *Nude & Rude: The Best of Iggy Pop* (Virgin, 1996); *King Biscuit Flower Hour* (King Biscuit Flower Hour, 1997); *Avenue B* (Virgin, 1999); *The Heritage Collection* (Arista, 2000); *Live in NYC* (King Biscuit Flower Hour, 2000); *Beat Em Up* (Virgin, 2001); *Skull Ring* (Virgin, 2003). **Stooges:** *The Stooges* (Elektra, 1969, 1977, 1982); *Fun House* (Elektra, 1970, 1977, 1982); *No Fun* (UK Elektra, 1980); *Rubber Legs* (Fr. Fan Club, 1987); *What You Gonna Do* EP (Fr. Revenge, 1988); *Live 1971* (Fr. Starfighter, 1988); *Live at the Whisky a Go Go* (Fr. Revenge, 1988); *My Girl Hates My Heroin* (Fr. Revenge, 1989); *1970: The Complete Fun House Sessions* (Elektra/Rhino Handmade, 1999). **Iggy and the Stooges:** *Raw Power* (Columbia,

The godfather of punk, Iggy Pop, is shown here in a particularly limber pose. *Photofest.*

1973; Columbia/Legacy, 1997); *Metallic K.O.* (Import, 1976); *I'm Sick of You* EP (Bomp!, 1977); *(I Got) Nothing* EP (Skydog, 1978); *I'm Sick of You* (Ger. Line, 1981, 1987); *Death Trip* EP (Fr. Revenge, 1987); *Gimme Danger* EP (Fr. Revenge, 1987); *Pure Lust* EP (Fr. Revenge, 1987); *Raw Power* EP (Fr. Revenge, 1987); *Iggy & the Stooges* (no label, ca. 1987); *Metallic 2xKO* (Fr. Skydog, 1988); *Raw Stooges Vol. 1* (Ger. Electric, 1988); *Raw Stooges Vol. 2* (Ger. Electric, 1988); *She Creatures of Hollywood Hills* (Fr. Revenge, 1988); *The Stooges* (Fr. Revenge, 1988); *Search and Destroy—Raw Mixes Vol. III* (Curtis, 1989); *Iggy and the Stooges* (Fr. Revenge, 1991); *I Got a Right* EP (Bomp!, 1991). **Iggy Pop and James Williamson:** *Jesus Loves the Stooges* EP (Bomp!, 1977); *Kill City* (Bomp!, 1978).

IRISH PUNK

Although there was no monolithic Irish punk scene, there were, and continue to be, numerous vital punk scenes in many cities in both Ireland and Northern Ireland. Perhaps the best-known scenes during the early years of punk were the prolific Derry scene that produced the **Undertones** and the Belfast scene that produced **Stiff Little Fingers** and **Radiators from Space.** Contrary to popular myth, the **Pogues** were a product of the dissolution of the London punk scene, where many émigrés such as Shane MacGowan had been members of the early punk scene.

IRON PROSTATE

New York City punk band led by punks who celebrated the power and finesse of punk's early years. The band featured ex-Ed Geins' Car front man Scott Weiss on lead vocals and guitarist **George Tabb,** who went on to form **Furious George.** The band was allegedly recording with Meat Loaf producer Jim Steinman (arguably a very nonpunk, or extremely punk, thing to do) when they dissolved due to the usual creative differences.
Discography: *Loud, Fast and Aging Rapidly* (Skreamin' Skull, 1991).

"I WANT TO BE SEDATED"

Although not a hit when it was released, this **Ramones** song is frequently overplayed at weddings and sweet-16 parties and (sadly) remains the best-known song of the Ramones, despite their rich and varied catalog.

I WAS A MURDER JUNKIE: THE LAST DAYS OF G. G. ALLIN

Book by Evan Cohen, former roadie for **G. G. Allin,** that recounts the escapades, chaotic gigs, and overall debauchery of life on the road with the notorious G. G. Allin during his infamous last tour before his timely death. (G. G. had been threatening to kill himself onstage for several years before accidentally dying of an overdose of cocaine and heroin.) Evan Cohen also played bass in punk author **George Tabb's Furious George** for some time.

JADE TREE RECORDS

Very popular and prolific punk label in the punk scene known for releases by bands such as Joan of Arc, Pedro the Lion, and Trial by Fire.

JAM, THE

Leaders of the mod revival that coincided and overlapped with punk in England during the 1970s. The Jam was enormously successful in England and very influential and popular among punks around the world. Led by controversial singer and guitarist Paul Weller (who identified as a Tory early on, much to his later regret), the Jam applied punk energy to a revival of the early mod sound and image as epitomized by the early Who. As the Jam grew older, Weller began to show less inclination to play straight rock and roll and chafed under the musical restrictions inherent in a three-piece lineup and began experimenting by adding additional instruments and more of a soul flavor to the band, a sound that he would pursue to more success in his next band, the Style Council. Paul Weller maintains an active solo career. Bass player Bruce Foxton has been a member of the reconstituted **Stiff Little Fingers** since the late 1980s.

Discography: *In the City* (Polydor, 1977); *This Is the Modern World* (Polydor, 1977); *All Mod Cons* (Polydor, 1978); *Setting Sons* (Polydor, 1979); *Sound Affects* (Polydor, 1980); *The Jam* EP (Polydor, 1982); *The Gift* (Polydor, 1982); *The Bitterest Pill* EP (Polydor, 1982); *Beat Surrender* EP (Polydor, 1982); *Dig the New Breed* (Polydor, 1982); *Snap!* (Polydor, 1983); *All Mod Cons/Setting Sons* (tape; Polydor, 1983); *Sound Affects/The Gift* (tape; Polydor, 1983); *Compact Snap!* (Polydor, 1984); *The Peel Session* (UK Strange Fruit, 1990); *Greatest Hits* (Polydor, 1991); *Extras* (Polydor, 1992); *Live Jam* (Polydor, 1993); *The Jam Collection* (UK Polydor, 1996); *Direction, Reaction, Creation* (UK Polydor, 1997); *The Very Best of the Jam* (UK Polydor, 1997); *This Is the Modern World and All Mod Cons* (Collector's Choice Music, 2000); *45 rpm: The Singles 1977–79* (UK Polydor, 2001); *45 rpm: The Singles 1980–82* (UK Polydor, 2001). **Bruce Foxton:** *Touch Sensitive* (Arista, 1984). **Style Council:** *A Paris* EP (UK Polydor, 1983); *Introducing the Style Council* EP (Polydor, 1983); *Café Leu* (UK Polydor, 1984); *My Ever Changing Moods* (Geffen, 1984); *Our Favorite Shop* (UK Polydor, 1985); *Internationalists* (Geffen, 1985); *The Lodgers* EP (UK Polydor, 1985); *Home & Abroad* (Geffen, 1986); *The Cost of Loving* (Polydor, 1987); *Confessions of a Pop Group* (Polydor, 1988); *The Singular Adventures of the Style Council (Greatest Hits Vol. 1)* (Polydor, 1989); *Here's*

Some That Got Away (Polydor, 1993); *The Style Council Collection* (UK Polydor, 1996); *The Style Council in Concert* (UK Polydor, 1997); *The Complete Adventures of the Style Council* (UK Polydor, 1998).

JAWBOX

Aggressive **Washington, D.C.,** band led by J. Robbins (formerly of **Government Issue**), who was known for his blistering and crunchy guitar-driven songs. The band released several consistent records on **Dischord Records** before jumping to a major label, Atlantic, where they had a minor hit with the song "Savory" in 1994. The band could not survive on a major label and split in the late 1990s, and Robbins went on to form Burning Airlines.
Discography: *Jawbox* EP7 (DeSoto/Dischord, 1990); *Grippe* (Dischord, 1991); *Novelty* (Dischord, 1992); *Savory + 3 EP* (Atlantic, 1994); *For Your Own Special Sweetheart* (Atlantic, 1994); *Jawbox* (Tag/Atlantic, 1996); *My Scrapbook of Fatal Accidents* (DeSoto, 1998). **Jawbox/Leatherface:** *Your Choice Live Series* (Ger. Your Choice, 1995).

JAWBREAKER

Berkeley, California, punk band with roots in New York City (the band formed after meeting as students at New York University) was a template for much of the early 1990s punk scene. The band was marked by an extremely tight and constantly shifting, stop-and-start musical approach and the scratchy and distinctive vocals of guitarist Blake Schwarzenbach, along with the ultratight rhythm section of bassist Chris Bauermeister and drummer Adam Pfhaler. Their first two records, *Unfun* and *Bivouac* (the second one recorded after Schwarzenbach suffered from seemingly inevitable throat trouble), set the sonic template for much of the early scene, and Schwarzenbach's highly personal lyrics addressed the issues of loss and authenticity with candor rarely seen in the punk scene. The breakthrough record, *24 Hour Revenge Therapy*, established Jawbreaker as one of the most important punk bands outside **Fugazi** and added a new dimension of sophisticated pop on songs such as "The Boat Dreams from the Hill" and "Do You Still Hate Me?" The band was then signed to DGC in the post–**Green Day** feeding frenzy and released one more album, the underrated but criminally overproduced *Dear You*, before calling it quits in 1996. After the band's demise, Schwarzenbach formed the stranger but compelling **Jets to Brazil.**
Discography: *Unfun* (Shredder, 1990); *Bivouac* (Tupelo Communion, 1992); *24 Hour Revenge Therapy* (Tupelo Communion, 1994); *Dear You* (DGC, 1995).

J CHURCH

Long-running and excessively prolific band led by constant member Lance Hahn, who moved from Hawaii and started the band with Cringer cofounder and bassist Gardner Maxam and a variety of other players. Hahn is a punk archivist who writes for *Maximum Rock 'n' Roll* and is also working on a book on the British anarchist bands of the 1970s. Hahn also played in Monsulo and runs the Honey Bear label. Current members of J Church include Ben White (of the diary comic *Snakepit*) on bass, David DiDonato on guitar, and Chris Pfeffer on drums. The band has toured extensively and sometimes releases as many as 10 records per year.
Discography: *Quetzalcoatl* (Allied, 1993); *Nostalgic for Nothing* (Broken Rekids, 1995); *Yellow Blue* (Allied, 1995); *Cat Food* (Damaged Goods, 1998); *One Mississippi* (Honest Don's Hardly, 2000); *Meaty, Beaty, Shitty Sounding* (Honey Bear, 2001); *Palestine* (Honey Bear, 2002); *Society is a Carnivorous Flower* (No Idea, 2004).

JERRY'S KIDS

Early Boston **hardcore** band that helped develop the Boston hardcore scene and was one of the most original bands of that time period. The original lineup included Bryan Jones on lead vocals, Chris Doherty on guitar, and Rick Jones on bass. After they first broke up, Doherty

left to form **Gang Green,** and the 1987 lineup featured Bob Cenci and Dave Aronson on guitar. The band veered in a more metallic direction for *Kill Kill Kill* before retiring again.
Discography: *Is This My World* (X-Claim, 1983; Ger. Taang!/Funhouse, 1987; Taang!, 2002); *Kill Kill Kill* (Taang!, 1989).

JERSEY BEAT

Long-running **zine** started in 1982 and published by rock writer Jim Testa (an insurance salesman form Weehawken, New Jersey). Testa also sometimes performs as a musician. The zine is one of the best and longest-running zines devoted to punk and indie music. It has a Web site at http://www.jerseybeat.com/.

JETS TO BRAZIL

Melodic punk band started in 1997 and led by Blake Schwarzenbach after the demise of **Jawbreaker.** The band featured Schwarzenbach on lead vocals, guitar, and keyboards, along with Chris Daly (from Texas is the Reason) on drums, Jeremy Chatelain on bass (from Handsome), and Bryan Maryansky on guitar.
Discography: *Orange Rhyming Dictionary* (Jade Tree, 1998); *Four Cornered Night* (Jade Tree, 2000); *Perfecting Loneliness* (Jade Tree, 2002).

JFA

Hardcore band from Phoenix, Arizona, whose name was short for Jodie Foster's Army, after the actress about whom John Hinckley (who shot **Ronald Reagan**) obsessed. The band was led by vocalist Brian Bannon (who also used to write for *Thrasher* magazine) with drummer Mike Sversvold. The band was also heavily involved in **skateboarding** and would only take members who could skate.
Discography: *Blatant Localism* EP (Placebo, 1981); *Valley of the Yakes* (Placebo, 1983); *JFA* (Placebo, 1984); *Mad Garden* EP (Placebo, 1984); *JFA Live* (Placebo, 1985); *Nowhere Blossoms* (Placebo, 1988); *Only Live Once* (Rotz, 1999); *We Know You Suck: Blatant Localism/Valley of the Yakes* (Alternative Tentacles, 2003).

"JILTED JOHN"

Novelty punk single by actor Graham Fellows that inexplicably went to chart in the British top 10.

JOY DIVISION

Increasingly influential **postpunk** band led by the tragic and brooding epileptic Ian Curtis, who composed much of the sonic palette for the postpunk and **New Wave** scenes. Curtis, a frustrated poet and songwriter from Manchester, England, is said to have been inspired by the **Sex Pistols'** legendary concert at the Lesser Free Trade Hall in Manchester on July 20, 1976. The band also featured Bernard Summers on guitar, Peter Hook on bass, and Stephen Morris on drums. Joy Division was influential on postpunk and the experimentations of numerous bands inspired by their more somber take on punk rock. After Curtis killed himself on May 18, 1980 (before setting out on what would have been a lucrative North American tour), the rest of the band eventually regrouped as New Order, one of the most successful of the New Wave bands.

Discography: *An Ideal for Living* EP (UK Enigma, 1978; UK Anonymous, 1978); *Unknown Pleasures* (Factory, 1979; Qwest, 1989); *Closer* (Factory, 1980; Qwest, 1989); *Still* (UK Factory, 1981; Qwest, 1991); *The Peel Sessions* EP (UK Strange Fruit, 1986, 1987, 1993); *Substance* (Qwest, 1988, 1990); *The Peel Sessions Album* (UK Strange Fruit, 1990); *Permanent Joy Division 1995* (Qwest, 1995); *All the Lyrics* (Ei, 1998); *Preston 28 February 1980* (live; Factory, 1999); *Complete BBC Recordings* (live; Varese, 2000); *Heart and Soul* (box set; Rhino, 2001); *Les Bains Douches 18* (live; Factory, 2001); *Before and After/BBC Sessions* (live with New Order; Varese, 2002); *Refractured Box One* (Phantom, 2003); *Les Bains Douches, Vol. 1* (live; Get Back, 2004); *Les Bains Douches, Vol. 2* (live; Get Back, 2004).

JUDGE

Straight edge hardcore band from New York City during the 1980s led by Mike Judge (Mike Ferraro, who formerly played drums with **Youth of Today** and Death before Dishonor and later became Supertouch). After touring with Youth of Today on the Break Down the Walls tour, Judge collaborated with John Procell of Youth of Today, Jimmy Yu of Death before Dishonor on bass (later replaced by Matt Pinkus), and Luke Abbey from **Warzone** (later replaced by Sammy Siegler from the band Judge) and released several records and became a major touring attraction. Judge broke up in 1991, and Mike Judge formed an acoustic project called Old Smoke.

Discography: *Bringin' It Down* (Revelation, 1989); *Storm* (Revelation, 1994); *No Apologies* (Lost & Found, 1995); *What We Said & Where It Went* (Lost & Found, 1996); *Judge This* (Executive Thug, 2002); *What It Meant: The Complete Discography* (Rev, 2005).

KENT, NICK

British journalist and rock critic who played a key part in early punk rock and roll both journalistically and as a member of the embryonic (pre-**Johnny Rotten**) version of the **Sex Pistols.** While working as a journalist and enamored of the Stooges, **MC5,** and **New York Dolls,** Kent met both **Malcolm McLaren** and Glen Matlock, who invited him to join their band Q. T. Jones & the Sex Pistols. This early version of the Sex Pistols consisted of Paul Cook on drums, Glen Matlock on bass, Wally Nightingale on guitar, and Steve Jones on vocals. Kent essentially replaced Nightingale and (according to him) introduced the band to the music of the **Modern Lovers** and **Iggy and the Stooges.** McLaren eventually fired Kent from the Sex Pistols before Rotten was inducted into the band (Kent had by then become a junkie) and maintained a relationship with the band until he was attacked and beaten with a bicycle chain at a Sex Pistols show by **Sid Vicious** and a knife-wielding Jah Wobble (later of **Public Image Limited**). Kent continues as a writer to this day.

KILLING JOKE

Punk/industrial band from London best known for their anthem "Eighties," Killing Joke was one of the more abrasive and aggressive bands of the **postpunk** era and became a template band for many of the industrial bands that followed in their wake. The band was formed in 1978 by Jazz Coleman on vocals, Geordie (Kevin Walker) on guitar, Youth (Martin Glover) on bass, and Paul Ferguson on drums. The band first broke up in 1988 and reformed in 1990 with new members Martin Arkins (of **Public Image Limited** and Brian Brain) on drums and Paul Raven on bass. They broke up again (various members formed Murder Inc.) and reformed again in 1994 with Coleman, Geordie, Youth, and new drummer John Dunsmore. Various members work in production, Youth collaborated with Paul McCartney as Fireman, and Youth and Coleman teamed up to record a symphonic Pink Floyd record with the London Philharmonic Orchestra. The band reunites sporadically for recording and tours.

Discography: *Almost Red* EP (UK Malicious Damage, 1979; UK Island, 1981; EG, 1990); *Killing Joke* (Malicious Damage/EG, 1980, 1990; Red international, 2003); *What's This For. . .!*(Malicious Damage/ EG, 1981, 1990); *Revelations* (Malicious Damage/EG, 1982, 1990); *"Ha"* EP*10* (Malicious Damage/EG, 982); *Fire Dances* (EG, 1983, 1990); Night Time (EG/Polydor, 1985; EG, 1990); *Brighter than a Thousand*

Suns (EG/Virgin, 1986, 1994); *Outside the Gate* (EG/Virgin, 1988, 1999); *The Courtald Talks* (Invisible, 1989); *An Incomplete Collection* (EG, 1990); *Extremities, Dirt & Various Repressed Emotions* (Noise International/RCA, 1990, 1998); *Laugh? I Nearly Bought One!* (EG/Caroline, 1992); *Pandemonium* (Big Life/Zoo, 1994); *Jana Live EP* (Butterfly Records/Big Life, 1994); *Millennium* (Zoo, 1994); *BBC in Concert* (UK Windsong, 1995); *Willful Days* (Blue Plate, 1995); *Democracy* (Zoo, 1996); *No Way out but Forward Go* (live; Pilot, 2001); *Love Like Blood* (Brilliant, 2002); *The Unperverted Pantomine?* (Pilot, 2003); *Chaos for Breakfast* (box set; Malicious Damage, 2004); *For Beginners* (Caroline, 2004); *Untitled* (Teichiku, 2005); *Ha! Killing Joke Live* (EMI, 2005). **Anne Dudley and Jazz Coleman:** *Songs from the Victorious City* (China/TVT, 1991). **Murder Inc.:** *Murder Inc.* (Invisible, 1992; Futurist/Mechanic, 1993); *Corpuscle EP* (Invisible, 1992). **Fireman:** *Strawberries Oceans Ships Forest* (UK Parlophone, 1993; Capitol/EMI, 1994). **Us and Them:** *Symphonic Pink Floyd* (Point Music, 1995).

KILL ROCK STARS

Prolific underground record label that released albums by bands such as **Huggy Bear** and early **Sleater-Kinney.** One of the key indie record labels in the United States.

KLEENEX/LILIPUT

Swiss female band from Zurich, formed in 1978, that helped define the **postpunk** sound with their off-kilter songs. The original lineup featured Regula Sing on vocals (replaced by Chrigle Freudn and later Astrid Spirit), Marlene Marder on guitar, Klaudia Schiff (Klaudia Schifferle) on bass, Lisolt Ha (Lisolt Hafner) on drums (later replaced by Beat Schlatter), and Angie Barrack (later replaced by Christoph Herzog) on saxophone. The band was forced to change its name to Liliput in 1980 after the Kleenex brand tissues threatened litigation. The band expanded their sound with a sax player before eventually calling it quits in 1983. Marder went on to form the band Dangermice in the 1980s.
Discography: *Liliput* (Rough Trade, 1982); *Some Songs* (Rough Trade, 1983). **Dangermice:** *Sound Session EP* (Swiss Sounds!, 1989).

KLOVER

Early 1990s punk band featuring guitarist Chris Doherty and drummer Brian Betzger, former members of **Gang Green,** with lead singer and guitarist Mike Stone. The band released one record featuring a cover of the Real Kids' "All Kinds of Girls" before folding and reviving Gang Green for subsequent tours and records. Klover was yet another band snapped up by anxious record company executives who, inspired by the **Green Day** juggernaut, threw contracts at any band with any kind of punk connection or look.
Discography: *Feel Lucky Punk* (Mercury, 1995).

KRAUT

Key early New York City **hardcore** band best known for their anthemic songs "Kill for Cash" and "You're All Twisted," later covered by **Civ.** The band featured Doug Holland (later of the **Cro-Mags**) on guitar (later replaced by Chris Smith from **Battalion of Saints**), Davy Gunner on vocals, and Johnny Feedback (John Koncz) on drums. The band was a key part of the metamorphosis of the New York City sound from hardcore to punk and was one of the key early New York bands. Highlights were opening for the **Clash** at Bonds Casino in 1981 and having former **Sex Pistol** Steve Jones play on their debut album. Smith drowned tragically, and Feedback and Gunner went on to form Gutterboy. Kraut has reunited sporadically in recent years.
Discography: *An Adjustment to Society* (Cabbage, 1983); *Whetting the Scythe* (Cabbage, 1984); *Night of Rage* (New Red Archives, 1989); *The Movie* (New Red Archives, 1990); *Complete Studio Recordings* (New Red

Archives, 1995); *Live at CBGB's* (New Red Archives, 2004). **Gutterboy:** *Gutterboy* (DGC, 1990); *Gutterboy* (Mercury, 1992).

K RECORDS

Record label led by Calvin Johnson of **Beat Happening.** Some may argue the relative punkness of both Johnson's musical endeavors and his label, but his economic independence, **DIY** aesthetic, and commitment to putting out records by women and the disenfranchised are all hallmarks of the latter-day punk aesthetic.

KRISHNA, HARE

Krishna exerted an influence on many members of the New York City **hardcore** scene in the 1980s and 1990s, most notably on Ray Cappo (formerly of **Youth of Today**), who went on to found the Krishna-core band **Shelter,** and several members of the original **Cro-Mags.** Sometimes branded a cult, the Hare Krishna movement came to the United States in the 1960s and took root in the poorer areas of many cities, including New York City's Lower East Side, where many young punks in the 1970s and 1980s were attracted to the idea of some kind of non-Western spirituality. Most punks who embraced Krishna belong to either the International Society for Krisha Consciousness (ISKCON), the largest group working outside of India, or one of its many offshoots. The group primarily is Indian in origin, going back at least 500 years, and primarily was spread in the United States by A.C. Bhaktivedanta Swami Prabhupada, who brought the mission to the Western world. Krishna devotees are known for their shorn heads and chanting of the mantra "Hare Krishna, Hare Rama," in which *Hare* refers to the energy from God and *Rama* and *Krishna* are two of the Sanskrit words for God.

KRISTAL, HILLY

Hilly Kristal is the proprietor of **CBGB's** (the full title of the club is CBGB & OMFUG, which stands for "County Bluegrass Blues" and "Other Music for Uplifting Gourmandizers"), the club he founded in 1973 at 315 Bowery in the heart of the then decrepit Bowery area of New York City. CBGB's hosted the first real appearances of bands such as the **Ramones, Television, Talking Heads, Blondie, Richard Hell,** and countless others. Hilly had previously operated other bars and wanted to start a new club that showcased the styles of music he liked best. In the divey, Hell's Angels atmosphere of early CB's, where a quarter purchased a pitcher of beer, however, Kristal was unable to make ends meet until Television and other bands started playing there in March 1974. The club soon became world famous, and Kristal was an omnipresent figure at the door, watching, with some bemusement, the various bands and audience members who tried to slip in for free or claim they were with the band. Kristal also tried his hand at managing groups, including the **Dead Boys** and latter-day punk's Riconstruction. In 2005, the existence of CB's came under attack by the Bowery Residents Committee, who tried to have CB's evicted due to issues with back rent. Kristal, who maintained that most of the estimated $2 million per year CB's received from merchandising and the CB's logo simply went back into the business, also organized several benefit concerts to save the club in August 2005.

KROQ

Los Angeles radio station famous for playing punk and underground music when few other stations in the United States would play such music. **Rodney Bingenheimer** started as a DJ there in 1976 and played music by local bands such as the **Dils,** Motels, and the **Ramones.** Gradually, this alerted many in Los Angeles that a new type of music was becoming prevalent.

LAGWAGON

Melodic Southern California band from Goleta, originally formed under the name Section 8, that played poppy **punk** in the traditional **Fat Wreck Chords** style. The lineup included Joey Cape on vocals, Chris Flippin on guitar, Chris Rest on guitar, Jesse Buglione on bass, and Dave Raun on drums. The band toured extensively and was widely regarded as one of the best of the Fat Wreck Chords groups that combined punchy punk hooks with melodic pop songs. The band toured extensively and played **Vans Warped tour** on many occasions.

Discography: Duh (Fat Wreck Chords, 1992); *Trashed* (Fat Wreck Chords, 1994); *Hoss* (Fat Wreck Chords, 1995); *Double Plaidinum* (Fat Wreck Chords, 1997); *Let's Talk about Feelings* (Fat Wreck Chords, 1998); *Let's Talk about Leftovers* (Fat Wreck Chords, 2000); *Blaze* (Fat Wreck Chords, 2003); *Live in a Dive* (Fat Wreck Chords, 2005).

LAPD

During the early to late 1980s, notorious incidents of violence occurred between the LAPD (Los Angeles Police Department) and members of the **punk** rock community. Although many cities had troubles between punks and locals, such as **London** and many cities in England during the 1970s and 1980s, nowhere was the antagonism between punks and local authorities more pronounced than in **Los Angeles.** Often, police would show up in full riot gear outside punk shows because of "complaints" by neighbors and would attack the show with tear gas and then beat the fleeing patrons with batons. Although the LAPD always justified these actions as breaking up potential riots, there were doubtlessly more attacks on punks than outright provocation by punks toward police officers. The band **MDC** (sometimes the initials stood for "Millions of Dead Cops") responded with the song "Dead Cops."

Black Flag documented the troubles in their song "Police Story," in which **Henry Rollins** sings "This fucking city is run by Pigs / They take the rights away from all the kids / Understand we're fighting a war that we can't win / They hate us, We hate them / We can't win." Although the songs by Black Flag and MDC (and many others by bands such as the **Dead Kennedys** and

Government Issue) attacked the police and often preached violence, most punk bands did not actually advocate armed struggle against the police. On the other hand, Black Flag and other bands endured regular police surveillance and harassment every time they attempted to play in Los Angeles. As Henry Rollins wrote in his book *Get in the Van*, "On any given night you could look out the window to the back parking lot and see an unmarked police car. They were watching us" (11). It was unclear why punk bands were regarded as such a threat by the LAPD, but it is possible that the way punks were portrayed in mass media may have helped fuel the perceptions on the part of police that punk was a dangerous and violent subculture. There were numerous problems between the police and **hardcore** bands across the country over the years, which have mostly dissipated because punks are not seen as dangerous as they were before, but the Los Angles punk scene will always be remembered for the number of confrontations that occurred between (mostly) peaceful punks and the police department. *See also* Black Flag; *Get in the Van*; MDC; Punk and Mass Media Representations.

LEAVING TRAINS

Los Angeles band led by Courtney Love's first husband, Falling James (James Moreland). Leaving Trains was equally infamous for James's transvestite look and for naming a record *Fuck*.

Discography: *Well Down Blue Highway* (Bemisbrain/Enigma, 1984); *Kill Tunes* (SST, 1986); *Fuck* (SST, 1987); *Transportational D. Vices* (SST, 1989); *Sleeping Underwater Survivors* (SST, 1991); *Loser Illusion Pt. 0* EP (SST, 1991); *The Lump in My Forehead* (SST, 1993); *The Big Jinx* (SST, 1994); *Drowned and Dragged* EP (SST, 1995); *Smoke Follow Beauty* (SST, 1996); *Favorite Mood Swings (Greatest Hits 1986–1995)* (SST, 1997); *Emotional Legs* (Steel Cage, 2001).

LEO, TED

Washington, D.C., solo performer with the Pharmacists. Ted Leo was known for his work that evoked both the **Clash** and the righteousness of early **punk.** Before his better-known solo work with his bands the Pharmacists and Citizens Arrest, Leo was originally in Chisel, which also featured Chris Norborg on bass and John Dugan on drums and released several records in the mid-1990s.

Discography: **Chisel:** *Nothing New* EP (Gern Blandsten, 1995); *8 a.m. All Day* (Gern Blandsten, 1996); *Set You Free* (Gern Blandsten, 1997). **Ted Leo:** *The Tyranny of Distance* (Lookout!, 2001).

LETCH PATROL

New York City antihardcore band formed in 1985 that founded the scum rock movement, which combined heavy metal and **punk** rock. The band was led by lead vocalist Harris Pankin, a former squatter from Detroit by way of San Francisco, and a rotating cast of musicians and released only one seven-inch in its brief existence, which included a prominent television appearance during the Tompkins Square Park riots. The name Letch Patrol indicated the band's favorite activity: spying on women. The **New York** press reported that in 2005, Pankin, who was homeless, played in the New York City Grand Central Neighborhood Services soccer team at the Homeless Cup of Soccer in Graz, Austria.

Discography: *Love is Blind/Axe to Grind* 7" (Electric Shaman, 1988).

LE TIGRE

Feminist, **queercore, punk** dance band led by singer Kathleen Hanna, formerly of the band **Bikini Kill.** The band featured Hanna, Johanna Fateman, and Sadie Benning, who was replaced by J. D. Samson on multiple instruments and vocals. Le Tigre played a subversively poppy and poppily subversive combination of **New Wave** dance rhythms, furious beats, and sometimes-punk guitars accompanied usually by Hanna's punk vocals. Most songs dealt with the impermanence of gender and asked the audience to question its assumptions about being straight, gay, or somewhere in between while the band danced up a storm.

LETTS, DON

Don Letts was a filmmaker, DJ, and former member of Big Audio Dynamite who contributed much to **punk,** not only by documenting the early scene via his ubiquitous camera but also by introducing many of punk's key players (such as the **Clash**) to **reggae** via his deejaying at punk shows and at **Acme Attractions,** one of the early punk fashion shops on King's Road. In 2005, Letts made the punk documentary *Punk Attitude,* which featured interviews with many of punk's original founders as well as members of the **New York** punk and **hardcore** scenes, including Arthur Kane from the **New York Dolls** just before his death, **Legs McNeil, Henry Rollins,** and members of the **Sex Pistols, Bad Brains,** and **Agnostic Front.**

LIFETIME

New Jersey **hardcore** band from the mid-1990s that released several seminal records. The band consisted of Arti Katz on lead vocals, Dan Yemin on guitar, Pete Martin on guitar, Dave Palaitis on bass, and Scot Golley on drums. The band broke up in 1997, and Yemin joined Kid Dynamite; Katz, Palaitis, and Golley formed Zero Zero.
Discography: *Lifetime* EP (New Age, 1991); *Background* (New Age, 1992); *Hello Bastards* (Jade Tree, 1995); *The Seven Inches* (Glue, 1996); *Jersey's Best Dancers* (Jade Tree, 1997).

LIPSTICK TRACES

Punk book published in 1989 and written by Greil Marcus (full title *Lipstick Traces: A Secret History of the Twentieth Century*) that tried to contextualize punk rock and the **Sex Pistols** in terms of historical, political, and artistic movements, highlighting connections between punk rock and movements such as the **situationists.** Although the connection was denied by many (including Sex Pistols front man **Johnny Rotten**), Marcus made a compelling point that punk did not simply spring out of nothing but came from a long tradition of artistic and social rebellion against the dominant power structures throughout history. The book was also a moving account of the potential power of underground movements and how the arts, philosophy, and social movements long had a tradition of rebellion that not only predated punk rock but also provided a pool from which punk rock could draw for philosophical and social statements. Overall, *Lipstick Traces* was one of the most intellectual looks at punk rock and the power of protest.

LIVERMORE, LARRY

Zine publisher and writer and founder of **Lookout Records.** Larry Livermore was one of the most influential people involved in the **punk DIY** movement and was responsible for the signings of numerous key bands and for his writing on punk in **zines.**

LONDON

Along with **New York,** London had one of the most vital and active **punk** scenes during the 1970s and later. Numerous bands, such as the **Sex Pistols,** were formed in and around London as the grim economic and social conditions of the city during the 1970s led to an inevitable back-lash against mainstream society. The London scene was one of the most fertile for punk groups, and the numerous contingents that formed around London, such as the **London SS** led by Mick Jones, later evolved into bands such as the **Clash, Generation X,** and the **Damned.** The London scene was inspired by a wide array of factors, such as the decline of the British economy and high unemployment, and included a few epicenters of discontent, such as fashion shops like **Malcolm McLaren's Sex** shop and **Acme Attractions,** where numerous musicians congregated to find out about the latest bands and fashions and to hear new music and **reggae** played by Acme Attractions DJ **Don Letts.** The crucible was the debut of the Sex Pistols, which also inspired numerous other bands to form and play in colleges, as opposed to the pub circuit, and places like the **100 Club** and the **Roxy,** where young people could be exposed to the new phenomenon. The scene soon spread beyond London as the Sex Pistols and others toured, spreading the word outside of a relatively small area. Mass media attention, such as the Pistols' notorious appearance of the *Today* show with **Bill Grundy,** led to a media frenzy that further exposed the scene's vitality. The scene changed quickly, however, and most of the early London bands (with the exception of the Clash and the Damned) quickly broke up, and **postpunk** replaced punk within a few years. New generations quickly picked up the torch, and **hardcore** bands began to dominate the scene within a few years for the next several generations. Today, London is still a musical and cultural capital, and new bands continually spring up to fill the void.

LONDON CALLING

The **Clash's** third record, released by Epic in 1979, was an awesomely ambitious double album that proved that the band had not lost its vision. Songs from the record, including the title track and the unlisted track "Train in Vain" (almost always misnamed by U.S. audiences as "Stand by Me"), established the Clash as more than a flash in the pan to U.S. audiences and almost single-handedly proved to numerous critics (if not to radio stations and music executives) that punk was no trend but a viable form of music. The record covered a vast array of styles, from **rockabilly** to funk to **dub** to jazz, and demonstrated that punk need not be held to one narrow stylistic movement but could embrace many disparate sounds as long as the proper attitude and energy were present. The album was rereleased in 2004 with a variety of bonus tracks and demos as well as a DVD with footage of the Clash. The design and style of the album was also groundbreaking, and the album cover featured bassist Paul Siminon smashing his bass on stage at the Palladium in a parody—or tribute, if you will—of the first Elvis Presley album, another reason why the nickname of the Clash was "the only band that matters."

LONDON SS

Early version of the **Clash** that featured, among others, Keith Levine (later of **Public Image Limited**), Tony James (later of **Generation X**), and Mick Jones. The sound of London SS was closer to glam rock or the **MC5** than to the sound that would make the Clash famous. Other members came and went, and the band was managed by Bernie Rhodes, the theorist and professional agitator who also worked extensively with the Clash later on. Chrissie Hyndes of the Pretenders was briefly a member, as was Bryan James who left to form the **Damned.** When Rhodes assumed greater control of the band and recruited **Joe Strummer,** the band mutated into the Clash. London SS never officially recorded (although the Clash song "Protex Blue" was supposedly written during this time period) and was best remembered for the numerous groups that members would later found.

LOOKOUT RECORDS

One of the key independent **punk** labels that put out records by **Green Day,** the **Donnas,** the **Mr. T. Experience, Operation Ivy,** the **Queers, Avail,** the Hi Fives, and many others. Lookout Records was founded in Berkeley, California, in 1987 by **Larry Livermore** and David Hayes. Hayes left in 1989 to form Very Small Records and Too Many Records, and Livermore ran the label though its most successful period until he sold the label to Chris Appelgran, who got his start working in the Lookout mailroom. Although the label had eclectic tastes, it was best known for the poppy style of punk that made them world renowned. Lookout endured considerable financial trouble, and several bands, angered over unpaid royalties, charged breach of contract and took back their masters from lookout. Avail reissued theirs on **Jade Tree Records, Screeching Weasel** took theirs to Asian Man, **Pansy Division** to **Alternative Tentacles,** and most importantly **Green Day** rescinded their masters on August 1, 2005, apparently forcing the cash-starved label to cancel any new releases and lay off two-thirds of the Lookout staff. The label's future remained unclear, which was sad in light of the enormous contribution the label made to independent and punk music.

LOS ANGELES

Key album from **Los Angeles** band **X,** released by the Slash label in 1980, that demonstrated to the rest of the United States (and the world) what a vibrant and active scene was going on there. The album was produced by Ray Manzarek from the Doors.

LOS ANGELES

One of the two key earliest **punk** scenes (along with **New York**) that stood as a remarkable testament to the diversity of early punk in the United States. Although there were some similarities to the New York scene and some bands and personalities that crossed over, the Los Angeles punk scene had a unique flavor and composition all its own and an equally early pedigree that led to a wide diversity of styles and art-based creative movements.

The Los Angeles scene had its roots in the days of glam and glitter rock in which bands such as Christopher Milk (who's lead singer Kurt Ingham poured hot wax on himself and bit people in the audience in a precursor to some of punk's more showier artists), the legendary space alien band **Zolar X** (all the members dressed as aliens in bubble helmets and stayed in character both before and after shows), Jobriath (an openly gay singer-songwriter who was an inspiration to Morrissey, among others), as well as androgynous Dolls-like bands such as the Berlin Brats played the Sunset Strip. The scene began to change in the early 1970s when bands such as **Iggy and the Stooges** migrated to Los Angeles and **Iggy Pop** began his downward spiral into junkiedom. (Iggy at one point was so desperate for drugs that he sold his legendary Raw Power Cheetah skin jacket to Stan Lee of the **Dickies** for **heroin.**) As more and more dissatisfied **protopunks** began to come to Los Angeles, the early scene began to congregate around **Rodney Bingenheimer'**s club, the English Disco, or the Sugar Shack, another popular place for underage Los Angeles scenesters to meet, have sex, and get drugs. Early participants in this scene included **Darby Crash,** who was then planning world domination in his band the **Germs,** as well as future members of the Go-Go's. Early **zines,** such *Back Door Man,* started by Phast Phreddie (Fred Patterson), that championed outsider music such as Eno, the Dolls, and Roxy Music also started to inform those in the Los Angeles scene of the early stirrings of a music revolution. Black Randy, a local musician, had seen and reported back on the **Ramones,** and soon Rodney Bingenheimer was playing the Ramones regularly in his clubs and on his radio show on **KROQ,** where he championed bands such as the Ramones as well as new local bands such as the **Dils** and the Motels. Soon, a vibrant artistic scene grew up around bands that valued art for art's sake, such as the Dadaist Weirdos, the performance art and pseudodrag of the **Screamers,** the poets in **X,** as well as the **Germs,** the fastest, sloppiest, and most aggressive of the early Los Angeles bands. The scene was also helped out immensely when Claude Bessey started *Slash* magazine, which provided another valuable source of information about Los Angeles bands of the time. When many local clubs such as the Whiskey a-Go-Go where initially reluctant to let punk bands play, the solution was provided by Scottish immigrant **Brendan Mullen,** who had a 10,000-foot basement space in the Hollywood Center building on North Cherokee Avenue, which opened as the **Masque,** a rehearsal and performance space where local bands could play. After a while, the punk bands were more accepted and could play outside of the Masque and house parties as more and more clubs such as **Madame Wong's** and the Hong Kong Café started to let punk bands play. Numerous bands from the Los Angeles scene were signed to major labels, including X, but by the end of the late 1970s, the scene was changing, inspired by the Germs' sound and eventual self-destruction.

Although the original scene had been centered around urban Los Angeles, the end of the 1970s saw a new group of bands grow up around the suburbs in subscenes such as Hermosa Beach, where **Black Flag** came from, or the **Orange County hardcore** scene, known for its violence and relative affluence that featured bands such as **TSOL** (True Sounds of Liberty). Bands from the South Bay area, such as the **Descendents, Minutemen, Red Kross (Red Cross)**, and Saccharine Trust, started a slightly geekier, less violent scene than that of Orange County or the earlier art punk scene of central Los Angeles. The early South Beach scene congregated around the Creative Craft center in Hermosa Beach, called the "church" by most of the locals, where Black Flag and others played until increasing violence caused the center to stop allowing bands. Although the heyday of the Los Angeles scene is over, numerous bands still play the Los Angeles circuit.

LOVE AND ROCKETS

Underground comic book started in 1982 by the three Hernandez brothers that chronicled the lives of Latin American neighborhoods, lesbian themes, science fiction, and various punks. *Love and Rockets* is not to be confused with the identically named band that featured former members of Bauhaus. The Hernandez brothers, primarily Jamie and Gilbert but occasionally Mario, were also among the most influential in underground comic books during the 1980s and 1990s, which was in many ways analogous with the punk movement in its connections to **DIY** and authenticity. The comic stopped publication in 1996 but resumed in 2001 after the brothers recharge their creative juices. Like alternative records, the Hernandez brothers also had to face charges of "selling out" because the comic style of *Love and Rockets* kept improving, and as it sold better it was considered by some elitist punks to be too mainstream. Along with *Hate* and *Eightball, Love and Rockets* was one of the most consistent adult comics created for an alternative audience.

LUNCH, LYDIA

New York City singer and poet who worked with the bands Teenage Jesus and the Jerks and collaborated with **Sonic Youth** and others. A key member of the no-wave movement in New York City in the early 1980s, Lydia Lunch (Lydia Koch) left an abusive home in Rochester and became part of the **New York punk** scene at an early age and began working as a waitress at **CBGB's.** She formed her first band, Teenage Jesus and the Jerks, with notoriously confrontational saxophone player James Chance and drummer Bradley Field to create a challenging and abrasive wall of noise, especially after Chance left to found his own band, James Chance and the Contortions (later James White and the Blacks), and Lunch brought in various bass players to play the music she labeled no wave. The band barely recorded (including several tracks on the *No New York* compilation of no-wave bands). In 1980, Lunch disbanded the Jerks and started a solo career with her pseudojazz record *Queen of Siam*. She returned to her own abrasive form with the formation of 8 Eyed Spy along with drummer Jim Sclavunos (later a member of Nick Cave and the Bad Seeds) and bassist George Scott, who later died of a **heroin** overdose before the band became popular. Lunch went on to collaborate with a dizzying array of musicians and writers, including Nick Cave, Michael Gira (of the Swans), Jim Thirwell (Foetus), **Sonic Youth Henry Rollins,** and Exene Cervenka, as well as appear in the films of Richard Kern. For the past several decades, Lunch concentrated mostly on writing and spoken word, in which her emotionally naked performances were challenging and difficult to watch.

LURKERS

English band from Uxbridge in the loud and fast pop style of the **Ramones.** The original four included the aptly named Arthur Bassick on bass, Howard Wall on lead vocals, Pete Stride on guitar, and Manic Esso on drums. The band went through numerous personnel changes and several breakups. A reunited version of the Lurkers tours today.

Discography: *Fulham Fallout* (UK Beggars Banquet, 1978; Captain Oi!, 2000); *God's Lonely Men* (UK Beggars Banquet, 1979, 2000); *Shadow* (UK Beggars Banquet, 1979); *Greatest Hit: Last Will and Testament* (UK Beggars Banquet, 1980, 1998); *Final Vinyl EP* (UK Clay, 1983); *This Dirty Town* (UK Clay, 1983, 1990, 1997); *Wild Times Again* (Weser, 1988, 1998); *King of the Mountain* (UK Link, 1989); *Live and Loud!!* (UK Link, 1990); *Totally Lurked* (Castle, 1992); *Ripped n' Torn* (Step 1, 1995); *Live in Berlin* (Released Emotions, 1995); *Non Stop Nitropop* (Weser, 1996, 1998); *Take Me Back to Babylon* (Receiver, 1997); *Last Will & Testament (Greatest Hits)* (Lowdo, 1997); *Beggars Banquet Singles Collection* (Anagram Punk UK, 1999); *Ain't Got a Clue* (Harry May, 2000); *BBC Punk Session* (live; Captain Oi!, 2000); *Wild Times Again/Non Stop Nitropop* (Captain Oi!, 2001); *Powerjive/King of the Mountain* (Anagram Punk UK, 2002); *The Punk Singles Collection* (Captain Oi!, 2002); *On Heat* (Ataque Frontal, 2002); *26 Years* (Ahoy, 2003); *Lurkin' Aboot* (live; Bassick Productions, 2004); *Live Freak Show* (Kotumba, 2004). **Pete Stride/John Plain:** *New Guitars in Town* (UK Beggars Banquet, 1980).

LYDON, JOHN

Former lead singer of the **Sex Pistols** (as **Johnny Rotten**) and **Public Image Limited** (under his own name). John Lydon is the author of the autobiographical *Rotten: No Irish, No Blacks, No Dogs* in which he presents his response to the allegations of **Malcolm McLaren** (both in print, in litigation, and in the movie *The Great Rock 'n' Roll Swindle*) that the Sex Pistols were merely puppets for the Svengaliesque McLaren. Lydon appeared in several TV shows and toured with the reunited Sex Pistols. *See also* McLaren, Malcolm; Public Image Limited; Punk; Rotten, Johnny; Sex Pistols.

LYNMAN, KEVIN

Founder of the enormously successful **Vans Warped tour,** which brings together large numbers of punk bands of varying ability and popularity to play relatively short sets during large package tours, akin to the rock and roll reviews of the 1960s meets the Lollapalooza festival. Many critics complain that the acceptance of corporate sponsorship, even by a product that many punks use and even if it creates greater awareness of punk bands and ideology, is still a betrayal of the nature of punk rock.

MACKAYE, IAN

Lead singer of **Minor Threat,** leader of **Fugazi,** and co-owner of **Dischord Records** in **Washington, D.C.** One of the most visible and admired people in **punk** rock and longtime advocate of radical causes, vegetarianism, and the **straight edge** lifestyle. MacKaye started as a skateboard fanatic in Washington, D.C., who listened to Ted Nugent (and was probably inspired to start the straight edge movement because of Nugent's aversion to drugs and alcohol). It was the **Cramps** and especially **Bad Brains,** a band Ian championed for many years, however, that transformed the young Ian MacKaye into a young punk. MacKaye formed an early band, the Slinkees, to espouse his clean-living lifestyle (a typical Slinkees song was called "I Drink Milk") in a humorous way. The Slinkees evolved into the **Teen Idles** with the addition of singer Nathan Strejeck and toured cross-country with roadie Henry Garfield (who later changed his name to **Henry Rollins** and formed **SOA** and then joined **Black Flag**). During the tour, MacKaye devised his famous X on the hand to signify that the punk wearing the X was at a show to listen to music and not drink, which soon became a movement in Washington, D.C., and was needed to see shows in bars, as opposed to strictly being a symbol of straight edge punk rock. In 1980, Dischord Records was formed by Ian MacKaye and Jeff Nelson to put out the first Teen Idles single (featuring a cover of two hands crossed with Xs on them), and MacKaye and Nelson ran Dischord from then on, putting out not only their own records but also records of bands (regardless of genre) from the Washington, D.C., area. In 1980, MacKaye, tired of not singing, broke up the Teen Idles and formed Minor Threat, which quickly became one of the most important and most influential bands in **hardcore.** MacKaye (who eventually became a **vegetarian** in 1984) was also increasingly alienated from the band because of his bandmates' reluctance to embrace the political and message-oriented lyrics he was writing, versus the more commercial direction the rest of the band wanted to go. When Minor Threat broke up in 1983, Ian concentrated on running Dischord Records for a while before deciding to put a new band together under the name Embrace. Embrace featured former members of Faith (including Ian's younger brother Alec), with Ivor Hanson on drums, Chris Bald on bass, and Mike Hampton on guitar and was radically different from Minor Threat, which confused many of MacKaye's fans. By this time, MacKaye was less concerned with commercial success and more concerned with political and social change, and in 1985 he was a major participant in the famous **Revolution Summer.** Despite its name, Revolution Summer was not an attempt to foster armed revolution but rather an attempt to create a new punk scene that was more inclusive and political than the previous Washington, D.C., scene. It included participants such as **Beefeater,** Grey Matter, and Rites of Spring (featuring Guy Picciciotto and Brendan Canty, who both later joined Fugazi) as well as Embrace. Revolution Summer was a call to liberate music from the constraints of the straight edge and hardcore movements, and even if the political goals of the various groups were not met the Revolution Summer did create a large catalog of music, including the only Embrace album released in 1986. Embrace ended in March 1986 after internal dissention and musical differences. After the demise of Embrace, Ian worked at Dischord and released the *Egg Hunt* single, his last collaboration with Jeff Nelson, before forming Fugazi in 1987. As a guitarist and vocalist in Fugazi, MacKaye was one of the most visible voices of the punk and **DIY** underground, and Fugazi was legendary for its marathon shows and strong and consistent beliefs about capitalism, merchandising, and door prices. As leader of Fugazi, Ian became even more political and released numerous records that challenged both mainstream society and the insularity of the punk community. Because Fugazi sold no merchandise and kept show prices low, MacKaye never became the punk millionaire some of his detractors called him, but he did lead a cultural revolution and remained consistent with his original beliefs. MacKaye now plays with the Evens because Fugazi seems to be on hiatus. Ultimately, Ian MacKaye is one of the most consistent (Fugazi refused to be interviewed by large corporate magazines that allowed ads for alcohol or cigarettes, keeping with Ian's beliefs) and well-respected members of the punk community and has been a mentor to numerous bands across the United States. Although some might find his communal, almost monklike, existence hard to emulate, Ian MacKaye remains one of the most important figures in punk history. *See also* Fugazi.

MADAME WONG'S

Los Angeles Chinese restaurant turned **punk** club where many of the bands from the early Los Angeles punk scene played. The club was known for its early embrace of punk, but later it switched to a more pop sound and started to book bands like the Knack.

MAINMAN

MainMan was the name of the management company set up by Tony Defries that handled both **David Bowie** in the United States as well as the **Iggy and the Stooges.** Photographer and manager **Leee Black Childers** was a vice president and was responsible for minding the **heroin**-addicted **Iggy Pop** as well as putting as much of the record label's money to good use. MainMan artists such as Iggy Pop were notorious for their antisocial behavior, and, while supported by MainMan, Iggy Pop would have died several times if not for the intervention (and sometimes swimming skills) of Childers.

MAOISM

Some punks were not only members of far-left groups or subscribed to various movements, some were also forthright in their condemnation of capitalism and their subscription to various political movements. Bands such as the **Dils** from **Los Angeles** and **Nation of Ulysses** from **Washington, D.C.,** were either avowed Maoists, aching to destroy all things American, or just critics of the

United States with tongue firmly planted in cheek. **Protopunk** band the **MC5** was also notorious for having stacks of Mao's Little Red Book in their communal living space (placed there no doubt by band Svengali John Sinclair, who honestly believed that the revolution was right around the corner). The actual meaning of many so-called political songs might depend on the listeners' critical stance or just what day of the week they happened to query the band members on the meaning of their manifestos or their ideology. Other bands such as the original Red Rockers and **Gang of Four** had similar positions that were probably better thought out and more nuanced than, for example, the **New York Dolls** in their infamous **Malcolm McLaren**–inspired red patent leather Communist final tour. Despite the labels of Communism, Maoism, or socialism, most punk bands work within the frame of capitalism and consumer culture, and even many small, independent record labels are either partially owned by major labels (**Epitaph** and Sub Pop), rely on them for distribution, or simply work on a profit-based economic system. Although many punks are and have been against capitalism, few have been able to survive without using or at least participating in the capitalist system to some extent, if only to distribute records to punks in towns that do not have access to the underground zine movement. The few bands and labels that reject the basic capitalist approach, such as **Fugazi** and **Crass,** are discussed elsewhere. *See also* Crass; Fugazi.

MASQUE

Illegal club and performance space run by **Los Angeles** scenester **Brendan Mullen,** considered by many to be the birthplace of Los Angeles **punk.** The club was located in a 10,000-foot basement in the Hollywood Center building on North Cherokee Avenue. Mullen was aided in opening the Masque by Fluxus artist Al Hansen, the grandfather of singer Beck Hansen. The Masque was originally a rehearsal space where a variety of bands practiced, before Mullen realized that he could also use the space as a performance venue in a town where many punks could not get a show at one of the major clubs on the Sunset Strip. The Masque, like **CBGB's** was run-down, filled with empty bottles and passed-out patrons, but was beloved by many in the Los Angeles scene for the bands that played there. The Masque was forced to close due to police harassment and the introduction of **hardcore,** which made the scene more violent and made many of the original punks drop out.

MAXIMUM ROCK 'N' ROLL

Long-running **zine** that evolved from an influential radio program, as equally authoritative as it is controversial. For its supporters, the zine is an arbiter of those who have not sold out and who remain true to the vision of **punk** as epitomized by early proponents of the scene. To its detractors, *Maximum Rock 'n' Roll* can appear as elitist and snobbish, obsessed with decreeing who is and is not punk due to a self-imposed criteria. Despite its detractors, the importance of *Maximum Rock 'n' Roll* on the punk scene for the last three decades cannot be underestimated. A positive review of a band can sell as much merchandise as a negative review can prevent. *Maximum Rock 'n' Roll* also served as an informal, pre-Internet way for punks around the world to network and trade **vinyl** singles and other paraphernalia. It also was an invaluable source of information on scenes outside the big cities (such as the well-documented and media-friendly cities of **Washington, D.C., Los Angeles,** and **New York**) as well as scenes in Europe and Asia. *Maximum Rock 'n' Roll* is still going strong despite the early death of its founder, **Tim Yohanon,** in the 1990s.

MAX'S KANSAS CITY

New York City club located at 213 Park Avenue South, where many of the influential predecessors to punk and many of the early punk bands played before the scene coalesced around **CBGB's.** Max's Kansas City was opened by entrepreneur and art connoisseur Mickey Ruskin and named Max's Kansas City on the recommendation of writer Joel Oppenheimer, who reasoned that the name evoked cuts of steak from Kansas. The restaurant and club started in the 1960s and went through several incarnations before finally closing in 1981. Max's was as exclusive as it was visionary; there was a strict door policy with a velvet rope (years before Studio 54 thought of the same trick), and artists such as Robert Rauschenberg, John Chamberlain, and, most especially, Andy Warhol called the club home. Warhol was an especially ardent customer during the late 1960s, holding court in the (in)famous back room at Max's with his entourage of superstars (such as Sugar Plum Fairy, Jackie Curtis, and Candy Darling, later immortalized in the **Lou Reed** song "Walk on the Wild Side"), drag queens, and junkies. Members of the **Velvet Underground, Iggy Pop,** and Alice Cooper were also early patrons who relied heavily in the notoriously uncollectible tabs given out by the ever-generous Ruskin to artists and performers he judged worthy of his indulgence. Other notables included **Leee Black Childers,** the famous punk rock photographer, manager, and former **MainMan** employee; **Patti Smith,** the punk poet; singer Cherry Vanilla; David Johansen; members of the **New York Dolls;** and noted punk transsexual **Wayne/Jayne County,** who was a DJ upstairs at Max's for several years.

During Ruskin's tenure, and especially after his departure, Max's became known as a mecca for live music, often booking bands that no one else would take a chance on. The Velvet Underground had a lengthy residence at Max's that led to a famous live album and ended with the band imploding onstage and the final departure of Lou Reed. During the early 1970s, the nascent glitter scene was represented by Iggy Pop, Alice Cooper (who performed in a dress with cones to simulate breasts), and others (all of whom despised the glitter label). The New York Dolls played Max's several times a week in their early incarnation. Ruskin closed Max's in 1974, and in 1975 it was reopened by Tommy Dean, who made it a prime breeding ground for punk bands during the mid- to late 1970s. There was an informal rivalry between the upscale and "uptown" Max's Kansas City and CBGB's, although many bands such as the **Heartbreakers** (who released a live album recorded at Max's Kansas City), **Television, Ramones,** and the Sic Fucks played both clubs. The rivalry was epitomized by a famous punk incident that, although it took place at CBGB's, was indicative of the divisions in the scene at that time. Handsome Dick Manitoba of the **Dictators** was well known for the good-natured abuse he heaped upon bands during sets, and Wayne County was a particular target of abuse one night at CBGB's. Wayne County responded in typical punk fashion by hitting Manitoba over the head with a microphone stand. After Manitoba pressed assault charges, a benefit was held at Max's that further polarized the punk scene and caused divisions based on who played the benefit and who did not (although charges were later dropped and 30 years later Handsome Dick and Wayne County appeared together on the same stage). **Sid Vicious** of the **Sex Pistols** also was a regular during the late 1970s and played at Max's with various pickup bands to varying degrees of success. Later, members of the **no wave** scene, including **Lydia Lunch** and James Chance, played the club in its last incarnations. In 1976, the album *Max's Kansas City 1976* was released, featuring Cherry Vanilla and her Staten Island Band, **Suicide, Pere Ubu,** the Fast, and Wayne County and the Back Street Boys. The club closed for good in 1981, and a deli currently occupies the space. In the 1990s, there was a brief revival of the club.

Discography of Music Relating to Max's: *The Velvet Underground Live at Max's Kansas City* (Cotillion, 1972); *Max's Kansas City 1976* (Roir, 1976); *Live at Max's Kansas City* (Max's Kansas City, 1979).

MC5

Protopunk band from the late 1960s, best known for its anthem "Kick Out the Jams" and its mixture of jazz riffs and brutal feedback-laden guitar sound. The band, led by manager, provocateur, and radical political activist John Sinclair, espoused a radical vision that many in the record industry did not find palatable, and the band's initial promise was doomed by poor sales, internal strife, and the conflict between Sinclair and almost anyone in a position of authority. Sinclair was a professional agitator and revolutionary who, although not a fan of the band's music, saw in MC5 the potential to use music to arouse the masses to revolution. The band quickly became known for the members' revolutionary politics (although apparently only Rob Tyner was actually politically involved). The MC5 was signed to the Elektra label by **Danny Fields,** the artist representative (A&R) and "house hippie" of Elektra. The band's first album was recorded live and released amid controversy due to the line "Kick out the Jams, Motherfuckers!" that started the song "Kick Out the Jams." The band was then banned not only in Boston but also by the Fillmore East and West, and finding gigs became a difficult task. This situation was not helped by a large Detroit store's, Hudson's, refusal to stock the record, leading the always-cautious MC5 to take out an ad in an underground paper saying "Fuck Hudson's" with the Elektra logo. After Elektra dropped the band, MC5 was singed to Atlantic and dropped Sinclair, who was subsequently sentenced to 10 years in jail for a pot arrest. The band released two more albums, *Back in the USA* and *High Time*, each one increasingly less political. The band was dropped by Atlantic, and the members scattered. Vocalist Rob Tyner died in 1991. Guitarist Fred Smith later married punk poet **Patti Smith,** and the two retired into relative obscurity to raise a family before Fred Smith's untimely death in 1995. Guitarist Wayne Kramer did a stint in prison and later played in the band Gang War with **Johnny Thunders** and now tours on his own and with the rhythm section of the MC5, with special guests taking over for the late Rob Tyner and Fred Smith. Despite the group's obscurity during their time period and despite the band's often lengthy jazzlike jamming, the band is still regarded as very influential on the early punk as well as the heavy metal scene. Some of their attitude wore off on political bands such as Rage against the Machine, and some of their lengthy jazzlike experimentations influenced bands in the sludge rock scene. The remaining members of the band tour with a changing roster of lead singers, billing themselves as DKT (the initials of the three surviving members) MC5, along with guest singers such as Mark Arm from Mudhoney. The band showcases music from the MC5's influential catalog.

Discography: *Kick Out the Jams* (Elektra, 1969, 1983); *Back in the USA* (Atlantic, 1970; Rhino, 1992); *High Time* (Atlantic, 1971; Rhino, 1992); *Babes in Arms* (Roir, 1983, 1997; Fr. Danceteria, 1990); *Do It* (Fr. Revenge, 1987); *Live Detroit 68/69* (Fr. Revenge, 1988); *Kick Out the Jams* (live; Elektra, 1991); *Power Trip* (Alive, 1994); *Black to Comm* (Receiver, 1994); *Looking at You* (Receiver, 1994); *American Ruse* (Total Energy, 1995); *Live 1969/70* (New Rose, 1995); *Teenage Lust* (live; Total Energy, 1996); *Phun City, U.K.* (Sonic, 1996); *Starship: Live at Sturgis Armory June 1968* (live; Total Energy, 1998); *Ice Pick Slim* EP (live; Alive, 1997); *Thunder Express* (Cleopatra, 1999); *'66 Breakout* (Total Energy, 1999); *Greatest Hits Live* (Cleopatra, 1999); *The Big Bang: The Best of the MC5* (Rhino, 2000); *Motor City Is Burning* (live; Trojan Us, 2001); *Human Being Lawnmower: The Baddest and Maddest of MC5* (Total Energy, 2002); *Extended Versions* (BMG Special Prod., 2003); *Take 2: High Time/Back in the USA* (Wea International, 2004); *Purity Accuracy* (box set; Easy Action, 2004); *Are You Ready to Testify: Live Bootleg Anthology* (Castle Us/ Ryko, 2005).

MCLAREN, MALCOLM

Situationist, entrepreneur of the influential London shop **Sex,** and manager and alleged Svengali behind the **Sex Pistols,** early incarnations of Adam and the Ants, Bow Wow Wow, and the last incarnation of the **New York Dolls.** Malcolm McLaren was also responsible for the movie *The Great Rock 'n' Roll Swindle,* which featured the Sex Pistols. He released several albums during the 1980s, some of which included hit singles such as the song "Double Dutch," which became a top-10 hit on the British charts in 1983, as well as the albums *Duck*

Malcolm McLaren was the Svengali behind the Sex Pistols and a master of the art of confusion. *Photofest.*

Rock and *Buffalo Girls*, which also became a hit and was one of the few records using rap to make the charts at that time. McLaren was an extremely controversial figure in the **punk** scene and was probably best known for his involvement with the Sex Pistols. He was also largely responsible, with his partner and ex-wife **Vivienne Westwood**, for introducing **punk fashion** to Britain at their notorious shop, where they sold bondage clothing and ripped T-shirts that were inspired by the look of **New York** punks such as **Richard Hell.** McLaren is a controversial figure not only for the way in which he tried to manipulate punks such as the New York Dolls and Richard Hell to adapt to his ideas about rebellion and fashion but also for (at times) claming sole credit for the look, attitude, and music of the Sex Pistols. His claims, along with his management company's, Glitterbeast's, financial turmoil, eventually cost McLaren millions as a result of the lawsuits that followed the demise of the Sex Pistols. McLaren was well known for his eye for talent, and at one point he was able to develop careers for Adam and the Ants and Bow Wow Wow, before they decided he was too controlling and escaped his clutches. McLaren also made numerous successful experimentations with other forms of music, such as hip-hop and opera, that were ahead of their times stylistically. The 1983 album *Duck Rock* was an early synthesis of rap and other styles with the Supreme Team. His next album, *Fans*, in 1984 was a combination of hip-hop with opera. Subsequent albums saw McLaren experimenting with African music, opera, funk (with Bootsy Collins), and various other music styles. McLaren returned to the Svengali business in 1998 with the band

JUNGK, an all-Asian girl band designed to emulate the Spice Girls. At this point, however, he seemed to lose interest in his project, and an attempt to run for mayor of London in 2000 also went nowhere. McLaren could also be credited for almost single-handedly bringing punk fashion to the United Kingdom and along with **Jamie Reid** was quite successful in marketing an image for the Sex Pistols.

Discography: *Duck Rock* (Charisma, 1983); *D'Ya Like Scratchin'* EP (Island, 1984); *Fans* (Island, 1984); *Swamp Thing* (Island, 1985); *Paris* (No!/Vogue/Gee Street/Island, 1995); *Buffalo Gals Back to Skool* (Priority, 1998). **Malcolm McLaren and the Bootzilla Orchestra:** *Waltz Darling* (Epic, 1989). **Malcolm McLaren Presents the World Famous Supreme Team Show:** *Round the Outside! Round the Outside!* (Virgin, 1990).

MCNEIL, LEGS

Gonzo-style journalist, author, and "resident punk" at **Punk** magazine in the mid-1970s. He wrote the authoritative book on the U.S. punk movement, *Please Kill Me,* and an oral history of the pornography industry, *The Other Hollywood: The Uncensored Oral History of the Porn Film Industry.* Legs McNeil helped both name the punk movement and create the punk aesthetic by championing bands such as the **Dictators, Ramones,** and **Lou Reed.** McNeil was younger than his friends **John Holmstrom** and Ged Dunn, who founded *Punk* magazine, and after the two of them had settled on becoming editor and publisher, respectively, it was left to Legs to become the "house punk" of *Punk* magazine. McNeil used this youthful exuberance (and a love of mind-altering substances) to write surrealistic interviews with real rock and rollers and with cartoon characters such as Boris and Natasha (from the *Rocky and Bullwinkle* television show) and Sluggo (from the comic strip *Nancy*). After *Punk* folded, McNeil worked as a journalist and editor for magazines such as *Spin* (he once famously went down the Mississippi River with old friend **Richard Hell**) and eventually turned to book writing, releasing in 1996 the definitive book about the punk revolution, *Please Kill Me,* with cowriter Gillian McCain.

MDC

The radical **punk** band whose moniker stands for either "Millions of Dead Cops" or "Multi-Death Corporation." MDC was unrelenting in its full-on attack on capitalism, homophobia, police brutality, racism, and the other perceived ills of the U.S. system. The band formed in 1978 in Austin, Texas, as the Stains and released the "John Wayne Was a Nazi: 7" before changing its name to Millions of Dead Cops. The original band featured Dave Dictor on vocals, Matt Van Curra on bass, drummer Al Batross, and guitarist Eric Mucho (numerous musicians came and went, and Matt Freeman from **Rancid** played bass in one version of the band). Millions of Dead Cops was among the most militant of the **hardcore** bands of the 1980s, and their music was as uncompromising and fierce as their name. The band lost momentum as the 1980s wore on and only performed and recorded sporadically, eventually going on several lengthy hiatuses before reforming and touring again. MDC continued to record and tour and played at the benefit concerts to save **CBGB's** in August 2005.

Discography: *Millions of Dead Cops* (R Radical, 1982; MDC, 1995); *Multi-Death Corporation* (R Radical, 1983); *Chicken Squawk 7"* (Boner Records, 1984); *Smoke Signals* (R Radical, 1986); *This Blood's for You* (R Radical/Boner, 1987; MDC, 1995); *More Dead Cops 1981–1987* (R Radical/Boner, 1988); *Elvis: In the Rheinland* (live; Destiny, 1989); *It's the Real Thing* (Boner, 1989, 1995); *Metal Devil Cokes* (We Bite, 1992; Goldr, 1994); *Elvis—In the Rheinland* (Ger. Destiny, 1989); *Hey Cop, If I Had A* (Radical, 1991; MDC, 1995); *Shades of Brown* (New Red Archives, 1993); *Thanks for Giving Me What I Didn't Want* (New Red Archives, 1993); *Now More Than Ever* (Beer City, 2002); *Now More Than Ever* (Cleopatra, 2002); *Magnus Dominus Corpus* (Sudden Death, 2004).

MEATMEN

Often vulgar and shocking band known for its scatological lyrics and obsession with all things relating to bodily functions and perversion, led by singer Tesco Vee (Bob Vermuellen), who toured for years with various incarnations of the band. Vee originally had run a fanzine called *Touch & Go* and later founded the record label **Touch and Go.** The first album, *We're the Meatmen . . . and You Suck,* featured their anthem "Crippled Children Suck" and an ode to the late Beatle John Lennon, "One Down Three to Go." Vee followed up the first record with *War of the Superbikes,* which featured Brian Baker and Lyle Presslar from **Minor Threat** on guitars. Subsequent albums were less popular, and recordings grew more sporadic as the 1990s wore on. The Meatmen will be remembered as one of the most vulgar and entertaining bands of the 1980s and 1990s.
Discography: *Blood Sausage* EP (Touch and Go, 1982); *Crippled Children Suck* EP (Touch and Go, 1982); *We're the Meatmen . . . and You Suck!* (Touch and Go, 1983); *War of the Superbikes* (Homestead, 1985); *Rock 'n' Roll Juggernaut* (Caroline, 1986, 1994); *We're the Meatmen . . . and You Still Suck!* (live; Caroline, 1989); *Crippled Children Suck* (Touch and Go, 1990); *Stud Powercock: The Touch and Go Years* (Touch and Go, 1990, 1991); *War of the Superbikes* (Homestead, 1994); *Pope on a Rope* (Pravda, 1995); *War of the Superbikes, Vol. 2* (Go Kart, 1996); *Evil in a League with Satan* EP (Go Kart, 1997). **Tesco Vee and the Meat Crew:** *Dutch Hercules* EP (Touch and Go, 1984).

MEAT PUPPETS

Arizona power trio that melded **punk** and country to create a unique sound and favorites of **Nirvana** front man Kurt Cobain, who covered (along with the Kirkwood brothers) three of the Meat Puppets' songs on the *Nirvana Unplugged* album and video. The classic Meat Puppet lineup was the Kirkwood brothers, Curt and Cris, on guitar, bass, and vocals, along with Derrick Bostrom on drums. Although the Meat Puppets were part of the early **hardcore** scene and some of the band's early music was quite fast and aggressive, they were also known for incredibly slow and drug-fueled takes on various songs that marked them as outsiders to a scene that looked upon long hair and musical experimentation as anathema to the hardcore scene of the mid-1980s. This did not daunt the band, and they responded with some of the most challenging music of its career, releasing the legendary trilogy of *Meat Puppets, Meat Puppets II,* and *Up on the Sun.* The band was one of the staples of the **SST** label but eventually decided to move to the major labels thanks to SST's notorious lack of skill in promoting bands (or successfully accounting for their money) and had a 1994 radio and video hit with "Backwater." Bostrom and Cris Kirkwood left the band after the *No Joke!* record due to Cris's increasing addiction to **heroin.** Curt Kirkwood formed a new band called the Royal Neanderthal Orchestra in Austin, Texas, but later changed the name of the band to Meat Puppets for several new releases. Cris Kirkwood went several stints in rehab and was arrested in December 2003 for attacking a security guard at a post office; in August 2004 he was sentenced to 21 months in prison. A Web site about him is at www.freecriskirkwood.org.
Discography: *In a Car* EP (World Imitation, 1981; SST, 1985; Rykodisc, 1999); *Meat Puppets* (Thermidor/ SST, 1982; Rykodisc, 1999); *Meat Puppets II* (SST, 1983; Rykodisc, 1999); *Up on the Sun* (SST, 1985; Rykodisc, 1999); *Out My Way* EP (SST, 1986; Rykodisc, 1999); *Mirage* (SST, 1987; Rykodisc, 1999); *Huevos* (SST, 1987; Rykodisc, 1999); *Monsters* (SST, 1989; Rykodisc, 1999); *No Strings Attached* (SST, 1990); *Forbidden Places* (London, 1991); *Too High to Die* (London, 1994); *No Joke!* (London, 1995); *Live in Montana* (Rykodisc, 1999); *Golden Lies* (Atlantic, 2000); *Live* (DCN, 2002); *Classic Puppets* (Rykodisc, 2004).

MEKONS

One of **punk's** strangest and longest-lasting bands (albeit with numerous personnel changes, especially early on), the Mekons experimented in almost every musical genre from country and western to **dub** and probably also invented some along the way. The original band was started in late 1977 in Leeds, England, by art students. The Mekons released their seminal first single, "Never Been in a Riot," in January 1978, which parodied both the **Clash** single "White Riot" and punk's halfhearted (at best) commitment to revolutionary politics. The original lineup included Jon Langford on drums, Mary on bass, Kevin Lycette and Tom Greenhalgh on guitars, and Mark White and Andrew Corrigan on vocals. After numerous personnel changes, the band solidified with Langford and Greenhalgh on guitars and singing most of the songs, abetted by Sally Timms on vocals and, occasionally, violinist Susie Honeyman and an ever-evolving rhythm section. The Mekons released a staggering number of records in their 30-year career and mostly released records outside of the machinery of major labels. Their 1985 album *Fear and Whiskey* was often looked upon as one of the first alt-country records and certainly one of the first attempts to fuse punk's attitude with country music's swagger. Despite years of acclaim and consistent touring (and far too many solo and side projects to be mentioned here), the Mekons were rarely on a major label (an EP on A&M being the exception in 1990), but that did not slow their remarkable output or put a damper on their revolutionary politics. The Mekons at their best made the personal intensely political, as in "He Beat Up his Boyfriend"; the political intensely personal, as in "(Sometimes I Feel Like) Fletcher Christian"; or an attack on U.S. imperialism seem longing and romantic, as in "Ghosts of American Astronauts," as any keyboard-driven **New Wave** dance classic of the 1980s. Cofounder Jon Langford now lives in Chicago and between frequent Mekons tours and working on various art projects records under the names Waco Brothers, Pine Valley Cosmonauts, and his own name. In 2005, he was commissioned by the Walker Arts Center in Minneapolis and Alverno College to create a multimedia stage version of his Pine Valley Cosmonauts record *The Executioner's Last Songs* for a stage tour.

Discography: *The Quality of Mercy Is Not Strnen* (UK Virgin, 1979; Blue Plate, 1990); *Devils Rats and Piggies a Special Message from Godzilla* (UK Red Rhino, 1980); *It Falleth Like Gentle Rain from Heaven—The Mekons Story* (UK CNT Productions, 1982; Feel Good All Over, 1993); *The English Dancing Master* EP (UK CNT Productions, 1983); *Fear and Whiskey* (UK Sin, 1985); *Crime and Punishment* EP (UK Sin, 1985); *The Edge of the World* (UK Sin, 1986; Quarterstick, 1996); *Slightly South of the Border* EP (UK Sin, 1986); *Honky Tonkin'* (Sin/Twin\Tone, 1987); *New York* (tape, Roir, 1987; Roir/Important, 1990); *So Good It Hurts* (Twin\Tone, 1988); *Original Sin* (Sin/Twin\Tone, 1989); *The Dream and Lie of . . .* EP (UK Blast First, 1989); *The Mekons Rock 'n' Roll* (Twin\Tone/A&M, 1990); *F.U.N. '90* EP (Twin\Tone/A&M, 1990); *The Curse of the Mekons* (UK Blast First, 1991); *Wicked Midnite/All I Want* EP (Loud Music, 1992); *I Y Mekons* (Quarterstick, 1993); *Millionaire* EP (Quarterstick, 1993); *Retreat from Memphis* (Quarterstick, 1994); *Mekons United* (Touch and Go, 1996); *I Have Been to Heaven and Back: Hen's Teeth and Other Lost Fragments of Unpopular Culture, Vol. 1* (Quarterstick, 1999); *Where Were You? Hen's Teeth and Other Lost Fragments of Unpopular Culture, Vol. 2* (Quarterstick, 1999); *Journey to the End of the Night* (Quarterstick, 2000). **Mekons/Kathy Acker:** *Pussy, King of the Pirates* (Quarterstick, 1996).

MELODY MAKER

British music magazine that extensively covered the **punk** movement, not always in positive terms. The magazine was founded in 1926 and focused early on outsider music such as jazz, although in the 1950s it gradually shifted its focus to rock and roll. The focus on rock made *Melody Maker* more popular than ever, and at its peak the circulation was more than 250,000 copies per week. During the heyday of punk, *Melody Maker* featured writers such as May Harron from *Punk* magazine ,who astutely covered the punk revolution. Poor circulation and a reluctance to adapt to new musical movements led to *Melody Maker's* demise in 2000, when it was forced to merge with *NME*.

MELVINS, THE

Sludge rock band from Aberdeen, Washington, that heavily influenced **Nirvana.** The band was formed in 1986 and originally featured Buzz "King Buzzo" Osbourne on guitar and vocals, Dale Crover on drums, and Matt Lukin (who later joined Mudhoney) on bass (replaced by Lori Black, who was replaced by Mark Deutrom and, later, Kevin Rutmanis). The band pioneered the fusion of the sludgy heavy metal riffs of Black Sabbath with **punk**'s energy, although played at a glacial pace. The band was briefly signed to Atlantic Records, no doubt because of the band's relationship with Nirvana, but returned to independent labels a few years later. The band continued to tour and record and was enormously influential on grunge, **postpunk,** and modern experimental heavy metal. The daughter of former child star Shirley Temple was a member for a short period.

Discography: *Melvins* EP (C/Z, 1986); *Gluey Porch Treatments* (Alchemy, 1986; Ipecac, 2000); *Ozma* (Boner, 1989); *Eggnog* EP (Boner, 1991); *10 Songs* (C/Z, 1991); *Your Choice Live Series, Vol. 12* (Ger. Your Choice, 1991); *Bullhead* (Boner, 1991); *Melvins* (Boner/Tupelo, 1992); *Houdini* (Atlantic, 1993); *Stoner Witch* (Atlantic, 1994); *Live* (X-mas, 1996); *Stag* (Mammoth/Atlantic, 1996); *Honky* (Amphetamine Reptile, 1997); *Singles 1–12* (Amphetamine Reptile, 1997); *Alive at the Fucker Club* (Amphetamine Reptile, 1998); *The Maggot* (Ipecac, 1999); *The Bootlicker* (Ipecac, 1999); *The Crybaby* (Ipecac, 2000); *Melvins at Slim's on 8-Track 6.17.99* (8-track; Life Is Abuse, 2000); *The Trilogy on Vinyl* (Ipecac, 2000); *Hostile Ambient Takeover 7" Singles* (Ipecac, 2000); *Electroretard* (Man's Ruin, 2001); *Colossus of Destiny* (Ipecac, 2001); *Hostile Ambient Takeover (H.A.T.)* (Ipecac, 2002); *26 Songs* (Ipecac, 2003); *Melvinmania: The Best of the Atlantic Years 1993–1996* (Atlantic, 2003); *Pigs of the Roman Empire* (Ipecac, 2004); *Mangled Demos from 1983* (Ipecac, 2005). **Snivlem:** *Prick* (Amphetamine Reptile, 1994). **FantomasMelvins Big Band:** *FantomasMelvins Big Band* (Ipecac, 2002). **King Buzzo:** *King Buzzo* EP (Boner/Tupelo, 1992). **Dale Crover:** *Dale Crover* EP (Boner/Tupelo, 1992). **Joe Preston:** *Joe Preston* EP (Boner/Tupelo, 1992).

METAL URBAIN

French **punk** band, and one of the first to play in the United Kingdom, best known for its anarchic combination of brash guitar and electric drums. Metal Urbain first released a single in October 1977, and its original members included Claude Panik on vocals, Eric Debris on synthesizer, and Nancy Luger and Herman Schwartz on guitars. Although the band sang entirely in French, they were still successful in the early British punk scene, and their use of a synthesizer instead of a drummer made them stand out even more. The band reunited several times for tours around the world. Metal Urbain is another example of how quickly the punk impulse spread around the world.

MINOR THREAT

Perhaps of the most legendary **hardcore** band, known for its ferocious music and for starting the **straight edge** movement and **Dischord Records.** There is almost no way to sum up the influence of Minor Threat on a political, social, and philosophical level on the lives of countless punks. Minor Threat was started by singer **Ian MacKaye** and drummer Jeff Nelson after the demise of their previous band, the **Teen Idles** (in which Ian had played bass while Nathan Strejeck sang), when Ian wanted to sing more and develop his new ideas about living straight and rejecting the false promises of drugs and alcohol. (Minor Threat was almost called Straight.) Minor Threat was started in November 1980, and the original lineup featured Lyle Presslar on guitar, Brian Baker on bass, Jeff Nelson on drums, and Ian MacKaye on lead vocals. The band became a quick success in the **Washington, D.C.,** scene with its electric shows that featured Ian flailing around the stage. The band's initial EPs, *Minor Threat* and *In My Eyes,* established Dischord as a source of imaginative and aggressive new music. The band broke up in 1981, however, when guitarist Presslar went to Northwestern University and Baker joined **Government Issue** on guitar. Presslar soon found college not to his liking, and Minor Threat reunited in March 1982 to even greater acclaim and national touring. Some fans cried sellout, leading Minor threat to pen the hilarious song "Cashing In," in which they joked that people who thought they were reuniting only for the money were correct. Minor Threat then added bassist Steve Hansgen as Baker moved to second guitar for the *Out of Step* EP. Hansgen did not gel well with the band and was asked to leave, but the damage had been done, and Minor Threat was almost through. With Baker and Presslar trying to write more commercial songs, MacKaye decided to leave the band after recording the *Salad Days* EP. The importance of Minor Threat can be underestimated, and their influence still resonates inside and outside punk scenes. Minor Threat not only recorded its own music, distributed its own records, and booked its own shows, it also was one of the few bands at that time to tour outside its local fan base, conducting two major tours and playing cities such as **New York** numerous times. The band helped spread the emerging straight edge scene to cities unfamiliar with straight edge and presented hardcore punk in a variety of towns where few bands had bothered to tour. The band material was collected on one CD available from Dischord. Ian MacKaye went on to play in the short-lived Embrace and **Egg Hunt** projects before founding **Fugazi.** Nelson continued to work with MacKaye on Dischord and worked on graphic design, most notably the "Meese Is a Pig" signs that seemingly sprouted out of thin air during **Revolution Summer.** After briefly working with Glenn Danzig, Presslar and Baker joined the **Meatmen,** and Presslar subsequently retired from playing. Baker founded **Dag Nasty,** briefly played in the heavy metal band Junkyard, and toured and performed with both Dag Nasty and **Bad Religion.** *See also* Bad Brains; Bad Religion; Dag Nasty; Dischord Records; MacKaye, Ian; Washington, D.C.

Discography: *Minor Threat* EP (Dischord, 1981); *In My Eyes* EP (Dischord, 1981); *Out of Step* (Dischord, 1983); *Minor Threat* (Dischord, 1984); *Complete* (Dischord, 1988). **Embrace:** *Embrace* (Dischord, 1987). **Teen Idles:** *Minor Disturbance* EP (Dischord, 1981).

MINUTEMEN

One of the ultimate **DIY** bands and light-years ahead of their time, the Minutemen left behind a musical and cultural legacy that was matched by few 1980s **punk** bands. Although the Minutemen started off as a punk band, they quickly went beyond punk rock in jazz- and funk-influenced jams that exposed the limitations inherent in many other bands' approaches to punk music. Musically, the Minutemen were extremely prolific during their brief recording period but will probably be best known for their double record *Double Nickels on the Dime,* an answer of sorts to **Hüsker Dü's** double album *Zen Arcade,* which also stretched the limits of punk's musical landscape. The band was often cited as a major influence on the nascent punk touring scene in the United States in the early 1980s. The band consisted of the larger-than-life D. Boon, who played guitar and sang, Mike Watt on bass and vocals, and Joe Hurley on drums. The band originally formed in 1980 as a four-piece called the Reactionaries but soon evolved into its key configuration, with D. Boon's songs and Watt's precision bass keeping things focused. Despite the musical experimentations, the Minutemen borrowed from the best of British **postpunk** in ideological commitment and focus as well as in musical experimentation. The Minutemen evolved even further by the time of the release of *What Makes a Man Start Fires?* and began to explore more of a loose, jazzy feel, perfected by Hurley's drumming, which could be a thundering gallop or a slow, swing-time waltz. With *Double Nickels on the Dime,* one of the best-selling records at the time on **SST,** the Minutemen also showed that the three-piece lineup was not inherently limiting musically. The members experimented with bizarre juxtapositions of politics and popular culture in songs such as "Political Song for Michael Jackson to Sing." *Project: Mersh*, their joking salute to selling out, added more instrumentation but did little to bring the band in an actual commercial direction, nor did the almost unlistenable daylong jam with **Black Flag's** instrumental players that was released as the *Minuteflag* EP. Tragically, at the same time as the release of the last album, *3-Way Tie (for Last)*, D. Boon was killed in a van accident. The band included a ballot on the last record, and the results of the fan voting led to the excellent posthumous *Ballot Result*.

After Boon's tragic death, Watt and Hurley formed the adventurous Firehose with guitarist and singer Ed from Ohio (later of Whiskeytown, which was led by Ryan Adams, who had a prolific solo career) and released several records in the late 1980s and early 1990s. After Firehose ran its course, Watt sporadically released solo records with various friends, such as Eddie Veder of Pearl Jam. Watt later played bass and recorded with the reconstituted **Iggy and the Stooges.** The Minutemen were one of the most important punk bands of the 1980s for their dedication to their ideals of political discussion and DIY and econo-style touring that influenced countless punk bands.

Discography: *Paranoid Time* EP (SST, 1980, 1990); *The Punch Line* (SST, 1981, 1992); *Bean-Spill* EP (Thermidor, 1982); *What Makes a Man Start Fires?* (SST, 1983, 1991); *Buzz or Howl under the Influence of Heat* (SST, 1983, 1991); *Double Nickels on the Dime* (SST, 1984, 1990); *The Politics of Time* (New Alliance, 1984, 1990); *Tour-Spiel* EP (Reflex, 1985); *. . . Just a Minute Men* (Virgin Vinyl, 1985); *My First Bells 1980–1983* (tape; SST, 1985); *Project: Mersh* EP (SST, 1985, 1993); *3-Way Tie (for Last)* (SST, 1985, 1990); *Ballot Result* (live; SST, 1987, 1990); *Post Mersh, Vol. 1* (SST, 1987, 1990); *Post Mersh, Vol. 2* (SST, 1987, 1990); *Post Mersh, Vol. 3* (SST, 1989, 1991); *Introducing the Minutemen* (SST, 1998). **Minuteflag**: *Minuteflag* EP (SST, 1986).

MISFITS

Horror **punk** band formed in the late 1970s from Lodi, New Jersey, that featured vocalist Glenn Danzig, who later went on to front Samhain and Danzig. The Misfits were well known for lyrics dealing with the supernatural, science fiction films, and other macabre subjects. The Misfits were formed in the mid-1970s by Danzig, who at that time played keyboards though a fuzzbox along with various sidemen. The band began to take shape in 1977 with the addition of bassist Jerry "Only" Caiafa, Frank Licata (Franche Coma) on guitar, and James "Mr. Jim" Catania on drums. The band recorded the *Static Age* album (which would not be released until 1995) and numerous singles on their own Plan 9 label (named after the Ed Wood cult film). After gigging around, the band changed lineups again, adding guitarist Bobby Steele and drummer Joey Image. In late 1979, after successfully opening for the **Damned** at Hurrahs in New York, the Misfits showed up almost literally on the Damned's doorsteps in late 1979 and asked to be added to the Damned's tour. Charmed by the Misfits' chutzpah, the Damned took the young U.S. band on tour with them, but after squabbles over pay, the Misfits left the tour and drummer Image quit the band. After a fight, Steele and Danzig also spent a night in jail in London, which led the Misfits to write the song "London Dungeon." Returning to the United States, Steele was bounced from the band and replaced by Caiafa's younger brother Paul "Doyle" Caiafa on guitar, and Arthur Googy was added on drums. By this time, the band members had already spent quite a bit of time and money developing a unique look, dressing in black leather, chains, and spikes, and gelling their hair down past their eyes in a sort of reverse Mohawk referred to as a Devillock. The band released its clearest and most concise mixture of pop and punk gloom in 1982, the *Walk among Us* album. After Googy departed, the band hired former **Black Flag** drummer Robo (the band members were good friends with Black Flag and **Henry Rollins,** and on the live version of "We Are 138" Rollins appears with a prominent Misfits tattoo on his arm) and recorded the speeded up and dark *Earth a.d.* album. After fighting with Danzig, Robo left the band and was replaced by Tod Swalla of the **Necros** on drums for a few final shows, after which the Misfits disbanded. Glenn Danzig formed the more gothic Samhain for several records before dissolving Samhain and forming the band called Danzig in the late 1980s and turning in a more metallic and commercial direction. The band Danzig scored a minor radio and **MTV** hit with the song "Mother." Danzig primarily played metal and resisted efforts at a true Misfits reunion. He was also infamous for an Internet video clip from July 2004 in which he was knocked out by a musician with whom he had been feuding backstage at a concert. Doyle and Jerry formed the hair metal band Kryst the Conqueror in 1987, and in 1995 the two re-formed the Misfits with new singer Michael Graves and drummer Dr. Chud for several tours and new records. When that lineup dissolved, Only Caiafa recruited former **Ramones** drummer Marky Ramone and former Black Flag and DC3 guitarist and singer Dez Cadena to form a reconstituted Misfits. Bobby Steele formed the Misfits-influenced Undead. Shortly after, Robo rejoined the Misfits in time to play a benefit show to save **CBGB's** in August 2005.

Discography: *Bullet* EP (Plan 9, 1978); *Beware* EP (UK Cherry Red, 1979); *Evilive* EP (Plan 9, 1982); *Walk among Us* (Ruby, 1982, 1988); *Earth a.d./Wolfsblood* (Plan 9, 1983); *Earth a.d./Die Die My Darling* (tape; Plan 9, 1984); *Legacy of Brutality* (Plan 9/Caroline, 1985); *Misfits* (Plan 9/Caroline, 1986); *Misfits* (Plan 9, 1986); *Evilive* (Plan 9/Caroline, 1987); *Static Age* (Caroline, 1995); *Collection II* (Caroline, 1995); *Box Set* (Caroline, 1996); *American Psycho* (Geffen, 1997); *Famous Monsters* (Roadrunner, 1999); *Cuts from the Crypt* (Roadrunner, 2001); *12 Hits from Hell* (Caroline, 2001). **Undead:** *Nine Toes Later* EP (Stiff, 1982); *Never Say Die!* (Ger. Rebel, 1986); *Act Your Rage* (Post Mortem, 1989); *Live Slayer* (Skyclad, 1991); *Dawn of the Undead* (Shagpile/Post Mortem, 1991; Shock/Post Mortem, 1997); *Evening of Desire* EP (Overground, 1992); *Til Death!* (Underworld/Post Mortem, 1998). **Samhain:** *Intium* (Plan 9, 1984; Plan 9/Caroline, 1986); *Unholy Passion* EP (Plan 9, 1985; Plan 9/Caroline, 1986); *November-Coming-Fire* (Plan 9/Caroline, 1986); *Final Descent* (Plan 9/Caroline, 1990); *Box Set* (E-Magine, 2000); *Samhain Live, 85–86* (E-Magine, 2002). **Kryst the Conqueror:** *Deliver Us from Evil* EP (Cyclopean, 1989).

MISSION OF BURMA

Short-lived but influential band from **Boston** best known for the songs "That's When I Reach for my Revolver" (later covered by Moby) and "Academy Fight Song." Mission of Burma was founded in 1978 by guitarist and singer Roger Miller after the breakup of his band Moving Parts, with bassist Chris Conley, and drummer Pete Prescott. After a few gigs as a three-piece, the band decided to expand its sound by adding Martin Swope, who "played" a tape machine that added tape loops and effects to the band's live sound. After playing around Boston for several years, Mission of Burma released an EP and their first complete album, *Vs.*, in 1982. The band was forced to call it quits relatively early due to the chronic tinnitus of guitarist Roger Miller (later to join the Alloy Orchestra and provide live soundtracks to silent films). The band re-formed without Swope and with new member Bob Weston (of Shellac) in 2002 and toured and released the album *OnOffOn* on Matador Records to critical acclaim in 2004. Prescott also played in the Volcano Suns and Kustomized.

Discography: *Signals, Calls and Marches* EP (Ace of Hearts, 1981); *Vs.* (Ace of Hearts, 1982); *The Horrible Truth About Burma* (Ace of Hearts, 1985); *Peking Spring* (Taang!, 1987); *Forget* (Taang!, 1987); *Mission of Burma* (Rykodisc, 1988); *OnOffOn* (Matador, 2004).

MODERN LOVERS

Punk and folk band led by Jonathan Richman. The Modern Lovers' only official release was recorded in 1972 as a collection of demos and not released until 1976. The album was extremely influential on many bands (the **Sex Pistols,** among others, covered the song "Roadrunner"), and Richman went on to a long and prolific solo career, including a memorable role in the film *There's Something about Mary.* Keyboard player Jerry Harrison joined **Talking Heads.**

Most Mohawks are not as ostentatious as this example, which is two feet tall! © *Derek Ridgers.*

Discography: Jonathan Richman and the Modern Lovers: *Jonathan Richman & the Modern Lovers* (Beserkley, 1977; Beserkley/Rhino, 1986); *Rock 'n' Roll with the Modern Lovers* (Beserkley, 1977; Beserkley/Rhino, 1986); *Back in Your Life* (Beserkley, 1979; Beserkley/Rhino, 1986); *The Jonathan Richman Songbook* (UK Beserkley, 1980); *Jonathan Sings!* (Sire, 1983; Sire/Blue Horizon/Warner Bros., 1993); *Rockin' and Romance* (Twin/Tone, 1985); *It's Time for Jonathan Richman and the Modern Lovers* (Upside, 1986); *Modern Lovers 88* (Rounder, 1987); *The Beserkley Years: The Best of Jonathan Richman and the Modern Lovers* (Beserkley/Rhino, 1987); *Jonathan Richman* (Rounder, 1989); *Jonathan Goes Country* (Rounder, 1990); *23 Great Recordings by Jonathan Richman and the Modern Lovers* (UK Beserkley/Essential/Castle Communications, 1990); *Having a Party with Jonathan Richman* (Rounder, 1991); *I, Jonathan* (Rounder, 1992); *¡Jonathan, Te Vas a Emocionar!* (Rounder, 1994); *You Must Ask the Heart* (Rounder, 1995); *A Plea for Tenderness* (UK Nectar Masters, 1995); *Surrender to Jonathan!* (Vapor, 1996); *I'm So Confused* (Vapor, 1998); *Her Mystery Not of High Heels and Eye Shadow* (Vapor, 2001). **Modern Lovers:** *The Modern Lovers* (Beserkley, 1976; Beserkley/Rhino, 1986); *Live* (Beserkley, 1977); *The Original Modern Lovers* (Bomp!, 1981); *Live at the Long Branch Saloon* (Fr. New Rose, 1992); *Precise Modern Lovers Order: Live in Berkeley and Boston* (Rounder, 1994); *Live at the Long Branch and More* (Fr. Last Call, 1998).

MOHAWK

Also known as the Mohican, this distinct hairstyle based on a Native American ritual haircut involved a variation on shaved sides, sometimes with the liberal use of gel and hairspray to elevate hair to spikes. In England, *Sounds* magazine reported the use of Mohawks in bands as early as April 1979, perhaps inspired by the movie *Taxi Driver*, in which Robert De Niro's character Travis Bickle wears his hair in a short Mohawk. Britain, however, often saw Mohawks that were six inches tall or taller that stood in a large symmetrical fin that covered the head. Famous examples of punks who wore Mohawks at least some of the time included Wattie Buchanan from the **Exploited;** Lars and Tim from **Rancid;** Ritchie Stotts, Jean Beauvoir, and Wendy O'Williams from the **Plasmatics; Joe Strummer** during the later days of the **Clash;** and numerous punks in pictures and on television. The covers of the *Punk and Disorderly* compilations also showed numerous punks with Mohawks. The Mohawk could certainly be regarded as one of **punk**'s most expressive forms of resistance to the fashion and cultural norms of society, and in the early days of punk, wearing a Mohawk (as well as sporting visible **tattoos**) made mainstream employment a difficult task. The actual styling of the Mohawk involved shaving the sides of the head and elaborately layering gel and hairspray to straighten the Mohawk. Its more elaborate version was the liberty spikes or crown, which involved a more specific configuration of spikes along the top of the head instead of the straight fin of most Mohawks). A reverse version was the Devillock, worn by the members of the **Misfits**, in which the hair was grown long and pulled into a lock on the forehead. During the 1980s, it was quite common to see groups of punks with Mohawks at punk shows, but things began to change when Mr. T. from the popular television show *The A Team* also wore a Mohawk and it began to be caricatured in mainstream media. Aside from certain British **hardcore** bands, the Mohawk largely fell out of favor in the late 1980s and early 1990s. With the punk revival of the 1990s and the emergence of fashion-heavy trends, however, the Mohawk became more permissible in mainstream culture. A less extreme version often called the faux hawk was worn by members of various economic classes, from record store clerks to world-famous soccer players. It is unclear if the adoption of this haircut by contemporary youth culture reflected the authentic resistant tendencies of punk rock or was merely a fashion statement. Several of the more popular bands that use punk style and play speeded-up pop music, such as Blink-182 and **Good Charlotte,** have had members that wore variations of the Mohawk at one point or another.

MONKS

Early 1960s **protopunk** band with distorted guitars and amateurish punk vocals. The group of U.S. servicemen stationed in Germany distinguished themselves by wearing monks' robes onstage and shaving the crowns of their heads in monks' tonsures. Their debut album, *Black Monk Time*, was released in the 1990s and led to a revival of interest in the band that sporadically re-formed for tours. A book chronicling the band's 1960s exploits titled *Black Monk Time: Coming of the Anti-Beatle* by Thomas Edward Shaw was published in 1995.
Discography: *Black Monk Time* (InfiniteZero/American, 1997); *Five Upstart Americans* (Omplatten, 1999).

MORDAM RECORDS

Mordam records is one of the largest independent distribution companies in the United States and acts as a distributor for **Alternative Tentacles, Lookout Records, Kill Rock Stars,** and others.

MORRIS, KEITH

Lead singer of an early version of **Black Flag** and the **Circle Jerks.** Well known for his excessive lifestyle, a cleaned-up Keith Morris sporadically re-forms the Circle Jerks for occasional tours and works as an artist representative (A&R) scout for a small record label.

MOTÖRHEAD

One of the more influential punk metal crossover bands, led by the legendary Lemmy Kilmister and a revolving cast of musicians. Lemmy started Motörhead after leaving legendary space rock band Hawkwind and anticipated many of the innovations started by **punk** and remains a perennial favorite of many punks. At one time, Motörhead was among the only metal bands considered acceptable to punks. Lemmy was also a **Ramones** fan who wrote the tribute song "R.A.M.O.N.E.S." on the *1916* album. The original lineup included Lemmy Kilmister on bass and lead vocals (original drummer Lucas Fox and guitarist Larry Wallis were not on the early releases but only appeared when *On Parole* was released a decade later), Phil "Philthy Animal" Taylor on drums (later replaced by Mikkey Dee, Pete Gill, and occasionally himself), and "Fast" Eddie Clark on guitar (later replaced by Brain Robertson, Wurzell, and Phil Campbell). Motörhead remains a key part of punk history, as epitomized in songs such as "Ace of Spades."

Discography: *Motörhead* (UK Chiswick, 1977; UK Big Beat, 1978; Roadracer Revisited, 1990); *Overkill* (UK Bronze, 1979; Profile, 1988); *Bomber* (UK Bronze, 1979; Profile, 1988); *On Parole* (UK Liberty, 1979; UK Fame, 1982; EMI America, 1987); *Motörhead EP* (UK Big Beat, 1980); *The Golden Years* EP (UK Bronze, 1980); *Ace of Spades* (Mercury, 1980; Profile, 1988); *No Sleep 'til Hammersmith* (Mercury, 1981; Profile, 1988); *Iron Fist* (Mercury, 1982; Roadracer Revisited, 1990); *Stand by Your Man* EP (UK Bronze, 1982); *What's Words Worth?* (UK Big Beat, 1983); *Another Perfect Day* (Mercury, 1983); *No Remorse* (Bronze, 1984; Roadracer Revisited, 1990); *Anthology* (UK Raw Power, 1985); *Born to Lose* (UK Dojo, 1985); *Orgasmatron* (GWR/Profile, 1986); *Rock 'n' Roll* (GWR/Profile, 1987); *EP* (UK Special Edition, 1988); *Another Perfect Day/Overkill* (UK Castle Comm., 1988); *No Sleep at All* (GWR/Enigma, 1988); *Blitzkrieg on Birmingham '77* (UK Receiver, 1989); *Dirty Love* (UK Receiver, 1989); *The Best of & the Rest of Motörhead Live* (UK Action Replay, 1990); *Welcome to the Bear Trap* (UK Castle Comm., 1990); *Bomber/Ace of Spades* (UK Castle Comm., 1990); *Lock Up Your Daughters* (UK Receiver, 1990); *The Birthday Party* (GWR/Enigma, 1990); *From the Vaults* (UK Sequel, 1990); *1916* (WTG, 1991); *Meltdown* (UK Castle Comm., 1991); *March or Die* (Sony, 1992); *Sacrifice* (CMC, 1995); *Overnight Sensation* (CMC, 1996); *Stone Dead Forever* (Receiver, 1997); *Snake Bite Love* (CMC, 1998); *Everything Louder than Everyone Else* (CMC, 1999); *We Are Motörhead* (CMC, 2000). **Motörhead and Girlschool:** *St. Valentine's Day Massacre* EP (UK Bronze, 1980).

MR. LADY RECORDS

Queercore independent label started by Kaia Wilson and girlfriend Tammy Rae Carlson that released records by Wilson's band **the Butchies.** Mr. Lady is another example of how even punks have to sometimes work outside of the punk mainstream to get their records released.

MR. T. EXPERIENCE

Despite the band's embarrassingly dated and ludicrous name (the band usually refers to itself as the less ridiculous MTX), Mr. T. Experience was one of the most lyrically confident and musically adventurous bands. The band started in October 1985, and was led by Dr. Frank (Portman, who had been a student of Greek and history at the University of California at Berkeley, which shows in his complex lyrics) from its inception. After going through numerous lineup changes and surviving the loss of coleader Jon Von, Dr. Frank is the only original member at this point. The band first released the fairly pedestrian *Everybody's Entitled to Their Own Opinion* in 1986. Dr. Frank released an eclectic solo record *Show Business Is My Life* in 1999.

Discography: *Everybody's Entitled to Their Own Opinion* (Disorder, 1986; Lookout!, 1990); *Night Shift at the Thrill Factory* (Rough Trade) 1988; (Lookout!, 1996); *Big Black Bugs Bleed Blue Blood* (Rough Trade, 1989; Lookout!, 1997); *Making Things with Light* (Lookout!, 1990); *Milk Milk Lemonade* (Lookout!, 1992); *Our Bodies, Ourselves* (Lookout!, 1993); *Taping Up My Heart* EP (Lookout!, 1995); *... And the Women Who Love Them* EP (Lookout!, 1994, 2002); *Alternative Is Here to Stay* EP (Lookout!, 1995); *Love Is Dead* (Lookout!, 1996); *Revenge Is Sweet and So Are You* (Lookout!, 1997); *Road to Ruin* (Skull

Duggery, 1998); *Show Business Is My Life* (Lookout!, 1999); *Alcatraz* (Lookout!, 1999); *Songs About Girls, Etc.* (Lookout!, 1999); *The Miracle of Shame* EP (Lookout!, 2000); *Yesterday Rules* (Lookout!, 2003).

MTV

Music Television Network started in 1980 and dedicated originally to playing the promotional videos of songs provided by record companies along with commentary by various VJs. MTV was once a relatively minor station, but now it is owned and operated by Viacom and is one of the crown jewels of the Viacom empire. Most punk bands have had an ambivalent attitude (at best) regarding MTV. Despite its cultural prevalence today and obsession with the equivalent of punk rock boy bands, early MTV was shunned by most punks. The **Dead Kennedys** even wrote a song called "MTV Get Off the Air" to critique the mindless images of consumer culture and anti-intellectualism that dominated the channel. Although some pop-punk bands, such as Sum 41 and Blink-182, have benefited from exposure on MTV, many bands, such as **NOFX,** refuse to have anything to do with the megaconglomerate. Now that MTV concentrates primarily on nonstop reality programming with musical content, it is unclear what involvement (if any) MTV will have with punk rock in the future. MTV has several sister stations, and before a format change M2 was a more free-form version of MTV that occasionally played videos by punk bands, such as **Black Flag's** "TV Party." Another video sister station occasionally plays early punk videos on their alternative show. *See also* Punk and Mass Media Representations.

MUD CLUB

New York club during the late 1970s and early 1980s where many punk bands played. The Mud Club was immortalized in the **Talking Heads** song "Life during Wartime."

MULLEN, BRENDAN

Scottish immigrant and **Los Angeles** resident who played a major role in the early Los Angeles scene with his legendary underground club the **Masque.** Brendan Mullen cowrote the definitive account of the Los Angeles scene in his 2001 book *We Got the Neutron Bomb* (named after a famous punk song by Los Angeles punk band the **Weirdos**) with coauthor Marc Spitz. Mullen's account was particularly noteworthy because he was present for many of the events chronicled in the book.

MUMMIES

San Francisco garage rock band formed in 1988 with a unique twist: The band performed dressed head to toe in bandages. The Mummies recorded for several years on minor labels and during their heyday refused to release material on CD. The original lineup consisted of Larry Winther on guitar, Maz Kattuah on bass, Trent Ruane on organ and saxophone, and Russell Quan on drums. The band performed for several years but, tiring of performing under wraps, called it quits in the mid-1990s. A CD compilation, *Death by Unga-Bunga!!,* was released in 2003 on the Estrus label.
Discography: *Never Been Caught* (Telstar, 1992, 2002); *Fuck CDs, It's the Mummies* (UK Hangman, 1992); *The Mummies Play Their Own Records* (Estrus, 1992); *Party at Steve's House* (Pin Up, 1994); *The Mummies* (no label, 1994); *Runnin' on Empty, Vol. 1* (Estrus, 1996); *Runnin' on Empty, Vol. 2* (Estrus, 1996); *Death by Unga Bunga!!* (Estrus, 2003).

MURPHY'S LAW

New York hardcore band fronted by Jimmy Gestapo (Jimmy Drescher) that was primarily popular during the late 1980s hardcore scene but still toured. The band released its first record in 1986 and went on a tour with the Beastie Boys, exposing New York hardcore to mainstream audiences across the United States. Problems with their record label and band conflict hurt Murphy's Law's chances for success, and the band went through several lineup changes until only longtime scene stalwart Jimmy Gestapo remained. Jimmy Gestapo continued to play and record with a new version of Murphy's Law.

Discography: *Murphy's Law* (Rock Hotel/Profile, 1986); *Back with a Bong!* (Profile, 1989, 1992); *The Best of Times* (Combat, 1991); *Murphy's Law/Back with a Bong!* (Another Planet, 1994); *Good for Now* EP (We Bite, 1995); *Dedicated* (Another Planet, 1996); *The Party's Over* (Artemis, 2001); *Beatles Karaoke* (Castle/Pulse, 2002).

MUSIC MACHINE

The Music Machine was one of the key 1960s bands considered **protopunk,** or anticipating **punk's** energy and stylistic contributions before the movement became formalized. The band formed as the Ragamuffins in 1965 but mutated into the Music Machine by 1966. The original lineup featured Sean Bonniwell on lead vocals, Keith Olsen on bass, Mark Landon on guitar, Ron Edgar on drums, and Doug Rhodes on organ, although only Bonniwell remained from the original lineup after 1967. The band's Farfisa organ style placed them on the garage and psychedelic side of the music scene. Music Machine is best known for the garage classic "Talk Talk."

Discography: *(Turn On) The Music Machine* (Original Sound, 1966); *Bonniwell's Music Machine* (Warner Bros., 1967); *Turns You On* (Repertoire, 1991, 1994); *The Music Machine* (Performance, 1994); *Beyond the Garage* (Sundazed Music, 1995); *Rock 'n' Roll Hits* (Castle, 1998); *Turn On: The Best of the Music Machine* (Collectables, 1999); *Ignition* (Sundazed Music, 2000).

NAPALM DEATH

Heavy metal (or grindcore or possibly noisecore or speedcore; it is hard to categorize) band, initially heavily influenced by the speed of thrash and **hardcore** but taken to ridiculous extremes in which songs became blurs of sound. Although there are often copious lyrics, the vocals often come out sounding like prolonged screams of agony. The records *Scum* and *The Peel Sessions* highlight the band at its early best, before they slowed down and became more conventional as they went through repeated personnel changes. Key member drummer Mick Harris went on to more experimental music with avant-jazz artists such as John Zorn and collaborations with former Faith No More singer Mike Patton.

Discography: *Scum* (Earache, 1986); *From Enslavement to Obliteration* (Earache, 1988); *The Peel Sessions* EP (UK Strange Fruit, 1989); *Napalm Death* EP (UK Rise Above, 1989); *Mentally Murdered* EP (UK Earache, 1989); *Harmony Corruption* (Earache/Combat, 1990); *Live Corruption* (UK Earache, 1990); *Suffer the Children* EP (UK Earache, 1990); *The Peel Sessions* (Strange Fruit/Dutch East India Trading, 1991); *Mass Appeal Madness* EP (Earache/Relativity, 1991); *Death by Manipulation* (Earache/Relativity, 1991); *Utopia Banished* (Earache/Relativity, 1992; Earache, 1996); *The World Keeps Turning* EP (Earache, 1992); *Nazi Punks Fuck Off* EP7 (Earache, 1993); *Fear, Emptiness, Despair* (Earache/Columbia, 1994); *Greed Killing* EP (Earache, 1995); *Diatribes* (Earache, 1996); *Inside the Torn Apart* (Earache, 1997); *Bootlegged in Japan* (Earache, 1998); *The Complete Radio One Sessions* (BBC/Fuel 2000/Var/Sarabande, 2000); *Leaders Not Followers* EP (Relapse, 2000); *Enemy of the Music Business* (Spitfire, 2001).

NATIONAL FRONT

Fascistic and racist movement native to England that caused controversy due to the prevalence of its members at punk shows in London during the original 1970s **punk** scene. Bands such as **Sham 69** had particular difficulty with National Front fans, including many who charged the stage during songs and attempted to shout propaganda or give Nazi salutes. Although most mainstream punk bands were not fans of the National Front and many worked on the **RAR** (**Rock against Racism**) concerts or denounced them in print and onstage, other bands such as **Skrewdriver** actively courted the movement's members as fans. Some bands, such as **Crass,** defended the right of the National Front and other fascists to be present at punk shows because they were the ones who were most likely to benefit from the strong antifascist message of the band. Although the National Front was an organized political party in England (with equivalent versions in other European countries, mostly organized under the banner of anti-immigration parties), there was no real equivalent in the United States. There was certainly an underground network of white-power punks and Nazi **skinheads,** however, as epitomized in the **Dead Kennedys'** classic rebuttal song "Nazi Punks Fuck Off!" Although many punks were lumped with the fascist tag, relatively few punks actually had fascist tendencies. *See also* Nazi Punks; Skrewdriver.

NATION OF ULYSSES

Perhaps the strangest, and certainly the snazziest dressers, on the **Dischord Records** label in the earl 1990s, Nation of Ulysses was a **straight edge punk** and dance band that made catchy songs about dismantling the state apparatus and getting one's groove on. The band featured Ian Svenonious on lead vocals and trumpet, guitarists Steven Kroner and Tim Green, bassist Steve Gamboa, and drummer James Canty (brother of Brendan Canty from **Fugazi**). The band seemed to waver between halfway serious statements such as "it was a simple matter of seceding from the union, issuing our own currency and penning our own national anthem" (liner notes to *13 Point Program to Destroy America*) to asserting that "Halloween is a potent instrument for revolt." Either way, they were an electrifying band, and after their inevitable dissolution (few revolutionary cells ever existed long without the inevitable schisms over ideology), Svenonious formed the equally dapper Make-Up.
Discography: *13 Point Program to Destroy America* (Dischord, 1991); *Plays Pretty for Baby* (Dischord, 1992).

NAUSEA

New York City band led by singer Neil Robinson and formed on the Lower East Side in 1987 by a variety of squatters. Robinson also ran the Tribal War label and booked shows at the popular independent club **ABC No Rio** in New York City. The band started out as fairly normal **punk** band, but after Robinson's departure soon developed a more grindcore style that incorporated death metal and psychedelic styles as well. The lineup consisted of John Jesse on bass, Victor Venom on guitar (formerly of **Reagan Youth**), Amy Miret (wife of Roger Miret of **Agnostic Front**) on second vocals, Roy Mayorga on drums, and Al Long on vocals after Robinson's departure. The band played numerous shows with Prong, Agnostic Front, Leeway, Reagan Youth, and others and stayed true to the members' anarchist principles until their dissolution in 1992.
Discography: *Extinction* (Profane Existence, 1990); *Cybergod* EP (Allied Records, 1991); *Punk Terrorist Anthology, Vol. 1* (Black Noise, 2004); *Punk Terrorist Anthology, Vol. 2: 1986–1988* (Alternative Tentacles, 2005).

NAZI PUNKS

A U.S. version of the England's National Front, comprising mainly **skinheads** and their allies in the Aryan Nation and White Brotherhood. Many of them participated in riots inside and outside shows and periodically attacked or taunted minority fans. **New York** and **Los Angeles** had particularly large contingents of Nazi punks in the early 1980s, inspiring the **Dead Kennedys** to write their anthem "Nazi Punks Fuck Off." The movement seemed to have faded during the 1990s, but the prevalence of the World Wide Web and other means of communication led to the movements' revival, and it continues in diminished form to this day. Even though few punks now (openly) identify themselves with racist or Nazi movements, some skinheads (although not all) are still allied with various white-power movements and can be identified by buttons and other paraphernalia that celebrate either the Aryan Nation or white power. Although many white-power and Nazi punks listen to regular punk bands (particularly **oi** music and skinhead bands), others seek out more extreme and openly racist or fascist music albums or bands such as **Skrewdriver.**

NECROS

Punk band from Maumee, Ohio, led by Barry Hennsler on vocals, Andy Wendler on guitar, Tod Swalla on drums, and future **Touch and Go** proprietor Corey Rusk on bass (later replaced by Ron Sakowski after Rusk broke his leg). The band began as a straightforward **hardcore** band but veered into more metallic territory in the mid-1980s and split acrimoniously with Rusk, who fought with the band over the early Touch and Go material.

Discography: *Necros* EP (Dischord/Touch and Go, 1981); *Conquest for Death* (Touch and Go, 1983); *Tangled Up* (Restless, 1987); *Live or Else* (Medusa, 1989); *Tangled Up/Live or Else* (live; Restless, 2005). **Necros/White Flag:** *Jail Jello* EP (Gasatanka, 1986).

NEGATIVE APPROACH

Detroit-based **punk** band featuring John Brannon on vocals. After Negative Approach's demise, Brannon formed the band Laughing Hyenas.

Discography: *Tied Down* (Touch & Go, 1983, 1988, 1991); *Live Your Life for You* (bootleg; no label, 1992); *Total Recall* (live; Touch & Go, 1992, 1994); *Ready to Fight, Demos Live and Unreleased 1981–83* (Reptilian, 2005).

NEGATIVE FX

Boston hardcore band that played very few shows but, nonetheless, was very influential on the Boston hardcore scene. Negative FX was led by front man Jack "Choke" Kelly, who later formed the bands Last Rites and **Slapshot.**

NEON BOYS

Original lineup of **Television** before the band broke up during the early **New York punk** scene. Neon Boys featured Richard Meyers **(Richard Hell)** and Tom Miller (Tom Verlaine), who had met at boarding school in the late 1960s. Billy Ficca later joined on drums, and when Richard Lloyd joined on guitar they changed the band's name to Television. Hell soon departed to join the **Heartbreakers** with **Johnny Thunders** and later formed his own band, Richard Hell and the **Voidoids.** *See also* Hell, Richard; Television; Voidoids.

NERF HERDER

Melodic **punk** band from Santa Barbara, California, named after an insult from the film *Star Wars*. The band played songs about nerdy subjects such as science fiction and being a heavy metal geek and was also known for providing the intro music to the cult TV show *Buffy the Vampire Slayer*. The original lineup featured Parry Grip on guitar and vocals, Steve "the Cougar" Sherlock on drums, and a succession of bass players, starting with Charlie Dennis, who was replaced by Pete Newbury, Marko 72, Justin Fischer, then Ben Pringle in 2002. Second guitarist Dave Ehrlich was added to beef up the band's sound in 1998. The band broke up briefly in 2003 then reformed in 2004.

Discography: *Nerf Herder* (My Records, 1995; Arista, 1996); *Foil Wrapped for Freshness* (self-release, 1995); *How to Meet Girls* (Honest Don's, 2000); *High-Voltage Christmas Rock* (self-release, 2000); *My* EP (My Records, 2001; Honest Don's, 2003); *American Cheese* (Honest Don's, 2002).

NEVER MIND THE BOLLOCKS, HERE'S THE SEX PISTOLS

The **Sex Pistols'** one and only legitimate album of recordings and a **punk** classic in its own right. *Never Mind the Bollocks* was the long-awaited record (released in 1977 on the Warner Bros. label) from the Sex Pistols that, ironically, was released long after many of the bands they inspired, such as the **Damned,** had already released long-playing records. The album collected classic punk singles such as "Pretty Vacant," **"Anarchy in the UK,"** and **"God Save the Queen"** as well as satirical attacks such as "EMI" (a song about one of the original labels that signed the Sex Pistols only to drop them a few days richer and a few thousand pounds poorer. Even though many critics at the time were disappointed by the album, it demonstrates the codification of the punk sound and remains one of the most influential records ever released. The record was also quite controversial, not only for its music but also for its situationist cover designed by **Jamie Reid** and for its use of the word *bollocks* in the title, which was considered offensive by many and led to a criminal trial against a record store owner who displayed the record. After a trial, the album was ruled not obscene and went on to become a top-10 success in England and enormously influential elsewhere.

NEW BOMB TURKS

Punk band from Columbus, Ohio, known for its high-speed songs and ferocious energy. New Bomb Turks started in the early 1990s and featured Eric Davidson on lead vocals and Jim Weber on guitar. The band played a combination of garage and punk rock inspired by early punk's manic energy.

Discography: *So Cool, So Clean, So Sparkling Clear* EP7 (Datapanik, 1992); *!!Destroy-Oh-Boy!!* (Crypt, 1992); *Drunk on Cock* EP (Engine, 1993); *Information Highway Revisited* (Crypt, 1994); *Pissing Out the Poison* (Crypt, 1995); *Scared Straight* (Epitaph, 1996); *At Rope's End* (Epitaph, 1998); *The Blind Run* EP10 (UK Epitaph Europe, 2000); *Nightmare Scenario* (Epitaph, 2000).

"NEW ROSE"

One of the first British **punk** singles and arguably the first to be released on a major label, **Stiff Records,** in October 1976. This punk single by the **Damned** was produced by pub rocker and fellow traveler Nick Lowe and backed with a version of "Help" by the Beatles, a band that many punks (Glenn Matlock aside) despised. The single paved the way for many other punk singles to be released by Stiff and for the punk rock feeding frenzy in England during the late 1980s. Stiff also released records by Elvis Costello and Nick Lowe, among many others.

NEW WAVE

A term much derided by punks, New Wave was the music industry's way of trying to repackage **punk** in a more friendly way for U.S. audiences. Although many in the punk scene despised the term, other bands such as **Blondie** embraced it and were marketed as less threatening music. Punk bands that were more abrasive (in theory) and less photogenic, such as the **Ramones,** were still stigmatized (to many in the general public) with the punk label, which meant sales in the thousands as opposed to the millions and guaranteed a lack of air play. Seymour Stein of Sire Records openly campaigned for the label New Wave, which he thought would be less threatening and more accessible to the general public. As the 1980s wore on, the term began to be used as a catchall to describe synthesizer-driven bands with a dancy edge, such as Flock of Seagulls and Haircut One Hundred. Eventually, most of punk music was marginalized, and record labels desperate to sell the punk acts they had signed often encouraged them to put out danceable synthesizer-driven singles that were presumably more palatable to the public from a sales standpoint. (Bands as disparate as the **Clash** and New Order often could be heard on the same radio stations and in the same dance clubs.) Ultimately, the term *New Wave* did more to sink the chances for commercial (and possibly political and social) changes that the original wave of punk had seemed to promise, and the commercial success enjoyed by bands, such as Blondie, that were marketed as New Wave was also a factor in convincing many early punks that the movement was over by the early 1980s. The rise of **hardcore** also music may have been partly inspired by the compromises many bands made to gain radio play and be considered New Wave. Although many in the punk scene embraced New Wave, many did not and found it to be a dilution of punk's promise, which also relates to issues of how many punks remain ambivalent about marketing and the relationship of punk rock to corporate culture.

NEW YORK

New York City arguably can be labeled the birthplace of punk rock. Early bands such as the **New York Dolls, Dictators, Ramones, Richard Hell** in his various bands, **Television,** and **Patti Smith** coalesced around a small number of clubs in New York City, such as **CBGB's** and **Max's Kansas City,** and founded a movement that went against the dominant rock orthodoxy of the time. For a few years, New York had an extremely large and vibrantly punk scene that showcased the true diversity of early punk, before it became more formulaic. (For a more detailed discussion of the early New York City scene, *see* Introduction; punk.)

Although most of the original New York punk bands had broken up or moved on by the early 1980s, a new scene was developing in a harder faster style that would later be labeled **hardcore** punk. New bands, such as **Reagan Youth,** the **Stimulators** (featuring a young Harley Flanagan, later of the **Cro-Mags,** on drums), **Kraut,** and Heart Attack (featuring a young Jesse Malin, later of **D Generation**), soon began to dominate the new scene. The arrival of **Bad Brains,** a Washington, D.C., transplant whose members consistently quarreled and sabotaged their own chances at success but were the most respected band in New York City in the early 1980s and recorded some of their crucial early material such as the "Pay to Cum" single in New York City, also changed the dynamic of the scene and inspired many New York bands to speed up their sounds in order to compete with the Bad Brains' legendary musical prowess. Jack Rabid (later of *Big Takeover* magazine) played the latest hardcore on WNYU radio, furthering awareness of the new scene and new clubs such as **A7** and recording studio 171A and leading to an increase in shows and musicians recording what was increasingly becoming a new form of punk rock. By 1982, newer bands such as the Undead (featuring Bobby Steele, formerly of the **Misfits**) played alongside Kraut (which had been one of the opening bands when the **Clash** played Bond's Casino in New York), Heart Attack, Even Worse (featuring Jack Rabid), False Prophets, and an embryonic version of the Beastie Boys (which then included future Luscious Jackson drummer Kate Shellenbach; the band began to become the Beastie Boys proper when friend Adam Yauch and **Young and the Useless** member Adam Horovitz joined). By 1983 to 1984, many New York punks had become **skinheads,** and the scene became exponentially more violent and the music even faster. New bands such as Cro-Mags (led by bassist Harley Flannagan of the Stimulators) and **Murphy's Law** (featuring longtime scene fixture Jimmy Gestapo) played increasingly violent matinee shows at CBGB's, and gangs of skinheads heightened the insularity of the scene. By the late 1980s, most of the early bands had broken up or gone metal, and a strong **straight edge** movement began to coalesce in New York City around bands such as **Youth of Today** and (now cleaned up) **Warzone,** both of which put out releases on **Revelation Records.** At that time, the scene was in disarray, but a new group of bands grew around New York City in the 1990s and beyond, featuring bands that were conscious revivalists, such as the Strokes, alongside newer and fresher bands such as **Iron Prostate,** Dirt Bike Annie, **Serpico,** the Ergs, Egghead, In Crowd, the Bullys, the Waldos, and the Kowalskis.

NEW YORK DOLLS

One of the last-missing links between **punk,** glam rock, and 1960s punk, the New York Dolls were a legendary band in their heyday in the early 1970s, but their influence had greater, far-reaching consequences. The band was also well known for spawning the careers of David Johansen, who later found a top-10 hit as Buster Poindexter, and **Johnny Thunders,** who died of an overdose in 1991. The New York Dolls originally formed in 1971 from a band called Actress, which featured Arthur Kane on bass, Billy Murcia on drums, John Gezale (Johnny Thunders) on guitar, and Rick Rivets on second guitar. Later, they added Sylvain Sylvain (Ronald Misrahi) on guitar, who replaced Rivets, and David Johansen on lead vocals. They debuted in March 1972 and quickly made a name for themselves playing around New York City in places as varied as a gay bath house but gained real notoriety when they established a residency at the Mercer Arts Center in the Oscar Wilde Room, where they played alongside bands such as **Suicide.** The Dolls soon began to draw a crowd of celebrities, including **Lou Reed** and **David Bowie** (who had been known to wear a dress or two in his time), and finally were signed to a management contract by Marty Thau. Seeking to drum up interest in the band, the New York Dolls undertook a tour of England in 1972 and opened for Rod Stewart and the Faces at Wembley Pool, where a young Glen Matlock (later of the **Sex Pistols**) was inspired by the band to start dreaming of his own possible future. The band drew a following, but tragedy struck in November 1972 when original drummer Billy Murcia overdosed on barbiturates in London and was placed in a bathtub to recover, whereupon he promptly drowned. The New York Dolls returned to New York City discouraged, but after a few weeks Murcia was replaced by former gang member Jerry Nolan. With Nolan in the band, the Dolls became even more aggressive and musically tight and signed a record deal with Mercury Records in March 1973. The New York Dolls' self-titled and Todd Rundgren–produced debut album was released to little commercial success but international critical acclaim, catching the notice of a young **Malcolm McLaren.** After releasing a second album, the all-too-aptly named *Too Much Too Soon,* produced by legendary girl group producer George "Shadow" Morton, in early 1974, the band was dropped by its record company. The band attempted to keep going, but Nolan's and Thunders's growing addictions to heroin, as well as Kane's problems with alcohol, complicated the band's problems. In an attempt to chance their image, the Dolls decided to work with Malcolm McLaren, who redesigned their image, clothing them in red leather outfits and placing a huge Communist hammer and sickle flag behind them, and took them on a disastrous tour of Florida, where the band was chased by locals, unimpressed with their sartorial splendor. Nolan and Thunders then left the band, and, despite Sylvain Sylvain and Johansen's best attempts, the band soon fell apart. Nolan and Thunders went on to form the **Heartbreakers** with **Richard Hell** and guitarist Walter Lure. Hell was eventually asked to leave the band and was replaced by bassist Billy Rath for the Heartbreakers definitive lineup, which had success on the early punk scene and went on tour with the Sex Pistols and the Clash in England during the first punk package tour. David Johansen and Sylvain Sylvain went on to solo careers of varying success. Johansen scored several chart hits during the early 1980s and eventually transformed himself into the ridiculously popular Buster Poindexter before returning to his blues roots and touring with the Harry Smiths. The band reunited in 2004 for some concerts, originally with Arthur Kane, who died of leukemia halfway through the tour, but continued on with Sylvain Sylvain and Johansen and various sidemen. The legacy of the New York Dolls can be felt in both punk and heavy metal, in the androgyny of many glam rock bands, as well as in former Smiths lead singer Morrissey, who is a huge fan of the New York Dolls and helped them reunite.

Discography: *New York Dolls* (Mercury, 1973); *Too Much Too Soon* (Mercury, 1974; Mercury/Hip-O Select; 2005); *New York Dolls* (Mercury, 1977); *Lipstick Killers: The Mercer Street Sessions 1972* (tape, Roir, 1981; CD, Roir/Important, 1990; Roir, 2000); *Red Patent Leather* (Fr. Fan Club, 1984); *Best of the New York Dolls* (UK Mercury, 1985); *Night of the Living Dolls* (Mercury, 1986); *Personality Crisis* EP

(UK Kamera, 1986); *Morrissey Presents the Return of the New York Dolls Live From Royal Festival Hall, 2004* (Attack/Sanctuary, 2004). **David & Sylvain:** *Tokyo Dolls Live!* (Fr. Fan Club, 1986). **The Original Pistols/New York Dolls:** *After the Storm* (UK Receiver, 1985).

NEW YORK HARDCORE—THE WAY IT IS

Compilation of **New York hardcore** bands such as **Youth of Today, Gorilla Biscuits,** and others on **Revelation Records.** The compilation was released in 1988, after the heyday of New York City hardcore.

NEW YORK ROCKER

New York Rocker was a magazine started in 1975 as a rival to **John Holmstrom's** *Punk* zine and covered much of the same music. The magazine was started and most successful when run by Alan Betrock, who served as publisher and editor. *New York Rocker* covered the **CBGB's** scene extensively and featured Steven Meisel, Roberta Bailey, and Duncan Hannah. Betrock later put out records on the Shake label, including releases by **Richard Hell,** the DBs, and the Smithereens.

NEW ZEALAND

Although many corners of the world were slow to catch on to **punk** rock, the island nation of New Zealand was quick to embrace punk in the mid-1970s, and the success of the **Sex Pistols** had an enormous impact on the local scene in Auckland. The first punk bands were the Scavengers and the Suburban Reptiles, followed quickly by the Masochists, all in Auckland, with Johnny Veloux and the Vauxhalls in Christchurch and the Enemy in Dunedin. The Scavengers included the legendary Paul Cooke (Johnny Volume) on guitar, Marlon Hart on bass, Des Truction (Simon Monroe) on drums, and Mike Simmons on lead vocals. The Suburban Reptiles featured Sally Slag (also known as Buster Stiggs [Claire Elliot]) on lead vocals, Shaun Anfrayd (Brian Nicols) on guitar, Sissy Spunk (Trish Scott) on guitar, Buzz Adrenalin (also known as Zero [Mark Hough]) on drums, Jimmy Vinyl (Brett Salter) on saxophone, and Billy Planet (Will Prendergast) on bass. These two bands inspired hundreds of other suburban youth to form their own bands and eventually paved the way for the fertile independent rock scenes of the 1980s and 1990s, as epitomized by the bands that released music on the Flying Nun label. A key player in the scene, Chris Knox of the band Toy Love, later went on to form the duo Tall Dwarfs with Alec Bathgate and released numerous records under that label and as a solo artist, becoming one of the most famous New Zealand musicians outside of New Zealand. The success and vitality of the New Zealand scene demonstrated that punk was a virus that could replicate under almost any conditions.

NICO

Nico (Christa Paffgen) was an Andy Warhol protégé and singer on the first **Velvet Underground** album as well as several critically acclaimed solo records. Nico struggled with **heroin** addiction for years and died in a bicycle accident in 1988. Before joining the Velvet Underground, Nico appeared in Federico Fellini's 1960 film *La Dolce Vita* and from there became a model and worked with Andy Warhol (she appeared in his film *Chelsea Girls*). Warhol decided to make her a member of the Velvet Underground, an experimental band featuring **Lou Reed** and John Cale that he was managing. The band performed as a collective with dancers and a light show as the Exploding Plastic Inevitable, and Nico soon began singing songs with the band, including "All Tomorrow's Parties," "Femme Fatale," and "I'll Be Your Mirror." Nico left the Velvet Underground after the first record and soon began a career as a solo artist, working with Reed, Cale, Morrison, and young folksinger Jackson Browne. Bob Dylan, Jackson Browne, and John Cale contributed songs to her first album, *Chelsea Girl*. She worked with Cale on her next record, the equally influential *The Marble Index* (her first two records would be cited for years by critics as precursors of the drone rock experiments of **postpunk**). After *The Marble Index*, however, her career went downhill and she became a virtual hermit, rarely touring and recording only sporadically. She died near her home in Ibiza, Spain, in 1988 after falling from a bicycle. Nico was also known for her many affairs, including liaisons with Jackson Browne, **Iggy Pop,** and Alain Delon, with whom she had a child. Nico's musical legacy can be seen in the artier and more experimental bands that adapted her sound and persona.

Select Discography: *Chelsea Girl* (PolyGram, 1967); *The Marble Index* (Elektra, 1968); *Desertshore* (Warner Bros., 1970); *The End* (Island, 1974); *Dram of Exile* (Aura, 1981); *Live in Denmark* (VU, 1983); *Camera Obscura* (Beggar's Banquet, 1985); *Behind the Iron Curtain* (Dojo, 1986).

NIHILISM

Philosophy that denies a belief in anything and says that the world has no meaning (from the Latin *nihil*, meaning "nothing"). Friedrich Nietzsche is probably the best known of the nihilist philosophers. Although many punks were accused of being nihilistic by the mainstream press, it is unusual to actually encounter a band that would admit to espousing a philosophy of simple nihilism. The term *nihilism* could certainly be applied to the "no future" themes prevalent in the music of the **Sex Pistols** and other bands from that time period, but many punk bands, especially **Crass** and many of the later **hardcore** bands, certainly had legitimate agendas that worked toward social change or specific social changes (such as people becoming **vegetarians** and resisting corporate culture). Although some bands were certainly nihilistic, the labeling of punks as nihilists probably had as much to do with media images of punks (such as in the infamous *Quincy* episode in which punks are murderers or movies such as *Return of the Living Dead* or *Class of 1984* in which punks have no useful societal function). In reality, many punks are involved in positive movements that use peaceful protest or the power of the underground media to agitate for social change. **Jello Biafra** (former lead singer of the **Dead Kennedys** and founder of the **Alternative Tentacles** label) even ran for mayor of San Francisco.

999

Long-running English **punk** band formed in **London** in 1976 that flirted with **New Wave** keyboards at various points, formerly known as 48 Hours. Best known for the song "Homicide" and the band's electrifying live shows. 999 featured vocalist and former pub rocker Nick Cash, guitarist Guy Days, bassist John Watson, and drummer Pablo LaBrittain, and the band first released an independent single, "I'm Alive," on LaBrittain Records in 1977. The first album *999*, released in February 1978, was good enough to make the charts, but it was the next release, *Separates*, in 1978, that featured the classic punk song (and one of the most collected songs on punk compilations) "Homicide." Other hits soon followed, such as the infectious "High Energy Plan." The lineup remained relatively stable, with drummer Ed Case briefly replacing an injured LaBrittain and original bassist Watson leaving to be replaced by Arturo Bassicak (Peter Arthur Billingsly), formerly of the **Lurkers,** to solidify the final 999 lineup. The band still toured with most of the original lineup as of 2005.

Discography: *999* (United Artists, 1978); *Separates* (United Artists, 1978); *High Energy Plan* (PVC, 1979); *Biggest Prize in Sport* (Polydor, 1980); *Biggest Prize in Sport (Live)* (Polydor, 1980); *Concrete* (Albion, 1981); *13th Floor Madness* (Albion, 1984); *Face to Face* (LaBrittain, 1985); *In Case of Emergency* (Dojo, 1986); *Lust, Power and Money* (ABC, 1987); *Live and Loud!* (Link, 1989); *The Cellblock Tapes*

(Link, 1990); *You Us It!* (Anagram Punk, 1993); *Live in L.A. 1991* (Triple X, 1994); *Scandal in the City* (Line, 1997); *Takeover* (Abstract, 1998); *Slam* (Overground, 1999); *English Wipeout: Live* (Overground, 1999); *Live at the Nashville* (Anagram Punk, 2002).

1991: THE YEAR PUNK BROKE

Documentary directed by David Markey and released in 1992 that chronicled the chart success enjoyed by **Sonic Youth** and **Nirvana** in 1991 and supposedly the mainstream acceptance of **punk** rock as a musical and cultural movement. The movie took as its main idea that most people were unaware of the indie underground of the 1980s and that mainstream acceptance was a positive step toward a larger assimilation of punk rock and its attendant ideology into mainstream culture. Although the film may have been overly optimistic and somewhat dubious in labeling all of the bands that made up the 1991 scene as "punk," the documentary featured many riveting performances and rare footage that ultimately made the film worthwhile, albeit as a document of somewhat unfounded optimism regarding punk's long-term commercial prospects. The film contained live performances by Dinasour Jr., Babes in Toyland, the **Ramones,** and Gumball.

NIPS

A band, also known as the Nipple Erectors, started by noted **punk** fanatic Shane MacGowan, who later found the famous Irish punk band the **Pogues.** The Nips were less a straight-ahead punk band and more of a combination of **rockabilly** and punk that gave no indication of how radically and powerfully MacGowan would change directions in the next few years. The lineup featured MacGowan on vocals and guitar, Shanne Bradley on bass, James Fearnley (later of the Pogues) on guitar, and Jon Moss (later of Culture Club) on drums. The band was done by 1980, but MacGowan was already planning his next project.
Discography: *Bops, Babes, Booze & Bovver* (UK Big Beat, 1987, 2000).

NIRVANA

The most popular and biggest-selling band associated with **punk** (and what was called the grunge movement) during the 1990s. Although many inside and outside the punk community often questioned the credentials of the band, and its commercial success, Nirvana still kept true (or paid lip service to) the punk ideals of authenticity and attitude. Late lead singer Kurt Cobain remains an iconic figure, and his image appears almost as often in popular culture as that of James Dean, Elvis Presley, and Marilyn Monroe as a doomed romantic poet, unable to stand the slings and arrows of outrageous fortune. Although Nirvana toured in several different formations for several years, the classic lineup of Kurt Cobain on vocals and guitar, Chris Novoselic on bass, Dave Grohl on drums and vocals, and, later, Pat Smear of the **Germs** on guitar was the focus of a media storm that helped bring punk rock back into the public eye when their album *Nevermind* went multiplatinum in the early 1990s. It is controversial to many as to whether Nirvana was a punk band, but most in the community agree that even if Nirvana did commit the ultimate sins of signing to a major label and getting massive airplay for their breakthrough single "Smells Like Teen Spirit," the band remained punk in spirit, donating money to punk causes and championing bands such as the Vaselines, **Meat Puppets** (who appeared on Nirvana's groundbreaking appearance on **MTV's** *Unplugged,* in which Nirvana played three Meat Puppets covers), and **the Melvins.** Nirvana was originally started by street punk Kurt Cobain and bassist Chris Novoselic and a variety of drummers. The band was signed to Sub Pop Records and released its acclaimed record *Bleach* in 1989. *Bleach* was a milestone, although it resembled some of the other records put out by the embryonic grunge scene of the time (such as the Melvins, and Green River), and Nirvana was busy working out a twisted combination of Black Sabbath (the premier sludge rock kings of heavy metal) and **Black Flag** that not only helped set the musical template of the 1990s but also demonstrated to many punks that they did not have to reject every band that was on a major label. Cobain committed suicide in 1994 and was memorialized in a media frenzy in Seattle that year, where his widow, Courtney Love, famously read his suicide note to the crowd via tape. Nirvana can be credited for fusing punk and heavy metal and underground music in a way that was accepted by fans of a variety of musical tastes and was long be remembered as one of the few bands with a punk orientation to cross over into the mainstream. **Discography:** *Blew* EP (Ger. Sub Pop/Glitterhouse, 1989); *Bleach* (Sub Pop, 1989, 1992); *Sliver* EP (Sub Pop, 1990); *Nevermind* (Sub Pop/DGC, 1991); *Hormoaning* EP (Japan DGC, 1992); *Incesticide* (Sub Pop/DGC, 1992); *In Utero* (Sub Pop/DGC, 1993); *MTV Unplugged in New York* (DGC, 1994); *Singles* (UK Geffen, 1995); *From the Muddy Banks of the Wishkah* (DGC, 1996).

NO FOR AN ANSWER

One of the first West Coast **straight edge** bands, formed by lead vocalist Dan O'Mahony. O'Mahony had been inspired by **Seven Seconds** and **Minor Threat** to form a band based on the antichemical and proyouth messages of both bands. O'Mahony published the book *Three Legged Race* dealing with his years in the **hardcore** and straight edge movements.

NOFX

Long-running Berkeley, California, band that incorporated elements of **ska** and **reggae** in their humorous songs. The members of NOFX are also well known for becoming political later in their careers and working to register voters for the 2004 election though **punkvoter.com.** The band started as a power trio in 1983, led by Fat Mike (Burkett) on bass and vocals (who also runs **Fat Wreck Chords,** a very successful **punk** label, with his wife, Erin) along with guitarist Eric Melvin and drummer Erik Sandin (who was replaced briefly by Scott Sellers for two EPs) The band also briefly had an alternate lead singer, Dave Allen, who died in a car crash in 1986. In 1987, the band added a second guitarist, Dave Casillas, who was replaced by Steve Kidwiller for the band's first album release, *S&M Airlines.* The lineup stabilized with the addition of guitarist and horn player El Hefe (Aaron Abeyta), who was a major reason for the band's incorporation of ska, reggae, and **dub** in its songs. NOFX was one of the most successful punk bands of the 1990s, touring successfully on its own and on the **Vans Warped tour.** Their records continued to sell well, and the 1994 album *Punk in Drublic* was certified gold in the United States, a rarity for a punk album. During the 2004 elections, NOFX surprised many by bringing politics to the forefront of their message and founding punkvoter.com. Despite the members' humor, NOFX was one of the most consistent underground punk bands for more than 20 years. **Discography:** *Liberal Animation* (Fat Wreck Chords, 1988; Epitaph, 1991); *S&M Airlines* (Epitaph, 1989); *Ribbed* (Epitaph, 1991, 1993); *E Is for Everything* (Mystic, 1991); *Liberal Animation* (Epitaph, 1991); *The Longest Line* EP (Fat Wreck Chords, 1992); *Maximum Rocknroll* (Mystic, 1992); *White Trash, Two Heebs and a Bean* (Epitaph, 1992); *Don't Call Me White* (Fat Wreck Chords, 1992); *Punk in Drublic* (Epitaph, 1994); *Bob Live* (Gema, 1994); *I Heard They Suck Live* (Fat Wreck Chords, 1995); *Heavy Petting Zoo* (Epitaph, 1996); *Eating Lamb* (Epitaph, 1996); *HOFX* (Fat Wreck Chords, 1996); *So Long and Thanks for All the Shoes* (Epitaph, 1997); *Pump Up the Valium* (Epitaph, 2000); *The Decline* EP (Fat Wreck Chords, 2000); *45 or 46 Songs That Weren't Good Enough to Go on Our Other Records* (Fat Wreck Chords, 2002); *War on Errorism* (Fat Wreck Chords, 2003); *Greatest Songs Ever Written (By Us)* (Epitaph, 2004).

NO NEW YORK

Compilation (Antilles, 1978) of the **New York no-wave** movement of the late 1970s, featuring tracks by James Chance and the Contortions, DNA (featuring a young Arto Lindsay), Teenage

Jesus, the Jerks (featuring a young **Lydia Lunch**), and other New York bands such as Mars. This influential compilation documented the reaction to the perceived stagnancy of New York City **punk** rock and a short-lived time period that would influence later bands such as Live Skull and, most prominently, **Sonic Youth.**

NOT ALL QUIET ON THE WESTERN FRONT

Influential compilation (Alternative Tentacles/Virus, 1982) released by *Maximum Rock 'n' Roll,* featuring numerous bands that would become extremely influential, such as **Seven Seconds**, and many that would never be heard from again, such as Intensified Chaos. It was an attempt to provide listeners of the Maximum Rock 'n' Roll radio show and a broader audience with an overview of what many of the new and cutting-edge bands sounded like.

NO TREND

Caustic **hardcore** band formed in 1982 in Ashton, Maryland, that played extensively in the **Washington, D.C., punk** scene and was known for attacking punk movements such as the **straight edge** scene of Washington, D.C., with a subversive wit that went against the punk rock political orthodoxy of the time. The band was antimovement and used to post **flyers** reading "No Trend, No Scene, No Movement" around places frequented by Washington, D.C., straight edge punks. The band consisted of founder Jeff Menteges on lead vocals, Jack Anderson on bass, Eric Leifert and Brian Nelson on saxophone, Dean Evangelista and Buck Parr on guitar, James Peachey on drums, and Frank Price on guitar. Despite the perceived openness and free-form nature of punk and **hardcore,** dress codes and rules of behavior (straight edge, in its most absurd extreme) were adopted, and many punks became a sort of punk police, trying to enforce the proper way to act, dress, and eat, and No Trend was a reaction against this. The band had much more in common with bands like the **Butthole Surfers** and **Flipper** than it did with the local Washington, D.C., bands like **Minor Threat.** Although the band was very successful and even had special guest **Lydia Lunch** of the **no-wave** movement in New York City sing on the song "A Dozen Red Roses," the band could only keep it going for so long, and after a ridiculous amount of turnover in band members decided to call it quits in 1988. No Trend was not well known except to a few in the hardcore scene who actually questioned the orthodoxy of the movement, but their legacy was still important in demonstrating that not all hardcore bands sounded alike or wanted to have anything to do with unity or the scene.
Discography: *Teen Love* EP (No Trend, 1983); *Too Many Humans* (No Trend, 1984); *A Dozen Dead Roses* (No Trend, 1985); *Heart of Darkness* EP (UK Widowspeak, 1985); *When Death Won't Solve Your Problems* (UK Widowspeak, 1986); *Tritonian Nash—Vegas Polyester Complex* (Touch and Go, 1986); *More* (described as their "lost" album; unknown label, 2001).

NO USE FOR A NAME

U.S. poppy **hardcore** band from the San Jose, California, scene, formed by Tony Sly on vocals and featuring Rorry Koff on drums. Members included Matt Riddle, formerly of **Face to Face,** on bass and Dave Nassie, formerly of **Suicidal Tendencies** and the dance-punk band Infectious Grooves, on guitar. No Use for a Name played an infectious melodic hardcore style reminiscent of **Bad Religion** and **NOFX** (they signed to Fat Mike's **Fat Wreck Chords** label), and in 2005 the band played the main stage on the **Vans Warped tour,** punk rock's biggest touring festival.
Discography: *No Use for a Name* EP (Woodpecker, 1989); *Let Em Out* EP (Slap a Ham, 1990); *Incognito* (New Red Archives, 1990); *Don't Miss the Train* (New Red Archives, 1992); *The Daily Grind* (Fat Wreck Chords, 1993); *¡Leche Con Carne!* (Fat Wreck Chords, 1995); *Making Friends* (Fat Wreck Chords, 1997); *More*

Betterness! (Fat Wreck Chords, 1999); *The NRA Years* (UK Golf, 2000); *Live in a Dive* (Fat Wreck Chords, 2001); *Hard Rock Bottom* (Fat Wreck Chords, 2002); *Keep Them Confused* (Fat Wreck Chords, 2005).

NO WAVE

Musical movement in New York City in the late 1970s that was a reaction to the corporate influences of major record labels and the perceived demise of the original **punk** scene. The no-wave movement featured bands such as DNA, James Chance, and Teenage Jesus and the Jerks. The movement was a reaction to both the failure of punk rock to catch on in the charts and to the marketing of watered-down, danceable versions of punk rock as **New Wave** by a nervous record industry. No wave was by its nature abrasive and experimental, and many of its proponents were known for their aggressive stage performances and challenging attitudes to the audience. Some artists, such as Chance (also known as James White), would sometimes physically, as well as verbally, abuse those who had come to see the band perform.

NUNS

Early female-led U.S. **punk** rock group from San Francisco led by singer Jennifer Miro and indie music legend Alejandro Escovedo. The Nuns broke up in the mid-1980s, and Escovedo formed Rank and File with Chip and Tony Kinman, formerly of the **Dils.** For the comeback album, Miro worked with other Nuns original member Jeff Oleaner.
Discography: *The Nuns* (Posh Boy/Bomp!, 1980); *Rumania* (PVC, 1986).

NYHC

The acronym NYHC stood for "New York Hardcore" and was used in various designs to indicate that one was a member of that scene. NYHC was also graffitied on the back of jackets, albums covers, and on **flyers** across New York City during the early 1980s. It implied the wearers' allegiance to a particularly confrontational style of **hardcore punk** rock, sometimes with metallic edges, depending on what point in the early to mid-1980s one wore the logo. Bands generally understood to fit into the genre included New York City legends **Agnostic Front, Cro-Mags,** and **Warzone.** It is interesting to note that many members of overtly identified metal bands also often wore this logo and attended hardcore matinees, and later many metallic bands cited NYHC as a major influence both musically and stylistically. (The design of the logo of **SOD** [Storm Troopers of Death] borrowed heavily from the design elements in NYHC logos; SOD did so musically as well.) Graffiti of this sort and the use of a common logo identified one's allegiance to both a style of music and in many cases a lifestyle (there was much crossover and cross-pollination between various punk movements, for example one could be a member of the straight edge scene and wear the logo just as easily as one could reject it for ideological or musical reasons), although it is also likely that many who wore the logo or identified with the overall New York City sound were unified by little else, despite the frequent assertions of unity by many bands. *See also* Hardcore; New York; Straight Edge.

OFFSPRING

One of the most successful punk bands of the 1990s, Offspring was known for its hit song and video "Keep'em Separated (Come out and Play)," which was featured in heavy rotation on **MTV** and ubiquitous on radio during the early 1990s. The band followed up with many other hit singles and courted controversy by leaving the independent label **Epitaph** for a major label in the mid-1990s. The band formed in 1987 in **Orange County** and played shows with many of the key bands of the time, finally releasing their first record in 1990 on Nemesis. The band consisted of Bryan "Dexter" Holland on lead vocals, Kevin "Noodles" Wasserman on guitar, Ron Welty on drums, and Greg K. on bass. The Offspring are also known for their energetic shows and encouragement of up-and-coming bands through their label Nitro. Lead Singer Bryan "Dexter" Holland joins the exclusive club of punk lead singers with Ph.D.s (which also includes Milo Auckerman of the **Descendents** and Greg Graffin of **Bad Religion**).

Selective Discography: *The Offspring* (Nemesis, 1989; Nitro, 1995); *Baghdad* EP (Nemesis, 1990); *Ignition* (Epitaph, 1992); *Smash* (Epitaph, 1994); *Ixnay on the Hombre* (Columbia, 1997); *Americana* (Columbia, 1998); *Conspiracy of One* (Columbia, 2000); *Splinter* (Columbia, 2003).

OI

British working-class musical and cultural movement circa the late 1970s that mixed skinhead, street punk, and working-class culture. The term is generally attributed to music critic Gary Bushell. The original bands lumped into the oi scene included **Slaughter and the Dogs,** the **Cockney Rejects,** the **Angelic Upstarts, Skrewdriver,** and, most importantly, **Sham 69,** all bands with anthemic sing-along choruses that were probably derived from the chants heard at English football games (sometime actually chanting "Oi! Oi! Oi!" or some variation of the word *oi*), with large contingents of working-class fans. Although the movement did include a fair number of **skinheads** in the early years, early oi was not inherently racist. By the early 1980s, however, bands such as Skrewdriver were openly identifying themselves as racist and allied with the **National Front,** and some members of the oi scene also identified with, or at least did not condemn, the racist elements within the punk, skinhead, and oi movements. A second generation of mostly skinhead bands formed in the early 1980s and included the Business, **4-Skins,** Combat 84, and others. The movement spread throughout the world and the United States, and although it was never as popular outside of England, numerous bands from the early years and more contemporary bands such as the Templars keep the spirit of oi alive. It remains to be seen if the music will ultimately be more associated with the racist followers who were some of is biggest proponents or the majority (although the majority was probably at least to the right of the political spectrum) who were simply looking for catchy music and a sense of unity. Oi certainly did indicate that a large section of working-class fans needed music that dealt with the day-to-day conditions of working-class life, not just songs about rebellion and anarchy.

100 CLUB

Famous **London** club that hosted many punk shows during the mid-1970s. The 100 Club was the sight of the 100 Club Punk Festival on September 20–21, 1976, where **Subway Sect** and **Siouxsie and the Banshees** made their debuts. The established bands that played included the **Clash,** the **Damned,** Stinky Toys (France), the **Vibrators** with guest guitarist Chris Spedding, the **Buzzcocks,** and, most notably, the **Sex Pistols.** A melee started by a thrown glass blamed (perhaps without justification) on Sex Pistols' fan and future bass player **Sid Vicious** led to punk bands being mostly banned from the club thereafter. **Alternative TV** was the last punk band to play the club in April 1978 before its demise as a rock club. In the 1980s, the club reinvented itself as a key spot for African Township music and featured artists such as Fela Kuti, Hugh Maskela, and Marion Makemba. In the early 1990s, the club turned to be-bop and new jazz but by the mid-1990s had switched to indie rock with bands such as Oasis, Suede, Cornershop, and Kula Shaker playing often. The club is open to this day and still hosts new bands.

101ERS

English pub-rock band, most notable as the starting point for future **Clash** front man **Joe Strummer.** The pre-Clash band featuring Strummer as lead vocalist played a combination of covers, original R & B–influenced material, and some future Clash songs in their embryonic forms. The band formed in September 1974 and took the name from a squat at 101 Walterton Road, where many members of the band then lived. The original lineup included Mole on bass, Clive Timperley on lead guitar, Richard Dudansky on drums (later a member of **Public Image Limited**), John Cassell on alto sax, Alvaro Pena on tenor sax, Jules on harmonica, and Joe "Woody" Strummer on vocals and guitar. The band eventually solidified when Mole was later replaced by Desperate Dan Kelleher on bass, keyboards, and vocals. The band was quite popular during the pub-rock scene of the early 1970s but was made all but redundant by the popularity of punk rock. Strummer left the band and joined the embryonic version of the Clash. A long-awaited CD version of the 101ers' session with 21 tracks, including original and mixes plus rare live and studio material, personally supervised by drummer Richard Norther with the cooperation of Strummer's widow, was finally released in 2005 after years of only poor-quality bootlegs available to the general market.
Discography: *Elgin Avenue Breakdown Revisited* (Astralwerks, 2005).

ONLY ONES

Poppy punk band lumped in with the early punk movement for commonality of style as opposed to ideological or sociological reasons. The Only Ones included lead singer and guitarist Peter Perret, Alan Mair on bass, Mike Kellie on drums (who had previously played with blues-rock

Spooky Tooth), and John Perry on guitar. The band is best known for its pop-punk singles "Lovers of Today" and "Another Girl, Another Planet," which would be covered by thousands of bands over the next several decades, including, notably, the **Replacements** in their live set. The Only Ones dissolved after three studio records in 1981, and Perret recorded sporadically after that, occasionally as the One, but to little success. The band was enormously influential on the indie rock scene, particularly on the work of Paul Westerberg and the Replacements.

Discography: *The Only Ones* (CBS, 1978); *Even Serpents Shine* (CBS, 1978); *Special View* (Epic, 1979); *Baby's Got a Gun* (Epic, 1980); *Remains* (Fr. Closer, 1984); *Alone in the Night* (UK Dojo, 1986); *Live* (Skyclad, 1989); *The Peel Sessions Album* (UK Strange Fruit, 1989). **England's Glory:** *Legendary Lost Recordings* (Skyclad, 1989).

OPERATION IVY

Another band that was far more influential after its demise than during its lifetime, Operation Ivy was the vanguard of the new **ska** revival in the United States, and guitarist Tim Armstrong and bassist Matt Freeman went on to form the far more successful **Rancid** several years after the demise of the band. During its heyday in the **Gilman Street** scene in Berkeley, California, the band was very popular for its anthems of unity within the scene and perceived authenticity. The band often played at Gilman Street in Berkeley, where their themes of unity against the outside world stuck a responsive chord with the local punk community. Although the band had only one official release on CD, *Operation Ivy*, and it was not well known outside of their local scene during their existence, it is now acknowledged as one of the most influential bands of the late 1980s.

Discography: *Hectic* EP (Lookout!, 1988); *Energy* (Lookout!, 1989).

ORANGE COUNTY

County in Southern California where many of the early California **hardcore** bands started out, including Middle Class (sometimes credited with having the first hardcore single, "Out of Vogue"), **TSOL, Agent Orange**, and the **Adolescents.** Many of the original punk elders of San Francisco, such as **John Doe** and Exene Cervenka from **X,** were later to blame the Orange County punks for bringing an element of danger and macho brutality to the scene, leading to the departure of many of the original scene members, especially women who found themselves increasingly unwelcome at shows and appalled by the more violent crowd who seemed more concerned with the pit than the actual music, as epitomized by TSOL, which had a notoriously violent following that often led to violence at shows. Gangs such as FFF, the Suicidals from Venice beach, and the LA Death Squad made shows less about the music and more about turf warfare. Later positive bands such as **Uniform Choice** (a **straight edge** band from Huntington) were almost as violent, and much of the scene was effectively over by the late 1980s, although new bands continue to form and tour from the Orange County scene.

OUTPUNK RECORDS

Independent U.S. record label specializing in queer punk bands started by zine publisher Matt Wobensmith, who also wrote a zine called *Outpunk*. The label released music by prominent queer, or queer-friendly, bands such as **Bikini Kill, Tribe 8,** Swine King, and **Pansy Division.** The label started off by releasing the influential compilations "There's a Faggot in the Pit" and "There's a Dyke in the Pit." Wobensmith ended Outpunk at the end of the 1990s and started the short-lived Queercorps label before founding the queer hip-hop label A.C.R.O.N.Y.M. Records.

PAGANS

Cleveland punk band from the first wave of the late 1970s, best known for their song "What's This Shit Called Love?" The Pagans were started as the Mad Staggers in 1974 by lead singer Mike Hudson on vocals and bass, his brother Brian on drums, and Lou Kolar on guitar, but by 1976 they had evolved into the Pagans with a new lineup that featured the Hudson brothers along with Mike "Tommy Gun" Metoff on guitar and Tim Allee on bass. The band fell apart while recording an album due to various financial and drug-fueled problems. The Pagans never recorded a proper album during their brief initial existence, but they released numerous classic punk singles.

Discography: *Shit Street* (Crypt, 2001); *The Pink Album* (Crypt, 2001).

PANSY DIVISION

Openly gay band from San Francisco, started in 1992, the band was one of the founders and one of the best known bands of the **queercore** movement. The band featured Jon Ginoli on guitar and vocals, Chris Freeman on bass, and a revolving drum chair, which created a sound that can best be described as a poppier **Ramones**-influenced band singing about the joys of sodomy and young, fem boys. Pansy Division first appeared on the *Outpunk Dance Party* compilation released by **Outpunk Records.** The band also released a record of mostly covers that included a hilarious **Nirvana** parody entitled "Smells like Queer Spirit." As promised in the queercore movement, Pansy Division is proof that the stereotype that gay men are only into dance music is patently false. Well, mostly. The current lineup also includes lead guitarist Patrick Goodwin and drummer Luis.

Discography: *Smells like Queer Spirit* EP (Lookout, 1992); *Undressed* (Lookout, 1993); *Deflowered* (Lookout, 1994); *Pile Up* (Lookout, 1995); *Wish I'd Taken Pictures* (Lookout, 1996); *More Lovin' from Our Oven* (Lookout, 1998); *Absurd Pop Song Romance* (Lookout, 1998); *Total Entertainment* (Alternative Tentacles, 2003).

PARENTS OF PUNKERS

Alarmist parents' group from California that advocated the "de-punking" of their children, basically as if young punks could be deprogrammed as if they belonged to a cult. The group regarded punks as inherently antisocial and nihilistic and saw punk as a dangerous lifestyle choice for their children. Parents of Punkers advocated a form of deprogramming to change children and teenagers back to normalcy, get them out of the seemingly garish outfits, and presumably stop their antisocial behavior. Founder Serena Dank appeared on talk shows such as *Donahue* with punks whom she had apparently "deprogrammed" back to normality and who talked about the violence inherent in punk (which was called a "violent cult") and demonstrated how to slam dance to presumably horrified parents. Other groups included the Back in Control Training Center and were mostly active in the early to mid-1980s, when the hysteria about punk rock reached its peak, before trailing off as more and more punk music and style were absorbed into mainstream culture. There are still several active groups among the born-again Christian community that attempt to convince young punks that they are living lives of sin (there are also Christian punk bands, the most famous being MXPX), but few parents are still trying to deprogram their children for owning a record by **Good Charlotte.** Supposedly, the band Suburban Menace had a song called "Serena Dank Fuck Off!"

PARTISANS

U.K. punk band formed in 1979 by Rob Harrington on vocals, Mark Harris on drums, Louise Wright on bass, and guitarist Andy Lealand, associated partially with the **oi** scene. After their first record in 1983, Dave Parsons replaced Wright and was eventually replaced by other bassists. The Partisans were in limbo from 1985 to 1999, when Harrington and Lealand got back together for reunion gigs, which continued sporadically.
Discography: *The Partisans* (No Future, 1983); *The Time Was Right* (Cloak and Dagger, 1984); *Police Story* (Anagram Punk, 2000); *Idiot Nation* (Dr. Strange, 2004).

PEACE PUNKS

Movement within the punk community that was more politicized and dedicated to anti-war protest and positive social change. Many of the U.S. peace punks were inspired by the **Ronald Reagan** administration to form or join groups such as the **Better Youth Organization** or **Positive Force** in order to organize protests against U.S. military incursions. Many peace punks refused to join any organizations (they opposed the concept of groups from an ideological standpoint), and many European peace punks and British peace punks supported local issues (such as protesting the Falklands War and excessive use of force by British police) and various international issues. (The many European, Asian, and African varieties of peace punks are beyond the scope of this work and should be investigated in more detail by those more familiar with the local scenes.) The heyday of peace punks' coverage in the media, and hence their visibility to many beyond the movement, was during the mid- to late 1980s and primarily concentrated on the **Washington, D.C.,** punk scene. Nonetheless, many punks still identify themselves as peace punks, and a new generation became politicized (although working within the system was also frowned upon by many in the punk community and some of the more extreme punks rejected any involvement with political systems or the capitalist enterprise) during the elections of 2000 and 2004 and the conflicts in Iraq, and some modern variants include Fat Mike's **Punkvoter.com.** The term remains ambiguous and is hardly accepted by all punks involved in political or social justice movements. *See also* Positive Force; Washington, D.C.

PEEL, JOHN

Influential and long-running British DJ known for his eclectic tastes and interest in new and independent music. Peel (John Robert Parker Ravenscroft) recorded live performances on radio show of almost every major band of the punk, **reggae,** hip hop, and electronic movements since the 1960s and had an uncanny sense of what the next exciting band or movement was going to be, despite his signature phrase bragging of being "the most boring man in Britain." His show aired on BBC radio from the 1960s until his untimely death from a heart attack in October 2004 while on a long-planned vacation. Not long before his death, Peel participated in an interview with the recently reformed **Undertones,** who had written "Teenage Kicks," what Peel had considered "the best song in the world." Peel had often remarked that he had wanted the line "Teenage Kicks so Hard to Beat" written on his tombstone. It is unclear as of this writing if his wishes had been carried out. His legacy continued in the numerous volumes of **Peel sessions,** recorded live during his radio program, that had been released and bootlegged for 30 years. Although some U.S. DJs had been sympathetic to punk rock (such as **Rodney Bingenheimer** in Los Angeles), it was John Peel who was the most sympathetic DJ involved in the punk movement, and his broad and eclectic tastes contributed immeasurably in disseminating punk (as well as other forms of underground and experimental music) to a wider audience.

PEEL SESSIONS

Recordings of bands live on the air on **John Peel's** show on BBC radio. These live sessions, such as by the **Undertones, Siouxsie and the Banshees,** the Cure, and numerous others, were recorded by the legendary DJ, who had pioneered inventive and outside-of-the-mainstream music since the 1960s. Some Peel sessions, such as the ones from the Undertones and **Napalm Death,** are just as essential as anything in the artists' catalogs. For many early bands, including those without recording contracts, this was also a convenient way to release material and gain publicity.

PENNYWISE

Ultrafast, melodic punk band from Hermosa Beach, California. The band first released the classic but dated EP *A Word from the Wise* in 1989, and the **Epitaph** label released their first full-length record, the eponymous *Pennywise,* in 1991. On *Pennywise* they finally distinguished themselves as different from the other punk bands crowding Southern California at the time. The original lineup featured Jim Lindberg on lead vocals, Jason Thirsk on bass, Bryon McMackin on drums, and Fletcher Dragge on guitar. Numerous other records followed in the same dynamic and powerful formula, and the band grew as extensive touring created a large and diverse fan base. Tragedy struck the band with the suicide of longtime bassist Jason Thirsk, who shot himself in 1996. The band paid tribute to Thirsk on the song "Bro Hymn Tribute" on the *Full Circle* album in 1997, and Ray Bradbury took over on bass. Pennywise was courted heavily by major-label bands during the post–**Green Day** feeding frenzy but decided they were better off selling hundreds of thousands of records on Epitaph rather then being mismarketed and eventually dropped by a major label. Pennywise continues and is one of the most popular U.S. **hardcore** bands.
Discography: *A Word from the Wise* EP (Theologian, 1989); *Pennywise* (Epitaph, 1991); *Wildcard* EP (Theologian, 1992); *Wildcard/A Word from the Wise* (Theologian, 1992); *Unknown Road* (Epitaph, 1993); *About Time* (Epitaph, 1995); *Full Circle* (Epitaph, 1997); *Straight Ahead* (Epitaph, 1999); *Live*

@ *the Key Club* (Epitaph, 2000); *Land of the Free?* (Epitaph, 2001); *From the Ashes* (Epitaph, 2003); *The Fuse* (Epitaph, 2005).

PERE UBU

Extremely long-running art-punk band from the fertile **Cleveland** punk scene led by lead singer Dave Thomas, who had formerly fronted the vastly influential (but hardly prolific) **Rocket from the Tombs** with Pete Laughner. Thomas formed Pere Ubu in 1975 following the demise of Rocket from the Tombs, and the original lineup included keyboard genius Allen Ravenstine and guitarist Tom Herman, who helped create the unique soundscapes that were Pere Ubu's signature, as well as drummer Scott Krauss and bassist Tony Mamione. In 1975, the band released its first single (and one of the first independent punk singles), "30 Seconds over Tokyo," and after the influential (but controversial) single "Final Solution," the band released its firsts album, *The Modern Dance*, in 1978. Equally adventurous albums followed in subsequent years, including *Dub Housing*. After innumerable personnel changes, the band still tours and records with Thomas and numerous new musicians. Pere Ubu's music remains almost uncategorical to this day, and new albums can be infuriatingly spotty as well as challenging. Pere Ubu may be one of the few bands that lived up to punk's promise of limitless creativity and experimentation. Pere Ubu's lyrics were also remarkable because they were written from Thomas's lifelong commitment to the Jehovah's Witnesses. In 2003, Thomas also re-formed Rocket from the Tombs, featuring Cheetah Chrome and Richard Lloyd (from **Television**), for tours and an album.
Select Discography: *The Modern Dance* (Blank, 1978); *Datapanik in the Year Zero* EP (Atlantic, 1978);*Dub Housing* (Chrysalis, 1978); *U-Men Live at the Interstate Mall* (Tricity, 1979); *New Picnic Time* (UK Chrysalis, 1979).

PETER AND THE TEST TUBE BABIES

Long-lasting English punk band that started in1978 and debuted on the *Vaultage 1978* compilation. The band featured singer Peter Bywaters, guitarist Derek "Del" Greening, bassist Chris "Trapper" Marchant, and drummer Nicholas "Ogs" Loizides. The band continued to record and tour, sometimes on the punk festival circuit.
Discography: *Mating Sounds of South American Frogs* (Trapper, 1983; Dr. Strange Records, 1997; Dojo, 1999; In&Out, 1999); *Soberphobia* (Hairy Pie, 1986; Castle, 1994; Captain Oi!, 2002); *Peter and the Test Tube Babies* (Rock Hotel, 1991); *Pissed and Proud* (No Future, 1982; Century Media, 1994); *Shit Factory* (Hp, 1990; Triple X Records, 1994; Goldr, 1999); *Rotting in the Fart Sack* EP (We Bite, 1995); *Journey to the Centre of Johnny Clarkes Head* (Dr. Strange Records, 1997); *Loud Blaring Punk Rock* (Hairy Pie, no date; Dr. Strange Records, 1997); *Test Tube Trash* (Dr. Strange Records, 1997); *Supermodels* (Dr. Strange Records, 1997); *Alien Pubduction* (Pub City Royal, 1998; Cargo, 2002); *Cringe* (Rebel, 1999); *Schweinlake* (We Bite, 1999); *The Punk Singles Collection* (Anagram Punk UK, 2000); *Best of Peter & Test Tube Babies* (Anagram Punk UK, 2001); *Loud Blaring Punk Rock* (Captain Oi!, 2002); *Live and Loud* (Step 1, 2003); *Paralitico* (Ryko, 2005).

PETTIBON, RAYMOND

Graphic artist, whose birth name is Raymond Ginn, and brother of **Black Flag** guitarist **Greg Ginn.** Pettibon did much of the artwork for album covers for bands such as Black Flag and the **Minutemen** and is best known as the "house artist" for Greg Ginn's **SST** label. Pettibon's work was challenging and controversial and often featured grotesque and blasphemous imagery in order to challenge his audience. A typical Pettibon cover was the album art of Black Flag's *Slip It In,* which featured a nun holding on to a muscular man. Although Pettibon was a prolific punk album cover designer, he was also a serious artist and became disillusioned because most punks did not appreciate his work as art. Today, his work is in major galleries across the United States, and the artist lives and works in Hermosa Beach, California. Some of his work is available online at the UBS Art Collection at http://www.ubs.com. Pettibon was one of a few select artists who helped create the look of the **Los Angeles hardcore** scene.

PHILOSOPHY OF PUNK

Book by Craig O'Hara, published in 1999, that tries to codify the disparate elements of punk. The book (the full title of which is *The Philosophy of Punk: More Than Noise*) argues that punk is by its nature antiestablishment, antiracism, antisexism, antihomophobia, profeminism, for animal rights, and inherently inclusive of diversity and difference. Although the book is an extremely worthy effort to give coherence to a massively incoherent and amorphous movement, it is unclear that the majority of those who identify themselves as punks would agree with the message in *Philosophy of Punk*. It is also unclear if a philosophy of punk can be, or should be, articulated due to the wide disparity of movements, cultures, and subcultures that exist within punk rock. It could be argued that O'Hara tried to articulate the philosophy of 1980s and 1990s North American **hardcore** punk rock, but even this is difficult to codify. Certainly hard-core anarchist punks would argue that you cannot try to reduce punk to one philosophy or that the philosophies of specific time periods and geographic locations have inherent differences; they are too vast to sum up in one book. The nature of punk rock and the **DIY** aesthetic makes it inherently difficult to try to sum up or explain punk rock. This point is further argued in the introduction to this encyclopedia.

PIT

One of the many names applied to the area where ritualistic dancing occurs during many punk shows. The most famous original punk dance was the **pogo,** a dance some claim **Sid Vicious** invented, which involved hopping up and down without much contact with other dancers. Later on, slamming became the norm at most punk shows, and the advent of **hardcore** punk led to a certain ubiquity and various parts of the pit being more dangerous than others. Most pits were hostile to women, and some were dominated by violent **skinheads,** who could be violent against those who were not from the local skinhead community, depending on location and what band was playing at the time. After the punk-metal crossover of the late 1980s, the term *moshing* became more prevalent as a way to describe activity on the floor. Many older punks violently decried the violence in the pit, and bands such as **Fugazi** often stopped shows that were too violent or too antiwomen or those pit dancers who would not allow women to dance or express themselves on their own. There were numerous forms of acceptable dancing, such as skanking, that varied from scene to scene and from band to band. Many women, especially in the **Washington, D.C.,** scene, were eventually disgusted by the groping and violence against women allowed in the pit and at some concerts fought back, either barring men from the pit as certain bands played or forming female-friendly pits where women could dance and express themselves. By the late 1980s, there was increasing concern about violence and antisocial behavior in the pit, and even **CBGB's,** home of the famous hardcore matinee, eventually decided to stop the matinees and ban most hardcore bands from the venue due to violence and lawsuits. After numerous lawsuits in various towns, many clubs stopped allowing pits to form or put up signs warning patrons that they danced at their own risk. Today, pits can be seen at many mainstream metal and hard rock shows, and the terms *mosh* and *moshing* are largely used to describe the dancing and physical activity that happens in front of the stage at concerts. The term *pit* is primarily a North American term that may be native to California and may not be in usage in other parts of the world. One of the many

A punk pit could be either exhilarating or frightening, depending on the crowd. © *Brian Sweeney.*

reasons that punk rock was considered to be violent by those outside of the punk community was media reports of violence in the pits or of the prevalence of the term *moshing*, which came to be associated with heavy metal concerts in the late 1980s and to the present. This does not mean that there were no pits simply devoted to communal and creative dancing and slamming. The pit was a key part of punk rock culture that was sadly tainted by violence, mostly from people outside of the scene or unaware of the communal nature of many punk rock scenes.

PIXIES

Noisy and raucous late 1980s and early 1990s U.S. band that laid the groundwork for the U.S. alternative movement of the 1990s and was one of the most influential bands of the 1980s and a prime influence on **Nirvana** and Radiohead, among many others. The Pixies were led by the enigmatic Black Francis (Charles Thompson), who later went by the name Frank Black in a semisuccessful solo career, and the oft-besotted Kim Deal (who early on went under the name of Mrs. John Murphy, her then-husband's name), who went on to form the enormously successful Breeders after the demise of the Pixies in 1992, along with guitarist Joey Santiago and drummer (and now magician) David Lovering. The Pixies were started by Black Francis, who early on had become obsessed with UFOs and outer space and had gained some of his fervent, almost preacherlike, vocals from his entire family becoming born-again Christians when he was 12. At the University of Massachusetts, Black Francis was paired with roommate Santiago, and the two decided to form a band. Kim Deal, who had previously (and again after the Pixies' demise) played in a band with her sister Kelley Deal, answered an ad for a female bass player for a band influenced by **Hüsker Dü** and Peter, Paul & Mary. After adding Lovering, a friend of Deal's husband, the band began playing as the Pixies. The band quickly established a style of its own with Black's lyrics, a bizarre mixture of David Lynch, biblical metaphor, and scene fiction allusions, as well as Santiago's unique guitar playing and the band's patented "whispered then shouted vocals" that demonstrated a complete disregard for what was occurring in the music scene during the late 1980s. Working with producer Gary Smith, the Pixies recorded what was then called the "Purple Tape," a collection of early songs that became *Come on Pilgrim*, the group's first EP for 4AD (others were released in 2003 by Spin Art as *Pixies*). Their first full-length EP, *Surfer Rosa*, recorded by antiproducer **Steve Albini,** was immediately hailed as a minor masterpiece upon its release in March 1988. After touring to enormous success (and causing friction with headlining band Throwing Muses when the Pixies' fans far outdrew Throwing Muses' fans), the band turned to English producer Gil Norton, who produced their breakthrough record, *Doolittle*, one of the most influential and important U.S. indie records of the decade. The Pixies scored minor radio and video hits with the songs "Monkey Gone to Heaven" and "Here Comes Your Man" and even cracked the U.K. top 10. A tour with the Cure exposed the Pixies to a newer group of fans, and the band reach the apex. Tensions soon arose between Black Francis and Deal over her intake of drugs and alcohol and her side project, the revived Breeders. The next album recorded with Norton took the Pixies in a more surf guitar direction, one that lost them some of their fan base. After more infighting, the rest of the band went to Los Angeles to work on their next record without telling Deal, who later was reluctantly asked to rejoin the band for the recording of their final album, *Trompe le Monde* in 1991. After supporting U2 on a U.S. tour, the Pixies were dissolved by Frank Black (Black Francis), who allegedly fired Deal by fax and the others via an interview about his first solo project. Deal went on to a huge success with the Breeders before her drug and alcohol intake sidelined her career. The Pixies reunited for a hugely successful string of shows in the United States and Europe in 2004 and continued to tour subsequently. The Pixies took the **DIY** aesthetic of punk rock and took punk's explorational side in a bold new direction that set the template for thousands of other bands and inspired the success of many of the most experimental bands of the early 1990s. They were one of the most significant U.S. punk bands.

Discography: *Come on Pilgrim* (UK 4AD, 1987; 4AD/Rough Trade, 1988; 4AD/Elektra, 1992); *Surfer Rosa* (4AD/Rough Trade, 1988; 4AD/Elektra, 1992); *Gigantic* EP (UK 4AD, 1988); *Doolittle* (4AD/Elektra, 1989); *Monkey Gone to Heaven* EP (4AD/Elektra, 1989); *Here Comes Your Man* EP (4AD/Elektra, 1989); *Bossanova* (4AD/Elektra, 1990); *Velouria* EP (UK 4AD, 1990); *Dig for Fire* EP (UK 4AD, 1990); *Trompe le Monde* (4AD/Elektra, 1991); *Planet of Sound* EP (UK 4AD, 1991); *Death to the Pixies* (4AD/Elektra, 1997); *At the BBC* (4AD/Elektra, 1998); *Complete B-Sides* (UK 4AD, 2000); *Pixies* (SpinArt, 2002).

PLASMATICS

Although the Plasmatics were one of the best known and most notorious punk bands of the late 1970s and early 1980s, they also had little to do with punk rock except for stylistic connections (such as the Mohawks sported by members Ritchie Stotts and Jean Beauvoir and singer Wendy O'Williams). O'Williams's outrageous antics, such as smashing television sets with a sledgehammer and exploding cars on stage while wearing little more than whipped cream or masking tape on her breasts, made the Plasmatics notorious and a bit of a joke to both the punk scene and to mainstream critics who used them to illustrate that there was no real message to punk other than **nihilism,** crass acts of autodestruction, and publicity stunts. The band was managed by O'Williams's companion Rod Swenson, who wrote many of the lyrics and helped the band generate controversy. Beauvoir left in 1981, and Stotts followed him after the *Metal Priestess* album, after which the newly reconstituted band recorded *Coup d'État* and then dropped the Plasmatics name and even recorded an ill-advised rap album. After several unsuccessful solo records, O'Williams retired to work for animal rights. She died of a self-inflicted gunshot wound in 1998.

Discography: *New Hope for the Wretched* (Stiff America, 1980); *Beyond the Valley of 1984* (Stiff America, 1981; PVC, 1991); *Metal Priestess* EP (Stiff America, 1981); *Coup d'État* (Capitol, 1982). **Wendy O'Williams:** *W.O.W.* (Passport, 1984); *Kommander of Kaos* (Gigasaurus, 1986); *Maggots: The Record* (Profile, 1987). **Ultrafly and the Hometown Girls:** *Deffest! and Baddest!* (Defest Disc/Profile, 1988).

PLASTIC BERTRAND

Belgian band featuring Roger Jouret (earlier of the famed Belgian punk rock band Hubble Bubble), formed in 1978. Their classic single "Ca Plane Pour Moi" can still be heard at sporting events in the United States. The band (Jouret, along with Lou Deprijk) sang silly, infectious, pop songs with French lyrics, an example of punk (later identified as **New Wave**) not taking itself all that seriously and somehow getting away with it to the tune of chart success. The band disbanded in 1982.

Discography: *Plastic Bertrand AN1* (UK Sire, 1978); *Ça Plane pour Moi* (Sire, 1978); *J'te Fais un Plan* (Bel. RKM, 1979); *L'Album* (Can. Attic, 1980); *Grands Succés/Greatest Hits* (Can. Attic, 1981); *Plastiquez Vos Baffles* (Can. Attic, 1982); *L'Essentiel: Best of Plastic Bertrand* (Emi, 2002); *King of the Divan: Best of Plastic Bertrand* (Emi, 2003).

PLEASE KILL ME

Oral history of the New York City punk movement written and compiled by original punks **Legs McNeil** and Gillian McCain and published in 1996 (full title *Please Kill Me: The Uncensored Oral History of Punk*). McNeil's strength is his close involvement with the early New York City punk scene and his close relationships with many of the musicians interviewed for the book. The book gives an account of punk's origins in the **protopunk** of the 1960s, and many of the major players of that decade, such as **Iggy Pop,** John Sinclair, the **MC5,** and **Lou Reed,** contextualize the nature of 1960s punk. When the book reaches the 1970s, McNeil himself becomes a participant because he (as the resident punk) and **John Holmstrom** of *Punk* magazine had a major influence not only in naming the new scene centered at **CBGB's** but also in interviewing and promoting the bands and artists they most enjoyed, such as the **Dictators** and the **Ramones.** The book is a noble attempt to document the often contradictory history of punk rock.

POGO

One of the early forms of crowd response to British punk shows, pogoing consisted of jumping up and down in place and sometimes from side to side. **Sid Vicious** is often credited as being the creator of the pogo, but its origins are unclear, and it is likely that many punks developed the pogo over time. After a while, the pogo became more interactive and gradually evolved into **slam dancing** (although many punks claim that they invented slam dancing and the concept of the pit). Occasionally, pogoing can be seen at the reunion tours of certain British punk bands, but the concept of the pogo seems as quaint today as the idea of **gobbing** (or spitting) on a band as they played. *See also* Gobbing; Pit.

POGUES

Irish punk band that mixed raucous punk energy with traditional Irish music, led by noted Irish writer, singer, and original **Sex Pistols** fan Shane MacGowan. The Pogues combined a love of traditional Irish music with the speeded up, frantic energy of punk rock and with the haunting and often brilliant lyrics of the troubled alcohol-fueled MacGowan, who can be regarded as one of the finest songwriters of the Irish tradition, even though he was born in Kent, England, and spent most of his life in London. The Pogues started playing in the

The Pogues, led by alcohol-fueled poet Shane MacGowan, fused Irish traditional music with punk. *Photofest.*

early 1980s when MacGowan decided to form a band that mixed traditional Irish music with punk's raw energy, and the band quickly became a major force in the Irish and punk scenes. MacGowan joined forces with drummer Andrew Rankin, bassist Cait O'Riordan (later to leave the band to marry Elvis Costello), Spider Stacey on tin whistle, banjo player and guitarist Gem Finer, and accordionist and multi-instrumentalist Jim Fearnley. In 1984, the band released their first album, *Red Roses for Me*, which mixed traditional Irish ballads with contemporary songs written by MacGowan, including the raucous "Boys of the County Hell," which indicated greater triumphs to come. The band expanded, adding more members, including guitarist Phillip Chevron, who had previously been in the Irish punk band Radiatorrs from Space, for the Elvis Costello–produced *Rum, Sodomy & the Lash*, which featured the hauntingly beautiful ballad "A Pair of Brown Eyes" and "The Sick Bed of Cuchulainn," which showed the depth of MacGowan's songwriting. An EP released after *Rum, Sodomy & the Lash*, *Poguetry in Motion*, contained one of MacGowan's finest moments, the ballad "A Rainy Night in Soho" and showed that his songwriting talents were growing by leaps and bounds. This was further confirmed by the Pogues masterpiece *If I Should Fall from Grace with God*, which featured a dizzying variety of songs, from the rave up title song to the party anthem "Fiesta" to the Pogues best-known song, "A Fairy Tale of New York," a duet with Kirsty MacColl, daughter of Irish songwriter Ewan MacColl, whose "Dirty Old Town" the Pogues had earlier covered. The Pogues had also expanded, replacing the departed O'Riordan with bassist Darryl Hunt and adding folk veteran Terry Woods on mandolin and other instruments. By *Peace and Love*, MacGowan's throat problems and excessive drinking had gotten out of control, and he wrote fewer songs, adding more contributions from Woods and Finer to the songwriting mix. An EP yielded the successful single "Yeah, Yeah, Yeah, Yeah," but the next album, the **Joe Strummer**–produced *Hell's Ditch*, which runs the gamut of styles from Irish to world music, found MacGowan becoming increasingly erratic, and he was asked to leave the band following the album's release. After touring with Joe Strummer as a lead vocalist, the band regrouped with Spider Stacey on lead vocals for the mediocre *Waiting for Herb*, which contained a few good numbers, including the lively "Tuesday Morning." The subsequent *Pogue Mahone* (the band's original name and an Irish saying meaning, essentially, "Kiss my ass"), without Woods, Chevron, or Fearnley, showed a lack of inspiration, and the band subsequently retired. MacGowan landed on his feet, first duetting with Nick Cave on the standard "What a Wonderful World" and then starting a new band, Shane MacGowan and the Popes. MacGowan toured and recorded sporadically with the Popes when alcohol or heroin didn't impair him. He was also hospitalized after a beating outside a London Pub. MacGowan may be one of the most brilliant and insightful songwriters of the twentieth century, but his excessive lifestyle and dissipated life may be for what he is best known. Shane maintained a fairly prolific solo career and in 2001 and 2004 reunited with the Pogues for several successful tours

Discography: *Red Roses for Me* (UK Stiff, 1984; Stiff/Enigma, 1986); *Rum, Sodomy & the Lash* (Stiff/MCA, 1985); *Poguetry in Motion* EP (Stiff/MCA, 1986; UK WEA, 1991); *St. Patrick's Night* EP (UK Pogue Mahone, 1988); *If I Should Fall from Grace with God* (Island, 1988); *Peace and Love* (Island, 1989); *Misty Morning, Albert Bridge* EP (UK WEA, 1989); *Yeah Yeah Yeah Yeah* EP (Island, 1990); *Hell's Ditch* (Island, 1990); *Essential Pogues* (Island, 1991); *The Best of the Pogues* (UK Warner Music, 1991); *The Rest of the Best* (UK Warner Music, 1992); *Waiting for Herb* (Chameleon/Elektra, 1993; Elektra, 1993); *Pogue Mahone* (UK Warner Music, 1995; Mesa, 1996); *The Very Best of the Pogues* (UK Warner Music, 2001). **Nick Cave & Shane MacGowan:** *What a Wonderful World* (Mute/Elektra, 1992). **Shane MacGowan and the Popes:** *The Church of the Holy Spook* EP (UK ZTT, 1994); *That Woman's Got Me Drinking* EP (UK ZTT, 1994); *The Snake* (UK ZTT, 1994, 1995; ZTT/Warner Bros., 1995); *Christmas Party* EP (UK ZTT, 1996); *The Crock of Gold* (UK ZTT, 1997); *Across the Atlantic* (UK Eagle Rock, 2001). **Popes:** *Are You Looking at Me?* EP (UK Scarlet, 1998); *Holloway Boulevard* (UK Scarlet, 1999; Snapper Music, 2000). **Various Artists:** *Straight to Hell* (Hell/Enigma, 1987). **Nips 'n' Nipple Erectors:** *Bops, Babes, Booze & Bovver* (UK Big Beat, 1987).

POISON GIRLS

British anarchist group allied with **Crass** and led by the older (for the time period) female vocalist Vi Subversa. The band started in 1977 when Subversa was inspired by the radical social and sexual politics of the time and decided to form a band with Richard Famous on guitar and Lance d'Boyle on drums. The band worked closely with Crass, particularly drummer Penny Rimbaud (J.J. Ratter), who produced the first two albums, and Crass vocalist Eve Libertine lent guest vocals to the first album. The band will be remembered not just for their attacks on the hypocrisy on social norms about family and the social system but for showing that the assumptions that punk was a movement purely for the young were premature, as demonstrated by Vi Subversa and Poison Girls becoming a major part of the anarchist punk movement in Britain.

Discography: *Hex* (Xntrix-Small Wonder, 1979); *Chappaquiddick Bridge* (UK Crass, 1980); *Total Exposure* (UK Xntrix, 1981); *Where's the Pleasure* (UK Xntrix, 1982); *I'm Not a Real Woman* EP (UK Xntrix, 1983); *7 Year Scratch* (UK Xntrix, 1984); *Songs of Praise* (CD Presents, 1985); *Statement: The Complete Recordings 1977–1989* (Cooking Vinyl, 1996); *Real Woman* (Cooking Vinyl, 1997); *Poisonous* (Recall Records UK, 1998).

POISON IDEA

U.S. **hardcore** band from Portland, Oregon, mostly active in the late 1980s and 1990s and led by the aptly named Pig Champion (Tom Roberts) on guitar along with Jerry Lang on vocals, Glen Estes on bass, and Dean Johnson on drums. The band's lyrics dealt with controversial subjects and were considered by some to be nihilistic and self-destructive and that they celebrated substance abuse and gluttonous eating. Poison Idea had a sound originally reminiscent of early punk bands with poor production, like the **Germs.**

Discography: *Pick Your King* EP (Fatal Erection, 1983; Taang!, 1992); *Record Collectors Are Pretentious Assholes* EP (Fatal Erection, 1985; Taang!, 1992); *Kings of Punk* (Pusmort, 1986; Taang!, 1992); *War All the Time* (Alchemy, 1987; Tim/Kerr, 1994); *Filthkick* EP (Shitfool, 1988); *Darby Crash Rides Again* EP (American Leather, 1989); *Ian MacKaye* EP (In Your Face, 1989); *Feel the Darkness* (American Leather, 1990; Tim/Kerr, 1994); *Official Bootleg* EP (American Leather, 1991); *Live in Vienna* EP (American Leather, 1991); *Dutch Courage* (Bitzcore, 1991); *Blank Blackout Vacant* (Taang!, 1992); *Pajama Party* (Tim/Kerr, 1993); *We Must Burn* (Tim/Kerr, 1993); *Religion & Politics Parts 1 & 2* EP (Tim/Kerr, 1994); *Your Choice Live Series* (Ger. Your Choice, 1994); *The Early Years* (Tim/Kerr, 1994); *Dysfunctional Songs for Co-Dependent Addicts* (Tim/Kerr, 1994); *Pig's Last Stand* (Sub Pop, 1996). **Jeff Dahl and Poison Idea:** *Jeff Dahl . . . Poison Idea* (Triple X, 1993).

POP GROUP, THE

One of the first and most strident **postpunk** bands that incorporated funk and **dub** into their incendiary attacks on capitalism and consumer culture. The band was formed in late 1977 in Bristol, England, featuring Mark Stewart on vocals, Simon Underwood on bass (replaced by Dan Catsis after the first album), Bruce Smith on drums, Gareth Sangeron on saxophone and guitar, and John Waddington on guitar. Influenced by john Cage and the anger of early punk, the Pop Group was noisy and aggressive postpunk and helped pioneer the style on their first album, *Y,* and on several essential punk singles, including a split single with the **Slits.** Like many of the bands at the time, the Pop Group took a more aggressive political stance, challenging not only the typical targets, such as the Tory government and Margaret Thatcher, but also directly attacking the hypocrisy of those in the punk movement who preached revolution, but they were largely silent on social issues. After the band broke up in 1980, lead singer Mark Stewart went on to form Mark Stewart and the Maffia, Gareth Sanger went on to form the band Rip, Rig & Panic, and Simon Underwood (who left after the first album) went on to form Pigbag. Lead singer Stewart continued to record under his own name.

Discography: **Singles:** "She Is beyond Good and Evil" (ADA, 1979); "We Are All Prostitutes" (Rough Trade, 1979); "Where There's a Will" (split single with the Slits; Rough Trade, 1980). **Full Length:** *Y* (UK Radar, 1979; WEA, 1996); *For How Much Longer Do We Tolerate Mass Murder?* (Y/Rough Trade, 1980); *We Are Time* (UK Y/Rough Trade, 1980); *We Are All Prostitutes* (Radar Records, 1998). **Pigbag:** *Dr. Heckle and Mr. Jive* (Stiff, 1982); *Lend an Ear* (UK Y, 1983); *Pigbag Live* (UK Y, 1983); *Favourite Things* (UK Y, 1983); *Discology: The Best of Pigbag* (UK Kaz, 1987). **Rip Rig & Panic Discography:** *God* (UK Uh Huh/Virgin, 1981); *I Am Cold* (UK Virgin, 1982); *Attitude* (UK Virgin, 1983). **Float up CP:** *Kill Me in the Morning* (Upside, 1985). **Mark Stewart and the Maffia:** *Learning to Cope with Cowardice* (UK Plexus, 1983). **Mark Stewart:** *As the Veneer of Democracy Starts to Fade* (UK Mute, 1985); *Mark Stewart + Maffia* (Upside, 1986); *Mark Stewart* (UK Mute, 1987); *Metatron* (Mute/Restless, 1990); *Control Data* (Mute, 1996); *Kiss the Future* (UK Soul Jazz, 2005).

POP PUNK

Pop punk is a term with multiple meanings, some of them derisive, and refers to punk that has harmonies, pronounced melodies, or, sometimes, commercial tinges. Contrary to much of the initial public perception, not all of punk rock was musically abrasive and rejected all of the conventions of traditional rock and roll. Many bands, especially early on, were trying to return to a more pop-based form of music that they felt had been rejected by the pomposity of 1970s art and progressive rock and roll. Many punk bands wore their allegiance to the quick and clever two- to three-minute pop song, and even early bands such as the **Ramones,**

Descendents, and **Bad Religion** were extremely indebted to pop music from the 1960s, as epitomized by harmony bands such as the Beach Boys, Big Star, and even the Brill Building songwriters and classic girl groups produced by Phil Spector during the early 1960s. (The Ramones were later to work with Spector on the ill-fated *End of the Century* album in a natural combination of the ultimate pop producer and the band that most epitomized the poppy hook-driven edge of early punk rock.) Many bands such as the Descendents and Bad Religion from the West Coast used harmonies and smoother, less aggressive vocals then many of their brethren on the East Coast, who would have decried the music as too soft. (An interesting parallel would have been to compare the vocals of a band such as the Descendents with New York's **Agnostic Front**). Although the movement more or less started with the Ramones, the **Dictators,** and other similar bands, the Ramones also played much harder, more metallic-tinged songs in their later years (and even embraced **hardcore** punk to a limited extent), and numerous bands followed in their wake. There are many different ways to describe pop punk, and many bands exist today that go by the name punk. **Green Day** is an example of a band that actually paid their dues on the punk scene while remaining very poppy, but the bands that imitated Green Day's style (who were imitating the Ramones, Descendents, Bad Religion, and any band that had a connection to pop music), such as Blink-182, Sum-41, **Good Charlotte,** and their brethren, have little connection to punk other than some fashion accoutrements and the poppy sound fostered by the earlier bands. Generally speaking, this is a U.S. phenomenon (there were also numerous bands from England, such as **Generation X,** and Ireland's the **Undertones** that could also have been described as pop punk, but British punk had significant stylistic differences with U.S. punk that led to many of their bands try to reject the trappings of the pop song). Today, the term is largely used as a pejorative by many in the punk community, and most bands reject the label, in much the same way that most bands who are saddled with the **emo** label also reject being called emo bands. Although some punk songwriters (such as the late **Joey Ramone**) were not ashamed to mention their love of pop music, the term is not universally accepted.

POSITIVE FORCE

Political punk movement started by Reno punk band **Seven Seconds** during the early 1980s and soon adopted by punks in numerous other cities, most famously in **Washington, D.C.,** where Positive Force worked closely with many in the punk community (including **Ian MacKaye** and Jeff Nelson from **Minor Threat** and **Dischord Records**) to combat the evils of weapons proliferation and the **Ronald Reagan** administration. The original Reno organization would book local shows and bands that Kevin Seconds, the cofounder of Positive Force and lead singer of **Seven Seconds**, wanted to play Reno, but the movement eventually fizzled out there as fewer people were involved. The group had it heyday in the mid- to late 1980s in Washington, D.C., but internal fighting and pressures soon led to many of the largest groups to cease functioning, schism, or revamps of themselves to operate as smaller, more effective coalitions. The best book-length account of the Washington, D.C., Positive Force scene is found in the book *Dance of Days: Two Decades of Punk in the Nation's Capital*, by Mark Andersen (who was, and still is, a member of Positive Force D.C.) and journalist Mark Jenkins, which details the intricacies and changes within the scene and within Positive Force. The Washington, D.C., version eventually had less to do with punk rock and more to do with community service, including delivering groceries to the elderly, and development of local groups and community centers. Positive Force has a Web site at http://www.positiveforcedc.org/, and Mark Andersen eventually wrote another book about the movement called *All the Power: Revolution without Illusion*.

POSTPUNK

Although any music after the initial wave of early to mid-1970s punk music could be labeled postpunk, the label specifically refers to a genre that arose out of the frustrations felt by many in the punk community that the initial punk musical "formula" was far too restricting for a movement that was supposedly based on experimentation. The term is usually applied to the movement circa the late 1970s and early 1980s and is usually used to refer primarily to bands such as **Public Image Limited** (led by former **Sex Pistols** singer **Johnny Rotten,** now going under his original name of **John Lydon**), Joy Division, **Gang of Four, the Pop Group,** the **Slits,** and others that expanded the musical palate of punk rock to include elements of **reggae, dub,** funk, and dance music. Postpunk in England was also a reaction to how punk had not been political enough and had failed to achieve any real social change. Many of those who first followed punk realized that the new generations of fans and second wave of punk and **hardcore** bands realized that the new fans and bands had come to the punk rock scene not just because of the celebration of difference but because of its conformity and the chance to play dress up and sing along. Other bands realized that the sonic experimentation of European bands such as Kraftwerk, Neu, and **Can** had shown the possibility of experimenting with instruments outside of the typical guitar, bass, and drums lineup, which dominated the punk scene. The other clear change brought about by postpunk was the influence of black musical styles such as **ska, reggae,** and disco, which were incorporated by many of the more adventurous of the postpunk bands. The **2 Tone** scene that dominated British music for a few years in the late 1970s and early 1980s can also be seen as a postpunk reaction to the political and musical limitations of punks. The term did not really get as much usage in the United States as it did in England, and the term **New Wave** was largely (an wrongly) used to describe the more electronic types of music that proliferated in the late 1970s and early 1980s in the United States. Numerous bands today such as Erase Errata and Interpol seek to re-create the postpunk sound and image.

PRETTY IN PUNK

A 2002 academic look at the role of women in punk by author Lauraine Leblanc. The book (full title *Pretty in Punk: Girls' Resistance in a Boys' Subculture*) examines how women are often marginalized and, at worst, abused by men and boys, who tend to forcefully dominate the various permutations of punk rock scenes. The book contains many interviews with street punks and provides a valuable insight into how many women feel marginalized, even in the supposedly more liberatory climate fostered by punk's anarchist ideology.

PROFANE EXISTENCE

Profane Existence (P.E.) is an influential and long-running punk **zine** that was created by an anarchist collective from Minneapolis that also runs a record label and distributes other small labels. The zine deals with **DIY** issues, punk social movements, and direct action against the system and advocates for change on social issues. Current issues can be obtained for free, and the zine also has a Web site at http://www.profaneexistence.com. *Profane Existence* has greatly contributed to the vitality of the DIY and underground scenes in the United States for the last several decades.

PROFESSIONALS

Post–**Sex Pistols** band with Steve Jones and Paul Cook and bassist Andy Allen (later replaced by Paul Meyers from **Subway Sect**). The band recorded one album before Jones relocated to the United States after being arrested for possession of **heroin,** essentially ending the band.

Discography: *Didn't See It Coming* (Virgin, 1981).

PROMISE RING, THE

Milwaukee **emo** punk band from the mid-1990s that recorded several records for **Jade Tree Records.** The band was one of the most prominent emo bands of the late 1990s and along with bands like Sunny Day Real Estate and Jimmy Eat World helped to popularize emo for a new generation of more mainstream fans. The band consisted of lead singer and guitarist Davey von Bohlen, John Gnewikow on guitar, Scott Bescheta on bass (later replaced by Tim Burton—not the filmmaker—and, later, Scott Schoenbeck), and Dan Didier on drums. The band went through various tragedies, including an almost fatal van crash and a benign brain tumor for von Bohlen, and broke up after releasing the more indie-rock-oriented *Wood/Water* in 2002.

Discography: *30 Everywhere* (Jade Tree, 1996); *Horse Latitudes* (Jade Tree, 1997); *Nothing Feels Good* (Jade Tree, 1997); *Very Emergency* (Jade Tree, 1999); *Wood/Water* (Anti, 2002).

PROPAGHANDI

Canadian punk rock band from Winnipeg, Manitoba, and one of the more literate and politically active bands of the 1990s, the members were active in a variety of causes, including vegetarianism and animal rights. The band consists of Chris Hannah on vocals and guitar, Todd Kowalski on bass and vocals (preceded by John Samson), and Jord Samolesky on drums and vocals. The band formed the label G7 Welcoming Committee Records.

Discography: *How to Clean Everything* (Fat Wreck Chords, 1994); *Less Talk, More Rock* (Fat Wreck Chords, 1996); *Where Quantity Is Job #1* (G7, 1998); *Today's Empires, Tomorrow's Ashes* (G7, 2001).

PROTOPUNK

Although there is some disagreement about the exact year or decade in which punk rock began, most scholars date punk rock from the early to mid-1970s and refer to bands and movements that preceded that period as *protopunk*. Examples of this genre would be **Iggy and the Stooges,** the **MC5,** the **Monks,** the **Seeds,** the **Music Machine,** the **Sonics,** and many other bands that are often today called *garage* or other terms (although some had called that brand of music punk during the late 1960s). The Nuggets' series of compilations of rare (and well-known) U.S. garage rock from the 1960s curated by future **Patti Smith** guitarist Lenny Kaye is also regarded as a treasure trove of protopunk. Most scholars identify the two primary 1960s protopunk bands as the Stooges and the MC5 (although some critics and scholars mention the influence of the Doors, and admittedly **Iggy Pop** owes much of his early image and look to those cultivated by Doors singer Jim Morrison), who are certainly two of the bands most cited by such early punk bands as the **Ramones** and the **Sex Pistols** in interviews as being bands that influenced their musical direction. The Stooges album **Raw Power** is regarded by many as a seminal prepunk album, and many punk bands covered the anthemic **"Search and Destroy."** Other bands sometimes lumped under the protopunk label are bands as diverse as the **Velvet Underground** (an influence on many in attitude and style and their lack of outside influences but musically not a band imitated by most in the early punk scene), Jonathan Richman and the **Modern Lovers** (the Sex Pistols were known to cover "Roadrunner"), and the **Dictators,** who certainly are a stepping stone between 1960s rock and early 1970s punk rock. Many of the best of the

1960s bands were captured on the Nuggets' albums (and boxed set) curated by musicologist Lenny Kaye, which illustrate how ubiquitous garage, or protopunk, was across the United States during the 1960s.

PSYCHOBILLY

Musical movement mixing **rockabilly** style and rhythm along with themes from science fiction and horror films and campy and often explicit sexual references and images. The **Cramps** are the best-known proponents of the movement, and the style is codified on the first few Cramps records.

PUBLIC IMAGE LIMITED

John Lydon's post–**Sex Pistols** band featuring original punk scene maker Jah Wobble (John Wardle), Keith Levine, formerly of the **London SS** and the earlier incarnation of the **Clash,** original drummer Jim Walker, along with conceptual artist Jeanette Lee. Their debut album, *Public Image*, was released in December 1978 and dealt with Lydon's disillusionment with the recording industry, organized religion, and the former management of the Sex Pistols. Although the first record was received by critics with mixed reviews, most critics were astonished by the second release, *Metal Box*, which came out with several 12-inch records inside a tin box, hence the Metal Box of the title (subsequent editions as well as reissues on CD were renamed *Second Edition*). The sound of Metal Box was as radical in its way as the original Sex Pistols sound and helped found a genre known as postpunk, which was a combination of punk, funk, **dub, reggae,** and abrasive noise. In a particularly bizarre moment on U.S. television, the band appeared on Dick Clark's *American Bandstand* in May 1980 to lip-sync to "Careering" and "Poptones," but, instead, a bored John Lydon waded into the audience, and the show nearly became a riot, much to Clark's delight. Despite television promotions and critical acclaim, *Metal Box* did not break the band into the United States, although it did make them a critical success. This work was achieved in a rare moment of relative calm in the Public Image Limited camp, and things were not to last. The band went through numerous personnel changes early on, and Wobble was asked to leave the band in a controversy over ownership of several music tracks. Levine left during the production of *This Is What You Want . . . This Is What You Get* in 1984, and subsequent albums such as *Album* (also released in a no-frills food style as *Tape* and *CD*) found Lydon working with a diverse group of musicians, including Ginger Baker and Steve Vai. Public Image Limited remained a draw in Europe and the United States and had several minor video and radio hits, but the band was never as inspired as they were for the first several records when breaking ground was the norm. Lydon soldiered on in Public Image Limited with various sidemen (although *Happy?* did feature John McGeoch from **Siouxsie and the Banshees** and Magazine along with Lu Edmonds from the **Damned**) until he dissolved the last version of Public Image Limited in the late 1990s. Lydon subsequently reformed the Sex Pistols for tours in 1996 and 2004 and appeared on several British and U.S. television shows such as *Rotten TV* and *Get Me out of Here, I'm a Celebrity*. The work of Public Image Limited is still considered as groundbreaking and influential as it was in the beginning, and even if it didn't live up to its ultimate potential, it paved the way for the experimentation of indie and underground music from the 1980s to the present.

Discography: *Public Image* (UK Virgin, 1978); *Metal Box* (UK Virgin, 1979); *Second Edition* (Island, 1980); *Paris au Printemps* (UK Virgin, 1980); *The Flowers of Romance* (Warner Bros., 1981); *Live in Tokyo* (UK Virgin, 1983; Elektra, 1986); *This Is What You Want . . . This Is What You Get* (Elektra, 1984); *Commercial Zone* (PiL, 1984); *Album* (Elektra, 1986); *Cassette* (tape; Elektra, 1986); *Compact Disc* (CD; Elektra, 1986); *Happy?* (Virgin, 1987); *9* (Virgin, 1989); *The Greatest Hits, So Far* (Virgin,

John Lydon's second band, Public Image Limited, proved that the Sex Pistols were no mere puppets working for Malcolm McLaren and thus established Lydon as the father of post-punk. *Photofest.*

1990); *That What Is Not* (Virgin, 1992); *Plastic Box* (UK Virgin, 1999). **John Lydon:** *Psycho's Path* (Virgin, 1997).

PUNK

A movement or series of cultural movements involving music, ideology, fashion, oppositional politics, and a *DIY* and antimainstream sensibility that is generally agreed to have been solidified in the early 1970s in New York City and in London as epitomized by bands such as the **Ramones, Richard Hell** and the **Voidoids, Television, Patti Smith,** the **Sex Pistols,** the **Clash, Buzzcocks,** and many others. Punk was preceded by many bands who can be considered pre-punk or **protopunk,** and although many considered it to have ended in a specific time period, it continued in different forms, such as **postpunk** and **hardcore,** and in various underground movements across the United States. There is no one acceptable definition of punk rock that is accepted by punks in the United States or in other countries, and the idea of punk is one that is the subject of much debate among punks on the local level and in larger **zines** such as *Punk Planet* and *Maximum Rock 'n' Roll.* See also Hardcore; Introduction; Postpunk; Protopunk.

PUNK

Very influential New York magazine started in late 1975 by illustrator and super music fan **John Holmstrom** along with his friends "resident punk" **Legs McNeil** and Ged Dunn. In the debut issue, Holmstrom and his crew of writers made a case for a new brand of underground rock and roll that challenged the mainstream rock that clogged the airwaves in the early 1970s. Holmstrom and his friends had been looking for a project to work on, and after rejecting the idea of founding a movie company, Holmstrom found a storefront complete with furniture that was perfect for working on a magazine. Holmstrom had become disillusioned with most of contemporary rock, had seen the **Ramones,** was aware of other bands such as the **Dictators, Iggy and the Stooges,** and Alice Cooper, and was known for his taste in music in a time when the music scene in the United States was filled with corporate rock bands. Holmstrom was aware that rock fans were craving more involvement with music. Holmstrom convinced McNeil, who wanted more to be a publicist, to be the resident punk of the magazine, due to his lack of rock critic credentials, and with several others helping out, the magazine was born. The magazine showed that it wanted to be something different when it featured in the first issue an interview with the Ramones and a cartoon cover of, and interview with, **Lou Reed.** The first issue of *Punk* came out in December 1975, although the name *Punk* had been used in various permutations previous to the start of the magazine (Lenny Kaye, among others, had used the term to describe garage rock bands; Holmstrom himself recalls first seeing the term in *Creem Magazine*). Holmstrom's magazine was the first one to use the term to describe the music scene at **CBGB's.** Holmstrom had wanted to name the band after a **New York Dolls** song, but McNeil had suggested that the term *punk* would sum up the philosophy of the magazine, which essentially was about the pop culture and new music that Holmstrom championed. The magazine was an instant success with a print run of at least 4,000, which sold out quickly, even with independent distribution, became an instant collector's item, and gained immediate acclaim from the *Village Voice* and other music newspapers that seemed to recognize that *Punk* "got" what was going on in new music and culture. (Complete sets are available on eBay now for several hundred dollars.) The next few issues were equally innovative and tried a variety of different forms, such as Fumetti issues (issues in which photos were assembled together to tell a story), which unfortunately were the least popular of *Punk*'s run. Subsequent issues highlighted the new bands around CBGB's and also featured the magazine's version of journalism, which included McNeil's interviews with celebrities such as Sluggo and Boris and Natasha. Holmstrom was essentially trying to re-create the sense of urgency and sense of involvement for music that had dominated the best prepunk and garage rock of the 1960s and that was reborn in New York City in the 1970s. The magazine ended far before its time with issue 18 completed but never seeing the light of day, thanks to several factors, including the demonization of punk by the media and Seymour Stein's memorandum to radio stations begging them to call the music by the less threatening term **New Wave.** Other magazines also sprang up that were inspired by punk, such as *Sniffin' Glue* in England, which feuded with *Punk*, not realizing that *Punk* was not only a commentary on the movement but also a parody of what it celebrated. The magazine made celebrities out of McNeil and Holmstrom and established them as key commentators on punk rock. Ironically, the best-selling issue of *Punk* was issue 16, the disco issue. *Punk* is still regarded as the most influential magazine that covered punk rock and popular culture at the time. Although it is much imitated (and often blatantly copied), there is no comparison between *Punk* and other **zines** and magazines.

PUNK AND DISORDERLY VOLS. I–III

Influential record compilations of largely British bands that celebrated the scene during the early 1980s. Bands such as **Vice Squad, Peter and the Test tube Babies,** the **Exploited,** the Expelled, Abrasive Wheels, the **Partisans,** UK Decay, the **Adicts,** and the **Dead Kennedys,** among others, were featured. The compilations are also referenced in a song by **NOFX** that celebrates a scenester so punk that he "should have been on the cover of *Punk and Disorderly.*"

PUNK AND GENDER. *See* Gender and Punk

PUNK AND MASS MEDIA REPRESENTATIONS

There has always been a tenuous relationship between punk and mass media. The reason for this is that, traditionally, most representations of punk music, or those who choose to identify as members of the punk subculture, have often struggled with representations in mass media that bore little resemblance to reality. From the **Sex Pistols'** appearance on England's *Today* show with Bill Grundy in which several of them caused outrage (when goaded by an obviously inebriated Grundy, they cursed on air) to the tabloids' subsequent outrage at the "foul mouthed yobs" and their dubbing the scene the "filth and the fury" to the scandalized approach and sensationalism of the U.S. press in which typical reactions included the famous *Quincy* episode in which punks are seen as potential killers moved by the incessant beat of punk to murder their friends to the violent punk so prevalent in movies such as *Class of 1984* and *Star Trek IV: The Voyage Home*. News reports in the United States were no less scandalized by the U.S. version of punk, and numerous articles have appeared since the mid-1970s decrying the punk invasion and even offering advice as how to "convert" your children back from being punks. For this, many punks distrust the representation of punk in mass media (with such exceptions as Penelope Spheeris's *Decline of Western Civilization* movies and smaller films that seemed to get it right: *Suburbia, Repo Man,* and even *Rock and Roll High School*). Many punks in recent years have worked on blogs, **zines,** films, and public-access cable programs to provide a more nuanced version of a much misunderstood subculture. The rise of skate punk and newer, less political bands that wear punk outfits, such as Sum-41, Blink-182, and **Good Charlotte,** have revived the image of the punk as party animal that so many political punks worked to change during the 1980s and 1990s. The fact that punk fashions can now be bought in most U.S. malls shows that although media representations may be stereotypical, they are also appealing to a younger generation of potential punks. Overall, since the start of punk, most representations have been stereotypical and have revealed more about the inherent prejudices toward youth cultures in mass media than they have revealed any great understanding of a complex and diverse subculture.

PUNK AND RACE

Punk has always had an ambiguous relationship with the issue of race. Although the punk ethos was one of inclusion, the scene was often hostile to outsiders, and, in particular, non-whites often had trouble within the scene. Although there was a complex relationship in England between the English punk bands and **reggae** music, aided by the efforts of DJ and filmmaker **Don Letts** and reggae fiends the **Clash,** the United States had a much more complex relationship with race issues. Even bands as forward thinking as **Minor Threat** and **Black Flag** wrote songs ("Guilty of Being White" and "White Minority") that could be (falsely) misconstrued as white-power anthems. Although the **Bad Brains** were one of the most popular acts in **hardcore** (and were also one of the least tolerant bands in hardcore) and there were probably very few white-power and **Nazi punks** in the United States, there were instances of violence at shows. D. H. Peligro of the **Dead Kennedys,** who was black, was occasionally the focus of racist taunts and was chased by **skinheads** who had no idea that he was the drummer for one of their favorite bands. The general lack of African Americans and other minorities in the punk and hardcore scenes in the United States was the focus of the documentary *Afro-Punk* by James Spooner.

The British scene also had a complex relationship with race, and although there were few actual black faces on the punk scene, there was much cross-pollination between the British punk scenes and the local reggae scenes. In the early days of punk, before many punk singles were released, DJ **Don Letts** would play mostly reggae singles before a band went on, and this may have led some punks to take an interest in a black-oriented (and in some cases antiwhite) musical form. Britain in the late 1970s, however, also saw numerous attacks by the racist and fascist **National Front** and had openly white-power bands such as **Skrewdriver.** Although the scene is slightly better integrated now, there remains a distinct problem in the punk and hardcore scenes regarding the issue of race and racism. *See also* Bad Brains; National Front; Minor Threat; Punk; Reggae; Skrewdriver.

PUNK AND TECHNOLOGY

Punk has often had an ambiguous relationship with technology in two ways. First, in the opposition of many punks, particularly **crust punks** and **peace punks,** to such forms of technology as factories, nuclear power, and weapons, some of the most famous punk demonstrations, such as the ones organized by **Crass** in England and around the world in the mid-1980s and the demonstrations in the **Washington, D.C.,** scene in the 1980s and 1990s, were also antitechnology in terms of being against nuclear weapons. The second concern is the ambivalence that many punks feel toward ways of expressing music (vinyl versus CD), recording music (analog versus digital), and distributing information (**zines** on paper versus Web sites). **Steve Albini,** in particular, has been extremely vocal as to what he considers the proper uses of technology in punk rock, and many musicians strive to use antique analog equipment in order to get a sound that is considered more "authentic." Many anarchist punk bands, in particular, were somewhat united in their rejection of the technologies that could be exploited for violence or destruction, and this ties in with the increasing prevalence of environmental activists in the punk movement.

PUNK BOOKS

This category can be divided into books about punk rock (such as autobiographies, biographies, critical examinations, histories, etc.) and books of fiction or semifiction that are written by punks or with a punk perspective. Some of the best-known books about the punk movement includes Jon Savage's *England's Dreaming,* **Legs McNeil's** and Gillian McCain's *Please Kill Me,* and Roger Sabin's *Punk Rock: So What? See* the Selected Bibliography for a more complete listing of works that examine punk rock from a variety of perspectives.

PUNK FASHION

Punk fashion depended upon the scene, country, and location and could range anywhere form the garish (safety pins, **Mohawks,** leather, and bondage outfits) to the seemingly mundane (suspenders, **Doc Martens,** sweatshirts, shaved heads, etc.). Initially, the U.S. scene as it started in New York City had no one uniform style. **Richard Hell** wore ripped clothing with safety pins and **Malcolm McLaren** was inspired by Hell to bring this look back to England and popularize it in his store. The members of **Television** and **Patti Smith's** band did not dress in a particularly memorable way, but the **Ramones,** with their stylized uniform of ripped jeans,

This punk girl wears a studded leather jacket, extreme makeup, nose ring, chains, and a dog collar. Punk is about individuality and self-expression. © *Derek Ridgers.*

sneakers, leather jackets, and bowl haircuts, started a stylistic revolution that inspired bands on both sides of the Atlantic. McLaren (who had previously changed the look of the **New York Dolls** from semidrag to red leather outfits), inspired by Hell's look, helped pioneer a new punk style of fashion that was soon imitated by countless punks

Hardcore punk involved several different styles, depending on the scene and what was predominant from city to city. Although people did sport Mohawks and liberty spikes and still dressed in leather, many in the hardcore scene adopted a more sedate fashion style. Many in the hardcore communities of **Los Angeles** and **Boston** dressed to intimidate as a reaction to the savage beatings and assaults that many punks had to endure for looking different. The shaved head, outside of the regimented skinhead look, was very often a preemptive strike against possible attackers. Many old-school hardcore punks made their own T-shirts with magic markers or dressed in "U.S." working-class style in ripped jeans, engineers' boots, chains, and sometimes leather jackets, the older and more worn in the better. Some punks such as the members of **Suicidal Tendencies** wore bandannas in specific colors to denote affiliations with scenes or gangs. Flannel shirts (which were pioneered by Mike Watt from the **Minutemen** and bands such as **Bad Brains**) were often worn (long before grunge appropriated the look) tied around the waist as a sort of cape, which was also a concession to the sometimes un-air-conditioned

A punk girl sports a red Mohawk. Punk hair was designed to stand out and mark the punk as part of a subculture. © *Ted Polhemus.*

clubs where shows were held during the summer or because of the sweat induced by a session in the pit. The ubiquitous **straight edge** X on the hand was also a fashion statement of a kind, and some members of the scene did not attend shows without clearly showing their allegiance to the straight edge movement. For footwear, Converse All Stars were often the sneaker of choice. Women often wore berets or caps, kilts or plaid schoolgirl skirts, and ripped sweaters. Hardcore hair could be shaved, but occasionally liberty spikes and spiked and mussed hair were common as well. **Tattoos,** as epitomized by the heavily inked **Henry Rollins** and many members of the New York City hardcore scenes, where members would get band names tattooed on their bodies to show allegiance or membership, became a form of **body art** in the 1980s for the U.S. scene, and gradually tribal art patterns and piercing began to become more common as well.

PUNK IS DEAD

By the late 1970s and early 1980s, especially in ever-impatient Great Britain, the music press (and many in the punk movement) was thoroughly disgusted by what appeared to be the inherent stagnation in the largely three-chord-based histrionics and empty posturing of latter-day punk bands such as **Slaughter and the Dogs, UK Subs,** and **Peter and the Test Tube Babies.** Many in the U.K. rock critics' scene also thought that punk had reached a dead end because it had failed (outside of the **Clash** and a few other notable exceptions) to incorporate other types of music (such as **reggae,** dance music, and disco) and that little social and political change had occurred, despite the urgency and political scope of early punk music. Other critics decried what they perceived as the insular and often xenophobic nature of the punk movement and disparaged punk for its latent homophobia and apparent racism in ignoring the (largely black and gay) dance music that was sweeping Britain at the time. Many others within the scene decried the involvement of major labels and large corporations and the fashionability of punk rock, as epitomized by runway shows and punk fashion being used in movies and television. Even punk bands such as **Crass** decried this loss of purity. On the other side of the Atlantic, many others, especially influential radio program and later zine *Maximum Rock 'n' Roll,* shared much of this attitude and began the almost endless internal debate in punk rock of what was truly "punk" and what was merely a pose adopted by trendy outsiders to take the look and attitudes of punk and commodify them. The **Clash** sang, "Huh, you think it's funny? Turning Rebellion into Money." By the early 1980s, this argument was later rendered moot by the demise and/or transformation of most of the original bands into **postpunk** or heavy-metal-influenced bands and the rise of hardcore punk in the United States and the United Kingdom, which attracted much of the youth subculture that would have followed the older bands. This notion of the "death" of punk seems to be debated every five years or so and will, no doubt, be debated far into the future. (This also relates to controversies in the so-called rockist and antirockist critical camps, which endlessly and tediously debate the critical approaches now necessary in a world that may—or may not be—post the era of rock and roll.) Whether punk rock is dead is a largely subjective question and remains a subject of fierce debate. Perhaps a better way to analyze punk rock would be to see it as a series of overlapping movements as opposed to a community. Perhaps the question itself it irrelevant or inadequate. *See also* the Hardcore; Introduction; Punk.

PUNK MOVIES

The tem *punk movie* is a difficult term to pin down because there are numerous films about punk, many with different degrees of success and authenticity in capturing the scene. On the one hand, punk filmmakers such as **Nick Zedd** and **Don Letts** captured punk on film at the time and/or made films inspired by punk rock. Numerous attempts were made to document the early scene, and Don Letts's *Punk Rock Movie* was instrumental in demonstrating the musical depth of the genre. There were numerous other punk documentaries as well, including *The Filth and the Fury, The Great Rock 'n' Roll Swindle, Afro-Punk, End of the Century,* the *Decline of Western Civilization Parts I and III,* and numerous others. Although many films about punk took their time to get the mood and music right (*Repo Man* and *Suburbia* and even *Rock and Roll High School*), numerous others just used punks for shock value, such as *Star Trek IV, Class of 1984,* and *Return of the Living Dead.*

PUNK PLANET

One of the most influential and widely read of punk **zines.** It was started by Daniel Sinker in 1994 as a bimonthly zine out of frustration with the orthodoxy of modern punk rock and to give exposure to bands and **DIY** activity that *Maximum Rock 'n' Roll* would not cover. The zine has also released books of interviews published in the zine over the years. *Punk Planet* remains one of the most highly respected zines in the history of punk rock, and its influence can be felt in how much more inclusive modern punk has become in terms of music and ideology.

PUNK ROCK AEROBICS

Punk rock workout classes, video, and book created by Maura Jasper and Hilken Mancini, designed to help aging punks shed pounds and tighten their beer guts. The book *Punk Rock Aerobics: 75 Killer Moves, 50 Punk Classics and 25 Reasons to Get off Your Ass and Exercise* was released in 2004. The book and classes received mainstream media coverage but were largely portrayed as a joke by television stations that covered Punk Rock Aerobics. The seriousness of the authors' intent is unclear, but they seem to be veterans of the punk scene and have a commendable knowledge of punk rock.

PUNK'S NOT DEAD

For every naysayer who proclaimed that punk was dead, new and old punk bands and luminaries proclaimed them wrong, or at least premature. One of the key songs by U.K. überpunks the **Exploited** proudly proclaimed that "Punk's Not Dead" in reaction to the prevailing trend in the music industry and in newspapers and magazines that punk rock was no longer viable and that it was time to move on to the next big thing. Many of the early U.S. punks in both the **Los Angeles** and **New York** punk scenes also proclaimed that punk rock was dead when major labels began to market bands such as **Blondie** as **New Wave** and **hardcore** punk replaced the early scenes in both cities. Later on in the United States, a movie featuring **Green Day, Sonic Youth,** and **Nirvana** labeled 1991 as *The Year Punk Broke,* indicating that punk was not dead (at least not by that point), and numerous others in the scene have variously wrote anthems declaring that punk was still a viable force. A problem may also be the sense of propriety that many in the early scenes had about their music and the newfound sense of indignation and ownership that many younger punks had after discovering the music for the first time. It is still an arguable point as to whether punk is dead or alive and whether or not punk has simply been constantly revived by different generations or whether punk is a continuous, uninterrupted movement that simply was ignored by mass media for prolonged periods of time or died and was resurrected by subsequent generations. The argument that punk (and other types of underground music) simply went underground and below the radar or mainstream media is persuasively made by Michael Azzerad in his book *Our Band Could Be Your Life* in which he documents such seminal 1980s punk bands as **Black Flag** and the **Minutemen,** which kept punk's spirit alive through relentless touring and underground promotion through **zines, flyers,** and other underground communication techniques.

PUNKVOTER.COM

Web site and movement started by Fat Mike of **NOFX,** dedicated to political change and defeating George W. Bush in the 2004 U.S. presidential election. Punkvoter.com made inroads in the sometimes apathetic punk scenes across the United States through relentless promotion on the **Warped tour** and through online promotions. Although it can be argued that Punkvoter.com was minimally successful in getting many punks to register to vote, it is nonetheless an indicator that many young punks in 2004 were taking the idea of voting more seriously and that some older punks who had long considered working within the parameters of a capitalist system to be selling out were becoming more involved in the political system.

"PUNKY REGGAE PARTY"

Solidarity anthem by **reggae** giant Bob Marley that acknowledged the affinity of early British punk and reggae as social movements concerned with social justice as well as having a good time. The song mentioned that fellow reggae fans such as the **Slits** and the **Clash** would also be in attendance at the punky reggae party, inexplicably alongside Dr. Feelgood, a pub rock band not overly concerned with politics. The song represents a key moment in which the usual one-sided embrace of reggae by punk bands was acknowledged by Bob Marley, the most popular reggae artist in the world at that time. The song might possibly also have been inspired by famed DJ and filmmaker **Don Letts,** who was renowned for playing reggae at punk clubs long before reggae was popular in the mainstream, and perhaps added to a sense of solidarity between two dispossessed cultures. Needless to say, "Punky Reggae Party" was eminently danceable.

PYRAMID BELTS

Belts with pyramid-shaped spikes. Latter-day punk fashion of choice.

QUAALUDES

Drug of choice for many in the **New York punk** scene and very prevalent at clubs such as **Max's Kansas City** and other places during the early scene. Some of the early punks used quaaludes to counter the high from other drugs.

QUEERCORE

Queercore was a movement designed to highlight one of the most ill-kept secrets in **punk rock**—the prevalence of gay men and lesbians as members of the scene and innovators within punk rock—as well as to demonstrate the discontent and anger felt by many in the punk community to the mainstream gay and lesbian communities, which in certain ways were seen as just as dogmatic as the insular punk community. Key bands (although not all of them accepted this label) included **Pansy Division** and **Tribe 8.** Although many early members of the scenes in **Los Angeles** and **New York** were openly gay, this was not the case in many scenes, particularly in the U.S. Midwest, where antigay slurs and violence sometimes occurred against same-sex affection. Even though members of **hardcore** bands such as **MDC** and the **Big Boys** were openly gay, the 1980s was not the most progressive decade in the U.S. punk community. By the 1990s, things had changed somewhat on the grassroots level, and many bands such as the extremely political Tribe 8 and **Team Dresch** were not only openly out but also fiercely confrontational about their sexual identify (or their rejection of the notion of a fixed sexual identity). The early zine *J.D.'s*, which was started by G.B. Jones and Bruce LaBruce in 1985, which originally used the term *homocore* to describe the new movement (which was later considered too limiting and replaced by the more inclusive *queercore* appellation), helped spawn the scene. Originally, Jones and LaBruce had published a manifesto entitled "Don't Be Gay" in *Maximum Rock 'n' Roll,* and that was a more or less wake-up call to the punk scene that its queer members were less than pleased by the marginalization of queer culture in what was supposed to be an all-inclusive movement. *J.D.'s* inspired the zines *Holy Titclamps* by Larrybob, *MomoCore* by Deke Nihilson, *Outpunk* by Matt Wobensmith, and *Chainsaw* by Donna Dresch, which provided queer youth within the punk movement a forum for discussion about greater diversity and establishing a uniquely queer **DIY** aesthetic. The first queercore compilation, *J.D.'s Top Ten Homocore Hit Parade Tape*, was released on cassette and included international queercore bands such as Fifth Column, Nikki Parasite, the Apostles, and Academy 23, some of which were not necessarily queer but supported the stance taken by queer punks. Although this marked the end of *J.D.'s*, the movement soon spread, and other bands such as God Is My Co-Pilot, Pansy Division, Team Dresch, Tribe 8, and Fifth Column demonstrated the musical breadth of the movement. Although many of the bands had to either form their own labels or join with friends' labels, such as Chainsaw and **Candy Ass Records,** soon indie labels such as **Lookout Records, Kill Rock Stars,** and **Alternative Tentacles** also began to showcase queercore bands. The queercore movement also embraced different musical styles and was not limited to hardcore, which many felt was too heteronormative in its musical and lyrical stance. This was reflected in newer bands such as Addicted 2 Fiction, Ninja Death Squad, and Excuse 17, which were far more diverse than the earlier bands. There are even queer **straight edge** bands such as Limp Wrist. In addition, festivals such as Homo a Go Go, held yearly in Olympia, Washington, provided a showcase for queer zines, bands, music, and film and acted as a gathering place for like-minded activists.

QUEERCORPS

Label that released numerous bands in the **queercore** and homocore movements during the 1990s.

QUEERS

Catchy, and despite the name, non-queercore band with a very obvious debt to the **Ramones** (they once covered the entire Ramones record *Rocket to Russia*) and Beach Boys. Led by Joe King, the Queers have been touring in one incarnation or another, making remarkably similar music, since 1982, although the band only really started to take themselves seriously when original lead singer Wimpy Rutherford left and King took over lead vocal duties. The classic lineup featured Hugh O'Neill on drums and B-Face on bass and released numerous albums during the 1990s that all were remarkably consistent (some critics would say derivative) in a never-ending quest to create first the ultimate Ramones homage and, later, the ultimate Beach Boys homage. Although not a joke band per se, the Queers music is dominated by a gleefully demented sense of humor, usually about the topics of girls ("Ursula Finally Has Tits," "She's a Cretin"), alcohol ("Next Stop Rehab," "I Only Drink Bud"), and the Ramones (almost every song). Hugh and B-Face were gone by the late 1990s, and King now tours with assorted sidemen under the Queers name. Hugh died of a brain tumor, and the band continued with a new lineup.

Discography: *Love Me* EP7 (Doheny, 1982); *Kicked out of the Webelos* EP7 (Doheny, 1984); *Grow Up* (UK Shakin Street, 1990; Lookout!, 1994); *A Proud Tradition* EP7 (Doheny, 1992; Selfless, 1993); *Too Dumb to Quit* EP7 (Doheny, 1993; Selfless, 1993); *Love Songs for the Retarded* (Lookout!, 1993); *Look Ma, No Flannel* EP7 (Clearview, 1994); *Beat Off* (Lookout!, 1994); *Surf Goddess* EP (Lookout!, 1994); *Rocket to Russia* (Selfless, 1994; Liberation, 2001); *Shout at the Queers* (Selfless, 1994); *Suck This* (Clearview, 1994, 1996); *The Queers Move Back Home* (Lookout!, 1995); *Surf Goddess* EP (Lookout!, 1995); *My Old Man's a Fatso* EP7 (Wound Up, 1995); *A Day Late and a Dollar Short* (Lookout!, 1996); *Bubblegum Dreams* EP7 (Lookout!, 1996); *Don't Back Down* (Lookout!, 1996); *Everything's O.K.* EP (Hopeless, 1998); *Punk Rock Confidential* (Hopeless, 1998); *Later Days and Better Lays* (Lookout!, 1999); *Beyond the Valley . . .* (Hopeless, 2000); *Today* EP (Lookout!, 2001); *Live in West Hollywood* (Hopeless, 2001).

QUICKSAND

Late 1980s and early 1990s experimental **hardcore** band that featured former members of **Gorilla Biscuits** and **Youth of Today** and Absolution guitarist Tom Capone and laid down crunchy metallic riffs over which lead vocalist Walter Shreifels screamed out lyrics. The band put out two highly acclaimed, but poor selling, albums and an EP before they broke up in 1995 and the members went on to various side projects and reunions with old bands.

Discography: *Quicksand* EP (Revelation, 1990); *Slip* (Polydor, 1993); *Manic Compression* (Island, 1995).

QUINCY

Long-running TV show featuring Jack Klugman as a medical examiner who solved crimes in his spare time. It is infamous among the punk community for attacking punk in an episode titled "Next Stop, Nowhere," which aired on December 1, 1982. In the episode, Quincy investigates the ice-pick–slaying of a young punk named Zack, who was killed while slam dancing. The conclusion of the episode is that the nihilistic lyrics of punk rock are at least partially to blame for the death of the young punk. Quincy wonders when will this madness end? Although this episode seems relatively innocuous, it is a key example of how mainstream media tried to assimilate and explain the punk movement to the United States, often using the most sensationalistic methods possible. As usual, the highly exaggerated and sensationalized version of punk shown on *Quincy* and in movies such as *Class of 1984* (and even *Start Trek IV: The Voyage Home*) was that of punks as violent predators and nihilists, blindly striking out at society. This image of punk was prevalent, especially during the late 1970s and early 1980s, and was reflected in reality by the often heavy-handed tactics of police in Los Angeles and New York City or crimes committed by punks or those who wore punk fashion. *See also* LAPD; Nihilism; Punk and Mass Media.

RADIATORS FROM SPACE

Irish **punk** band that featured a future member of the **Pogues.** Originally formed in Dublin as Greta Garbage and the Trash Cans, an idea of Stephen Rapid (Stephen Averill), members included Philip Chevron on guitar, who later joined the Pogues, Peter Holidai on guitar, Mark Megaray on bass, and James Crash on drums. The band changed its name to the Radiators and released its debut record in July 1979. The band reunited—and included Cait O'Riordan, who also played bass in an earlier version of the Pogues and who later married and divorced Elvis Costello—and continued to tour sporadically.

Discography: *TV Tube Heart* (UK Chiswick, 1977); *Ghostown* (UK Chiswick, 1979, 1989); *Buying Gold in Heaven: The Best of the Radiators (from Space)* (Hotwire, 1985); *Dollar for Your Dreams: The Radiators Live!—Aid to Fight AIDS Benefit, Dublin, September 13th, 1987* (Comet, 1988); *Cockles and Mussels: The Very Best of the Radiators* (Chiswick, 1995); *Alive-Alive-O! Live in London (1978) + Rare Studio Tracks* (Chiswick, 1996); *TV Tube Heart* (Big Beat UK, 2005).

RADIO BIRDMAN

Australian **punk** band led by the Michigan-born Deniz Tek, who played in a style reminiscent of the Stooges (the band's name comes from the Stooges' 1970 song). Radio Birdman influenced a brand of raw guitar rock that both predated and anticipated punk. The band did not last long, but Sub Pop reissued its music in 2001, which led to a reunion tour.

Discography: *Burn My Eye* EP (Aus. Trafalgar, 1976); *Radios Appear* (Aus. Trafalgar, 1977; Sire, 1978); *Living Eyes* (Aus. WEA, 1981); *More Fun!* EP (Aus. WEA, 1988); *Under the Ashes* (Aus. WEA, 1988); *Radio Birdman: The Essential 1974–1978* (Sub Pop, 2001).

RADIO TOKYO

Studio in **Los Angeles** where many early **punk** singles were recorded.

RAMONE, DEE DEE

Founder and bass player (born Douglas Colvin) for most of the history of the **Ramones.** Many of the Ramones' most influential songs were written by Dee Dee and referenced his problems with substance abuse and mental illness. Dee Dee was one of the key people involved in early **New York punk,** and his tough-guy persona may not have been an act (as indicated in the song "53rd and 3rd") because Dee Dee had worked as a male hustler and may have been provoked to violent acts against his johns. Dee Dee seemed to the British punks to be the epitome of the tough New York City street punk, and **Sid Vicious** was particularly taken with Dee Dee's persona, even to the extent of imitating aspects of Dee Dee's look. After years of turmoil and after not speaking to members of the Ramones for many long and unsettling van drives across the United States, Dee Dee finally quit the Ramones in 1989 and was replaced by C.J. Ramone, who eventually sang several of Dee Dee's songs live. Although he never rejoined the band, Dee Dee did write songs for the Ramones sporadically and worked with Marky and C.J. Ramone in Dee Dee's solo projects after the Ramones broke up. Infamously, Dee Dee produced a solo rap record as Dee Dee King in 1989, which was not exactly groundbreaking in terms of rap. As he struggled to stay clean and healthy, Dee Dee toured sporadically with bands that included other Ramones and occasionally his new wife. Shortly after the Ramones were inducted into the Rock and Roll Hall of Fame, Dee Dee Ramone died of a **heroin** overdose in California. He was featured in a documentary titled *Hey Is Dee Dee Home?*, which played to some acclaim. Dee Dee Ramone will be remembered as a pioneer of punk whose songs were essential to the Ramones success and also, sadly, as a poster boy for the rock star as dissolute artist struggling with a drug problem.

Discography: *Standing in the Spotlight* (Sire Records, 1989).

RAMONE, JOEY

Founder and lead singer (born Jeffrey Hyman) of the **Ramones.** A legendary front man who loomed large across both the concert stage and **punk** history. Joey Ramone was as rooted in 1960s garage rock as he was in the intricacies of the Phil Spector wall of sound prevalent in the girl groups he enjoyed so much. It was his unique voice, along with Johnny Ramone's guitar wall of noise, that made the Ramones the enormously influential band that they were. Joey never enjoyed good health, and after falling in New York, his lymphoma reoccurred and he died of it in 2001. After his death, a solo record was released (one he had been working on for several years with frequent collaborator Daniel Rey) that highlighted his health crisis and his love of girl groups, pure pop songs, and television stock market analyst Maria Bartilomo. The album fittingly contained a version of the Louis Armstrong classic "What a Wonderful World," demonstrating Joey's place in the pantheon of U.S. singer-songwriters. Longtime friend **Legs McNeil** is writing a biography of Joey Ramone. *See also* Ramone, Dee Dee; Ramones.

Discography: *Don't Worry about Me* (Sanctuary Records, 2002).

RAMONES

Along with the **Sex Pistols** one of the two most influential bands in **punk** rock history and arguably the band that either created or at least first articulated the 1970s version of punk. The influence of the Ramones is vast, and almost every punk band learned or stole ideas from the "brothers" from Queens. The original lineup included Johnny Ramone (John Cummings), **Dee Dee Ramone** (Douglas Colvin), **Joey Ramone** (Jeffrey Hyman), and Tommy Ramone (Tommy Edrelyi). The Ramones came from Forest Hills, Queens, New York, and came together to form the Ramones in the early 1970s. The Ramone's first gig was on March 30,

1974, and the band played around the city for a few months before learning about the new scene that was developing at **CBGB's,** where the Ramones quickly started a residency. The fans were first repelled, and then enraptured, by the new sound and the band's lightning-speed sets, punctuated only by shouting matches between the Ramones about what song to play next. A key moment in punk rock history occurred on July 4, 1976, when the Ramones gave a legendary performance at the Roundhouse in London. The performance was attended by members of the **Clash, Damned,** Sex Pistols, and numerous other punk bands who later indicated that a key impetus in them forming bands was watching the Ramones' legendary show. The band was signed by Seymour Stein to Sire Records and recorded their first album, the self-titled *Ramones,* in 1976. The record was laid down in record time and with a low budget but accurately reflected the Ramones' sound and velocity, which led to numerous instances of DJs playing the record for a few seconds and then flinging it across the room. The Ramones continued to be popular in New York, but the rest of the United States proved a harder nut to crack. The Ramones began their legendary cross-country tours in a small van, a practice that would see the band playing thousands of shows until the band retired in 1996. Several other records followed, but, despite critical acclaim and extremely devoted fans in the major cities, the Ramones could not find a home on radio, even when producing incredibly poppy songs that were played at lightning speed.

The Ramones were given some exposure in the United States, most notably in the film *Rock and Roll High School.* Roger Corman, the king of the B-movie industry, set out to make a film that capitalized on the disco craze but was dissuaded from this and decide to film a movie about

The Ramones were truly one of the most influential punk bands of all time. *Photo by Roberta Bayley/ Evening Standard/Hulton Archive/Getty Images.*

rebellion at a high school in Los Angeles. After going through several title changes, concepts (from "Heavy Metal High School" to "Disco High School"), and potential bands (Tod Rundgren and Cheap Trick were both considered), the Ramones were chosen to become punk movie stars. In late 1979, the Ramones filmed their scenes in the Roger Corman low-budget extravaganza *Rock and Roll High School* in California, arriving onscreen singing "I Just Wanna Have Something to Do" in a convertible driven by Los Angles DJ **Rodney Bingenheimer.** During the filming of *Rock and Roll High School*, the band, needing more tour money than the $5,000 that Corman was paying for their time spent filming, played three disastrous gigs with Black Sabbath during which the Ramones endured more abuse from hostile fans. More trouble ensued when they had to take Dee Dee Ramone to the hospital after he took pills that fans were throwing at the Ramones while on set. After the completion of *Rock and Roll High School*, the Ramones embarked on their most ambitious doomed project to date, recording the album *End of the Century* with legendary producer Phil Spector. The work with Spector proved to be disastrous, and Spector spent 10 hours listening to the opening chord of *Rock and Roll High School* and eventually threatened the Ramones with a loaded pistol. Even with Spector's glossy wall-of-sound production, the record did not sell many more copies than previous records (although the album did sell more than any Ramones album to that date, it did not enter the U.S. top 40), although it did spawn a British top-10 single with "Baby I Love You," a charting the band had not accomplished previously. After the disappointing recording sessions with Spector, the Ramones returned to their relentless touring schedule and continued to produce records, always with diminishing returns. The band went through several painful personnel changes, first in 1978 with the retirement of original drummer and Ramones visionary Tommy Ramone, who desired to work more in production and songwriting for the band (a notion quickly shot down by the band's stern taskmaster, Johnny Ramone), then replacement Marky Ramone (Mark Bell, the original drummer for **Richard Hell** and the **Voidoids**) left in 1983 due to problems with alcoholism and was replaced by Ritchie Ramone (Ritchie Beau), who left after three years because he was not paid the same as a full-time member. Marky returned in 1987 and stayed with the band until the Ramones disbanded in 1996. Many fans were disappointed when founding member Dee Dee Ramone quit the band in 1989 and was replaced by C.J. Ramone, who adopted Dee Dee's look and even sang some of his songs in concert. Due to Joey's failing health and the general rigors of touring, the band decided to retire in 1996 after several farewell tours that saw packed houses of rapturous fans. In particular, the band had become enormously popular in Latin and South America, where they played in stadiums and to screaming fans who mobbed their cars. After the Ramones retired, Johnny Ramone sold his legendary Mosrite guitar and moved to California, and Joey became a vocal supporter of numerous bands in the **New York** scene. The story of the Ramones was later documented in a film called *End of the Century,* which was released in 2004 and shown on public television in 2005. The documentary was an open and frank account of the dissension within the band (precipitated by Johnny Ramone marrying Joey's girlfriend, Johnny's role as the taskmaster of the group, Dee Dee Ramone's drug problems, and Joey's struggles with obsessive-compulsive disorder). Joey Ramone died of lymphoma in 2001. Dee Dee Ramone died of a **heroin** overdose in June 2002. Johnny Ramone died of cancer in September 2004. The Ramones were much more popular in the United States after their careers were over than they were during their lifetimes, and their songs could be heard in movies, commercials, and in baseball stadiums across the country. The lasting legacy of the Ramones was as producers of the template for punk rock that, literally, thousands of bands borrowed and stole from to lesser effect. The Ramones remained respected and loved by those who discovered the secret knowledge of the founders of punk rock.

Discography: *Ramones* (Sire Records, 1976); *Leave Home* (Sire Records, 1977); *Rocket to Russia* (Sire Records, 1977); *Road to Ruin* (Sire Records, 1978); *It's Alive* (UK Sire, 1979); *Rock and Roll High School*

(Sire Records, 1979); *End of the Century* (Sire Records, 1980); *Pleasant Dreams* (Sire Records, 1981); *Subterranean Jungle* (Sire Records, 1983); *Too Tough to Die* (Sire Records, 1984); *Animal Boy* (Sire Records, 1986); *Halfway to Sanity* (Sire Records, 1987); *RamonesMania* (Sire Records, 1988); *Brain Drain* (Sire Records, 1989); *All the Stuff (And More) Volume I* (Sire Records, 1990); *All the Stuff (And More) Volume II* (Sire Records, 1991); *Loco Live* (Sire Records, 1992); *Mondo Bizzaro* (Radioactive, 1992); *Acid Eaters* (Radioactive,1994); *Adios Amigos* (Radioactive, 1995); *Greatest Hits Live* (Radioactive, 1996).

RANCID

Rancid was one of the few commercially popular **punk** bands of the mid- to late 1990s that was still regarded by its fans as keeping its punk integrity. Rancid was led by Tim Armstrong (ex-husband of Brody Dalle of the Distillers), who took the sound of his former band **Operation Ivy** (in which he played guitar under the name Lint) and combined it with obvious influences from the **Clash** and other late-1970s punk bands to create a commercially successful version of punk rock. The band started as a trio in the early 1990s with Armstrong, former Operation Ivy bassist Matt Freeman, and drummer Brett Reed to release the heavily Clash-influenced first album, *Rancid*. After the first record's success, the band decided to augment its sound with the addition of second guitarist and vocalist Lars Frederickson (who had also played in British punk stalwart the **UK Subs**) in 1993, and the next record, *Let's Go*, proved to be one of the few punk crossover records to gain airplay on major radio stations and **MTV**. The next record, . . . *And Out Come the Wolves*, was a major breakthrough that showed Rancid experimenting with **ska, reggae,** and **dub** on songs like "Roots Radicals" and the hits "Ruby Soho" and "Time Bomb," which established Rancid as one of the most popular punk bands in the world. *Life Won't Wait* continued the formula to more artistic and creative, but less commercial, success. The following record, *Rancid*, was a return to the band's **hardcore** roots but seemed to put Rancid in a holding pattern that would last for the next four years. When Rancid finally returned with a new album in 2003, *Indestructible*, the band had lived though the deaths of close friends, Armstrong's messy divorce, and bouts with alcoholism. The renewed creative energy, diverse musical styles and arrangements, and the theme of the record—Rancid as a community—reestablished them as one of the best bands in the United States. Although the band faced continual criticism for signing to a major label and sounding like the Clash, Rancid remained one of the most vital and imaginative musical forces on the contemporary U.S. punk scene. Armstrong also ran **Hellcat Records** and played in the joke punk/rap band the Transplants.

Discography: *Rancid* (Epitaph, 1993); *Let's Go* (Epitaph, 1994); . . . *And Out Come the Wolves* (Epitaph, 1995); *Life Won't Wait* (Epitaph, 1998); *Rancid* (Hellcat/Epitaph, 2000); *Indestructible* (Hellcat, 2003). **Operation Ivy:** *Hectic* EP (Lookout!, 1988); *Energy* (Lookout!, 1989).

RAR (ROCK AGAINST RACISM)

British social movement designed to raise awareness of racist and Nazi movements in England in the late 1970s. Numerous **punk** bands played at Rock against Racism benefits (most of the gigs took place in and around London from 1977 to 1978). The movement also may have been partly inspired by Eric Clapton's infamous onstage remark in Birmingham in 1976 when he claimed that he "wanted to keep Britain white" as well as comments by **David Bowie** and other musicians. The British police often used heavy-handed tactics against members of the organizations that sponsored Rock against Racism, as documented in the **Ruts** song "Jah War." It is unclear how many punk bands supported Rock against Racism; **Siouxsie and the Banshees** wrote songs with questionable ethnic slurs. Most of the concerts were successful, however, and many punks worked to fight against racism in both England and the United States.

RAT

Boston club where many of the early **Boston punk** bands such as **Unnatural Axe** played during the heyday of punk. The club persisted long into the age of punk and **New Wave** and continued to showcase Boston's best as well as touring bands until its demise.

RAW POWER

Album by **Iggy and the Stooges** that is seen by most as the missing link between the **protopunk** of the 1960s and the aggressive but artistic punk of the 1970s. The album was recorded in 1973 by the reconstituted Stooges, featuring James Williamson on guitar and longtime guitarist Ronnie Asheton switching to bass. The album is considered by many to be a precursor to 1970s punk, especially in songs such as the title song, "Search and Destroy," and "Gimme Danger." Many fans complained about the original mix by **David Bowie,** and subsequent rereleases featured alternate mixes, including a 1997 remix by **Iggy Pop** that restored some of the power of the original album.

RAZORCAKE

Influential zine from **Los Angeles** that covers **punk** rock and popular culture with contributors such as Nardwuar and Rev. Norb. *Razorcake* is one of the most popular and most influential **zines** in the United States and does not conduct the punk litmus tests so common to other zines that deal with the punk rock scene. The zine has a Web site at http://www.razorcake. com. Razorcake also sponsors an independent book publisher, Gorsky Press.

REAGAN, RONALD

Focal point for much **punk** outrage in the 1980s and referenced in many punk songs such as "I Shot Reagan" by **Suicidal Tendencies** and "Intensified Chaos" by Intensified Chaos. An anarchistic punk band took the title **Reagan Youth** during the early 1980s, and in the mid-1980s a notorious campaign of civil disobedience by punks in the **Washington, D.C.,** scene opposed Reagan's foreign and domestic policies through open protest, benefit concerts, creative graffiti, and posters that decried various members of the Reagan administration.

REAGAN YOUTH

Reagan Youth was a classic **New York hardcore,** anarchist, **crust punk, peace punk** band formed in 1980 by Dave Insurgent (Dave Rubenstein) and Paul Cripple (Paul Bakija) on guitar when the members were still in high school. Reagan Youth made its mark on the New York City scene alongside bands such as **Agnostic Front** and the **Cro-Mags,** with whom the band played many **CBGB's** hardcore matinees on Sunday afternoon during the 1980s. The band broke up in the late 1980s after President Ronald Reagan left office and the band's name became obsolete. Various members played in loose aggregations after the band's demise but never had the level of success enjoyed by Reagan Youth. Rubenstein spiraled into drug addiction along with his girlfriend Tiffany, a prostitute who was killed by Long Island serial killer Joel Rifkin, and Rubenstein subsequently committed suicide.
Discography: *Fist* LP (New Red Archives, 1984); *Volume 1* (New Red Archives, 1989); *Volume 2* (New Red Archives, 1990); *A Collection of Pop Classics* (New Red Archives, 1994); *Live & Rare* (New Red Archives, 1998); *Punk Rock New York* (LoveCat Music, 2004).

RED KROSS (RED CROSS)

Originally recording as Red Cross, the MacDonald brothers, Jeff and Steve, formed this Los Angeles band in 1978 when Jeff was 14 and Steve was 11. Their first public performance was at an eighth-grade graduation party, which also starred an embryonic **Black Flag.** The MacDonald brothers formed the band as a reaction to their antipathy for the local surf bands and as an outlet for the MacDonald brothers' creativity. The original band featured the MacDonald brothers, along with Greg Heston on guitar and John Stelia on drums (replaced soon by Ron Reyes, who replaced Keith Morris in Black Flag). Numerous personnel changes shook the band (including Dez Cadena, pre–Black Flag, on guitar) before settling on a lineup of Tracey Marshak on guitar and Janet Housden on drums (a rare example of female representation in an early **hardcore** punk band) for the *Born Innocent* record. The band then changed directions, and Jeff and Steve grew their hair and changed the band's name to Red Kross so as to not be confused with the charitable organization. Even though the band made the cover of *Flipside,* Red Kross had by then abandoned hardcore for a more melodic, hippie-inspired, psychedelic sound, as epitomized by *Neurotica* in 1987.

Discography: *Red Cross* EP (Posh Boy, 1980, 1987); *Born Innocent* (Smoke 7, 1982; Frontier, 1986); *Teen Babes from Monsanto* (Gasatanka, 1984); *Neurotica* (Big Time, 1987; Five Foot Two/Oglio, 2002); *Third Eye* (Atlantic, 1990); *Phaseshifter* (This Way Up/Mercury, 1993); *2500 Red Kross Fans Can't Be Wrong* EP10 (Sympathy for the Record Industry, 1994); *Show World* (This Way Up, 1997). **Various Artists:** *Desperate Teenage Lovedolls* (Gasatanka, 1984); *Lovedolls Superstar* (SST, 1986). **Tater Totz:** *Alien Sleestacks from Brazil* (Gasatanka/Giant, 1988); *Sgt. Shonen's Exploding Plastic Eastman Band Request Mono! Stereo* (Gasatanka/Giant, 1989); *Tater Comes Alive!* (Sympathy for the Record Industry, 1992). **Anarchy 6:** *Hardcore Lives!* (Gasatanka/Giant, 1988); *Live Like a Suicidal* (tape; Dutch East Tapes, 1991).

REED, LOU

Often regarded as one of the founding fathers of **punk** rock for his groundbreaking and influential work with his legendary band the **Velvet Underground** and for his decadent and adventurous work in the early 1970s. Reed's work was influential in the **New York** punk scene of the early 1970s in particular, and he was featured on the cover of the first issue of *Punk* magazine. Reed was a prolific pop songwriter and student of legendary writer Delmore Schwartz, who formed the band the Velvet Underground in 1965. After the demise of the Velvet Underground, Reed took several Velvet's songs and recorded his first album with Rick Wakeman and Steve Howe (both of art rock band Yes!) as session musicians. The *Lou Reed* album was a constrained continuation of the work Reed had been doing with the Velvet Underground, and it wasn't until the *Transformer* record, produced by **David Bowie,** that Reed reached his full potential on songs such as "Vicious," "Perfect Day," and the radio hit "Walk on the Wild Side," all of which celebrated the decadence of the New York glam and factory scenes. (Most of the characters in the song "Walk on the Wild Side" were members of Andy Warhol' entourage.) With *Berlin,* Reed turned more somber, perhaps reflecting his own personal disintegration into drug and alcohol dependency, but he proved his vitality with the aggressive live album *Rock n Roll Animal,* cementing his position as a proponent of what would soon be called punk rock. Reed was the feature story and was on the cover (via a **John Holmstrom** illustration) of the first issue of *Punk* magazine, demonstrating the debt the scene owed Reed. After *Rock n Roll Animal,* Reed's work, in many cases, became much less inspired and deliberately difficult, as in the case of the notoriously unmistakable *Metal Machine Music,* which Reed supposedly recorded in an attempt to get out of his contract with RCA Records. Other good work followed on *The Blue Mask* and *The Bells,* but Reed settled into apparent complacency until returning strongly with the *New York* concept record and the collaboration with old pal John Cale on the Andy Warhol tribute *Songs for Drella.* Reed continued to experiment and even re-formed the Velvet Underground for a tour and live record in 1996 and toured and recorded extensively since then.

Discography: *Lou Reed* (RCA, 1972); *Transformer* (RCA, 1972, 1981); *Berlin* (RCA, 1973, 1981); *Sally Can't Dance* (RCA, 1974); *Rock n Roll Animal* (RCA, 1974, 1981); *Lou Reed Live* (RCA, 1975); *Metal Machine Music: The Amine β Ring* (RCA, 1975; Buddah, 2000); *Coney Island Baby* (RCA, 1976); *Rock and*

Roll Heart (Arista, 1976); *Walk on the Wild Side: The Best of Lou Reed* (RCA, 1977); *Street Hassle* (Arista, 1978); *Live Take No Prisoners* (Arista, 1978); *The Bells* (Arista, 1979); *Growing Up in Public* (Arista, 1980); *Rock and Roll Diary 1967–1980* (Arista, 1980); *The Blue Mask* (RCA, 1982); *I Can't Stand It* (UK RCA, 1982); *Legendary Hearts* (RCA, 1983); *Live in Italy* (UK RCA, 1984); *New Sensations* (RCA, 1984); *City Lights: Classic Performances* (Arista, 1985); *Mistrial* (RCA, 1986); *New York* (Sire, 1989); *Retro* (UK RCA, 1989); *Magic and Loss* (Sire, 1992); *Between Thought and Expression: The Lou Reed Anthology* (RCA, 1992); *Set the Twilight Reeling* (Warner Bros., 1996); *Different Times: Lou Reed in the '70s* (RCA, 1996); *Perfect Night* (Warner Bros., 1998); *The Definitive Collection* (Arista, 1999); *Ecstasy* (Warner Bros., 2000); *NYC Man: The Collection* (BMG Heritage/RCA, 2003); *The Raven* (Warner Bros., 2003). **Lou Reed/John Cale:** *Songs for Drella* (Sire/Warner Bros., 1990).

REGGAE

Reggae has had an enormous impact on **punk** rock both in England and in the United States. Numerous bands, such as the **Clash, Public Image Limited,** and the **Slits,** frequently drew on the rhythms of reggae and **dub.** In the United States, bands such as **Bad Brains** (whose members actually converted to Rastafarianism), **Operation Ivy, Rancid,** and **NOFX** also draw upon reggae's rhythms and subject matter. The history of punk and reggae can be traced to England, where disaffected Caribbean immigrants settled in mostly urban areas and resisted police harassment and inspired the local punk community, which was looking for other outlaw figures they could identify with in a music and cultural scene that marked both punks and Rastas as outsiders. Super reggae fans such as Paul Siminon and **Joe Strummer** of the Clash helped incorporate reggae rhythms into their music, and the Clash went on to cover numerous reggae songs, such as "Police and Thieves" by Junior Murvin and "Pressure Drop" by Toots and the Maytals, and also worked with reggae producers such as Mikey Dread and Lee "Scratch" Perry. The Clash also tried to articulate how the members were inspired by Rasta's resistance to authority in songs such as "White Riot" and "White Man in Hammersmith Palais," which detailed their frustration about how white punks were not as unified or politically as active as Rastafarians. Other punks such as **Johnny Rotten** (who allegedly had the largest reggae collection in England in the 1970s) spent time in Jamaica with reggae heroes such as Dr. Alimentado. Punk filmmaker and key DJ of the time, **Donn Letts,** played reggae and dub music at his DJ sets at **Acme Attractions** and the **Roxy,** partly because of the lack of acceptable punk singles to play during the mid-1970s but also because of the perceived affinity between punk and reggae. In a display of solidarity between dispossessed peoples, Bob Marley wrote a song called **"Punky Reggae Party,"** in which he noted the "Slits, the Clash, and the Feelgoods" will be there alongside the Wailers in a party at which all men are "rejected by society, treated with impunity, protected by their dignity." The implicit connections between Rastafarians and punks in England were key to early punk and the development of punk into **postpunk,** and the revolutionary advances made by bands such as PIL and the Slits cannot be imagined without the influence of reggae bands. English punk's resistance to the norms of society cannot be imagined without the ready-made antiestablishment views espoused by reggae artists. Later, the **2 Tone** movement led by bands such as the **Specials,** the Beat, the Selecter, and Madness helped fuse a black-and-white coalition in an effort to fight racism and the **National Front,** although these bands mostly were influenced by reggae's predecessors, **ska** and rock steady.

Although many U.S. bands are and were influenced by reggae, many of them were influenced by ska more than reggae, although there are several important exceptions. The Bad Brains were credited with introducing reggae to most U.S. punks, and they were militant Rastafarians, torn between the desire to play punk and the need to reconcile their religion with a largely antireligious scene. The Bad Brains successfully combined punk and reggae and influenced countless bands, most notably **Fugazi,** whose members acknowledged the enormous debt they owed to the Bad Brains. Unfortunately, the Bad Brains also absorbed the less-inclusive aspects of the Rastafarian religion and were blatantly antihomosexual, which led to an enormous conflict between them and the **Big Boys,** which had an openly gay singer. The Bad Brains' influence on other punk and metal bands was strong, and it is doubtful that all of those bands understood the contradictory nature of reggae music. Other U.S. bands, such Operation Ivy and Rancid, the band Tim Armstrong and Matt Freeman formed after its demise, also incorporated reggae and ska rhythms, although they also owed a debt to the Clash's use of reggae. Today, numerous bands such as NOFX incorporate reggae into their music, and guitarist El Hefe acknowledged the way in which the resistance to modern society embedded in reggae was influential in the band's political awakening. Numerous bands still try to fuse the aggression of punk with reggae's musical and ideological approach, which in its purest form is a positive step but in terms of the less savory aspects of Rastafarian culture (their apocalyptic nature, the antipathy about homosexuality, and some sects' reverse racism) brings into question whether the ideology of reggae can be separated from many punks' embrace of the music.

REID, JAMIE

A **situationist** and conceptual artist born in 1947 who is best known for his early work on the **flyers** and graphic design for the **Sex Pistols.** Artist Jamie Reid was influenced by the cut-and-paste montage style inspired by Guy Debord, who designed flyers and albums for the Sex Pistols and helped define the punk appropriation of disparate images that would define the **DIY** art style used by numerous punk bands. Reid met **Malcolm McLaren** in 1968 (the year of massive protests in Europe and a particularly significant year for the situationist movement) while organizing a student protest at Croydon Art College. After college in 1970, Reid founded Suburban Press, where he worked to develop his unique cut-and-paste style that turned advertisements from images of suburban society into something much more sinister and subversive. When McLaren needed help in getting the Sex Pistols a unique design style, he turned to Reid, who took the safety pins and ripped clothing of punk and combined them in unique, new ways with cut-and-pastes that emphasized the political and tribal nature of punk rock and placed it firmly in the camp oppositional to popular culture. Reid's most prominent work for the Sex Pistols were the album cover for *Never Mind the Bollocks, Here's the Sex Pistols* and the singles sleeves for "**Anarchy in the UK,**" "**God Save the Queen,**" "Holidays in the Sun," and "Pretty Vacant." Reid is now a world-famous artist who exhibits his work at major shows, at dance clubs, as well as online, on CDs, and in major museums such as the Centre Pompidou in Paris. Reid also worked on major projects such as the Ten Year project at the Strongroom Studios in London, which celebrated Reid's anarchist and Druidic beliefs. His Web site is http://www.jamiereid.uk.net/home.html.

REPLACEMENTS

Bratty and shambolic **punk,** pop, classic rock, and indefinable band of misfits led by Paul Westerberg that started out as a more sloppy **hardcore** band on albums such as *Sorry Ma, Forgot to Take Out the Trash* and *The Replacements Stink* before shifting course radically on *Hootenanny* and becoming one of the most diverse and influential bands in 1980s and 1990s alternative rock. The band was started by the Stinson brothers, Bob on guitar and Tommy on bass (who was only 14 when the band began), with drummer Chris Mars. They were joined by singer and guitarist Paul Westerberg, who apparently heard the band rehearsing through a basement window and asked if he could join. After joining the band, Westerberg quickly took over as songwriter, and the band released its first single, "I'm in Trouble," followed by the album *Sorry Ma, Forgot to Take Out the Trash*, which featured numerous hilarious hardcore songs, many clocking in at only a minute or so. The band had already begun to mature musically by the second EP, *The Replacements Stink*, which also contained its share of thrash and powerful anthems but also featured slower, more melodic songs. If the Replacements were getting more mature musically, they were also devolving into a drunken and stoned mess on stage, with gigs a haphazard prospect at best as members wandered drunkenly on- and off-stage or took audience requests to play songs they barely knew. (This is captured in all its debauched glory on the cassette-only release *The Shit Hits the Fans*). Bob Stinson was the biggest offender and eventually became too much for even the heavy-drinking Westerberg to take. Bob was fired and replaced by guitarist Slim Dunlap after the more commercial release *Tim* and after one album as a trio, *Pleased to Meet Me*. Westerberg began to chafe under the limitations of the group, and the last record, *All Shook Down*, was essentially a Westerberg solo record featuring limited contributions from the rest of the band. By the last tour, Mars had been sacked and replaced by drummer Steve Foley. Westerberg sobered up and started a financially semisuccessful and critically acclaimed solo career. Bassist Tommy Stinson later joined the latter-day version of Guns N' Roses and somehow managed to put out several solo records while putting up with Axl Rose. Drummer Chris Mars put out several solo records with covers that illustrated his abilities as a painter as well as an all-around musician. Bob Stinson tried to start a variety of new bands before his career of substance abuse caught up with him; he died in 1995.

Discography: *Sorry Ma, Forgot to Take Out the Trash* (Twin\Tone, 1981); *The Replacements Stink* EP (Twin\Tone, 1982, 1986); *Hootenanny* (Twin\Tone, 1983); *Let It Be* (Twin\Tone, 1984); *The Shit Hits the Fans* (tape; Twin\Tone, 1985); *Tim* (Sire, 1985); *Boink!!* (UK Glass, 1986); *Pleased to Meet Me* (Sire, 1987); *Don't Tell a Soul* (Sire/Reprise, 1989); *All Shook Down* (Sire/Reprise, 1990).

REPO MAN

One of the few commercial films of the 1980s to deal with **punk** in a realistic way, and *Repo Man* was ostensibly science fiction. *Repo Man* was directed by Alex Cox, produced by former Monkee Mike Nesmith, and starred Emilio Estevez as a young punk named Otto caught up in a quest for the supposed treasure hidden in the back of a stolen car. The film featured a group of punk stalwarts in cameos, including the **Circle Jerks** as a lounge band singing their song "When the Shit Hits the Fan" (Otto, the hero, disdainfully shrugs, "I can't believe I used to like these guys!"). The film's soundtrack also featured a diverse group of punk songs by bands such as **Suicidal Tendencies, Black Flag, Iggy Pop** (who sang the title song), the Circle Jerks, **Fear,** and the Plugz, which also provided some moody instrumentals. The film was not only known for having a punk soundtrack but also seemed to have some knowledge of the desperation of the punk life, no doubt influenced by the contributions of director Alex Cox and screenwriter Dick Rude. The scene in which numerous punks dance outside a club because they were too poor to get in is particularly evocative of the early 1980s punk scene. The film is available on DVD.

RESISTANCE RECORDS

White-power and Nazi label that distributed the music of **Skrewdriver** and other racist and white-power bands in the United States during the 1980s and 1990s. Resistance is an important part of the white-power and racist movements in the United States.

REVELATION RECORDS

Record label formed in Connecticut in 1987 by Jordan Cooper and Ray Cappo of **Youth of Today** that released records by **Warzone, Sick of It All,** Youth of Today, **Bold, Supertouch,**

Gorilla Biscuits, and the compilation *New York Hardcore—The Way It Is.* Although many of the records released by Revelation (especially during the early years) were by **straight edge** bands, the label was never a primarily straight edge label. Cappo left the company in 1988 to concentrate more on **Krishna** Consciousness. The label started with a Warzone seven-inch single in 1987 and released more than 120 records by artists such as **Civ,** Sick of it all, Gorilla Biscuits, Bold, **Judge,** and Ignite. The label is now based in Huntington Beach, California.

REVOLUTION SUMMER

A term first used by **Washington, D.C.,** stalwart Amy Pickering (later of **Dischord Records**) who was working a job at the Neighborhood Planning Council in the U.S. capital when she decided to create an uprising against an unpopular supervisor. Pickering started sending notes that read "Be on your toes . . . this is Revolution Summer" to a variety of Georgetown punks. The punks became energized by the potential of real revolutionary change, and the term became a self-fulfilling prophecy and was later used to describe the political and social protests led by punks and **Positive Force** in Washington, D.C., in summer 1985. Many punks engaged in measures of resistance against the **Ronald Reagan** administration, and Dischord cofounder and former **Minor Threat** drummer Jeff Nelson famously placed numerous signs and posters around town that said Attorney General Edwin Meese was "a Pig." Summer 1985 also saw the rise of a new generation of more emotional and politically active bands such as Rites of Spring and **Beefeater.** Although there were no long-lasting political ramifications of the Revolution Summer, it demonstrated the fact that many punks were not apolitical and, with proper mobilization, could organize to demand change.

RICH KIDS

Bassist Glenn Matlock's band after he was unceremoniously ousted from the **Sex Pistols.** Rich Kids featured Matlock on bass and vocals, Midge Ure on guitar and vocals, Steve New on guitar, Rusty Egan on drums, and, from the Faces, Ian McLagen on keyboards on the first album, *Ghosts of Princes in Towers.* The band split in mid-1979, and Midge Ure went on to join Ultravox. Matlock went on to several reunion tours with the Sex Pistols in the 1990s and in 2003 and to release new, poppy, **punk** solo records after that.
Discography: *Ghosts of Princes in Towers* (EMI, 1978; Fame, 1983).

RIOT GRRRL MOVEMENT

The Riot Grrrl movement was one of the most influential punk movements (*Grrrl* is intentionally spelled with three Rs to symbolize how it is different and more powerful symbolically than the often derogatory *girl*). Although many women were considered key figures in the early Riot Grrrl movement, the key instigators were Allison Wolfe and Molly Neuman (later of the band **Bratmobile**) of the zine *Girl Germs,* who, along with **Kathleen Hanna,** produced a manifesto that celebrated a hypothetical "girl riot." The manifesto noted the lack of encouragement women faced in a boy-band-dominated atmosphere and mentioned their refusal to assimilate the standards set by boys and boy bands and, while denying they were reverse sexists, laid claim to being the "TRUEPUNKROCKSOUL CRUSADERS THAT WE KNOW we really are." The label stuck and was applied to bands such as Bratmobile and **Bikini Kill,** which wore the title proudly, but was also universal enough in the true spirit of **DIY** to encourage female bands and **zines** across the country and the world to make the term their own and start their own bands, zines, or other outlets for artistic expression. Although there was a manifesto, there was no dogma, so Riot Grrrl was whatever combination of feminism and self-expression could be created in a place safe from the standards set by the male-dominated punk rock scene. Riot Grrrl shows and artistic events were often associated, so even when boys were allowed in, they would dominate the pit or the happening through numbers, force, or intimidation. Mainstream magazines and newspapers such as *Newsweek* and *Rolling Stone* were not sure what to make of Riot Grrrl, and the movement was increasingly categorized by mainstream media as either "man-hating" or a fad that was embraced by mostly middle-class white girls. Although the term is not used today by either the media or many bands to describe themselves, it was an important moment in punk music when women decided to create an inclusive movement dedicated to women's empowerment and taking control of the often male-dominated punk scene. The legacy lives on in many of the **queercore** bands and continuing projects of founders such as Hanna in her band **Le Tigre.**

RIVERDALES

Ramones-esque side project of most of the members of **Screeching Weasel.** The Riverdales followed the same sonic template as Screeching Weasel but in a poppier, Ramones style. The band featured Ben Weasel (Ben Foster) on guitar and vocals, Dan Vapid (Dan Schafer) on bass and vocals, and Dan Panic (Dan Sullivan)on drums.
Discography: *Riverdales* (Lookout, 1995).

ROACH MOTEL

Florida **punk** band from the early 1980s that featured George Tabb, later of the band **Furious George.** The band did a notable tour of Florida with **Black Flag** in 1981 when relatively few punk bands played in the Sunshine State. Tabb later went on to play in False Prophets and **Iron Prostate** before forming his own band Furious George.

ROBINSON, TOM

Although much of Tom Robinson's work (especially after the late 1970s and early 1980s) was tangential to **punk** rock, his first two records with the Tom Robinson Band and his influence on the early scene during the late 1970s were quite substantial. Robinson was also notable as one of the foremost openly gay musicians in the early English punk scene, which he celebrated in his controversial anthem "Glad to be Gay," released as a single in 1978.
Discography: Tom Robinson Band: *Power in the Darkness* (Harvest, 1978; Razor & Tie, 1993); *TRB Two* (Harvest, 1979; Razor & Tie, 1993); *Tom Robinson Band* (UK EMI, 1981; UK Fame, 1982); *Rising Free: The Very Best of TRB* (UK EMI Gold, 1997). **Sector 27:** *Sector 27* (IRS, 1980); *Complete* (UK Fontana, 1996). **Tom Robinson:** *North by Northwest* (IRS, 1982); *Cabaret '79: Glad to Be Gay* (UK Panic, 1982; UK Castaway Northwest, 1997); *Atmospherics* EP (UK Panic, 1983); *Hope and Glory* (Geffen, 1984; UK Castaway Northwest, 1997); *Still Loving You* (UK Castaway Northwest, 1986; UK Blueprint, 1998); *The Collection 1977–1987* (UK EMI, 1987); *Last Tango: Midnight at the Fridge* (UK Dojo, 1987; UK Castaway Northwest, 1997); *Back in the Old Country* (UK Connoisseur Collection, 1989); *Living in a Boom Time* (UK Cooking Vinyl, 1992); *Love over Rage* (Rhythm Safari/Priority, 1994); *Having It Both Ways* (Cooking Vinyl, 1996); *The Undiscovered* (Cooking Vinyl, 1998); *Home from Home* (UK Oyster, 1999).

ROBO

Popular **punk** drummer for the **Misfits** and **Black Flag.** Robo was a bit of a mystery and had contentious relationships with both Black Flag and the Misfits. Robo played again with the Misfits and played at the August 2005 benefit shows to save **CBGB's.**

ROCKABILLY

Rockabilly, both in its original form during the 1950s and also though its frequent revivals during the 1960s and 1970s, is one of the influences on **punk** both musically and stylistically, and bands such as the **Cramps** prove what a great influence this style of music had on punk's development. Many bands from the 1970s onward, such as the Reverend Horton Heat and the Supersuckers, attracted a crossover of punk and rockabilly fans. Much of **punk fashion,** such as boots, bandannas, and gelled hair, has its roots in rockabilly styles, and at certain shows there are numerous mixtures of the various looks and attitudes of punk and rockabilly.

ROCK AND ROLL HIGH SCHOOL

Exploitation film featuring the **Ramones** made by Roger Corman's production company, directed by Alan Arkush, and released in 1979. Originally envisioned as a typical Corman exploitation film called "Disco High School," *Rock and Roll High School* was reenvisioned as a vehicle for the new generation of rebellious **punk** bands, and the Ramones were seen as the epitome of punk by many young punks. The film featured a particularly muted performance by bassist **Dee Dee Ramone** (who also was taken to the hospital after ingesting pills thrown at the band by punk fans), who needed several takes just to say the line "Oh boy, pizza!" Although the film was low budget and unrealistic, it nonetheless was appealing for its portrayal of a fantasy world where punk fans were popular and the Ramones were the biggest band in the world.

ROCKET FROM THE TOMBS

Cleveland band influenced by the absurdist music and humor of **Frank Zappa.** The band's original lineup included David Thomas (Crocus Behemoth) on vocals; Pete Laughner on guitar; Gene O'Conner, who would later change his name to Cheetah Chrome, on guitar; Johnny Mandansky, later Johnny Blitz in the **Dead Boys;** and Craig Bell of the Mirrors on bass. The band was legendary on the Cleveland scene, but internal tension over the role of Thomas and his unique voice soon split the band into different camps, and after trying out a young Stiv Bators on vocals and members of the band individually singing their songs, the band decided to break up. Members of the band would later go on to form **Pere Ubu** and the Dead Boys. Several of the surviving members of the band, including Thomas and Chrome, with **Television** guitarist Richard Lloyd, reunited for reunion tours as Rockets from the Tombs almost 30 years after the band's demise.

ROIR RECORDS

Roir Records (Reach out International Records) is an eclectic and influential tape-only label that released seminal music from **Bad Brains** and **Suicide** and numerous **dub** and **reggae** classics. The label initially was founded by Neil Cooper as a cassette-only label, devoted to an eclectic mix of what would later be referred to as world music and specializing in dub, reggae, and **punk** music. Other bands that have released records on Roir include the Skatalites, **MC5,** the Raincoats, Suicide, and **Television.** Due to declining sales for cassettes, the label switched to CDs as well. The label has a Web site at http://www.roir-usa.com/.

ROLLINS BAND

Henry Rollins's solo band after he left **Black Flag** in the late 1980s. The band went through various permutations and lineup changes but managed several radio and **MTV** hits during the early 1990s after it successfully toured with the first Lollapalooza tour in 1991. The Rollins Band had several semisuccessful singles in the mid-1990s, such as "Low-Self Opinion" and "Liar." The band originally featured rhythm section Sim Cain and Andrew Weiss, from Gone and Regressive Aid, along with guitarist Chris Haskett and released several **punk**-influenced EPs and several albums. The Rollins Band toured relentlessly and showcased Rollins's new stage persona, which was equal parts singer, screamer, and actor (Rollins also gained numerous small roles in films after Black Flag's demise). A typical show would start in chaos and end when Rollins would roll around the stage in his shorts. Rollins later reconstituted the Rollins Band, without Haskett, Cain, and Weiss, in a more hard rock direction, to diminishing returns, and concentrated primarily on his spoken-word tours and other ventures.

Discography: **Rollins Band:** *Life Time* (Texas Hotel, 1988; Buddha, 1999); *Do It* (Texas Hotel, 1989); *Hard Volume* (Texas Hotel, 1989; Buddha, 1999); *Turned On* (Quarterstick, 1990); *The End of Silence* (Imago, 1992); *Electro Convulsive Therapy* EP (Japan Imago, 1993); *Weight* (Imago, 1994); *«Come in and Burn»* (DreamWorks, 1997); *Insert Band Here: Live in Australia 1990* (Buddha, 1999); *Get Some Go Again* (DreamWorks, 2000); *Nice* (Sanctuary, 2001).

ROLLINS, HENRY

Punk singer, writer, and spoken-word artist (born Henry Garfield) who came to fame as the lead singer of **Black Flag** after a stint in the early **Washington, D.C.,** punk band **SOA.** Rollins was perhaps one of the best-known and prolific of the public faces of punk rock, thanks to his numerous appearances in movies and documentaries, on **MTV,** and on spoken-word tours and book readings, not to mention his appearances with the **Rollins Band** throughout the 1990s. Although Rollins will always be known to most punks for his stint in Black Flag in the early to mid-1980s, it was only after Black Flag broke up that he rose out of relative obscurity to become a punk celebrity. Rollins became a successful solo artist with the Rollins Band and was also the publisher of **2.13.61** books and records. Rollins was one of the most sought-after professional punks for interviews by mainstream media and often appeared on news programs, on television specials, particularly on MTV, and in documentaries on punk and independent music. Rollins also toured and recorded live concert films of his spoken word, which evolved further from poetry into what could be seen as a form of stand-up comedy. *See also* Black Flag; 2.13.61; Washington, D.C.

Discography: *Hot Animal Machine* (Texas Hotel, 1987; Buddha, 1999); *Big Ugly Mouth* (Texas Hotel, 1987; Quarterstick, 1992); *Sweatbox* (Texas Hotel, 1989; Quarterstick, 1992); *Live at McCabe's* (Texas Hotel, 1990; Quarterstick, 1992); *Human Butt* (2.13.61/Quarterstick, 1992); *The Boxed Life* (Imago, 1993); *Get in the Van* (2.13.61/Time Warner Audio Books, 1994); *In Conversation* (UK Tabak, 1995); *Everything* (2.13.61/Thirsty Ear, 1996); *Black Coffee Blues* (2.13.61/Thirsty Ear, 1997); *Think Tank* (DreamWorks, 1998); *A Rollins in the Wry* (Quarterstick, 2001). **Henrietta Collins and the Wifebeating Childhaters:** *Drive by Shooting* EP (Texas Hotel, 1987). **Henry Rollins/Gore:** *Live* (Hol. Eksakt, 1987). **Rollins Band:** *Life Time* (Texas Hotel, 1988; Buddha, 1999); *Do It* (Texas Hotel, 1989); *Hard Volume* (Texas Hotel, 1989; Buddha, 1999); *Turned On* (Quarterstick, 1990); *The End of Silence* (Imago, 1992); *Electro Convulsive Therapy* EP (Japan Imago, 1993); *Weight* (Imago, 1994); *Come in and Burn* (DreamWorks, 1997); *Insert Band Here: Live in Australia 1990* (Buddha, 1999); *Get Some Go Again* (DreamWorks, 2000); *Nice* (Sanctuary, 2001). **Lydia Lunch/Henry Rollins/Hubert Selby Jr./Don Bajema:** *Our Fathers Who Aren't in Heaven* (UK Widowspeak, 1992). **Wartime:** *Fast Food for Thought* EP (Chrysalis, 1990). **S.O.A.:** *No Policy* EP (Dischord, 1981). **Various Artists:** *Four Old 7"s on a 12"* (Dischord, 1985).

ROTTEN, JOHNNY

Name taken by **John Lydon** as singer for the **Sex Pistols.** The nickname Rotten was originally given to Lydon to highlight his disregard for dental hygiene but soon also became appropriate as a description of his withering sarcasm and biting comments and lyrics. Rotten had an ambivalent relationship with the name and persona of Johnny Rotten and often used his given name, especially in his work with **Public Image Limited** and in his collaborations. Rotten was one of the best-known punks from the English punk revolution (next to **Sid Vicious**), both to punks and especially to the mainstream audiences that relied on mass media for their images of **punk.** Rotten provided the perfect face of punk rock, with his ever-present sneer, hunchback demeanor, and complete contempt for almost everyone who dared to talk to him. Onstage, Rotten was an electrifying and somewhat demonic stage presence, and his voice, rather than the actual music of the Sex Pistols, defined the band as punk rock. **Malcolm McLaren** often tried to take credit for the persona of Johnny Rotten, as epitomized by his claims in the film *The Great Rock 'n' Roll Swindle* in which he lays out his manifesto for creating a punk band. Rotten and the other Sex Pistols later refuted this, and Rotten made the authoritative claim that he had been the author of his own image and lyrics in his 1994 book *Rotten: No Irish, No Blacks, No Dogs* and in the movie *The Filth and the Fury*. Rotten was also known for his eclectic taste in music and once had a formidable **reggae** and **dub** collection. On July 16, 1977, Rotten appeared as a special guest on DJ Tommy Vance's radio program on Capital Radio in London, and his selections included cuts by **David Bowie,** Kevin Coyne, **Captain Beefheart, Nico, Can,** John Cale, and reggae selections by Culture, Fred Locks, Peter Tosh, and Dr. Alimantado. Lydon largely abandoned the name Rotten for most of the 1980s and 1990s but revived it for two Sex Pistols reunion tours. Rotten also appeared an MTV interview show called *Rotten TV* and also appeared on the British reality television show *Get Me Out of Here, I'm a Celebrity*.

ROUGH TRADE

Influential British music label that released many seminal **postpunk** records and continued to release challenging and innovative music from the new wave of postpunk bands. The label was started by Geoff Travis as a record store in London in 1976 but became a label in 1978, issuing many key European postpunk releases. The label was acquired by Zomba in the late 1990s, and its back catalog was purchased by One Little Indian Records. Current artist on Rough Trade include Adam Green, British Sea Power, the Libertines, Babyshambles, Cornershop, Belle and Sebastion, and the Unicorns.

ROXY

Legendary **London** club where many of the original **punk** bands played during the mid- to late 1980s. **Crass** wrote the protest song "Banned from the Roxy" about the supposedly exclusionary practices of the club in its later incarnations.

RUDE BOY

One of the early **punk** films, made in 1980 by Jack Hazan and David Mingay about a roadie for the **Clash** and featuring members of the Clash and various concert scenes. The film brilliantly blurred the line between documentary and staged footage, often switching quickly between the two.

RUDIMENTARY PENI

English anarchist punks who recorded on the **Crass** label before leaving and working on their own.
Discography: *Death Church* (Corpus Christi, 1983); *The EPs of RP* (Corpus Christi, 1987); *Cacophony* (Outer Himalayan, 1988); *Pop Adrian 37th* (Outer Himalayan, 1995); *The Underclass* (Outer Himalayan, 2000).

RUNAWAYS

Female group formed by **Los Angeles** Svengali **Kim Fowley** that played a raw form of rock and roll very reminiscent of **punk** rock and featured Joan Jett and Lita Ford before their successful solo careers during the 1980s. The band was initially founded by Fowley with lyricist Kari Krome and Joan Jett. Other members included Cherie Currie on vocals, Sandy West on drums and vocals, and Michael Steel on bass and vocals (who later went on to considerably more success in the Bangles and who was replaced by Jackie Fox on bass and later by Peggy Foster and Laurie McAllister). The Runaways were formed deliberately as a girl rock group by Fowley, who had previously worked as a songwriter and performer. Fowley recruited Kari Krome to write songs for the band and wanted to create a raw, sexualized, all-female band that could rock as hard as any male band but still remain under his control. After grueling tours and several years of abuse by Fowley, Jackie Fox quit, followed shortly by Cherie Currie. After Jett sang for a spell, the band finally dissolved amid much acrimony. Although talented, the Runaways were still best known for the careers launched by members after the band's demise. Jett later had a successful solo career and produced the first and only **Germs** album.

Discography: *The Runaways* (Mercury, 1976; Cherry Red, 2003); *Queens of Noise* (Mercury, 1977; Cherry Red, 2003); *Live in Japan* (Mercury, 1977; Cherry Red, 2004); *Waitin' for the Night* (Mercury, 1977; Cherry Red, 2004); *And Now . . . the Runaways* (UK Cherry Red, 1979; Cherry Red, 1999); *Flaming Schoolgirls* (UK Cherry Red, 1980; Cherry Red, 2004); *Little Lost Girls* (Rhino, 1981; Rhino, 1990); *The Best of the Runaways* (Mercury, 1982; Mercury/Universal, 2005); *I Love Playing with Fire* (UK Laker/Cherry Red, 1982); *Born to Be Bad* (Marilyn Records, 1991).

RUTS

Mid-1970s **punk** band influenced by **reggae,** also notable for the early overdose death of singer Malcolm Owen. The band hailed from the **London** suburb of Southhall and featured Dave Ruffy on drums, Paul Fox on guitar, Malcolm Owen on vocals, and John "Vince Segs" Jennings on bass. Lead singer Owen died of a **heroin** overdose after the band released one record, *The Crack*, in 1979. The Ruts were known for the members' social conscience and played many **RAR (Rock Against Racism)** gigs and worked with the People Unite offices, which were attacked during a police action that later inspired the song "Jah War." The Ruts were also a fairly experimental band and experimented with **dub** on such songs as "Jah War," but the Ruts were best known for the single "Babylon's Burning." The band extensively supported the RAR concerts and organization, and through RAR the band met the **reggae** band Misty in Roots, which in 1978 released the Ruts' first single, "In a Rut," on Misty in Roots' People Unite record label, which led to the band being signed by Virgin in 1979. While getting ready for a new album, the band briefly fired Owen in an attempt to get him to tackle his heroin addiction, but after Owen's reinstatement in the band, he overdosed in July 1980. It is unclear how far the Ruts would have gone in experimenting with punk and reggae, but the band's story clearly illustrates the ravages of drugs in the punk community. The band toured without Owen after his death, replacing him with saxophone player and keyboardist Gary Barnacle and renaming themselves Ruts DC (from the Italian term *da capo*, which translates as "from the beginning"). As Ruts DC, the band released two dub- and reggae-inspired albums and a collaboration with dub hero Mad Professor before the band finally called it quits in 1983 after several tours. Numerous live albums and collections were released after the demise of the Ruts, making their catalog look much more prolific than it was during the band's brief existence.

Discography: *The Crack* (Virgin Int'l, 1979; Virgin, 1988; Blue Plate, 1991); *Grin & Bear It* (Virgin, 1980); *The Peel Sessions* EP (UK Strange Fruit, 1986); *The Ruts Live* (UK Dojo, 1987); *Live and Loud!!* (UK Link, 1987); *You Gotta Get Out of It* (Virgin, 1987); *The Peel Sessions Album* (UK Strange Fruit, 1990). **Ruts DC:** *Animal Now* (Virgin, 1981); *Rhythm Collision* (Bohemian, 1982). **Ruts DC and the Mad Professor:** *Rhythm Collision Dub, Vol. 1* (tape; Roir, 1987).

SAINTS

Australian punk band known for the incendiary 1977 single "I'm Stranded." Not all of the quintessential bands of the first wave of punk rock were from England or the United States. In particular, the Saints, which formed in 1976 with Chris Bailey on vocals, Ed Kuepper on guitar, Ivor Hay on drums, and Kym Bradshaw on bass, demonstrated that punk was not a regional occurrence, but that it had more to do with attitude than the British preoccupation with class struggle. Essentially a speeded-up rock-and-roll band, the Saints recorded well into the late 1980s, before disbanding around 1988. Although the band had a long history and a vast catalog, they were best known for the single and album *I'm Stranded*. After Kuepper left the band, Bailey kept it going through the 1980s with a revolving cast of musicians and a direction change toward more straight-ahead blues-based rock and roll. Bailey revived the Saints name in the late 1990s, toured again under that moniker, and did occasional solo projects. Kuepper, who wrote many of the classic songs, left in 1978 to form his own solo band, the Laughing Clowns, and then released several dozen solo records within a relatively short period of time. In the early 1990s, Kuepper also formed the band the Aints (originally with fellow Australian and **Celibate Rifles** member Kent Steedman) as a Saints cover band for one live record, put out 1960s-based, raucous rock and roll for a time, and recorded his own material in a variety of styles and formats.

Select Discography: *I'm Stranded* (Sire, 1977); *Eternally Yours* (Sire, 1978); *Prehistoric Sounds* (UK Harvest, 1978); *Prehistoric Song* (Fr. Harvest, 1978).

SCENES

The word *scene* is usually associated with regional punk movements, usually based around large urban centers, and frequently cited examples are the early punk scenes of **London,** Manchester, **New York, Washington, D.C.,** and **Cleveland.** Although it is almost impossible to list the variety of scenes and different permutations of punk that existed from city to city and from suburb to suburb and in towns throughout the world, it is important to note that punk was not monolithic in the approaches its fans and practitioners took to it. Scenes varied dramatically, often within small geographic distances and between time periods, as in the case of New York, **Los Angeles,** and the Washington, D.C., scenes, where the music evolved from the earlier, artier punk to the later permutations of **hardcore** that became predominant within a few years. Some scenes were more political than others, some more **straight edge,** and some more peace punk. Some scenes were breeding grounds for major labels and have been well chronicled in various books and articles, whereas other scenes were largely ignored, except in local lore, oral tradition, and perhaps in the regional scene reports published by major **zines** such as *Maximum Rock 'n' Roll.* There were often disputes between various scenes that were geographically close, including feuds between **Boston** and New York bands, particularly during the straight-edge hardcore scenes, and between the Washington, D.C., and New York scenes over issues such as straight edge, vegetarianism, and conduct in the **pit.** Also, as **Henry Rollins** chronicles in his autobiographical book **Get in the Van,** there were also rivalries between English bands and U.S. bands, and U.S. bands touring Europe during the early 1980s could sometimes expect verbal as well as physical abuse from not only the more boisterous members of the audience but also from the bands that supposedly shared a common philosophy. Much of the history of regional scenes is unwritten, and it will remain to be seen if many punk scenes in the United States (not to mention the rest of the world) are ever fully documented. Some indications of the diversity of today's scenes can be found in the regional reports in *Maximum Rock 'n' Roll* and in a variety of zines and Web sites that detail local events.

SCREAMERS

Early 1970s **Los Angeles**–based performance artist and band. The band was reportedly one of the most vital and important bands on the early Los Angeles scene but never made a proper recording of their music (except for some poorly recorded live tracks). The band was started by performance artists Tomato du Plenty, KK Barrett, David Brown, and Tommy Gear, who had previously been in an experimental theater troupe that performed in drag. Although the Screamers were one of the most popular and experimental of the Los Angeles punk scene, there are no proper recordings of the band, and its legend is largely based on reputation rather than lasting musical legacy.

SCREECHING WEASEL

Chicago-based, prolific pop-punk band in the **Ramones** vein led by lead singer Ben Weasel (Ben Foster) that has been recording since 1986. The original lineup featured Johnny Jugghead on guitar, Ben Bovine on bass, and Steve Cheese on drums. The band went through various permutations and short breakups over the years, and the most stable lineup was the early 1990s group consisting of Dan Vapid (Dan Schafer) on guitar, Danny Panic (Dan Sullivan) on drums, and Dave Naked on bass (although there were some subsequent switches on bass as well). Ben Weasel was also a prolific writer and columnist for **zines** such as *Maximum Rock 'n' Roll.* Vapid, Panic, and Weasel also make up the **Riverdales,** another band with an obvious debt to the Ramones.
Discography: *Screeching Weasel* (Underdog, 1987); *Boogadaboogadaboogada* (Roadkill, 1988); *My Brain Hurts* (Lookout, 1991); *Ramones* (Selfless, 1992); *Wiggle* (Lookout, 1993); *Anthem for a New Tomorrow* (Lookout, 1993); *How to Make Enemies and Irritate People* (Lookout, 1994); *Kill the Musicians* (Lookout, 1995); *Bark Like a Dog* (Fat Wreck Chords, 1996); *Television City Dream* (Fat Wreck Chords, 1998); *Emo* (Panic Button, 1999); *Thank You Very Little* (Panic Button/Lookout, 1999).

"SEARCH AND DESTROY"

Before it was well known as one of the themes behind a Nike commercial, the song "Search and Destroy" by **Iggy and the Stooges** was the highlight of the *Raw Power* record and is perhaps one of the most covered songs in punk history.

SEARCH AND DESTROY

Search and Destroy was a pivotal San Francisco zine that covered not only the San Francisco scene but also the **punk** and **postpunk** movements in general. The zine was founded and published by V. Vale, who later went on to found Re/Search Publications. *Search and Destroy* is available in two reprints from Re/Search: Volume one covers issues 1 through 6, and volume two covers issues 7 through 11.

SEEDS

Protopunk garage and psychedelic band of the 1960s led by the enigmatic Sky Saxon and best known for the song "Pushing Too Hard," which originally appeared on the first album. The band was remarkably different and much more abrasive than many of its contemporaries and is considered, along with bands such as the **Sonics** and the **Music Machine,** to be the band that inspired punk rock years later. Sky Saxon continued to tour with a version of the Seeds.
Selective Discography: *The Seeds* (GNP Crescendo, 1966); *A Web of Sound* (GNP Crescendo, 1966).

SEPTIC DEATH

U.S. **hardcore** band formed in 1981, inspired by British anarchist punk like **Rudimentary Peni,** and led by the controversial but brilliant artist, writer, and musician Brian "Pushead" Schroeder. Schroeder did artwork for Metallica and wrote extensively in **zines** and magazines such as the **skateboarding** magazine *Thrasher,* where he was the music editor and wrote the "Puszone" column about hardcore and heavy metal music. To quote Pushead on why the name and philosophy of the band are called Septic Death, he writes, "Septic Death represents when you die, you are dead. There is nothing else that will happen; no guiding light, no angels, no heaven or hell. You are deceased, your body rots away. The brain's stored knowledge is idle. Septic Death is like a fear that people create things to escape reality. People are afraid to die, afraid to think that tomorrow it might be all over" (originally from an interview on *Flex Your Hear,* available at http://www.flexyourhead.net/interview_display.php?id=59). As well as his work recording with Septic Death, writing, and producing art, Pushead also created the labels Pusmort and Bacteria Sour.
Discography: *Barricaded Suspects* LP (Toxic Shock Records, 1983); *Empty Shells* (Self Release, 1983); *Need So Much Attention ... Acceptance of Whom* (Pusmort, 1984); *P.E.A.C.E.* (R Radical Records, 1984); *Now That I Have Your Attention What Do I Do With It* (Pusmort, 1984); *Time Is the Boss Aaarrggh It's Live* (Deluxe, 1984); *Live Dirt up a Side Track Carted Is a Putrid Evil Flexi* (Kalv and Dig, 1985); *Cleanse the Bacteria* (Pusmort, 1985); *Part of Compilation: Wild Riders of Boards—Skate Rock Volume 3* (Thrasher Magazine, 1985); *Burial Mai So* (Pusmort, 1987); *Part of Compilation: Pusmort Sampler* (Pusmort, 1987); *Part of Compilation: Road Rash—Skate Rock Volume 6* (Thrasher Magazine, 1988); *Part of Compilation: North Atlantic Noise Attack* (ManicEars, 1989); *Kichigai* (Pusmort, 1988); *Nightmare Takes a Nap Box Set Volume 1* (Pusmort, 1990); *Attention* (Pusmort, 1991); *Theme from Ozo Bozo* (Toy's Factory Records, 1992); *Rocket from the Crypt* (Pusmort, 1992); *Daymare* (Pusmort, 1992);*Nightmare Takes a Nap Box Set Volume 2* (Pusmort, 1993; with RFTC, Pusmort, 1993); *Part of Compilation: Pusmort View* (Toy's Factory Records, 1994); *Decade of Disaster* (Toxic Shock, 1994); *Barricaded Suspects* (Toxic Shock, 1994); *Taste* (Pushead Bacteria Sour, 1995); *None of Your Attention* (Pusmort, 1995); *Somewhere in Time* (Lost and Found, 1997); *Nightmare Takes a Nap Box Set Volume 3* (Pusmort, 1998); *Part of Compilation: Bacteria Sour Catalog Volume 2* (Bacteria Sour, 1998); *Desperate for Attention* (Flex 16, 1998); *Crossed Out Twice* (Bacteria Sour, 1999); *Uncontrollable Proof* (Sourpus, 1999); *Victim of a Thought Crime* (Sourpus, 2000); *Septic Death* (Pusmort, 2000); *Chumoku* (Prank Records, 2002).

SERPICO

One of the **New York** bands of the mid- to late 1990s most popular in Europe, led by guitarist and sometime lead singer John Lisa. The band was originally formed as Sleeper, but the British band of the same name bought the name from band leader John Lisa, and the band changed its name to Serpico in 1994 after one of the band's better known songs. The band was formed in Staten Island and existed in too many forms to be taken seriously from 1991 until an ugly and embarrassing death in September 1998. The original group included John Lisa on guitar, John Telenko on vocals, Hobi Klapuri on guitar, Lew Dimmick on bass, and T.J. Quatrone on drums. Serpico released its debut seven-inch record on J. Lisa's homegrown Tragic Life label. Typical band problems, temper tantrums, creative differences, and laziness led to nearly a dozen lineup changes, trips across the country, shaky flights to Europe, onstage nakedness, phlegm, blood, and a ton of hard feelings and irreparable damages to previously solid friendships. Michael Thomas DeLorenzo on guitar, Marc Treboschi (later of In Crowd) on bass, and Chris "Niser" Guardino on drums joined the fold after the departure of most of the original lineup. Sal Cannestra of In Crowd was also a guitar player on several records and got kicked out, much to Lisa's later regret.

Rumble, Serpico's final Equal Vision CD and swan song, cost the label thousands to record but only brought in two-fifths of the initial investment, prompting Equal Vision's Steve Reddy to proclaim, "That's the LAST fucking time I sign a non-**Krishna** band." The band called it quits shortly after the *Rumble* tour to re-form only temporarily with the help of Darien's Greg Swanson and Murdock's Rob Marinelli. J. Lisa's very latent homosexuality (at 30 years old) came to full bloom in 1998 when he left the European farewell tour because he missed his Mexican boyfriend back in New York. "We just could never catch a groove," he said, "but now at least I get laid regularly."

Easily the best of Serpico's output was their 1996 single "I'm Not Dead," which was released by C.I. records and hand-numbered to 1,000. Powerful, raw, and melodic, they finally got to where they wanted to be, though only 1,000 people listened globally. Not much to brag about for a seven-year run. C'est la vie.

Discography: Sleeper: *Display Debut* 7" (Tragic Life, 1991); *Time and Tide* 12" LP (Ger. 42 Records, 1993); *Splinter* 7" (Allied Records, 1993); Split 7" with Gutwrench (Excursion Records, 1993); *Preparing Today for Tomorrow's Breakdown* LP/CD (Excursion records; also released as *Serpico* on CD, 1994). **Serpico:** *Feel Bad Rainbow* LP/CD/CS (Equal Vision, 1995); *They Shoot Babies Don't They?* 7" (Day After, 1995); *Rumble* LP/CD/CS (Equal Vision Records, 1996); Split 7" with Three Steps Up (Struggle, 1996); Split 7" with Walleye (Food Not Bombs, 1996); Split 7" with J-Church (Ded Beat, 1996); *I'm Not Dead* 7" (C.I., 1996); *The Weakest Boy in the Troop Award Singles Collection* (Excursion, 1996); *Heroes of the Bomb Scare* 7" (Day After, 1998).

7 SECONDS

Original title of the band **Seven Seconds.** The band later dropped the number seven in their logo in favor of Seven Seconds.

SEVEN SECONDS

Long-running punk bad from Nevada that ranks as one of the most influential and melodic **hardcore** bands. Led by the charismatic Kevin Seconds (Kevin Marvelli) along with long-term members Steve Youth (Kevin's brother) on bass and guitar and drummer Troy Mowatt (along with a variety of other bass and guitar players, most notably Bobby Adams), Seven Seconds continued for more than 25 years. The band originally formed as a reaction to the conservative nature of their hometown and connected with **Ian MacKaye** and **Henry Rollins** (then Garfield) via the post office, the only means of communication for punks before the Internet. The band pioneered the skeeno sound (named after the area encompassing Reno, Lake Tahoe, and Sparks) and developed a distinctive tribal look by drawing black lines below their eyes, much like athletic sun protection or Indian tribal paint. After playing some shows with **Minor Threat,** Seven Seconds began to tour outside of their home base and started to mentor other U.S. bands such as **Youth of Today.** Kevin Seconds also wrote for *Maximum Rock 'n' Roll* on the Reno scene. Although Seven Seconds did not necessarily identity as a **straight edge** band, the band did reject drugs and alcohol and dedicated themselves to clean living and helping punks though their record label **Positive Force,** which also grew to a multistate organization dedicated to political and social change. Seven Seconds put out some of the fastest yet most accessible music of the early 1980s and covered both Nena's "99 Red Balloons" and Nancy Sinatra's "These Boots Are Made for Walking." After several classic records such as the anthemic ode to unity *Walk Together, Rock Together* and *New Wind,* Seven Seconds mutated at one point in the 1980s. Kevin Seconds and the other band members grew their hair, and the band changed their style of music (reminiscent of U2 or REM), as documented on the live record *Live! Plus One.* The band even interpolated a section of "Cuyahoga" by REM in the middle of a song. The band continued to tour and release new music far more reminiscent of their original sound than the music they recorded for much of the 1980s and 1990s. Seven Seconds also worked with the local and national punk communities to provide information about venues touring bands could play and also created a network of activist punks who could work on social and political issues. Kevin Seconds also released work under various other names, including his own name, Drop Acid, Five Foot Ten, and Mustard. *See also* Positive Force.

Discography: *Socially Fucked Up* (tape; Vicious Scam, 1981); *3 Chord Politics* (tape; Vicious Scam, 1981); *Skin, Brains and Guts* EP7 (Alternative Tentacles, 1982); *Committed for Life* EP7 (Squirtdown, 1983); *The Crew* (Better Youth Organization, 1984, 1994); *Walk Together, Rock Together* (Positive Force/BYO, 1985; Better Youth Organization, 1994); *Blasts from the Past* EP7 (Positive Force, 1986); *New Wind* (Positive Force/BYO, 1986; Better Youth Organization, 1994); *Praise* EP (Positive Force/BYO, 1987); *Live! One Plus One* (Positive Force/Giant, 1987, 1995); *Ourselves* (Restless, 1988, 1993); *Soulforce Revolution* (Restless, 1987 or 1989, 1993); *Old School* (Headhunter/Cargo, 1991); *Out the Shizzy* (Headhunter/Cargo, 1993); *alt.music.hardcore* (Headhunter/Cargo, 1995); *The Music, the Message* (Immortal/Epic, 1995); *7 Seconds (+ Bonus Tracks)* (Byo, 1997); *Good to Go* (SideOneDummy, 1999); *Scream Real Loud . . . LIVE!* (SideOneDummy, 2000); *Better Youth Years* (Golf Records, 2001); *Take It Back, Take It On, Take It Over* (SideOneDummy, 2005). **Jackshit:** *Hicktown* EP (Squirtdown, 1984). **Drop Acid:** *Making God Smile* (Restless, 1991); *46th & Teeth E.P.* (Headhunter/Cargo, 1992). **Kevin Seconds/5'10":** *Rodney, Reggie, Emily* (Earth Music/Cargo, 1994). **Kevin Seconds:** *Stoudamire* (Earth Music/Cargo, 1997); *Heaven's Near Wherever You Are* (Headhunter/Cargo, 2001). **Mustard:** *Mostaza* (Sunspot, 1996).

76% UNCERTAIN

Early 1980s Connecticut **hardcore** punk band featuring Mike Spadacini on guitar and Chip Moody on drums. Numerous personnel changes and lack of recording support led to the band calling it quits by the end of the 1980s. After the death of Jeff Robinson in a car accident, the band reunited in 1997 for benefit shows for Robinson's family and continued to reunite sporadically.

Discography: *Estimated Starting Time* (Shmegma, 1984); *Nothing but Love Songs* (Schmegma, 1986); *Hunk Hunka Burning Log* (Grant, 1990).

SEX

London fashion boutique at 430 Kings Road in Chelsea owned by **Malcolm McLaren** and partner **Vivienne Westwood** where the **Sex Pistols** formed and most of **punk fashion** in Britain was developed. The store started out as Let It Rock in 1971 when McLaren and a partner bought the store and sold Teddy Boy gear and 1950s records. The store quickly mutated into Too Fast to Live Too Young to Die, and they sold motorcycle jackets and paraphernalia and zoot suits. At this point the store attracted a clientele that included Alice Cooper, **Lou Reed,** and the **New York Dolls,** whom McLaren managed in 1974. When McLaren returned from the United States, he was inspired by the punk style he had seen on the Dolls and **Richard Hell.** He rechristened the shop Sex and stocked it with bandage gear and leather and rubber costumes, sold by shop assistants such as Chrissie Hyndes (later of the Pretenders), Glenn Matlock, and the enigmatic Jordan, who later became one of the most famous faces of British punk rock. The Sex Pistols were formed in the shop, and soon all of the early punks such as Siouxsie Sioux and Mick Jones became regulars. The shop evolved into Seditionairies: Clothes for Heroes in December 1976, and it outfitted most of the class of 1977. The shop eventually evolved into World's End, which it remains.

SEX PISTOLS

Along with the **Ramones,** one of the two most influential bands of the 1970s punk rock scene. They pioneered a sound, look, and aesthetic that was enormously influential on both the British and U.S. punk rock scenes, and the Sex Pistols created a media storm that became

Johnny Rotten of the Sex Pistols was punk's ultimate provocateur. *Photofest.*

the dominant definition of punk rock for most people unfamiliar with punk's nuances. Their first and only proper record, *Never Mind the Bollocks, Here's the Sex Pistols*, is one of the most imitated and well known of punk records and features some of the most famous songs in punk history: **"God Save the Queen," "Anarchy in the UK,"** and "Pretty Vacant." The group was equally well known for its provocative lyrics and the controversy, chaos, and confusion caused by the band wherever it went. The Sex Pistols have been the subject of much controversy as to how much control their Svengaliesque manager, **Malcolm McLaren,** had over the group during their brief existence. Bass player **Sid Vicious** is revered by many punks for his brief and tumultuous life that ended in murder and an overdose in 1978. The band was formed by Malcolm McLaren, proprietor of influential bondage and fetish boutique **Sex,** who was looking to form a band inspired by the experiences he had managing the **New York Dolls** and the exotic look he had seen on New York pioneer **Richard Hell.** The original members were Steve Jones on lead vocals, Wally Nightingale on guitar, Paul Cook on drums, and Glenn Matlock on bass. British journalist **Nick Kent** was also an early member but left soon due to his growing drug problem. Nightingale was kicked out of the band (even though he provided the rehearsal space), and Steve Jones shifted to guitar. After McLaren spent fruitless months searching for a lead singer, asking at different points Sylvain Sylvain and **Johnny Thunders** from the New York Dolls to front his new group, eventually he found the proper singer in the misanthropic but compelling John Lydon, After auditioning with his back to the band, singing along to Alice Cooper's "Eighteen," the charismatic Lydon (soon to change his name to **Johnny Rotten**) was asked to join the band, and the Sex Pistols began to look for gigs.

Their first gig was on November 6, 1975, at St. Martin's Art College, and they soon began playing art colleges such as St. Albans and Chelsea School of Art, often under assumed names. Soon the band graduated to larger clubs like the Marquee, supporting bands such as Eddie and the Hot Rods, a gig that was reviewed by the *New Music Express* (*NME*) and started a string of positive press that McLaren expertly manipulated into gigs at larger venues like the **100 Club.** After fans Howard Devoto and Steve Shelley of the embryonic **Buzzcocks** organized a show at the Manchester Free Trade Hall in June 1976, numerous other bands inspired by the Sex Pistols' look and attitude started to form, including the members of **Joy Division,** Morrisey, and Tony Wilson of Factory Records. By July 1976, the Pistols had already worked out many of their best-known songs, such as "Anarchy," "Pretty Vacant," and "Seventeen."

From there, their notoriety spread via word of mouth and a few rave reviews in the British press, which was much more open to punk rock than its U.S. counterparts would later prove to be. On December 1, 1976, thanks to the rock band Queen canceling at the last minute, the Sex Pistols were booked on Bill Grundy's TV show *Today.* The band, accompanied by several friends, including Siouxsie and Sue Catwoman, drank heavily before the cameras rolled. The subsequent furor led to tabloid headlines such as "The Filth and the Fury," to Bill Grundy being suspended for two weeks, and to the cancellation of many dates for the Sex Pistols' upcoming tour of the United Kingdom with the **Heartbreakers, Damned,** and the **Clash.** The Damned were kicked off the tour for offering to play a show at which the other bands declined to play because the Sex Pistols were asked to play beforehand for the approval of the local town council. The tour ended acrimoniously, with most dates canceled and much money lost by the band. After returning from a brief tour of Holland in 1976, they were unceremoniously dumped from their label EMI due to allegations of improper behavior in the airport en route to Holland. The Sex Pistols signed shortly thereafter to A&M records and were subsequently dumped again after yet another violent debacle featuring the irrepressible Sid Vicious. They then signed to Virgin Records and released the "God Save the Queen" single in May 1977, leading to an almost immediate ban from the airwaves. The band embarked on a cruise down the River Thames on June 7, during which they played a seven-song set and were asked to dock by police, who eventually

Susie Catwoman had one of the most engaging looks in British punk fandom. *Photo by Ray Stevenson/Rex Features.*

arrested one person. "God Save the Queen" went to number one on the British charts that month despite an almost complete lack of airplay. The album *Never Mind the Bollocks, Here's the Sex Pistols* was released in England in October 1977 to immediate notoriety and controversy. In late 1977, a shopkeeper was brought to court for displaying a mock-up of the album cover, but after testimony, including some by professors on the origins and common usage of the word *bollocks*, the case was dismissed in late 1977. After much discussion and many aborted attempts, the band began a truncated U.S. tour in January 1978 that skipped the major venues in Los Angeles and New York City but concentrated on the South and Midwest, starting at the Great Southeast Music Hall. To no avail, Sid was given a babysitter by the label, but his continued search for **heroin** in an unfamiliar country led him into frequent fights and childish behavior. Other stops included Austin and the Longhorn Ballroom in Dallas, a place where country legends had played for years. The tour ended at the Winterland Ballroom in San Francisco on January 14, 1978. Johnny Rotten ended the chaotic show by taunting the audience with the now-classic line "Did you ever feel that you had been cheated?" This was the last live performance of the Sex Pistols before reunion tours in 1996 and 2003 with Glenn Matlock on bass to replace the departed Sid Vicious. Following the Winterland show, Sid found solace with some fans who scored him some heroin, leading to an overdose. The band effectively ended when Steve Jones and Paul Cook informed Johnny Rotten that they no longer wanted to work with him. Johnny flew to New York City to release some steam, and Steve and Paul flew down to Rio de Janeiro, Brazil, to record with noted English fugitive **Ronnie Biggs.**

Johnny went off in February to sign bands for Richard Branson of Virgin Records along with **Don Letts,** the punk filmmaker and DJ who would later go on to form Big Audio Dynamite with Mick Jones from the Clash. Sid Vicious went to Paris to film the video for his cover of the Frank Sinatra standard "My Way." Shortly after Sid and Nancy Spungen arrived in the United States, Nancy was found dead of a stab wound at the Chelsea Hotel, and Sid Vicious was arrested and charged with the killing. After getting into a fight with **Patti Smith**'s bother, Sid was returned to the prison at Rikers Island. When he was released from jail after seven weeks, he overdosed in a Greenwich Village apartment.

John Lydon sued Malcolm McLaren to dissolve the Sex Pistols' assets, and in February 1979 the judge ruled against McLaren. Part of the lawsuit's resolutions was the quick release of the soundtrack to the Sex Pistols' film put together by Malcolm. *The Great Rock 'n' Roll Swindle* was released quickly to recoup any money owed the group. The album was a collection of odds and ends and new recordings made by various permutations of the band without Johnny Rotten (now going by his real name, John Lydon), who launched a lawsuit against McLaren and his company Glitterbeast that would last for eight years. In retrospect, the influence of the group in both sociological and aesthetic terms cannot be underestimated. Along with the Ramones, they were the most influential of the punk bands, and most of what people know about punk rock in terms of music and look came directly from the Sex Pistols and their progeny. Overall, the Sex Pistols had the most influence on the look and attitude of punk over the last 30 years, especially impressive for a band that recorded only one proper album and a handful of singles during its brief initial life span. The Sex Pistols reunited with original bassist Glenn Matlock for tours in 1996 and 2003. McLaren went on to various projects and ran for mayor of London. Steve Jones had a radio show in Los Angeles. Most recently, Johnny Rotten appeared on the British reality television show *Get Me out of Here, I'm a Celebrity.*

Discography: *Spunk* (UK Blank, 1977); *Never Mind the Bollocks, Here's the Sex Pistols* (Warner Bros., 1977); *The Great Rock 'n' Roll Swindle* (UK Virgin, 1979); *Some Product Carri On* (UK Virgin, 1979); *Flogging a Dead Horse* (UK Virgin, 1980); *The Heyday* (tape; UK Factory, 1980); *The Mini Album EP* (UK Chaos, 1985; Restless, 1988); *The Original Pistols Live* (UK Receiver, 1985); *Live Worldwide* (UK Konexion, 1985); *Best of the Sex Pistols Live* (UK Bondage, 1985); *Anarchy in the UK Live* (UK, 1985); *Where Were You in '77* (UK 77, 1985); *Power of the Pistols* (UK 77, 1985); *We Have Cum for Your Children (Wanted: The Goodman Tapes)* (Skyclad, 1988); *Better Live Than Dead* (Restless, 1988); *The Swindle Continues* (Restless, 1988); *Anarchy Worldwide* (UK Specific, 1988); *Cash for Chaos EP* (UK Specific, 1988); *Pirates of Destiny* (I Swirled, 1989); *The Mini Album Plus* (UK Chaos, 1989); *Live and Loud!!* (UK Link, 1989); *No Future U.K.?* (UK Receiver, 1989); *Live at Chelmsford Top Security Prison* (Restless, 1990). **The Original Pistols/New York Dolls:** *After the Storm* (UK Receiver, 1985). **Sid Vicious:** *Sid Sings* (UK Virgin, 1979); *Love Kills NYC* (UK Konexion, 1985).

SHAGGS

Group of three sisters, Dot, Helen, and Betty, who were active in the 1960s and known for their amateurish mangling of songs that would later be looked upon as a foretelling off the **DIY** aesthetic of punk rock. The Shaggs were put together as a band by their ambitious father, Austin Wiggin, who encouraged his children and, presumably, thought the girls were more talented than they were. The three sisters took music lessons and began homeschooling to allow more time for practicing. The first album, *Philosophy of the World,* is an amateurish and primitive version of outside rock and roll that soon went out of its limited print run. A second album, *Shaggs' Own Thing,* featured a fourth sister, Rachel, on bass but was musically very similar. The Shaggs best-known song was the charming "My Pal Foot Foot," which displayed the sisters at their most inspired. Many rock critics valued the Shaggs for the amateurish, but seemingly innocent, nature of their music, and many punk bands emulated the inspired amateurishness of their album.

Discography: *Philosophy of the World* (Third World, 1969; Red Rooster/Rounder, 1980); *Shaggs' Own Thing* (Red Rooster/Rounder, 1982).

SHAM 69

Anthemic band from the gutters of Hersham, England, formed in 1975, that made music with loud football-stadium choruses and (unfortunately) attracted a large contingent from the racist, fascistic **National Front.** The band was formed by singer Jimmy Pursey on lead vocals, Billy Bostick on drums, Albie Slider on bass, and Johnny Goodfornothing and Neil Harris on guitars. The band's name came from graffiti in their home neighborhood; the graffiti said "Hersham 69," but the *Her* was torn away, so the band adopted that as their name. Sham 69 was plagued by personnel changes early on, with Bostick, Goodfornothing, and Harris leaving. They were replaced by Mark Cain on drums and Dave Parsons on guitar, then Albie left as well and was replaced by Dave Tregunna on bass. Their first album, *Tell Us the Truth*, was released in 1978 and featured one live side and one side of studio recordings. Although the band wished to focus on the music, this was nearly impossible due to the band's working-class credentials, and many shows were plagued with violence by **skinheads** and members of the National Front who responded to the ambiguity of the band's lyrics. Sham 69 was unfairly lumped in with other **oi** bands that emulated British working-class culture and uniforms. Although the band never declared themselves as followers of the National Front, they also (along with more avowedly anarchist bands such as **Crass**) refused to bar racist skinheads from their shows, although this may also have been a logistical problem. The band struggled on but eventually broke up in 1980 after four records. Guitarist Dave Parsons and lead singer Jimmy Pursey reunited over the years and toured to celebrate the band's 30th anniversary. Dave Tregunna later went on to form the Lords of the New Church with Stiv Bators from the **Dead Boys** and Brian James from the **Damned.**

Discography: *Tell Us the Truth* (Sire, 1978); *That's Life* (Polydor, 1978); *The Adventures of the Hersham Boys* (Polydor, 1979); *The Game* (Polydor, 1980); *Information Libre* (Creative Man, 1995); *Kings and Queens* (Dojo, 1995); *Soapy Water and Mr. Marmalade* (Plus Eye, 1995); *The X Files* (Cleopatra, 1997); *Direct Action: Day 21* (Resurgent, 2001); *Live at CBGB's* (Harry May, 2002).

SHAW, GREG

Publisher of fanzines *Mojo Navigator* (from 1966) and *Who Put the Bomp* (from 1970). Shaw hired writers such as **Lester Bangs** and Grail Marcus and released records as Bomp Records. Artists who recorded for Bomp Records included the Flaming Groovies (Shaw founded Bomp to give the Groovies a U.S. outlet for their music), **Iggy Pop,** Stiv Bators, and the notable series of Pebbles anthologies of 1960s pop nuggets. Shaw died of a heart attack in October 2004 in Los Angeles.

SHELTER

Krishna-core band from New York City led by Ray Capo and Porcell, formerly of the influential New York City **straight edge** band **Youth of Today.** The band espoused the doctrines of the **Hare Krishna** sect in their music, and most lyrics reflect the doctrines of Krishna Consciousness. After the breakup of Youth of Today, Ray Capo struggled for some time to determine if music and a spiritual life were mutually incompatible, and Shelter was the compromise in which music and spirituality were mixed with equal fervor. Eventually, Porcell left the band, and Shelter went on for a while without him before calling it quits in the early 1990s. Members subsequently reunited for new albums.

Discography: *Perfection of Desire* (Revelation, 1990); *Quest for Certainty* (Equal Vision, 1991; Revelation, 1998); *Attaining the Supreme* (Equal Vision, 1993); *Mantra* (Supersoul/Roadrunner, 1995); *Beyond Planet*

Earth (Supersoul/Roadrunner, 1997); *Chanting, Prayers & Meditations* (Son of Yashoda, 1997); *When 20 Summers Pass* (Victory, 2000).

SHIBBOLETH

Autobiography of **Crass** leader Penny Rimbaud (JJ Ratter), published in 1998, that is slight on the history of Crass and heavy on philosophical musing on the nature of **anarchy** and violent fantasy sequences. The book (full title *Shibboleth: My Revolting Life*) ostensibly details Ratter's life and his admiration for Phil (Wally Hope Russell), a hippy leader and founder of the Stonehenge festivals, which were initially opposed by the British authorities and often crushed violently. Although the book is purportedly an autobiography, few biographical details are provided and are all too often interspersed with (presumably) fantasy sequences (for example, when Ratter kills a pimp and disrupts traffic with the judicious use of explosives, all in the name of revolution against the dominant corporate culture). The book ends up more or less a manifesto outlining the development of Ratter's beliefs and his eventual rejection of pacifism as a part of anarchism. Ratter also released several works of fiction, including *The Diamond Signature*.

SHONEN KNIFE

All-female Japanese band from Osaka founded in 1981 and influenced by the **Ramones** and U.S. pop punk that became one of the most popular bands to tour the West from Japan. (The band's name literally can be translated as "boy's knife.") The band, founded by sisters Naoko Yamano on vocals and guitar and Atsuko Yamano on drums (who also does much of the design work for the group) and Michie Nakatani vocals and bass, who retired from the band in June 1999 and was replaced by Atsuko on bass, with a new drummer stepping in to complete the group. The band was inspired by U.S. pop music, especially the Beatles (the band later covered the song "Rain" on a record), **Red Kross (Red Cross),** and **White Flag** (Shonen Knife did tribute songs to both bands). The band had commercial success in the United States in the 1980s with several videos on **MTV** and a spot on several successful tours. Although Shonen Knife had numerous songs that sound (and very often are) very silly to U.S. ears, the band is actually very challenging in the ways that it deals with consumer culture and how to maintain the balance between being female in a male-dominated industry (especially in Japan, where traditionally far fewer women were allowed positions of authority) and playing a U.S. art form in a culture that has its own unique take on rebellion and how people can express themselves in a **DIY** way. A particularly important way in which they do this is by taking control of their own image through drummer-turned-bassist Atsuko Yamano's designs for the band, which mark them as being far removed from the Japanese *idoru* (female idols, mostly manufactured in the manner of U.S. boy bands). The band was quickly championed by bands such as Red Kross and **Sonic Youth** and after several unreleased albums in Japan was finally able to cross over to U.S. markets in the 1990s with the compilation of rerecorded songs *Lets' Knife*. The band continued to tour and record.

Discography: *Burning Farm* (Japan Zero, 1983; tape, K, 1985); *Yama No Attchan* (Japan Zero, 1984, Japan MCA Victor, 1995); *Pretty Little Baka Guy* (Subversive, 1986; Oglio, 2004); *Shonen Knife* (Gasatanka/Giant, 1990); *Pretty Little Baka Guy + Live in Japan!* (Gasatanka/Rockville, 1990); *712* (Gasatanka/Rockville, 1991); *Let's Knife* (Virgin, 1993); *Rock Animals* (UK Creation, 1993; Virgin, 1994; EMI Special Markets, 1998); *Brown Mushrooms and Other Delights* EP (Virgin, 1993); *We Are Very Happy You Came* (UK Creation, 1993); *Favorites* EP (Japan MCA, 1993); *Greatest History* (Japan MCA, 1995); *The Birds and the B-Sides* (Virgin, 1996); *Super Mix* (Japan MCA Victor, 1997); *Brand New Knife* (Big Deal, 1997); *Explosion!* EP (Big Deal, 1997); *Ultra Mix* (MCA Victor, 1998); *Happy Hour* (Big Deal, 1998); *Strawberry*

Sound (Japan Universal Victor, 2000); *Millennium Edition* (Japan Universal Victor, 2001); *Heavy Songs* (Confidential, 2003); *Genki Shock* (Pv, 2005). **Various Artists:** *Every Band Has a Shonen Knife Who Loves Them* (Gasatanka/Giant, 1989).

SICK OF IT ALL

New York City **hardcore** band with a ferocious, raw, and aggressive sound. Founded in 1985 by brothers Lou Koller on lead vocals and Pete Koller on guitars, the band also featured Armand Majidi on drums and Rich Cipriani on bass; later Craig Setari played bass. The band was a massive draw in the New York City hardcore scene during the 1980s and 1990s and found itself the subject of unwanted controversy when teenager Wayne Lo killed several classmates in a massacre at his Massachusetts prep school while wearing a Sick of It All T-shirt. Although some in the mainstream media reported that Lo had been influenced by the band, the *New York Times* actually provided a forum for the band to explain why its lyrics were not about violence and that the student had willfully misinterpreted its philosophy. This is a rare example of a band actually getting a chance to defend itself from the usual mainstream suspicions about the links between punk and violence. Majidi also played in the band Rest in Pieces.

Discography: *Sick of It All* (Revelation, 1987, 1997); *Blood, Sweat, and No Tears* (Relativity, 1989); *We Stand Alone* EP (Relativity, 1991); *Just Look Around* (Relativity, 1992); *Scratch the Surface* (EastWest, 1994); *Live in a World Full of Hate* (Lost & Found, 1995); *Spreading the Hardcore Reality* (Lost & Found, 1995); *Built to Last* (Elektra, 1997); *Potential for a Fall single* (Fat Wreck Chords, 1999); *Call to Arms* (Fat Wreck Chords, 1999); *Yours Truly* (Fat Wreck Chords, 2000); *Live in a Dive* (Fat Wreck Chords, 2002); *Relentless Single* (Bridge Nine, 2003); *Life on the Ropes* (Fat Wreck Chords, 2003); *Outtakes for the Outcast* (Fat Wreck Chords, 2004). **Rest in Pieces:** *My Rage* (One Step Ahead, 1986; Blackout, 1994); *Under My Skin* (Roadracer, 1990).

SIDE BY SIDE

New York City **hardcore** band from the 1980s that was popular on the hardcore matinee scene of the 1980s. The band was formed by Jules Massey on lead vocals, with Eric Fink on lead guitar, Alex Brown on rhythm guitar, Billy Bitter on bass, and Sammy Siegler on drums. The band played the local scene and recorded an EP and a full-length album for **Revelation Records** before calling it quits. After the demise of Side by Side, Massey formed the band Alone in a Crowd.

Discography: *You're Only Young Once* EP (Revelation, 1988); *You're Only Young Once* LP (Revelation, 1997). **Alone in a Crowd:** *S/T* (Flux, 1989).

SIMPSONS

Many punks see an affinity with the popular and often-subversive animated Fox television show. The **Ramones** were featured in one episode singing "Happy Birthday" to Mr. Burns. Numerous punk **flyers** and album covers paid tribute to the *Simpsons* (just as other cartoon cultural icons such as Calvin and Hobbes were also used in an homage and subversion of the original intent), and *Change Zine* put together a tribute compilation to the *Simpsons* titled *This Is Springfield, Not Shelbyville* (which is also a tribute and parody to the well-known punk compilation **This Is Boston, Not LA**), featuring bands doing tributes to the *Simpsons* or covers of songs from the series. *Simpsons* tattoos can also be seen in the **pit** at many punk shows.

SIOUXSIE AND THE BANSHEES

Quintessential and long-lived band claimed by both the punk and goth camps—although lead singer Siouxsie Sioux (Susan Dallion) has long been uncomfortable with both of those labels—that created some of the moodiest and most atmospheric music of the early punk scene. The band, led by stalwarts Siouxsie Sioux and bassist Steve Severin (later joined by drummer Budgie and occasionally with the help of Cure leader Robert Smith), created a unique sound and look that inspired many young men and women to experiment with gender and identity. Siouxsie, along Steve Severin, was a member of the **Bromley Contingent,** which was a group of fans who followed the **Sex Pistols.** Siouxsie was sitting behind the Sex Pistols during their appearance with Bill Grundy on his *Today* show, and Grundy openly flirted with her, much to her disgust. The original band was formed in September1976 by Bromley Contingent members and **David Bowie** fanatics Siouxsie and Steve Severin after the breakup of their first group, the **Flowers of Romance** (later the title of a **Public Image Limited** album). Their show at the **100 Club** punk festival with drummer **Sid Vicious** (who refused to play cymbals) and guitarist Marco Pironi (who later went on to more success as a member of Adam and the Ants) was an unqualified attention getter that revealed Siouxsie's electrifying stage presence. After Vicious and Pironi left the band for greener pastures, the band decide to take itself more seriously. In 1977, the group solidified with the addition of John McKay on guitar and Kenny Morris on drums. Early gigs were rife with controversy as Siouxsie sometimes wore a swastika onstage (apparently to demystify it, but both she and Severin often gave contradictory accounts of this in interviews at the time) and sang about there being "too many Jews for my liking" in the song "Love in a Void" (which she later clarified as meaning "too many fat businessmen"). These and similar statements, as well as Siouxsie's love of bondage clothing, guaranteed the band attention, both the wanted and unwanted sort. The band became a sort of joke as being the longest-running unsigned punk band, but after months of gigging without success, they finally managed to score a record deal with Polydor records and release their first LP, *The Scream,* in October 1978. Their second album, *Join Hands,* was released in 1979, but the band splintered when Morris and McKay abruptly quit shortly before a gig in 1979. Siouxsie and Severin soldiered on with replacements, including Budgie on drums from the **Slits,** who would remain a member until the band eventually fell apart in the late 1990s, and Robert Smith of the Cure, who did double duty with both bands for a few years before turning his full attention to the Cure and was replaced by guitarist John McGeoch of Magazine, who died in late 2004. Smith returned for a while but was eventually forced to quit and concentrate on the Cure again and was replaced by John Carruthers, who stayed for several records before being replaced by Jon Klein of Specimen. The band grew in popularity as the 1980s went on, Siouxsie (slightly) toned down her image for mass consumption, and the band moved into a more sophisticated musical phase with tribal beats and eerie soundscapes. The band was also one of the bands of the first Lollapallooza tour, along with **Henry Rollins** and **Butthole Surfers.** Siouxsie now largely tours and records either by herself or as part of the Creatures with drummer Budgie, although Siouxsie and the Banshees have had sporadic reunions since the mid-1990s. Overall, despite her controversial and designed-to-shock comments, look, and attitude, Siouxsie was one of the first, and certainly the longest-lasting punk original, to prove that it was not just a boys' club, and she paved the way for women from **hardcore, punk,** and the **riot grrrl movement** to have a say in the music industry and in punk rock scenes.

Discography: *The Scream* (Polydor, 1978; Geffen, 1984); *Join Hands* (UK Polydor, 1979; Geffen, 1984); *Kaleidoscope* (PVC, 1980; Geffen, 1984); *Juju* (PVC, 1981; Geffen, 1984); *Arabian Knights* EP (PVC, 1981); *Once upon a Time/The Singles* (PVC, 1981; Geffen, 1984); *A Kiss in the Dreamhouse* (UK Polydor, 1982; Geffen, 1984); *Nocturne* (Wonderland/Geffen, 1983); *Hyaena* (Wonderland/Geffen, 1984); *The Thorn* EP (Wonderland/Polydor, 1984); *Cities in Dust* EP (Geffen, 1985); *Tinderbox* (Wonderland/ Geffen, 1986); *Through the Looking Glass* (Wonderland/Geffen, 1987); *The Peel Sessions* EP (UK Strange Fruit, 1987); *Peepshow* (Wonderland/Geffen, 1988); *The Peel Sessions* EP (UK Strange Fruit, 1988); *The*

Peel Sessions (Strange Fruit/Dutch East India Trading, 1991); *Superstition* (Wonderland/Geffen, 1991); *Twice upon a Time—The Singles* (Wonderland/Geffen, 1992); *The Rapture* (Wonderland/Geffen, 1995). **Creatures:** *Wild Things* EP (UK Polydor, 1981); *Feast* (UK Wonderland/Polydor, 1983); *Boomerang* (Geffen, 1989). **Glove:** *Blue Sunshine* (Wonderland/Polydor, 1983; Rough Trade, 1990).

SITUATIONISTS

Originally a French social and political movement of the 1950s and 1960s founded by Guy Debord, who wrote the influential book *The Society of the Spectacle*. Many scholars, such as Greil Marcus in his book *Lipstick Traces: A Secret History of the Twentieth Century*, have found a connection between the situationists and **Malcolm McLaren's** work with the **Sex Pistols. Jamie Reid,** the artist who did most of the flyers and record artwork for the Sex Pistols, was certainly influenced by the situationists in his cut-and-paste art style in which different images and words were juxtaposed, often in a manner that evoked a ransom note. Although the individual members of the Sex Pistols were later to deny both the extent of McLaren's control and involvement in any movement, especially situationism, there does seem to be some connection on the stylistic level and between situationism and certain of the anarchist collectives and **squats** in England during the first punk wave in the 1970s. *See also* McLaren, Malcolm; Punk and Fashion; Reid, Jamie; Sex Pistols.

SKA

Ska was a Jamaican precursor to **reggae** that achieved great popularity in the early 1960s and was epitomized by bands such as the Skatalites and Desmond Dekker. Since the 1960s, numerous punks bands in both Europe and the United States have been influenced by ska. The relationship between **punk** and ska can be examined on several levels. On one hand, the use of ska was a recurring motif in many punk scenes, from the **2 Tone** movement in England in the late 1970s and early 1980s to the U.S. scenes of the 1980s and the 1990s. The English version, however, at least in the 2 Tone days, was much more overtly political than most of the U.S. bands that jumped on the bandwagon in the 1990s. The popularity of ska in England also resurrected British problems with racism and cultural assimilation due to the large number of Caribbean immigrants who lived in the poorer neighborhoods in London and in many major cities. Many of the original members of ska bands were also influenced by the early nonracist skinhead scene in which young disaffected British men and women adopted the uniform of the working class and listened to imported ska and rerecords from Jamaica. The vestiges of the skinhead scene (which had splintered into various factions), the rise and influence of movements such as **RAR (Rock against Racism),** which combined reggae and punk bands on the same bill, the demise of the first wave of punk in England, and the many bands (such as the **Clash** and the **Ruts**) already using reggae music led to a generation of new musicians who saw the limitations in punk and decided to both move beyond it and adopt a new style that had its roots in the early 1960s. Ska, in the British scene, became a powerful force for social commentary in the hands of bands such as the **Specials,** Selecter, and English Beat, most of whom recorded early on for 2 Tone, the rerecord label started by Specials keyboard player Jerry Dammers. The British ska scene, although it did not last long, also influenced numerous U.S. bands, in particular **Operation Ivy.**

Operation Ivy was a Californian band that adopted ska and reggae rhythms in its music and was extremely influential in its abbreviated life span. The band sang about unity as it played around the Berkeley scene and released little material during its lifetime but led to the formation of many ska bands in the United States in the late 1980s to mid-1990s, including far less political bands such as Reel Big Fish and No Doubt in its early days. Guitarist Tim Armstrong from Operation

Ivy went on to form the band **Rancid.** Ska in the United States could be political, as demonstrated by Operation Ivy and some of the music of Rancid, but largely it lacked the intense political edge that the best of British ska possessed. *See also* Clash; Operation Ivy; Reggae; Ruts; 2 Tone.

SKANK

A form of slam dancing in the **pit,** usually called skanking because of the position assumed by the dancer. The origins of the term are in some dispute, but an early reference is the **Circle Jerks** song "I Just Want Some Skank." The term is also sometimes a pejorative used by sexist punks against women, as also seen in the song by the Circle Jerks. *See also* Pit.

SKATEBOARDING

Skateboard enthusiasts and punk culture have a long and varied history, with most of the earliest alliances coming from the **Orange Country,** California, scenes. Many of the early Southern California bands were skateboard aficionados, and the outlaw culture that went along with skateboarding fit in well with the early **hardcore** punk scenes. Today, many street punks can be seen in major cities with their skateboards covered in their favorite bands logos.

SKATE PUNK

During the 1980s, numerous people involved in the skateboarding and surfing subcultures of Southern California became interested in punk bands such as **Black Flag,** the **Circle Jerks,** and **JFA,** some of whom also skated. The young skateboarders found punk's energy and aggression to be the perfect background music for their athleticism. Later on, the **Big Boys** launched their own line of skateboards. *Thrasher* magazine also highlighted the connection during the 1980s and released skate videos with punk soundtracks and the photography of Glen Friedman, whose photos for many early skate magazines and of the punk scene also helped make the connection much more explicit. Skate punk is enormously popular in the United States, and there are venues from television to live tours, such as the Warped tour, that feature skate punk bands as well as demonstrations of skateboarding. Some punks question the involvement of large corporations as sponsors of skate punk, and in July 2005, Nike's skateboard division angered many punk fans by releasing a flyer and Web advertisement for their Major Threat skate tour. Nike not only evoked the name of legendary **hardcore** band **Minor Threat** but also accompanied the almost identical logo with an image clearly meant to evoke the cover photo of the first Minor Threat album. Under protest, Nike withdrew the advertisement, but this illustrates the ambiguity of punk rock associating with major corporations.

SKINHEAD MOONSTOMP

Early ska record beloved by **skinheads** before the movement coalesced into its less inclusive form. *Skinhead Moonstomp* was released by Symarip (also known as the Pyramids), featuring Johnny Orland on vocals, Montgomery Neysmith on keyboards, Roy Ellis on vocals, and various backing musicians. Symarip is generally known as the first skinhead band, doing music from and for skinheads, who were increasingly attracted to their shows when skinheads were fans of rock steady and **ska** music. The song is loosely based on Derrick Morgan's "Moon Hop," but such sampling is common in the world of reggae music. The band was an early skinhead icon and demonstrated the more positive side of the skinhead movement, which was about camaraderie and dancing as opposed to violence.

Discography: *The Pyramids* (President, 1969); *Skinhead Moonstomp: The Album* (Trojan, 1969, 2003); *Skinhead Moonstomp: The Best of Symarip* (Trojan, 2004).

SKINHEADS

Skinheads make up a subdivision of punks that predate punk and are one of the most controversial and sometimes reviled groups in punk, known for their specific fashion styles and codes, distinctive haircuts, and reputations for violence and racism. The skinhead movement is largely traced back to its roots in 1960s British working-class culture. Initially, it was not racist, and the members were followers of **reggae, ska**, and rock steady who wore the traditional working-class outfits of factory workers, including steel-toed boots, suspenders, straight-legged denim jeans, and extremely short hair. This movement more or less coalesced around the rock-steady bands that played clubs where white and black performers such as Symarip and Judge Dread played for an audience that mingled freely and was united by its class boundaries more than race. Different skinheads began associating themselves in a tribal style by adopting variations in dress and hairstyle, with shorter-haired suede-heads and smoothies adopting their own distinct look. By the 1970s, when punk became popular in England, skins, as some preferred to call themselves, began to divide further, with a large contingent joining forces with militant football fans and right-wing nationalistic movements such as the **National Front,** whose brand of jingoism and appeals to patriotism were found attractive by the mainly lower-class skinheads. The British media picked up on the violence at shows by **Skrewdriver** and other right-wing bands and began to demonize skins as much more violent than most of them were in reality. In the United States, many were first introduced to the skinhead look through the music of underground **hardcore** bands and the shaved head. The shaved head was not automatically a skinhead identifier in the United States, and it could also be associated with other movements such as **straight edge** punk or simply a devotion to hardcore and a rejection of the excesses of punk fashion. Many skinheads, alarmed by the bad publicity the movement was receiving from the media, formed groups such as SHARP (Skin Heads against Racial Prejudice) in the late 1980s, and members began to identify themselves by signs such as shoelace color that denote

Skinheads often have a reputation for violence and racism and are known for their fashion codes and distinctive shaved heads. © *Gavin Watson.*

whether the wearer was a communist, fascist, or simply a tolerant skin. Modern skin styles include dress shirts, "wife beater" T-shirts, suspenders, flight jackets, jeans rolled at the cuff for men, and boots, **Doc Martens** in particular, with laces that denote whether or not one is in favor of white power or racial unity or possibly communism. Men's hair is generally shorn close but not completely off, and women usually sport a fringe on the front and back. Musically, most skins listened to a variant of the **oi** music of the 1970s as epitomized by bands such as **Sham 69, Angelic Upstarts,** and Blitz, whereas many U.S. fans identified with bands such as **Agnostic Front, Warzone,** and the **Cro-Mags.** Modern skinhead bands such as the Templars, Anti-Heroes, and Niblick provided much of the modern skinhead soundtrack.

SKINS

The word *skins* is a shorthand term for **skinheads,** sometimes used interchangeably and often used in songs such as "Skins, Brains and Guts," an early song by the band **Seven Seconds.**

SKREWDRIVER

Skrewdriver was a notorious white-power band that had its roots in the original punk movement but quickly embraced a skinhead look and Nazi and racist philosophy as epitomized by the band's involvement with the **National Front.** Lead singer and white-power agitator Ian Stuart MacDonald lead various versions of the band throughout the 1980s and early 1990s, spewing racist swill until his death in a car accident. Although the band's later material is racist heavy metal, their first album is apparently fairly pedestrian punk rock typical of its time. All subsequent releases were on racist, white-power labels. Skrewdriver played as a regular punk band in its first incarnation (the band originally started as a Rolling Stones tribute band), which lasted until 1979. Stewart re-formed the band in 1982 and greeted his audience with a Nazi salute to indicate Skrewdriver's new direction and his newfound involvement with the National Front, the British white-power, anti-immigrant political group. In 1983, the band released the "White Power" single, which definitively established the band's new direction, as did the album *Hail the New Dawn.* Despite setbacks (such as Stewart being sentenced to a year in jail for a racially motivated beating), the band soldiered on, and Stewart formed a new organization Blood and Honor and a **rockabilly** band called the Klansmen and released new material from Skrewdriver, including a racist reworking of the song "Sweet Home Alabama" by Lynyrd Skynyrd. Stewart died in a car crash in 1993, and Skrewdriver ended with his death. The ultimate legacy of Skrewdriver may well be its negative emphasis on the darker side of punk rock and the skinhead movement. Not all skins are racist thugs, but Skrewdriver did nothing to soften this reputation. *See also* Punk and Race; Skinheads.
Select Discography: *Skrewdriver* (Chiswick, 1977); *Hail the New Dawn* (Blood and Honor, 1984).

SLANDER

Zine that offers a queer Asian American perspective on punk, by Mimi Nguyen, who also wrote for *Punk Planet* and *Maximum Rock 'n' Roll* and who recently finished her doctorate degree. *Slander* is a key zine from an actual outsider punk perspective.

SLAPSHOT

Straight edge hardcore band from Boston that gradually became more metallic after time. The band was started by Steve Risteen, Mark McKay, Jack Kelly, and Jordan Wood on guitar and over the years featured Darryl Sheppard on guitar, Jonathan Anastas on bass, Jamie Sciarappa on bass, Chris Lauria on bass, and Barry Hite on drums in the mid-1990s.

Discography: *Back on the Map* (Taang!, 1985); *Step on It* (Taang!, 1988, 1991); *Sudden Death Overtime* (Taang!, 1989); *Live at South 36* (Caroline, 1994); *Blast Furnace* (Caroline, 1995); *Unconsciousness* (Caroline, 1995); *16 Valve Hate* (Taang!, 1996); *Olde Tyme Hardcore* (Taang!, 1997); *Greatest Hits: Slashes & Crosschecks* (Bridge Nine, 2003); *Digital Warfare* (Bridge Nine, 2003); *Tear It Down* (Thorp, 2005).

SLASH

Los Angeles zine and record label that was influential in promoting local bands and, later, for releasing pivotal music from the Los Angles scene. The zine *Slash* was one of the first punk-related **zines** in the United States and was founded in 1977 by Claude "KickFace" Bessy, who had previously worked on several **reggae**-related zines, and Philomena Winstanley. The zine focused mostly on Los Angeles acts such as the **Screamers,** the **Weirdos,** and **X** as well as bands the editors admired, such as the **Damned.** The zine helped expose many of the early Los Angeles bands to readers outside of the immediate area and let others know about the thriving punk seeds being germinated in Los Angeles. Although the zine folded in 1980, the Slash record label was founded in 1980 by Bob Biggs as an outlet for releasing local music. Slash was sold to London records in 1986 and was distributed by Warner Brothers records from 1982 to 1996 and featured acts such as X, the Plugz, **Gun Club,** and the **Germs** as well as national acts such as Violent Femmes, Los Lobos and Faith No More. Slash's slogan was "Small enough to know the score, big enough to settle it." In 2003, the label was revived by Bob Biggs as Slash/BiggMassive.

SLAUGHTER AND THE DOGS

Early punk band from Manchester, England, around 1976 that put out sporadic singles on the pioneering Rabid label until the release of their album *Do It Dog Style* on Decca records. The band sporadically re-formed in subsequent decades and was led by singer Wayne Barrett (later replaced by Eddie Garrity) with guitarist Mike Rossi, bassist Howard Bates, Billy Duffy, later of the Cult, and included (according to rumor) a brief stint by future Smiths singer Morrisey on vocals. Some members later formed a band called the Studio Sweethearts with Billy Duffy.

Discography: *Do It Dog Style* (Decca, 1978; Damaged Goods, 1989); *Live Slaughter Rabid Dogs* (UK Rabid, 1979); *Live at the Factory* (Thrush, 1981); *Rabid Dogs* (UK Receiver, 1989); *The Slaughterhouse Tapes* (UK Link, 1989). **Slaughter:** *Bite Back* (DJM, 1980).

SLEATER-KINNEY

Sleater-Kinney is an all-female trio from Olympia, Washington, formed in 1994, that became one of the most commercially successful punk bands in the United States during the 1990s. The band was started after the demise of earlier bands lumped into the **riot grrrl movement** such as Heavens to Betsy, which featured singer and guitarist Corin Tucker, Carrie Brownstein from Excuse 17, and several drummers (including Misty Farell and Lora Macfarlane, who played on the first two records) before the band settled on Janet Weiss (who also played in the band Quasi with her former husband, Sam Cooms). Their eponymous debut record was released on Donna Dresch's Chainsaw label in 1995 and caused a minor sensation, but the band hit its stride with the electrifying *Call the Doctor* in 1996, which featured the song "I Wanna Be Your Joey Ramone," which situated the band as challengers of the gender assumptions inherent in punk rock. After moving up to major indie label **Kill Rock Stars,** the demise of Brownstein and Tucker's relationship, and the addition of Weiss, the next record, *Dig Me Out*, was even more emotionally charged and one of the most successful records on an indie label. In 2001, Tucker and her husband had their first child, the aptly named Marshall Tucker Bangs, and this newfound sensibility as a mother and feminist icon gave added depth to their new record, *One Beat*, in 2002. Sleater-Kinney continued to grow in songwriting and musical ability over the next few records and quickly became one of the most politically articulate and musically powerful bands in modern punk rock.

Discography: *Sleater-Kinney* (Chainsaw, 1995; Villa Villakula, 1995); *Call the Doctor* (Chainsaw, 1996); *Dig Me Out* (Kill Rock Stars, 1997); *The Hot Rock* (Kill Rock Stars, 1999); *All Hands on the Bad One* (Kill Rock Stars, 2000); *One Beat* (Kill Rock Stars, 2002).

SLITS

One of the earliest and most influential all-female punk groups, the Slits (although the name can be taken as a double entendre, it was not originally meant that way) were also known for their experiments with **reggae,** funk, and **dub** music and can be categorized as **postpunk.** The original lineup consisted of Palmolive (Paloma Romero, who got her punk name from **Clash** bassist Paul Simonon and who had previously lived with **Joe Strummer** for two years) on drums, guitarist Kate Korus, bassist Suzy Gutsy, and Arianna "Ari Up" Foster (Ari Up's mom would marry **Johnny Rotten**) on vocals. Before the band was a few weeks old, Gutsy and Korus left and were replaced by Vivian Albertine on guitar and Tessa Pollit on bass, who had previously played in the band **Flowers of Romance.** The band started off as a primitive punk band but soon was playing opening gigs for the Clash and other bands. The band waited a long time to record its first record, and in that time their primitive punk sound evolved into a fusion of reggae, funk, and dub that had little to do with the loud and fast punk rock being made around them. The Slits made a conscious decision to try to play music that was more organically "female" as opposed to the inherently male music that dominated most of punk rock and most of rock and roll. When the band began to record its first record, "Cut" Budgie (later of **Siouxsie and the Banshees**) replaced Palmolive (who later went on to play with the Raincoats) and played on most of the tracks. The first album, with its provocative cover of the women in the band posing topless and covered with mud, both parodied and debunked the notion of using women's bodies as tools to sell a record. The mud covering the Slits played with the idea of nakedness being both dirty and life affirming and as being close to the Earth. After touring and replacing Budgie with drummer Bruce Smith from **the Pop Group,** the Slits broke up at the end of 1981 after putting out the harder, more dub inflected *Return of the Giant Slits*. Ari Up moved to Jamaica and recorded solo records and she and Viv Albertine worked in Adrian Sherwood's New Age Steppers. In 2005, Ari announced a Slits reunion, featuring her, bassist Tessa Pollit, Pollit's daughter, Paul Cook's daughter, and Mick Jones's daughter as well as contributions from Marco Pironi (from Adam and the Ants) and Paul Cook. The Slits were not only the most important all-female band of the 1970s, but their experimental use of reggae, dub, and funk also paved the way for the experimentation of the 1980s and 1990s and remained largely ahead of its time.

Discography: *Cut* (Island, 1979); *Untitled (Retrospective)* (Rough Trade, 1980); *The Return of the Giant Slits* (UK CBS, 1981); *The Peel Sessions* (Strange/Fruit, 1989).

SMITH, PATTI

Influential punk poet, singer, writer, and performer; the poet queen of the early New York City punk rock scene; as well as a major influence on later singers such as P.J. Harvey. Patti Smith and her band, the Patti Smith Group, brought (along with **Richard Hell** and Tom Verlaine) a poetic and romantic sensibility to **New York** punk rock that helped distinguish it from the working-class British version that tried hard to disassociate itself with anything romantic or poetic. Born in Chicago in 1946, she later moved to the wilds of New Jersey, where she gave birth to a child given up for adoption and worked in a factory (later dramatized in her first single, "Piss Factory"). She originally came to New York City in fall 1967, met longtime friend and photographer Robert Mapplethorpe, and quickly made a name for herself on the Bowery poetry scene during the early 1970s. Her readings with guitarist Lenny Kaye, her fierce intensity, and her rock-and-roll edge that she borrowed form her hero Keith Richards surprised the established poets such as Jim Carroll. She also became involved with playwright Sam Shepard and wrote and performed the play *Cowboy Mouth* with him in 1971. Smith at that time was unsure about becoming a rock and roll star, and, inspired by the French poet Rimbaud, she concentrated more on her writing, releasing the book of poems *Seventh Heaven* in the early 1970s, but also pursued other creative avenues. Her readings with Kaye on guitar and, later, Richard Sohl on keyboards began to resemble songs more than poems set to music, and soon the possibility of playing at rock clubs and making recordings were taken much more seriously. Eventually, to augment their sound, Kaye and Smith added keyboard player Sohl and then solidified the classic lineup with the addition of Ivan Kral on bass and J.D. Daugherty on drums. The album *Horses*, released by Clive Davis's Arista label and produced by John Cale, was the first record from a member of the **New York** punk scene and was a powerful indication that the New York scene was as influenced by the romantic poets as it was by the grime and **nihilism** of the Lower East Side. After touring and solidifying as a band, the Patti Smith Group returned to the studio in late 1976 to record *Radio Ethiopia*, which took the band farther in an almost mystical direction. Aided by Smith's dynamic stage presence and manic intensity, *Radio Ethiopia* found her sometimes chanting, sometimes singing her lyrics, depending on the way in which the band took the song. The band toured to support the record, but disaster loomed. While touring with the Bob Seger band, Patti Smith fell onstage and cracked a vertebrae in her neck, forcing her to withdraw from making music for a year when the band could have been at its most successful point. The band released the record *Easter*, which contained their biggest hit, the song "Because the Night," written by Bruce Springsteen, but by then Sohl had been replaced by Bruce Brody, and some of the magic was gone. After recording *Wave* and after a final performance at a stadium in Florence, Italy, for 70,000 fans, Patti Smith decided to retired and marry Fred Smith (of the **MC5**), move to Detroit, and raise a family. Patti Smith came out of retirement in the late 1980s with her album *Dream of Life*, featuring the anthemic "People Have the Power," and then went back on hiatus for several more years until the release of *Gone Again*, which marked her return to music following immense personal tragedy. Her husband, Fred Smith, and brother Tod Smith both died in 1995, and keyboard player Sohl died in 1990. Smith continued to tour and record with a reconstituted band that featured Kaye and Daugherty and put out music that justified her vision as the poet laureate of punk rock.

Discography: *Horses* (Arista, 1975); *Dream of Life* (Arista, 1988); *Gone Again* (Arista, 1996); *Peace and Noise* (Arista, 1997); *Gung Ho* (Arista, 2000); *Trampin'* (Sony, 2004). **Patti Smith Group:** *Radio Ethiopia* (Arista, 1976); *Easter* (Arista, 1978); *Wave* (Arista, 1979).

SMITH, WINSTON

Punk artist and graphic designer, best known for designing the famous **Dead Kennedys'** DK logo. Smith also worked in the U.S. version of **RAR (Rock against Racism)**.

SMOKEWAGON

Punk band from Brooklyn influenced by Johnny Cash, Nick Cave, Ennio Morricone, and other outlaws. SmokeWagon is known for its lyrics' evocative imagery, its musical mixture of punk, blues, goth, country, and **postpunk,** and interesting covers, including a slowed-down, countrified version of "Skulls" by the **Misfits.** The trio included Jesse James Howard on drums, Pat Fondiller on bass (who also played with Michael Gira of the Swans), and Kevin Omen on guitar and vocals.

Discography: *Smokewagon* (Smokewagon, 2002); *Deuce* (Smokewagon, 2006).

SNIFFIN' GLUE

Popular British zine, inspired by the first **Ramones** album, founded in mid-1976 by Mark Perry as a photocopied handout. Perry became nervous about being part of the journalistic mainstream and encouraged readers to start their own **zines.** He released a book-length compilation, *Sniffin' Glue: The Essential Punk Accessory* in 2000.

SOA

Early **hardcore** band from **Washington, D.C.,** fronted by **Henry Rollins** (Garfield), Michael Hampton on guitar, and, later, drummer Ivor Hanson, who would play in Embrace with **Ian MacKaye** and in Faith with his brother Alec.

SOCIAL DISTORTION

Long-running punk band led through various incarnations by punk stalwart Mike Ness. The band enjoyed success in the 1990s with hits "Ball and Chain" and "Story of My Life." The original lineup featured Ness along with Casey Royer and Rik Agnew (who later went on to form the **Adolescents** and **DI**), and soon Dennis Darnell joined to solidify the lineup. Ness became a catalyst for the Orange County local scene at his home and crash pad, the "Black Hole." In 1983, Social Distortion released the classic punk record *Mommy's Little Monster,* which featured the classic title track, and they appeared in the film *Another State of Mind,* which documented their troubled and drug-fueled tour with **Youth Brigade.** Ness struggled with drug problems for many years, leading to the first dissolution of the band before their resurgence in the late 1980s. Guitarist Dennis Darnell died from a brain aneurysm in 2000 at the age of 38. After a brief hiatus, the band continued with guitarist Johnny Wickersham.

Discography: *Mommy's Little Monster* (13th Floor, 1983; Triple X, 1990; Time Bomb, 1995); *Prison Bound* (Restless, 1988; Time Bomb, 1995); *Social Distortion* (Epic, 1990); *Story of My Life . . . and Other Stories* EP (Epic, 1990); *Somewhere between Heaven and Hell* (Epic, 1992); *Mainliner (Wreckage from the Past)* (Time Bomb, 1995); *White Light, White Heat, White Trash* (550 Music/Epic, 1996); *Live at the Roxy* (Time Bomb, 1998). **Mike Ness:** *Cheating at Solitaire* (Time Bomb, 1999); *Under the Influences* (Time Bomb, 1999).

SOD

The New York City band SOD's name is an abbreviation of Stormtroopers of Death, a thrash/ **hardcore** joke band led by Billy Milano, featuring Scott Ian, drummer Charlie Banante from **Anthrax,** and Dan Lilker from Nuclear Assault. Their first record, *Speak English or Die*, led to some crossover popularity and influenced numerous metal fans to embrace the thrash/ hardcore scene. The band continued to tour and record sporadically, and Milano often toured with his more metal-oriented band, MOD.

Discography: *Speak English or Die* (Megaforce, 1985); *Live at Budokan* (Megaforce, 1992); *Bigger Than the Devile* (Nuclear Blast, 1999).

SONICS

One of the little-known but often-cited progenitors of 1960s garage rock that later would influence numerous members of the 1970s punk scene. The Sonics best-known songs,

"Strychnine" and "The Witch," showcased lead singer Gary Roslie's punkesque voice and manic singing to a small group of dissatisfied youth looking for better music in the 1960s. **Discography:** *Here Are the Sonics* (Etiquette, 1965).

SONIC YOUTH

Sonic Youth is an extraordinarily influential and long-lived noise-punk band that inspired numerous bands though their experimentation and consistency. Formed in New York City in the early 1980s and led by singer guitarist Thurston Moore (who had previously worked with avant-garde composer Glenn Branca); his wife, singer and bassist Kim Gordon; guitarist Lee Renaldo; drummer Steve Shelley; and late addition third guitarist Jim O'Rourke. Sonic Youth began as an offshoot of the work that Renaldo and Moore had been doing with composer Glenn Branca in the late 1970s and early 1980s, and the band formed in order to continue this experimentation. The band used alternative forms of tuning and intentional dissonance, often created via the use of drum sticks or screwdrivers applied to guitars (Sonic Youth often used as many as 20 backup guitars, each with its own tuning, to create the effects that were necessary for different material). The first EP with original drummer Richard Edson (who acted in numerous underground films, most notably by Jim Jarmusch) was as noisy and dissonant as anything on the **New York** art scene, but had few songs that actually had traditional song structure. With the addition of Bob Bert for *Confusion Is Sex*, the band began to find a middle ground between the noise experiments and its secret love of pop music and created an entirely new form of pulsating **postpunk** or post–**New Wave** that would be extremely influential on later bands of the 1980s indie scene. *Bad Moon Rising* was a step closer to conventional rock and provided a look back at their New Wave past, which was provided in the song "Death Valley 69," featuring Lydia Lunch singing with Gordon. With *EVOL*, the band added drummer Steve Sheely (formerly of the **Crucifucks**), and signed to indie giant **SST,** one of the key indie labels of the 1980s. At SST, Sonic Youth produced some of its most compelling music, including the epic "Expressway to Yr. Skull," which on the 12-inch single has a listed time of infinity, thanks to a well-placed flaw in the record that keeps the final drone playing in a continuous skip. After a few records, the band grew tired of the lackadaisical accounting practices at SST and jumped to Enigma for their breakthrough record, *Daydream Nation*. That record established them as one of the key bands in the U.S. independent music scene and led to them being signed to major label DGC (home of Sonic Youth fans **Nirvana**). A friendlier production team led to the band gaining more popularity through **MTV** with the single "Kool Thing" and its video (featuring Chuck D. of Public Enemy). After appearing in the film *1991: The Year That Punk Broke,* which documented the increasing popularity of bands such as Nirvana and **Green Day,** Sonic Youth began to grow tired of the attention of the mainstream media and started working on more obtuse and experimental records that lost them a considerable share of their growing fan base. Although the band was getting more experimental, they also retained their love of pop culture and produced *The Whitey Album* as Ciccone Youth, in an homage to Madonna, with guests **Mike Watt** and **Greg Ginn.** As the 1990s wore on, Sonic Youth became less concerned with success and more concerned with the experimentations of their youth, leading to a host of collaborations and a revitalization of the band when Jim O'Rourke joined. Although Sonic Youth may not have been as popular as they had been a decade ago, they remained one of the most important U.S. independent bands. Sonic Youth was also well known for championing other bands and working with other musicians in organized and improvisational combinations far too numerous to catalog.

Select Discography: *Sonic Youth* EP (Neutral, 1982; SST, 1987); *Confusion Is Sex* (Neutral, 1983; SST, 1987; DGC, 1995); *Kill Yr. Idols* EP (Ger. Zensor, 1983); *Sonic Death: Sonic Youth Live* (tape, Ecstatic Peace!, 1984; SST, 1988); *Bad Moon Rising* (Homestead, 1985; DGC, 1995); *Death Valley 69* EP

Thurston Moore of Sonic Youth appears on NBC's *Last Call with Carson Daly* in 2002. *Photofest.*

(Homestead, 1985); *EVOL* (SST, 1986; DGC, 1994); *Sister* (SST, 1987; DGC, 1994); *Master Dik* EP (SST, 1988); *Daydream Nation* (Blast First/Enigma, 1988; DGC, 1993); *Daydream Nation* EP (Blast First/Enigma, 1988); *Goo* (DGC, 1990); *Dirty* (DGC, 1992); *Experimental Jet Set, Trash and No Star* (DGC, 1994); *Made in USA* (Rhino, 1995); *Screaming Fields of Sonic Love* (DGC, 1995); *Washing Machine* (DGC, 1995); *SYR1: Anagrama* EP (Sonic Youth, 1997); *SYR2: Slaapkamers Met Slagroom* EP (Sonic Youth, 1997); *A Thousand Leaves* (DGC, 1998; Sonic Youth, 1998); *Hold That Tiger* (Goofin, 1998); *Silver Session for Jason Knuth* (Sonic Knuth, 1998); *SYR 4: Goodbye 20th Century* (Sonic Youth, 1999); *NYC Ghosts & Flowers* (Geffen, 2000); *Murray Street* (DGC/Geffen, 2002); *Sonic Nurse* (Geffen, 2004). **Sonic Youth/Jim O'Rourke:** *SYR 3: Invito al Cielo* (Sonic Youth, 1998). **Ciccone Youth:** *The Whitey Album* EP (Blast First/Enigma, 1988); *The Whitey Album* (Blast First/Enigma, 1988; DGC, 1995). **Sonic Youth/ Eye Yamatsuka:** *TV Shit* EP (Ecstatic Peace!, 1994). **Lee Ranaldo:** *From Here to Infinity* (SST, 1987); *Scriptures of the Golden Eternity* (Father Yod, 1993; Father Yod/Drunken Fish, 1995); *Broken Circle/Spiral Hill* EP (Starlight Furniture Company, 1994); *East Jesus* (Atavistic, 1995). **Jim Sauter/Don Dietrick/ Thurston Moore:** *Barefoot in the Head* (Forced Exposure, 1990). **Thurston Moore:** *Psychic Hearts* (DGC, 1995). **Kim Gordon/D.J. Olive/Ikue Mori:** *SYR 5* (Sonic Youth, 2000).

SPECIALS

Original **2 Tone** band formed in 1979 and led by Jerry Dammers and originally designed to bridge the gap between **punk** and **reggae** before it shifted courses slightly and pioneered the

Led by Jerry Dammers, the Specials fused ska and punk and inspired countless bands. *Photo by Eugene Adebari/Rex Features.*

British **ska** revival of the late 1970s. The band scored numerous hits and influenced numerous bands in both the British revival and the U.S. revival of the 1990s. The original lineup consisted of Jerry Dammers on keyboards, Neville Staples and Terry Hall on vocals, Lynval Golding and Rodney Radiation on guitar, John Bradbury on drums, Rico Rodriguez on trombone (who had been in one of the original ska bands, the Skatalites), and Sir Horace Gentleman (Panter) on bass. The band was essentially a vehicle for Dammers's political and social views, and various permutations of the band continued after most of the original band dissolved. Hall, Golding, and Staples left for the more pop-oriented Fun Boy Three.

Discography: *The Specials* (2 Tone/Chrysalis, 1979); *More Specials* (2 Tone/Chrysalis, 1980); *Ghost Town* EP (2 Tone/Chrysalis, 1981); *The Peel Sessions* EP (UK Strange Fruit, 1987); *The Singles Collection* (Chrysalis, 1991). **Special A.K.A.:** *The Special A.K.A. Live!* EP (UK 2 Tone, 1980); *In the Studio* (2 Tone/Chrysalis, 1984).

SPIKE

A character on the TV show *Buffy the Vampire Slayer* and the *Buffy* spin-off *Angel*. Spike was a 200-year-old vampire and supposed friend of **Sid Vicious** who in dress and attitude epitomized the punk aesthetic circa 1977. Although the character is British, Spike was played by U.S. actor James Marsters. At numerous points in the show, Spike referenced punk music and was often seen driving while punk music played in the background.

SPIKED HAIR

Spiked hair is hair elevated or otherwise kept upright via hairspray, gel, or other products. In some of the more elaborate configurations, such as **Mohawks** and liberty spikes, glue or another strong substance was used to achieve the right effect. Although punk does not have one particular hairstyle, the original punk look was largely inspired by the spiked and disheveled hair as epitomized by **Richard Hell. Malcolm McLaren** had been inspired by Hell's look and had attempted to duplicate it in his fashions and also tried to get others to emulate Hell's distinctive look. Hell and others may have been inspired by **David Bowie's** semispiked hair during the Ziggy Stardust period. Spiked hair and short hair were also a conscious reaction to the legacy of hippies and art rock, which espoused long hair and a distinctive look.

SPIKES

Bracelets with metal studs or spikes and leather jackets with spikes or studs attached were very popular in the second wave of punk rock, particularly as epitomized in British bands such as **Discharge,** the **Exploited,** and **Anti-Nowhere League,** which helped to popularize the heavily spiked look. Although early band such as the **Sex Pistols,** especially **Sid Vicious,** wore some leather and spikes, and some of **Malcolm McLaren** and **Vivienne Westwood's** designs came from bondage outfits and included chains and spikes, the look did not really catch on as a **punk fashion** statement until the second generation of punks wore them. The look can still be seen today in many street punks who adorn their belts, wrist bracelets, and jackets with spikes to make them look more ferocious. The look also spread to members of the heavy metal scene in the mid-1980s, and bands such as WASP took the look to ridiculous extremes.

SPIRAL SCRATCH EP

One of the first independent **DIY** record releases from punk band the **Buzzcocks.** *Spiral Scratch* was not the first British punk single (that distinction belongs to the song "New Rose" by the **Damned,** released by **Stiff Records** in October 1976). It was released on the Buzzcocks' own New Hormones label in January 1977 and was recorded for the sum of £500 with producer Martin Hannett (along with the calming presence of Pete Shelley's father, who was presumably there to make sure his son's band was getting the most for their money). The single, expected to sell a few hundred copies, quickly sold more than 16,000 copies and remains a key collectors item. Lead singer Howard Devoto left the band shortly after the single was released to form the band Magazine, but *Spiral Scratch* had already made the reputation of the Buzzcocks and had inspired numerous other bands across England to start their own labels to release music outside the mainstream. This trend continues.

SQUATS

Places where loose aggregations of punks lived, usually illegally, in more or less communal fashion. Squats varied from city to city, and there were famous punk squats in Amsterdam, **London,** Manchester, **New York,** and **Washington, D.C.,** among many other places.

SSD

Boston's first and most important **hardcore straight edge** band from the 1980s. The band, led by guitarist Al Barile, was one of the more vocal proponents of straight edge and was also one the hardest Boston bands, with a distinct metallic edge. The band featured Barile, also known as Lethal, on guitar, bassist Jamie Sciarappa, drummer Chris Foley, and lead singer Phil "Springa" Springs. SSD pioneered Boston hardcore and allowed a scene to grow, which included bands such as **DYS** (featuring Dave Smalley, later of **Dag Nasty, All,** and **Down by Law**), **Gang Green, F.U.'s,** and **Jerry's Kids,** who drank beer and were not as closely associated with the SSD

scene. SSD had a loose aggregation of 20 or so superfans known as the Boston Crew who were known by their shaved heads, straight edge militancy, and ferocity in the **pit.** The band founded the XClaim! label in 1982. After the band broke up, bassist Jamie Sciarappa joined **Slapshot** before joining My Eye. Foley was in a variety of bands, including Crime & Punishment.
Discography: SS Decontrol: *The Kids Will Have Their Say!* EP (XClaim!, 1982); *Get It Away* (XClaim!, 1983). **SSD:** *How We Rock* (Modern Method, 1984); *Break It Up* (Homestead, 1985); *Power* (Taang!, 1993).

SST

Label founded by **Greg Ginn** and Chuck Dukowski of **Black Flag.** Originally designed to release records by Black Flag, the label grew early to put out seminal records from almost every major punk, indie, and experimental band of the 1980s. Artists that have recorded for SST include Black Flag, the **Minutemen, Sonic Youth, Bad Brains, Meat Puppets, Hüsker Dü,** and **Descendents.** Ginn had originally formed a company called SST Electronics, which dealt with ham radio equipment, and it later became SST Records to release the first single and EP from Black Flag. Although SST was one of the most influential record labels of the 1980s, its talent roster was quickly depleted during the late 1980s, and the label became an outlet for Greg Ginn's solo work and avant-jazz artists. Many of the label's recording artists, such as the Meat Puppets, have had their catalogs rereleased by other record labels.

STAGE DIVING

Stage diving, or being hoisted up on stage by members of the audience, making a brief statement, and diving (or if the bouncers catch up, being thrown) off the stage, is another long-standing punk ritual that is related to the **pit,** slam dancing, and crowd surfing. Although the ritual started at punk shows, it made its way into heavy metal culture and is mainstream at most thrash metal shows. Although stage diving is an old tradition at punk shows, it is considered a nuisance by some bands, which often hire extra security to keep nonband members off stage. Some bands embrace stage diving, however, and openly encourage their fans to come onstage, usually during the encores. Stage diving can be dangerous, and **Circle Jerks** lead singer Keith Morris once broke his back diving off a stage and had to live in a back brace for months.

STANDELLS

Protopunk band from the 1960s from Los Angeles (although they did claim in their most famous song that Boston was their home), best known for its hit single "Dirty Water" and an appearance on the TV show *The Munsters.*

STIFF LITTLE FINGERS

Northern Ireland punk band, featuring Jake Burns on vocals and guitar, Henry Cluney on guitar, Ali McMordie on bass, and Brian Faloon on drums (replaced in 1979 by Jim Reilly, followed in 1981 by Brian "Dolphin" Taylor). The band released its first record, the incendiary single "Suspect Device," in March 1978 but did not release a proper album until February 1979. Led by the charismatic Burns, the band sang songs that reflected the turbulence and violence of everyday life in Northern Ireland; most of the songs were written by Gordon Ogilvie, a journalist who wrote for the *Daily Express.* The band started out as a Deep Purple cover band called Highway Star before being inspired by punk and changing its name to Stiff Little Fingers (after a song by the **Vibrators**). The group called it quits in 1983 but re-formed in 1987 with a new lineup featuring Burns, Cluney, and former **Jam** bassist Bruce Foxton. A revised lineup including Burns and Foxton still tours and consistently releases new material.

Discography: *Inflammable Material* (Rough Trade, 1979; with bonus tracks, Restless, 1990, 1993, 2005); *Christmas Album/Live in Sweden* (unknown label, 1979); *Broken Fingers/Live in Aberdeen* (unknown label, 1979; EMI, 2002); *Nobody's Heroes* (Chrysalis, 1980; with bonus tracks, Restless, 1990, 2005); *Hanx!* (Chrysalis, 1980; Restless, 1990, 2005); *Go for It* (Chrysalis, 1981; Restless, 1990; with bonus tracks, EMI, 2004); *Now Then …* (Chrysalis, 1982; with bonus tracks, EMI, 2004); *All the Best* (Chrysalis, 1983; One Way Records, 1995); *The Peel Sessions* EP (UK Strange Fruit, 1986); *Live and Loud!!* (UK Link, 1988); *No Sleep 'til Belfast* EP (Skunx, 1988; Castle, 1994); *No Sleep 'til Belfast* (UK Kaz, 1988); *See You up There!* (Caroline, 1989); *The Last Time* EP (UK Link, 1989); *The Peel Sessions Album* (UK Strange Fruit, 1989); *Flags & Emblems* (with bonus tracks, Castle, 1991, 2004); *Fly the Flags* [live] (Castle) 1991; (Snapper UK 1998); *Get a Life* (Castle) 1994; w/ Bonus Tracks 2004); *BBC Radio 1 Live in Concert* (Windsong, 1993; Griffin, 1995); *Pure Fingers Live: St. Patrix 1993* (Original Masters, 1995, 1999); *Tinderbox* (Taang!, 1997; EMI, 2002); *And Best of All? Hope Street* (EMI, 1999); *Hope Street? Greatest Hits Live* (Oxygen, 1999); *Stand up & Shout* (Origi, 1999); *Tin Soldiers* (Harry May, 2000); *Live Inspiration* (UK Recall Records, 2000); *Complete John Peel Sessions* (Strange Fruit, 2002); *Anthology* (EMI, 2002); *The Radio One Sessions* (Strange Fruit, 2003); *No Sleep 'til Belfast* (BMG International, 2003); *From the Front Row Live* (Silverline, 2003); *BBC Live in Concert* (Strange Fruit, 2003); *Guitar and Drum* (Kung Fu Records, 2004); *Backs against the Wall* (EMI, 2004); *Song By Song* (Phantom, 2004); *Wasted Life? Live* (Phantom. 2004).

STIFF RECORDS

English punk and rock label that released the earliest English punk seven-inch single, "New Rose," by the **Damned** in October 1976, beating out the **Sex Pistols'** debut by two months. Stiff also released records by artists such as Elvis Costello, Wreckless Eric, Madness, Dave Edmunds, and Graham Parker. The label was started by Dave Robinson and Jake Rivera and early on put out records by Dave Edmunds and Nick Lowe and had an early distribution deal with Island Records, which allowed their material wider release than most small labels. Rivera left in 1984 to form Radar Records, and Stiff Records was eventually acquired by Island and then ZTT. Stiff was also know for its slogans, such as "If it ain't Stiff, it ain't worth a fuck." The label also put out the first Damned record, *Damned, Damned, Damned*, also produced by Nick Lowe, who produced many records for Stiff. Stiff also put out **Richard Hell's "Blank Generation"** single as well as the first Elvis Costello records and singles.

STIMULATORS

Early New York City **punk hardcore** band that featured a young (11 years old when the band started) Harley Flannagan, later of the **Cro-Mags,** on drums, with vocalist Patrick Mack, guitarist Denise Mercedes, and bassist Anne Gustavson (later replaced by Nick Marden). The band was eclipsed by other bands, particularly the **Bad Brains,** and was more or less gone from the scene by 1981. The lead singer, Patrick Mack, died of AIDS in 1983.
Discography: *Loud Fast Rules* (live; Roir, 1982).

STOOGES, IGGY AND THE

Iggy Pop and his band the Stooges were one of the key bands from the 1960s that were hugely influential in influencing punk rock. Iggy Pop (James Osterberg), often called the "godfather of punk," founded the band the Stooges in 1968 with guitarist Ron Asheton, his brother, drummer Scott Asheton, and bassist David Alexander. In 1966, super music fans Ron Asheton and Dave Alexander, inspired by an electrifying Who performance they had seen in England, decided to form a band, and eventually Iggy Pop, who was then drumming for a blues rock band called the Prime Movers, decided to team up with the Asheton brothers and Alexander. The Stooges quickly became well known for their raucous shows and Iggy Pop's Jim Morrison–inspired persona. While the Stooges played their dronelike trance music, Iggy

Pop, sometimes dressed in glitter and body paint, writhed around the stage and contorted his body into various positions when not smearing himself in peanut butter, rolling in broken glass, or simply antagonizing the audience to see if they would react. The Stooges were friends with the **MC5** (who considered the Stooges their "baby brother" group) and through their connections were signed along with the MC5 by **Danny Fields** to Elektra records in 1968. John Cale of the **Velvet Underground** produced their first record, which contained the classic songs "Now I Wanna Be Your Dog" and "No Fun," which would both be covered by many punk bands later in the 1970s. Iggy Pop was also dating Nico from the Velvet Underground at the time, and she taught him how to modulate his voice, which he would use to great effect on the three Stooges records. When the first album, *The Stooges,* was released in August 1969, it caused many future punk pioneers to take notice, including **Patti Smith,** Alan Vega of **Suicide,** and Scott Kempner of the **Dictators,** although the album did not make much of an impression on the general public. The second record, *Fun House,* was as revolutionary as the first, incorporating jazz riffs courtesy of saxophone player Steve MacKay (Miles Davis had played with the Stooges before and was a fan) and even more intense songs such as "TV Eye." At the same time, the Stooges were introduced to **heroin** by road manager and ex-junkie John Adams, who showed the band how to snort and shoot up the drug, leading to a lengthy addiction for Iggy Pop. At this point, Dave Alexander had been replaced by James Williamson, and Danny Fields became the Stooges de facto manager after leaving Elektra. Elektra declined to pick up the option on the Stooges' third album, and Fields left after becoming frustrated with the band's constant drug abuse. **David Bowie,** who had yet to become popular in the United States, became interested in Iggy Pop and signed him to his **MainMan** management company, while Iggy Pop also signed a deal with Clive Davis at CBS records. Iggy Pop began to record with Williamson on guitar and, after auditioning others, invited the Asheton brothers back, this time with Ron Asheton on bass to record the seminal *Raw Power* record in England. *Raw Power* was another seminal prepunk album that featured the powerful title song and the instant classic **"Search and Destroy."** The record typically failed to make a dent in the charts, however, and Iggy and the Stooges decamped to the Beverly Hills Hotel, where they and minder **Leee Black Childers** descended into a pit of debauched behavior and drug addiction. The band traveled to New York City and played **Max's Kansas City,** where Iggy Pop notoriously cut himself so badly on stage he needed several stitches. After CBS dropped the group, Iggy Pop went on to work with David Bowie on several critically acclaimed solo records and recorded and performed regularly, becoming even more legendary in the process. The Asheton brothers went on to a variety of different projects, most notably New Order (not the **New Wave** dance band featuring former members of **Joy Division**). In 2004, the Stooges reunited for several tours with Mike Watt from the **Minutemen** and Firehose playing bass, alongside the Asheton brothers and saxophonist Steve MacKay. Iggy and the Stooges were one of the most important 1960s **protopunk** bands and influenced almost all of the early punk pioneers, including the **Ramones,** Dictators, Patti Smith, the **Sex Pistols** (both **Sid Vicious** and **Johnny Rotten** were clearly influenced by Iggy Pop's persona, and the band would cover the Stooges song "No Fun"), as well as countless other punk and heavy metal bands from the last 40 years. Iggy Pop eventually conquered his heroin addiction and today is healthier than many of the musicians he influenced both musically and in choice of lifestyle. *See also* Bowie, David; Childers, Leee Black; Heroin; Iggy Pop; MC5.

Discography: Stooges: *The Stooges* (Elektra, 1969, 1977, 1982); *Fun House* (Elektra, 1970, 1977, 1982); *No Fun* (UK Elektra, 1980); *Rubber Legs* (Fr. Fan Club, 1987); *What You Gonna Do* EP (Fr. Revenge, 1988); *Live 1971* (Fr. Starfighter, 1988); *Live at the Whisky a Go Go* (Fr. Revenge, 1988); *My Girl Hates My Heroin* (Fr. Revenge, 1989); *1970: The Complete Fun House Sessions* (Elektra/Rhino Handmade, 1999). **Iggy and the Stooges:** *Raw Power* (Columbia, 1973; Columbia/Legacy, 1997); *Metallic K.O.* (Import, 1976);

I'm Sick of You EP (Bomp!, 1977); *(I Got) Nothing* EP (Skydog, 1978); *I'm Sick of You* (Ger. Line, 1981, 1987); *Death Trip* EP (Fr. Revenge, 1987); *Pure Lust* EP (Fr. Revenge, 1987); *Raw Power* EP (Fr. Revenge, 1987); *Gimme Danger* EP (Fr. Revenge, 1987); *She Creatures of Hollywood Hills* (Fr. Revenge, 1988); *The Stooges* (Fr. Revenge, 1988); *Metallic 2xKO* (Fr. Skydog, 1988); *Raw Stooges, Vol. 1* (Ger. Electric, 1988); *Raw Stooges, Vol. 2* (Ger. Electric, 1988); *Search and Destroy—Raw Mixes Vol. III* (Curtis, 1989); *Iggy and the Stooges* (Fr. Revenge, 1991); *I Got a Right* EP (Bomp!, 1991); *Iggy & the Stooges* (no label, ca. 1987). **Iggy Pop & James Williamson:** *Jesus Loves the Stooges* EP (Bomp!, 1977); *Kill City* (Bomp!, 1978).

STRAIGHT AHEAD

New York City **hardcore** band from the 1980s.
Discography: *Show Me the Way* (Straight Ahead, 2001).

STRAIGHT EDGE

The straight edge movement was a punk movement in which participants did not drink, do drugs, have promiscuous sex, or, in many cases, eat meat or other animal products. The movement was unofficially founded and given its name by the **Minor Threat** song "Straight Edge" (and also other songs, such as "Out of Step with the World"), which calls those who use chemicals to alter their consciousness essentially "The Living Dead." Although lead singer **Ian MacKaye** had not meant to start a movement and had been publicly ambivalent toward straight edge in subsequent years, many bother bands took up the banner, including **Youth of Today, SSD, Seven Seconds, Gorilla Biscuits, Bold, Uniform Choice,** and **Straight Ahead.** Early straight edge, as epitomized by Ian MacKaye's first band, the Teen Idles, came up with the idea to allow underage punks into bars by marking an *X* on their hands, and soon the movement spread, with the *X* becoming the unofficial symbol of straight edge. Other symbols, such as the *XXX*, also indicated that a punk was extremely straight edge, and the "True till Death" tattoo that many straight edge punks wore indicated that they had not merely jumped on a trend but had dedicated their lives to being straight edge, to the extreme of getting a permanent reminder to themselves and their friends. There are many divisions in the straight edge movement as to what constitutes straight edge, and a particularly ardent debate continued as to whether someone can be straight edge if he or she consumed or used animal products in any way. Many punks involved in the straight edge scene either became strict **vegans** or at least stopped using animal products, although this is also a gray area. Many punks, such as those from the **Boston** straight edge scene, espoused the virtues of meat, but most of those from the **New York** and **Washington, D.C.,** scenes tried to avoid meat as much as possible.

Although many older and more traditional punks who had been raised in the drug-and alcohol-filled scenes in major cities rejected the straight edge movement, many younger punks, especially in the second generation of straight edge from the mid- to late 1980s, saw straight edge not only as a way of standing out from the nonpunk crowd but also as a rebellion against the codified culture that the older punks had embraced. In the words of Beth Lahickey, in her book *All Ages: Reflections on Straight Edge*, "Straight edge provided an untraditional form of rebellion—rebelling against traditional forms of rebellion" (xvii). Although the straight edge scene continued, it did not have the prominence or exposure it did during the glory days of the New York and Washington, D.C., scenes, where bands such as Youth of Today played numerous shows that provided a primer to young punks as to the positive outcome of leading a clean lifestyle. Although it is often difficult to categorize which bands were straight edge (some bands, such as Seven Seconds, never really used the term, other bands, such as the **Descendents,** espoused "good clean fun" and still allowed promiscuous sex, and other bands, like **Crucial Youth,** seemed much more like a parody of straight edge), most of the key bands in the scene identified as such. Some, such as Ray Cappo of Youth of Today, later moved on to become followers of Krishna Consciousness, which they saw as a natural conclusion to remaining true to the precepts of straight edge punk. *See also* Krishna, Hare; Minor Threat; New York; Vegans; Washington, D.C.

STRANGLERS

Originally named the Guilford Stranglers, the English band formed in 1974 with bassist and singer Jean-Jacques Burnel, drummer Jet Black (Brian Duffy), keyboard player Dave Greenfield (notorious for having a mustache, a punk rock fashion faux pas), and guitarist singer Hugh Cornell. The band was as famous for the members' paranoia and punk feuds as it were for its incendiary music. The Stranglers had a sort of gang that followed them known as the Finchley Boys, and Burnel, a martial arts expert, was famous for his fights with **Clash** bassist Paul Simonon and writer Jon Savage. The band was also well known for its interest in science fiction, paranoia, and misogyny. The Stranglers first album, *Rattus Norvegicus*, was released in 1977, and by the time of the band's third album, *Black and White*, the band had descended into paranoia, worried about the "men in black" (secret government operatives who silenced those who knew too much about UFOs, as later immortalized in the science fiction film *Men in Black*), and had started to use drugs more heavily. Women's groups began to picket the Stranglers performances because of the alleged misogyny of their lyrics and the strippers that were occasionally featured in the band's live shows. In November 1979, Cornell was arrested and spent some time in jail for possession of **heroin.** The band members found themselves again in trouble after a riot at a French gig led to a brief stay in jail, but luckily the band received a suspended sentence. The Stranglers continued on to diminishing returns, although they did release several singles and videos that charted in the United States, including "Skin Deep," but the band's drug addictions and paranoia kept them from releasing material on a consistent basis. After fighting for almost 15 years, Cornell left the band in 1990, but the band continued to record and tour with Burnel, Jet Black, Greenfield, and new singer Paul Roberts.

Discography: *IV Rattus Norvegicus* (A&M, 1977); *No More Heroes* (A&M, 1977); *Black and White* (A&M, 1977); *The Stranglers* EP (Japan UA, 1977); *Live (X Cert)* (UK UA, 1979); *The Raven* (UK UA, 1979; EMI, 1985); *Don't Bring Harry* EP (UK UA, 1979); *IV* (IRS, 1980); *The Meninblack* (UK Stiff, 1981; UK Fame, 1988); *La Folie* (UK Liberty, 1981; UK Fame, 1983); *The Collection 1977–1982* (UK Liberty, 1982; UK Fame, 1989); *Feline* (Epic, 1982); *Great Lost* (Japan UA, 1983); *Great Lost Continued* (Japan UA, 1983); *Aural Sculpture* (Epic, 1984); *Off the Beaten Track* (UK Liberty, 1986); *Dreamtime* (Epic, 1987); *All Day and All of the Night* EP (UK Epic, 1987); *IV Rattus Norvegicus* (A&M, 1988; UK Fame, 1982); *All Live and All of the Night* (Epic, 1988); *Rarities* (UK Liberty, 1988); *The Evening Show Sessions* (UK Nighttracks/Strange Fruit, 1989); *Singles (The UA Years)* (UK Liberty, 1989); *10* (Epic, 1990); *Greatest Hits 1977–1990* (UK Epic, 1990; Epic, 1991); *The Stranglers* EP (A&M, 1991); *No More Heroes* (A&M, 1991; UK Fame, 1987). **Hugh Cornwell & Robert Williams:** *Nosferatu* (UK Liberty, 1979). **J.J. Burnel:** *Euroman Cometh* (UK UA, 1979; UK Mau Mau, 1987); *Un Jour Parfait* (Fr. CBS, 1989). **D. Greenfield & J.J. Burnel:** *Fire & Water (Ecoutez Vos Murs)* (UK Epic, 1983). **Hugh Cornwell:** *Wolf* (Virgin, 1988); *Another Kind of Love* EP (UK Virgin, 1988); *hi fi* (Koch Progressive, 2001).

STRUMMER, JOE

Former lead singer of the **Clash** and Mescaleros and one of the founders of British **punk.** Strummer was a key proponent of the use of world music and rhythms in his music and was also key in the Clash's embrace of **reggae** music in their middle and later work. Strummer had a sporadic solo career after the Clash broke up, releasing his first proper solo work, *Earthquake Weather*, in 1989 and doing soundtrack work for Alex Cox for the films *Walker* and *Sid and Nancy*. Strummer also appeared as an actor, most notably in the Jim Jarmusch film *Mystery*

Punk legend Joe Strummer of the Clash was one of the most respected of the British punks. *Photofest.*

Train. After an almost decade-long hiatus from music, Strummer formed a new band, the Mescaleros, and released several albums that were amalgamations of world music, funk, punk, and reggae. Strummer died of a heart attack in December 2002 at the age of 50, leaving behind a musical and political reputation as inspiring as anyone in punk rock. The life and work of Joe Strummer have inspired several posthumous works, including the compilation *Let Fury Have the Hour: The Punk Rock Politics of Joe Strummer*, edited by Antonino D'Ambrosio.

SUBHUMANS (CANADIAN)

Activist Canadian punk band from Vancouver formed in 1978. The band featured bassist Gerry Useless (Gerry Hannah), who was also a member of the militant group Direct Action, which engaged in bombings and acts of civil disobedience. Hannah was charged in the bombing of a Litton Industries factory that made parts for U.S. cruise missiles and served five years in jail for conspiracy, which led to the group's demise. The band originally started as an offshoot of the Canadian band the Skulls, which featured future members of both **DOA** and the Subhumans. Hannah was later the subject of the documentary *Useless* in 2004.

Discography: *Subhuman* (Quintessence, 1979); *Incorrect Thoughts* (Friend Records, 1980); *No Wishes, No Prayers* (SST, 1983).

SUBHUMANS (U.K.)

Band formed in 1980 in England by vocalist Dick Lucas. (There was also another band from Canada that recorded under the name Subhumans.) The band was originally discovered by Flux of Pink Indians and put out early singles before it formed its own label, Bluurg, which released the group's records. Lucas went on to form the band Citizen Fish after the demise of the original Subhumans. The band reunited for several tours.

Discography: *The Day the Country Died* (Bluurg, 1982); *From the Cradle to the Grave* (Bluurg, 1983); *Worlds Apart* (Bluurg, 1985); *Alive in a Dive* (Fat Wreck Chords, 2004); *Unfinished Business* (Bluurg, 2004); *All Gone Live* (Cleopatra, 2004).

SUBURBIA

Penelope Spheeris movie from 1983 that detailed the lives of aimless suburban youth, including a young Flea (Michael Balzary) before he founded the Red Hot Chili Peppers. The movie was loosely based on the story "The Connected" by Aimee Cooper and dealt with the traumas faced by street punks in Los Angeles. The film bears no resemblance to the 1996 Richard Linklater film of the same name.

SUBWAY SECT

Subway Sect, also known as Vic Godard & the Subway Sect, was a British band from punk's first wave in England, led by the artistic Vic Goddard and influenced more by traditional pop, French music, swing bands, Frank Sinatra, and **rockabilly.** The band's original lineup included Vic Godard on lead vocals, Paul Meyers on bass, Paul Packham on guitar, and Barry "Baker" Auguste drums. The band had close ties to the **Sex Pistols,** and **Malcolm McLaren** was instrumental in forming the band. Subway Sect was more musically ambiguous than most of its peers at the time, and although the band toured with the **Clash** on the White Riot tour in 1977, it was clear that they would not be constrained by punk's limitations. The band broke up for the first time in 1978 but re-formed in 1980 with a new lineup that featured Rob Marche on guitar, Chris Bostock on bass, Dave Collard on keyboards, and Sean McLusky on drums. Godard went solo in 1982 and continued to put out music when not working his day job as a mailman in London. Godard also founded the Motion label.

Discography: *What's the Matter Boy?* (Oddball/MCA, 1980, 1982; Demon, 1996; with bonus tracks, Universal, 2000; PolyGram, 2001); *Songs for Sale* (London, 1982); *A Retrospective (1977–81)* (Rough Trade, 1985); *Holiday Hymn* (MCA, 1985); *20 Odd Years the Story Of?* (Motion Pace, 1999); *Subway Sect Sansend* (Motion Pace, 2002); *Singles Anthology* (Motion Pace, 2005). **Vic Godard:** *T.R.O.U.B.L.E.* (Upside, 1986); *The End of the Surrey People* (Postcard, 1993); *We Oppose All Rock and Roll* (Overground, 1996); *In T.R.O.U.B.L.E. Again* (Tugboat, 1998); *Long Term Side-Effect* (Tugboat, 1998).

SUICIDAL TENDENCIES

Gang-related **hardcore** punk (later heavy metal) band formed by Mike Muir and best known for the punk classic "Institutionalized." The band started out with a relatively straight-ahead sense of humor that won legions of fans with their classic self-titled first album, featuring the punk classic "Institutionalized" as well as the hyperfast "I Shot the Devil" and "I Won't Fall in Love Today." By the second record, Suicidal Tendencies had begun their long, slow, painful descent into straight-ahead heavy metal and funk rock. The band even made an ill-advised song-for-song remake of their first record, *Still Cyco after All These Years,* because Mike Muir was apparently upset at no longer owning the rights to the original. The classic lineup featured Mike Muir on lead vocals, Rocky George and Mike Clark on guitars, Robert Trujillo (later of

Metallica) on bass and R. J. Herrera on drums. The band was almost entirely mainstream metal by the time of *Lights. . .Camera. . .Revolution!* Mike Muir also found some success with the funk rock band Infectious Grooves as well as a solo career as the slightly more punk Cyco Miko.
Select Discography: *Suicidal Tendencies* (Frontier, 1983); *Join the Army* (Caroline, 1987); *How Will I Laugh Tomorrow. . .When I Can't Even Smile Today* (Epic, 1988); *Controlled by Hatred/Feel Like Shit . . . Déjà vu* (Epic, 1989); *Lights. . .Camera. . .Revolution!* (Epic, 1990); *The Art of Rebellion* (Epic, 1992); *Still Cyco After All These Years* (Epic, 1993); *Suicidal for Life* (Epic, 1994).

SUICIDE

Early New York City band and performance-art duo featuring Alan Vega on vocals and Martin Rev on synthesizer. The band's aggressive and abrasive sound influenced both the nascent **punk** movement and the industrial and goth scenes. Suicide may also be among the earliest bands to use the word *punk*, in its title of a performance-art piece in 1971, "Punk Rock Mass." They often played at the Mercer Arts Center in New York City with like-minded bands such as the **New York Dolls** before the (literal) collapse of that venue. Suicide was founded by artist Alan Vega and Martin Rev, a free-jazz guitarist. Both of them were inspired by **Iggy Pop**'s stage persona and the experimental music of the Silver Apples. The band started as a four piece before pairing down to a minimalist duo, with Vega's shouting and menacing the audience, often with a weapon such as a bike chain. The band did not really gel with the other bands at **CBGB's** or **Max's Kansas City,** but they were eventually signed by Marty Thau. The band's first record, *Suicide,* was released in 1977 and still feels years ahead of its time, at once minimalist and at other times as daunting as anything produced by a full band. Suicide was clearly influential on numerous young bands of the time, particularly the Cars, who brought Suicide on tour, and Ric Ocasek produced Suicide's second record. None of Suicide's records were ever popular, but they influenced countless bands from Soft Cell to Depeche Mode. Suicide went on frequent hiatuses and released records sporadically during the 1980s and 1990s. The band continues to tour.
Discography: *Suicide* (Red Label, 1977); *Alan Vega and Martin Rev: Suicide* (Restless, 1980); *Half Alive* (Roir, 1981); *Ghost Riders* (Roir, 1986); *A Way of Life* (Wax Trax!, 1989); *Why Be Blue* (Brake Out/ Enemy, 1992).

SUPERCHUNK

Pop punk band from Chapel Hill, North Carolina, that became one of the most successful indie bands of the 1990s. The band started as Chunk (named after the drummer, but the name was used by another band) and quickly changed its name to Superchunk in time for their first album in 1990, which demonstrated their raucous poppy punk as orchestrated by lead singer and guitarist Mac McCaughan. The band was formed in 1988, and the original lineup was McCaughan, Laura Ballance on bass, Chunk on drums (replaced by Jon Wurster after *On the Mouth*), and guitarist Jim Wilbur. The *Foolish* record was the slowest and most thought-out and was devoted thematically to the breakup of Ballance and McCaughan. Subsequent records saw the band refining its sound and musical breadth but still staying comfortably in the Superchunk style. Lead singer McCaughan also plays in Portastatic.
Discography: *Superchunk* (Matador, 1990; Merge, 1999); *The Freed Seed* EP7 (Merge, 1991); *No Pocky for Kitty* (Matador, 1991; Merge, 1999); *Tossing Seeds (Singles 89–91)* (Merge, 1992); *Hit Self-Destruct* EP (Aus. Hippy Knight, 1992); *On the Mouth* (Matador, 1993; Merge, 1999); *Foolish* (Merge, 1994); *Driveway to Driveway* EP (Merge, 1994); *On Paper It Made Perfect Sense* EP (Aus. Fellaheen, 1994); *Incidental Music 1991–95* (Merge, 1995); *Here's Where the Strings Come In* (Merge, 1995); *The Laughter Guns* EP (Merge, 1996); *Indoor Living* (Merge, 1997); *Hello Hawk* EP (Merge, 1999); *Come Pick Me Up* (Merge,

1999); *1,000 Lbs.* EP (Merge, 2000); *Late-Century Dream* EP (Merge, 2001); *Here's to Shutting Up* (Merge, 2001). **Portastatic:** *I Hope Your Heart Is Not Brittle* (Merge, 1994); *Scrapbook* EP (Merge, 1995); *Slow Note from a Sinking Ship* (Merge, 1995); *The Nature of Sap* (Merge, 1997); *De Mel, del Melão* (Merge, 2000); *Looking for Leonard* (Merge, 2001); *The Perfect Little Door* EP (Merge, 2001).

SUPERTOUCH

New York City **straight edge hardcore** band from the mid-1980s formed by former members of Altercation. The band was led by lead singer Mark Ryan (formerly of Death before Dishonor) and featured Jimmy Yu on bass and Mike Judge (later of the bands Judge and Old Smoke) on drums.

Discography: *The Earth is Flat* (Revelation, 1990, 1994).

SWA

Band featuring **Black Flag** bassist Chuck Dukowski after he left that band. SWA had several records released by the **SST** label and featured Merill Ward on lead vocals, Chuck Dukowski on bass, Richard Ford on guitar, and Greg Cameron on drums.

Discography: *Your Future if You Have One* (SST, 1985); *S.W.A.* (SST, 1985); *Sex Dr.* (SST, 1986).

TABB, GEORGE

Punk author and leader of the band **Furious George,** Tabb is known for his books *Playing Right Field: A Jew Grows in Greenwich* and *Surfing Armageddon: A Memoir*, autobiographical depictions of his Jewish and punk identity, and is also known for his long-running columns in the New York Press. He formerly played in bands such as **Iron Prostate** and False Prophets but is best known for his band Furious George, which was the target of a long-running lawsuit for copyright infringement from the Curious George children's books franchise.

TALKING HEADS

Artistically innovative and later hugely successful band that played in the early days of **CBGB's,** when the definition of punk was broader and more inclusive. Talking Heads, led by the prolific David Byrne, became one of the most popular bands of the late 1970s and 1980s with such hit singles as "Burning down the House" and "Nothing but Flowers," establishing the band as (along with **Blondie**) the most commercially successful to emerge from the CBGB's scene. Talking Heads was started in the early 1970s by the Rhode Island Institute of Technology (RIT) students David Byrne on guitar and vocals, Tina Weymouth on bass, and Chris Frantz on drums. The band became more successful after the members moved to New York City in the early 1970s and began playing gigs at CBGB's, soon augmenting their sound with the addition of Jerry Harrison on keyboards. After such early successes as "Psycho Killer," the band began to expand its sound with back up signers and additional percussionists, as documented in the live concept film *Stop Making Sense*, a film that featured lead singer Byrne in the now notorious oversize suit that helped cement his reputation as an eccentric genius. After several successful records, the band broke up in 1990, and Byrne went on to a solo career. The band was inducted into the Rock and Roll Hall of Fame and reunited for the induction only. Bassist Tina Weymouth and drummer Chris Frantz also play in the dance rock band Tom Tom Club. Keyboard and guitar player Jerry Harrison formerly played with the **Modern Lovers** with Jonathan Richman.

Discography: *Talking Heads: 77* (Sire, 1977); *More Songs about Buildings and Food* (Sire, 1978); *Fear of Music* (Sire, 1979); *Remain in Light* (Sire, 1980); *The Name of This Band Is Talking Heads* (Sire, 1982); *Speaking in Tongues* (Sire, 1983); *Stop Making Sense* (Sire, 1984); *Little Creatures* (Sire, 1985); *True Stories* (Sire, 1986); *Naked* (Sire, 1988).

TATTOOS

Many punks began to use tattoos as a way of demonstrating their loyalty to a variety of bands or movements within punk rock. Many band members, such as the members of seminal punk band **Black Flag,** tattooed the band's logo on themselves as a sign of their commitment to the band. **Henry Rollins,** in particular, epitomized the mid-1980s look that was soon adopted by many in the scene (particularly the **New York** scene where Harley Flannagan of the **Cro-Mags** introduced the extensive use of tattoos into the scene), and many punks saw the use of visible tattoos to mark their outsider status from mainstream America. Facial tattoos, in particular, were markers that the recipient did not want to work in a corporate job. Today, many punks in **hardcore** and **emo** bands sport tattoos, and the practice is quite widespread, although the meaning can vary from punk to punk. Tattoos can often be signs of tribal allegiance, markers of rites of passage, or simply body decorations.

TEAM DRESCH

U.S. **queercore** band named after guitarist and scene leader Donna Dresch (who was responsible for Chainsaw Records and the Chainsaw Dream). The band featured Dresch on guitar, Jody Bleyle on bass and vocals, Marci Martinez on drums, and Kaia Wilson on guitar. After the first record, Martinez was replaced by Melissa York. Kaia Wilson later went on to form the **Butchies,** one of the key bands in the queercore movement and also one of the bands that helped expose younger members of the queer community to punk rock.
Discography: *Personal Best* (Chainsaw/Candy-Ass, 1994); *Captain My Captain* (Chainsaw/Candy-Ass, 1996). **Kaia:** *Kaia* (Chainsaw/Candy-Ass, 1996); *Ladyman* (Mr. Lady, 1997); *Oregon* (Mr. Lady, 2002). **Butchies:** *Are We Not Femme?* (Mr. Lady, 1998); *Population 1975* (Mr. Lady, 1999); *3* (Mr. Lady, 2001). **Infinite X's:** *The Infinite X's* (Chainsaw, 2001). **Adickdid:** *Dismantle* (G, 1993).

TEENGENERATE

Japanese punk band that incorporated elements of garage and **protopunk** into their sound. The band started as the American Soul Spiders and took the name Teengenerate from a **Dictators** song and was one of the most popular Japanese punk bands to play worldwide. The original lineup consisted of Fink on lead vocals and guitar, Fifi on guitar and vocals, Sammy on bass, and Sho on drums (later replaced by Shoe). The band broke up in the mid-1990s but reunited for several shows in mid-2005.
Discography: *Audio Recording* (Cruddy Record Dealership, 1993; Pop Llama, 1995); *Savage!!!* (Sympathy for the Record Industry, 1994); *Get Action!* (Crypt, 1994); *Smash Hits!* (Estrus, 1995); *Savage* (Sympathy for the Record Industry, 1996); *Live at Shelter* (Target Earth, 2001). **Tweezers:** *Already!* (Japan, Time Bomb, 1997). **Raydios:** *Original Demo Recordings* (Ger. Screaming Apple, 1998).

TEEN IDLES

Early Washington, D.C., **hardcore** band featuring both **Ian MacKaye** and Jeff Nelson, future members of **Minor Threat,** as well as lead singer Nathan Strejeck, who later went on to form the Washington, D.C., based **Youth Brigade** and was an early member of **Dischord Records** before he left the punk scene. The band was one of the earliest hardcore bands in **Washington, D.C.,** and one of the first to tour outside that city. The band was also the impetus for the Dischord label when the members decided to release an EP of material upon the demise of the band and recorded the EP that would be Dischord's first release.

TELEVISION

One of the first New York City "punk" bands to coalesce in the mid-1970s and extremely influential, although not in a stereotypical punk style. Television was also the band that convinced **CBGB's** owner **Hilly Kristal** to let bands play there on nights when nothing else was going on. The band started out in the early 1970s as the Neon Boys with guitarist Tom Verlaine (Tom Miller), **Richard Hell** (Richard Meyers, an old friend of Verlaine's from boarding school who had also written poetry with Verlaine under the name Theresa Stern) on bass, and Billy Ficca on drums. After not finding a suitable second guitarist, the band eventually reformed as Television, with Richard Lloyd on second guitar. After a falling out and Verlaine gradually cutting Hell's songs from the band, Hell left and was replaced by bassist Fred Smith from **Blondie,** and Hell went on to join the **Heartbreakers** before forming Richard Hell and the **Voidoids.**

Television released its first single, "Little Johnny Jewel," in August 1975, which hinted at the dual guitar experimentation for which Television would eventually become famous on their first two albums. They pioneered a more artistic twin guitar attack that was a major influence on current New York City bands such as the Strokes, who borrow freely from the band's rhythmic experiments and singer Tom Verlaine's vocal style. The first album, *Marquee Moon*, featured the epic title track and such other classics as "Venus De Milo" and "Friction," all of which demonstrated the vitality and fluidity of Lloyd and Verlaine's dueling guitars, something that was not only unheard of in the early punk scene but was also rarely emulated in punk. (This does not mean it was not emulated in indie rock bands; **Sonic Youth** clearly owes a debt to Television.) After releasing a less successful second record, *Adventure*, in 1978, the band split due to conflicts between Verlaine and Lloyd, and both went on to solo careers of varying success, with Lloyd eventually becoming a session guitarist for artists such as Mathew Sweet. Ficca went on to drum with various bands, most notably the Waitresses, who had a minor hit with the song "I Know What Boys Like." Television reformed in 1992 and recorded a self-titled third album to critical acclaim but poor sales. The band continued to reunite and tour sporadically, although it has not released new material in a decade.

Discography: *Marquee Moon* (Elektra, 1977); *Adventure* (Elektra, 1978); *The Blow-Up* (tape, Roir, 1982; CD, Fr. Danceteria, 1989, 1993); *Television* (Capitol, 1992). **Tom Verlaine:** *Tom Verlaine* (Elektra, 1979); *Dreamtime* (Warner Bros., 1981; Infinite Zero, 1994); *Words from the Front* (Warner Bros., 1982); *Cover* (Virgin/Warner Bros., 1984); *Flash Light* (IRS, 1987); *The Wonder* (UK Fontana, 1990); *Warm and Cool* (Rykodisc, 1992); *The Miller's Tale* (UK Virgin, 1996).

TELEVISION PERSONALITIES

Quirky British punk band that veered off into left field after their early **Jam** and punk-influenced singles. The band was started by Dan Treacy and Ed Ball (Ball later left to form the Times) and had an early critique of the punk poseurs on their song "Part-Time Punks." Treacy eventually became a **heroin** addict and served time in prison.

Discography: *Where's Bill Grundy Now?* EP7 (UK Kings Rd., 1978; UK Rough Trade, 1979; UK Overground, 1992); *... And Don't the Kids Just Love It* (UK R ough Trade, 1981; UK Fire, 1991; Razor and Tie, 1995); *Mummy Your Not Watching Me* (UK Whaam!, 1982; UK Dreamworld, 1987; UK Fire, 1991); *They Could Have Been Bigger than the Beatles* (UK Whaam!, 1982; UK Dreamworld, 1986; (UK Fire, 1991); *The Painted Word* (UK Illuminated, 1985; UK Fire, 1991); *Chocolat Art* (Ger. Pastell, 1985, 1993); *Salvador Dali's Garden Party* EP (UK Fire, 1989); *Privilege* (Fire, 1990); *Camping in France* (UK Overground, 1991); *How I Learned to Love the Bomb* EP (UK Overground, 1992); *Closer to God* (Fire/Seed, 1992); *Not Like Everybody Else* EP7 (Ger. Little Teddy, 1993); *You, Me and Lou Reed* EP (UK Fantastic

Planet, 1993); *Far Away & Lost in Joy* EP (UK Vinyl Japan, 1994); *The Prettiest Girl in the World* EP7 (UK Overground, 1994); *Yes Darling, but Is It Art? (Early Singles and Rarities)* (Fire/Seed, 1995); *Do You Think if You Were Beautiful You'd Be Happy?* EP (UK Vinyl Japan, 1995); *I Was a Mod before You Was a Mod* (UK Overground, 1995); *Top Gear* (UK Overground, 1996); *Paisley Shirts & Mini Skirts* (UK no label, 1996); *Made in Japan* (Ger. Little Teddy, 1996); *Mod Is Dead* (UK Teenage Kicks, 1996); *Prime Time Television Personalities 1981–1992* (UK Nectar Masters, 1997); *Don't Cry Baby … It's Only a Movie* (UK Damaged Goods, 1998); *Part Time Punks: The Very Best of Television Personalities* (UK Cherry Red, 1999); *The Boy Who Couldn't Stop Dreaming* (UK Vinyl Japan, 2000); *Fashion Conscious* (Ger. Little Teddy, 2001).

THIS IS BOSTON, NOT LA

A response to the prevalence of press about the Los Angeles punk scene, featuring the then cream of **Boston hardcore** bands such as **Jerry's Kids, Gang Green, the Freeze,** and the Proletariats, released by Modern Method Records. The compilation inspired many in the Boston scene to join the growing scene. The title refers to the fact that the Boston scene was just as lively and engaging as those in other large cities.

THROBBING GRISTLE

The first industrial noise band form London that raised the ante on punk's abrasiveness. Led by the chameleonlike Genesis P-Orridge (originally named Neil Megson, who took his new name from a school nickname and the food on which he used to survive while trying to work on his original projects), Throbbing Gristle basically created industrial music and led punk to become more noisy and experimental. The band—really more of an art collective (originally based on P-Orridge's revelation of the idea of the COUM Transmissions Group, which was established to create art and music in a collective sense)—started in London in 1975 with Genesis P-Orridge, guitarist Cosey Fan Tutti (Christine Carol Newby, originally P-Orridge's girlfriend and collaborator in COUM), tape operator Peter Christopherson, and keyboardist Chris Carter (Chris Severin). Early shows were timed to a punch clock and featured art exhibits as well as musical performances and Genesis's sometimes provoking and attacking the audience. The band started out trying to shock the audiences not through mindless slogans and punchy guitars but through disquieting musical soundscapes and lyrics that discussed controversial and alarming topics such as "Hamburger Lady" and quietly subversive titles such as the bordering-on-accessible *20 Jazz Funk Greats*, which disguised itself as a relatively pleasant-looking album but was sure to shock any listener who had bought it under false pretenses. To release their work when no other record company would sign them, they formed Industrial Records, in effect starting the industrial music revolution. After releasing *Heathen Earth* in 1980, the band decided to break up, and Carter and Fan Tutti began a new project as Chris and Cosey. P-Orridge and Christopherson went on to form the even more shocking Psychic TV before Christopherson left to form the slightly more accessible Coil. P-Orridge remains the most active of the group, playing under a variety of new names, working in magic rituals to disrupt complacency, and apparently on his way to creating a new gender. P-Orridge was also one of the first punks to practice body modification through scarring, tattoos, and piercing, including several weighty piercings on his genitals. There were many live albums, reissues, and compilations released after the band broke up, most of dubious quality. Throbbing Gristle was not only a link between the art communes of the 1960s and punk rock but was also a powerful and much more subversive project than almost any punk group of the 1970s who espoused anarchy without any real idea of what it meant. Throbbing Gristle pushed music and meaning so far that most bands are still playing catch-up 30 years later. In subsequent volumes of works on art and music, Throbbing Gristle will one day be regarded as important as the Dadaist or surrealist movements were in their time. The band reunited for a concert in 2004 and announced plans to record and tour in the future.

Discography: *The Second Annual Report of Throbbing Gristle* (Mute, 1977); *DOA: The Third and final Report of Throbbing Gristle* (Mute, 1978); *Throbbing Gristle* (Fetish, 1978); *20 Jazz Funk Greats* (Industrial, 1979); *First Annual Report* (Industrial, 1979); *At the factory Manchester (Live)* (Industrial, 1980); *At Sheffield University (Live)* (Industrial, 1980); *Heathen Earth* (Industrial, 1980); *Beyond Ja Funk* (Rough Trade, 1981); *Funeral in Berlin (Live)* (Zensor, 1981); *Mission of Dead Souls (Live)* (Mute, 1981); *Raffters/Psychic Rally* (World, 1981); *Live at Death Factory* (No label, 1982); *Thee Psychick Sacrifice* (Illuminated, 1982); *Editions … Frankfurt Berlin Live* (Illuminated, 1982); *Further Dermenscheit* (American Phono, 1983); *Once upon a Time (Live at the Lyceum)* (Casual Abandon, 1983); *Live at Heaven* (Rough Trade, 1985); *Live Vol. 1* (Grey Area, 1996); *Live Vol. 4* (Grey Area, 1996); *Greif* (Thirsty Ear, 2001); *The First Annual Report of Throbbing Gristle* (Thirsty Ear, 2001); *TG+* (Mute, 2004); *Nothing Short of a Total War* (Cause for Concern, 2004).

THUNDERS, JOHNNY

Brilliant but drug addicted guitar player for both the **New York Dolls** and his own band, the **Heartbreakers,** instrumental in both the musical and stylistic directions that punk took in the mid-1970s. Thunders was born John Gezale and joined the embryonic New York Dolls in the early 1970s. The Dolls sound and gender-bending look was an important precursor to punk, and although the New York Dolls owed more to the Rolling Stones and 1960s pop and girl group sounds, the band's reputation and appetite for assorted substances made them legends. When the Dolls splintered in 1975, Thunders, along with drummer Jerry Nolan, left to concentrate more on their shared tastes for more aggressive music and **heroin.** They formed the Heartbreakers in New York along with **Richard Hell** on bass, who had recently quit the band **Television,** and guitarist Walter Lure. The band quickly became known for the members' out-of-control behavior, which was marketed by manager **Leee Black Childers** (formerly of **David Bowie**'s **MainMan** company), who promoted the Heartbreakers with a Roberta Bayley picture of the band with gushing gunshot wounds and the provocative slogan "Catch them while they're still alive." After arguing over creative direction, Hell left the band to form his own Richard Hell and the **Voidoids** and was replaced by Billy Rath. The Heartbreakers played New York unsuccessfully for a time and then joined the **Sex Pistols,** the **Damned**, and the **Clash** on the Anarchy tour in 1976. Although most of the gigs were canceled, Johnny Thunders was credited with one lasting effect on the tour: introducing British punks to heroin. After the demise of the Heartbreakers, Thunders recorded sporadically, although his first solo record, *So Alone*, featuring guest appearances from Phil Lynnott from Thin Lizzy and Peter Perrett from the **Only Ones,** contains his signature tune, "You Can't Put Your Arms around a Memory." The album also featured contributions from Steve Jones and Paul Cook from the ashes of the **Sex Pistols.** Thunders toured and recorded sporadically throughout the 1980s with different aggregations of musicians, most notably the collaborations with Wayne Kramer of the **MC5** on the *Gang War* sessions and Patti Paladin on the Copycats records, and developed an increasing dependence on drugs. An ill-fated attempt to form a punk supergroup with Stiv Bators (**Dead Boys** and Lords of the New Church) and **Dee Dee Ramone** in Paris in 1990 ended in acrimony when Dee Dee accused Thunders of stealing and threw bleach over Thunders' clothing and smashed his guitar. Thunders returned to the United States, where he died under mysterious circumstances, apparently of a heroin overdose, in 1991 in New Orleans.

Discography: *So Alone* (Real, 1978; Sire/Warner Bros., 1992); *In Cold Blood* (Fr. New Rose, 1983); *Diary of a Lover* EP (PVC, 1983); *New Too Much Junkie Business* (tape; Roir, 1983; Roir/Important, 1990); *Hurt Me* (Fr. New Rose, 1984); *Que Sera, Sera* (UK Jungle, 1985); *Stations of the Cross* (tape; Roir, 1987; Roir/Important, 1990); *Bootlegging the Bootleggers* (UK Jungle, 1990). **Jimmy K:** *Trouble Traveller*

The legendary Johnny Thunders performs at the Peppermint Lounge. © *Robert Barry Francos.*

(Japan Meldac, 1986). **Johnny Thunders & Patti Paladin:** *Copy Cats* (Restless, 1988). **Johnny Thunders & Wayne Kramer:** *Gang War* (Zodiac/DeMilo, 1990). **Heartbreakers:** *L.A.M.F.* (Track, 1977; Jungle, 1984); *Live at Max's Kansas City* (Max's Kansas City, 1979); *D.T.K.—Live at the Speakeasy* (UK Jungle, 1982). **Johnny Thunders & the Heartbreakers:** *L.A.M.F. Revisited* (UK Jungle, 1984); *D.T.K. L.A.M.F.* (UK Jungle, 1984); *Live at the Lyceum Ballroom 1984* (ABC, 1984; Receiver, 1990).

TODAY

British television show on ITV in the London area on which on December 1, 1976, the **Sex Pistols** (replacing the band Queen who canceled at the last moment) caused a sensation by arguing and cursing with the bored and tipsy host, Bill Grundy, who dared the band to "do something outrageous." The Pistols responded by calling him a "dirty bastard" and "dirty fucker" on live television, supposedly causing a father watching at home to kick in his television set after his son was exposed to the Sex Pistols' expletives. The tabloid press in Britain had a field day with the incident, and headlines denounced the "filth and the fury" (later the name of a documentary film about the Sex Pistols) that the Sex Pistols had caused. The Sex Pistols profile was raised by the incident, and Grundy was suspended in the ensuing outrage. From that moment on, the British press and television began to examine punk rock in more detail. Today, the clip can be seen in numerous documentaries on punk, including the film **The Filth and the Fury.**

TOKEN ENTRY

New York City **hardcore** band from the mid-1980s that was a key skate punk band. The original lineup featured Anthony Comunale on vocals (who later joined Killing Time and then Raw Deal), Ernie Parada on drums(who later joined the Arsons), Mickey Neal on guitar, and Arthur Smilios on bass (who also played bass for **Gorilla Biscuits,** and later **Civ**), and Timmy Chunks later joined on vocals. Some of the later records were produced by Gary "Dr. Know" Miller, the guitarist for **Bad Brains.**

Discography: *Ready or Not Here We Come* EP (Turnstyle Tunes, 1985); *From beneath the Streets* (Positive Force, 1987; Go Kart, 1998); *Jaybird* (Hawker, 1988; Go Kart, 1998); *The Weight of the World* (Emergo, 1990).

TOM ROBINSON BAND

Band well known for its poppy socialistic anthems and openly gay lead singer, Tom Robinson. The band also featured Mark Amberon on keyboards, Brian Taylor on drums, and Danny Kustow on guitar. Robinson, a songwriter and gay activist, signed to EMI and put out first the single, "2-4-6-8 Motorway" (over the more controversial "Glad to Be Gay"), in August 1977. His first album, *Power in the Darkness*, was a minor British hit. After a second record failed to chart, Robinson dismissed the rest of the band and began a long solo career that encompassed numerous genres and stylistic experiments.

TOO MUCH JOY

Punk band from Scarsdale, New York, known for its insight and humorous lyrics courtesy of front man Tim Quirk, alongside guitarist Jay Blumfield, drummer (and former New York City cop) Tommy Vinton, and bassist Sandy Smallens (later replaced by producer William Whitman). The band played numerous shows and toured relentlessly, releasing several classic albums such as *Cereal Killers* and *Son of Sam I Am*, but never really made a dent in the marketplace. The band did gain notoriety in numerous ways, however. In the early 1990s, they played a set of Too Live Crew covers in Florida as a protest against restrictive obscenity laws, and all of the band members except for drummer Vinton were arrested. Too Much Joy was also known for inadvertently inspiring the Republican revolution of the mid-1990s when staffers to then congressman Newt Gingrich adopted the bands refrain "to create, you must destroy" from their song "Theme Song" on the *Cereal Killers* album. After years of relentless touring, the band called it quits after the . . . *Finally* album, and Quirk is now a music writer in San Francisco.

Discography: *Green Eggs and Crack* (Stonegarden, 1987); *Son of Sam I Am* (Alias, 1988); *Cereal Killers* (Alais/Giant/Warner, 1991); *Nothing on My Mind* EP (Giant/Warner Brothers, 1991); *Mutiny* (Giant, 1992); . . . *Finally* (Discovery) 1996).

TOP JIMMY

Los Angeles punk scene maker from the early experimental days of **Los Angeles** punk rock.

TOUCH AND GO

Originally a **zine** founded by **Meatmen** singer Tesco Vee, eventually it evolved into a record label run by Corey Rusk (formerly of the **Necros**), who still releases records on the label. Bands that have appeared on Touch and Go include the **Butthole Surfers** and **Big Black.**

TRIBE 8

Queercore band of fiercely independent and determined lesbians who worked to smash dominant perceptions of gender though their raunchy stage shows. The band featured Leslie Mann on guitar, Lynn Payne on bass, Slade Bellum on drums (later replaced by Jen Savage), and Lynn Breedlove on lead vocals. The band released their early records on small labels before moving to the relatively larger **Alternative Tentacles.** Lyrically, the band eschewed political correctness and sang songs that openly proclaimed the joys of sexuality and demonstrated the band's refusal to be pinned down to any one political agenda. A Tribe 8 show was not so much

a concert as an event to explore or destroy the dominant notions of gender in society. Often a strap-on dildo was used by Breedlove to demonstrate that sexuality and power were one and the same and that the audiences' expectations of the norms of "straight" or "gay" were limited concepts. Tribe 8 broke up in the late 1990s, but their legacy as out punks and their challenges to the dominant punk orthodoxy make them an important addition to punk history.
Discography: *Pg Bitch* EP (Harp, 1991); *By the Time We Get to Colorado* EP (Revolver, 1993); *Fist City* (Alternative Tentacles, 1995); *Roadkill Care* EP (Alternative Tentacles, 1995); *Snarkism* (Alternative Tentacles, 1996).

TRUE TILL DEATH

Straight edge slogan (and occasionally tattoo) that signified one's commitment to the straight edge movement. True till Death meant that despite the temptations that adulthood would bring, the individual would remain devoted to straight edge and not drink, use drugs, and in some cases stay vegetarian or vegan.

TSOL

TSOL (True Sounds of Liberty) is one of the key early **hardcore** bands from California's Orange County, known for their violent shows and the ever-changing lineup (at one point a version of the band was touring without any original members). TSOL was started by vocalist Jack Grisham and drummer Todd Barnes (who had previously played together in Vicious Circle, also well known for the rampant violence at its shows) along with guitarist Ron Emory and Mike Roche on bass. The band started playing at affluent friends' house parties, but their inherent love of vandalism soon forced them to gig professionally. TSOL released its first self-titled EP in 1981 and followed it with the hardcore classic *Dance with Me*, which moved the band into a less political and more Gothic direction (sometimes known as Death Rock), which confused some in their fan base, and continued in this direction for the *Beneath the Shadows* record in 1983, which alienated even more fans. After a show in Los Angeles turned into a riot, Grisham quit TSOL to play similar music in the band Cathedral of Tears and later toured and recorded in the 1990s as Joykiller. After Barnes quit as well, TSOL added guitarist and singer Joe Wood and drummer Mitch Dean to record several metal-tinged TSOL records. The original TSOL reunited at the end of the 1990s and continued to record and tour, although original drummer Todd Barnes died soon thereafter.
Discography: *T.S.O.L.* EP (Posh Boy, 1981); *Dance with Me* (Frontier, 1981; Epitaph, 1996); *Weathered Statues* EP7 (Alternative Tentacles, 1982); *Beneath the Shadows* (Alternative Tentacles, 1982; Restless, 1989; Nitro, 1997); *Change Today?* (Enigma, 1984; Restless, 1997); *Revenge* (Enigma, 1986; Restless, 1997); *Hit and Run* (Enigma, 1987; Restless, 1997); *Thoughts of Yesterday 1981–1982* (Posh Boy, 1988; Rhino, 1992); *TSOL Live* (Restless, 1988); *Strange Love* (Enigma, 1990; Restless, 1997); *Hell and Back Together 1984–1990* (Restless, 1992); *T.S.O.L./Weathered Statues* (Nitro, 1997); *Live '91* (Nitro, 1997); *Disappear* (Nitro, 2001); *Divided We Stand* (Nitro, 2003); *Who's Screwin' Who?: 18 TSOL Greatest Non-Hits* (Anarchy, 2005). **TSOL/Slayer:** *Abolish Government* EP7 (Sub Pop, 1996). **Cathedral of Tears:** *Cathedral of Tears* EP (Enigma, 1984). **Tender Fury:** *Tender Fury* (Posh Boy, 1988); *Garden of Evil* (Triple X, 1990); *If Anger Were Soul, I'd Be James Brown* (Triple X, 1991). **Jack Grisham/Mike Roche/Ron Emory/Todd Barnes:** *Live 1991* (Triple X, 1991). **Joykiller:** *The Joykiller* (Epitaph, 1995); *Static* (Epitaph, 1996); *Three* (Epitaph, 1997); *Ready Sexed Go!* (Epitaph, 2003).

"TV PARTY"

Ironic **Black Flag** song about the numbing power of television, later used in the movie ***Repo Man*** and in the last season of the Fox animated series *Futurama*. During the end credits of the show, the characters sing "TV Party," substituting shows used as plot points on *Futurama*.

2.13.61

Publishing company run by punk provocateur **Henry Rollins** and named after his birthday. The company, which specializes in cult authors and Rollins' own considerable body of work, has so far released numerous volumes of Rollins' spoken word, poems, and musings that sometimes resemble stand-up comedy. The company also has released books by other artists Rollins admires, such as Nick Cave, Michael Gira (from the Swans), the late legendary author Henry Miller, Exene Cervenka, Hubert Selby Jr., Glen E. Friedman, who took many of the classic early punk and skateboarding photos, and spoken-word CDs by Rollins, Cervenka, and Hubert Selby Jr.

2 TONE

Record label started by Jerry Dammers of the **Specials** as an imprint for the Chrysalis label. The label released records by the Specials, Specials A.K.A., Madness, the Selecter, Elvis Costello, the Beat (called the English Beat in the United States for contractual reasons), and others. The label was started by Dammers, who was inspired by labels, such as Motown, that had a recognizable style and musical direction and that also fit into Dammers' plan to release music by multiracial bands such as his own and the Selecter. The label was largely active during the late 1970s to early 1980s and was instrumental in exposing many in the English scene to **ska** and rock-steady rhythms that regularly cracked the top 10. After the original Specials dissolved, with members leaving to form Fun Boy Three, Dammers reconstituted the Specials under its original name of Specials A.K.A., and the label had its last major hit with the antiapartheid classic "Free Nelson Mandela." Most of the 2 Tone bands have reunited in some form or another and released new music or toured.

UK SUBS

Formed in the late 1970s by leader and vocalist Charlie Harper, the UK Subs first recorded some live tracks for the Farewell to the Roxy. Harper (original name Manuel Vader) was the founder of the band, and the original lineup included Peter Davies on drums, Paul Slack on bass, and Nicky Garratt on guitar. Charlie Harper (who had previously been in a type of R & B band, called the Marauders, similar to **Joe Strummer's** the **101ers**) formed the band in late 1976 as the Subversives with guitarist Nicky Garratt, bassist Steve Stack, and several drummers, and eventually the most consistent was Pete Davis. The band recorded a live set at the **Roxy** club in 1977 that was not released until 1980 and recorded Peel sessions with **John Peel** in 1977. Their first record, *Another Kind of Blues*, was released on Gem in 1979. The band played many gigs with the like-minded **Crass** and fostered a sense of working-class pride absent from some of the artier permutations of punk rock and **postpunk** at the time, The band instead specialized in speeded up anthems such as "Stranglehold," "CID," and "Telephone Numbers." The UK Subs were featured in a rarely seen film by Julien Temple called *Punk Can Take It*. Bassist Alvin Gibbs later played with **Iggy Pop** and recounted his experiences in the book *Neighborhood Threat: On Tour with Iggy Pop*. Later members included Lars Frederickson of **Rancid,** and the band soldiered on until the early 2000s.

Discography: *Another Kind of Blues* (RCA, 1979); *Brand New Age* (Gem, 1980); *Crash Course* (Gem, 1980); *Live Kicks* (Universe, 1980); *Diminished Responsibility* (Gem, 1981); *Endangered Species* (Nems, 1982); *Flood of Lies* (Scarlet-Fall Out, 1983); *Demonstration Tapes* (Konexion, 1984); *Gross out USA* (Fall Out, 1985); *Left for Dead: Alive in Holland '86* (Roir, 1986); *Raw Material* (Killerwatt, 1986); *Jan Today* (Enigma, 1988); *Down on the Farm* (Castle, 1994); *Pun Is Back* (Cannon, 1995); *Occupied* (Amsterdamned, 1997); *Riot* (Cleopatra, 1997); *Sub Mission: The Best of the UK Subs 1982–1998* (Fallout, 2000); *Mad Cow Fever* (Fallout/Jungle, 2001); *Universal* (Captain Oi, 2002); *Before You Were Punk* (Anarchy Music, 2004).

UNDERDOG

Straight edge band from **New York** featuring Ritchie Birkenhead on lead vocals (Birkenhead later went on to join and then leave **Youth of Today** before reforming Underdog and

The Undertones were known as the "Irish Ramones" in their original legendary lineup. *Photo by Graham Wright/Rex Features.*

then leaving to form Into Another), Russ Wheeler on bass (who also played in **Murphy's Law**), Danny Derella on guitar, and Dean Joseph on drums. The band played extensively in the New York **hardcore** scene in the mid-1980s and worked in elements of **reggae** into their straight-ahead melodic sound.

Discography: *True Blue* EP (New Beginning, 1986); *Vanishing Point* (Caroline, 1989; Go Kart, 1998); *The Demos* (Revelation, 1993, 1996).

UNDERTONES

Northern Ireland's answer to the **Ramones,** best known for their ode to young love, "Teenage Kicks," as well as numerous pop-punk anthems and being the favorite band of the late English DJ **John Peel.** The Undertones were formed in Londonderry, Northern Ireland, in late 1975, with lead singer Feargal Sharkey, brothers John and Damian O'Neil on guitars, Mickey Bradley on bass, and Billy Doherty on drums. They finally released their first record, *The Undertones*, in May 1979. Seymour Stein of Sire records was apparently so enamored with the band that when he heard the song "Teenage Kicks" on the radio, he pulled his car over and decided right then and there that he had to sign the band. The resulting first record was a gloriously innocent exploration of the joys of being a teen, which was doubly surprising considering both punk's limited subject selection and where the Undertones had grown up. *Hypnotised* was a step forward but still concentrated on short, poppy songs about (as one song went) "chocolate and girls." The record also included the sarcastic "My Perfect Cousin" and the beautiful "Wednesday Week," which showed that the Undertones were far more than the Irish Ramones and had a distinct pop sensibility all of their own. By their later albums, however, they were consumed by their lack of popularity and hamstrung by the need to advance the sound but not lose old fans. A move in a more soulful direction (possibly influenced by Sharkey, as demonstrated by his own attempts at soul once he went solo) was less successful, and the band called it quits after the album *The Sin of Pride.*

After the demise of the Undertones, Damian and John O'Neil later went on to form the band That Petrol Emotion, which had some success during the 1980s and 1990s. The Undertones reunited, without singer Feargal Sharkey, in 1999 with new singer Paul McLoone (who somehow channels Feargal Sharkey's voice) and toured and recorded successfully. Thanks to the ceaseless efforts of John Peel, the Undertones will be remembered as one of the finest punk bands and certainly one of the poppiest.

Discography: *Teenage Kicks* EP7 (UK Good Vibrations, 1978); *The Undertones* (Sire, 1979; Rykodisc, 1994; Castle/Sanctuary, 2003); *Hypnotised* (Sire, 1980; Rykodisc, 1994; Castle/Sanctuary, 2003); *Positive Touch* (Harvest, 1981; Rykodisc, 1994; Castle/Sanctuary, 2003); *The Love Parade* EP (UK Ardeck, 1982); *The Sin of Pride* (UK Ardeck, 1983; Rykodisc, 1994; Castle/Sanctuary, 2003); *All Wrapped Up* (Ardeck/Capitol, 1983); *Cher 'o Bowlies* (UK EMI, 1986); *The Peel Sessions* EP (UK Strange Fruit, 1986); *The Peel Sessions Album* (UK Strange Fruit, 1989); *The Very Best of the Undertones* (Rykodisc, 1994); *True Confessions* (Singles = As + Bs; Castle/Sanctuary, 2003); *Get What You Need* (Sanctuary, 2003). **Feargal Sharkey:** *Feargal Sharkey* (Virgin/A&M, 1985); *Wish* (Virgin, 1988); *Songs from the Mardi Gras* (UK Virgin, 1991).

UNIFORM CHOICE

Straight edge hardcore punk band from **Orange County**, California, that imitated **Minor Threat** in look and musical style. The band featured Pat Dunbar on vocals, Victor Maynes on guitar, and Pat Longrie on drums. Dunbar and Longrie started the Wishing Well label, and Dunbar went on to play in Mind Funk. The band was also known for the skirmishes among fans at shows.

Discography: *Screaming* (WIS, 1980); *Staring into the Sun* (Positive, 1980); *Region of Ice* (Giant, 1995); *Getting the Point Across* (live; Lost & Found, 1996); *Screaming for Change* (Wishing Well, 1999).

UNNATURAL AXE

Early U.S. punk band from Dorchester, Massachusetts, that played the **Boston** punk scene during the late 1970s. The band was best known for the songs "They Saved Hitler's Brain" and "Three Chord Rock." The band featured Rich Parsons on guitar and vocals, Tom White on guitar, Frank Dehler on bass (later replaced by Joe Harvard), and Dom Deyoun on drums (later replaced by Bob Woodbury, Tommy Taylor, and others). The band played extensively on the Boston scene at the **Rat,** Cantone's, and the Space and famously opened for the Police before breaking up as the 1980s dawned. All of the band's material was later collected on a CD by Lawless records in the late 1990s. The band reformed sporadically after 2000.

Discography: *They Saved Hitler's Brain* EP (Varulven, 1978); *The Man I Don't Want to Be* EP (Varulven, 1982); *3 Chord Rock* EP (Varulven, 1990); *Unnatural Ass Is Gonna Kick Your Ass* (Lawless, 1997).

URBAN WASTE

Early 1980s **New York hardcore** band featuring Billy Phillips on vocals (later replaced by Kenny Ahrens), Johnny Waste on guitar, Andy Apathy on bass, and Johnny "Feedback" Dancy on drums. The band broke up by 1983, and Phillips, Waste, and Dancy later formed Major Conflict. Waste also played in **Agnostic Front.**

Discography: *Urban Waste* (Mob Style, 1982; Hungry Eye, 2004; Mad at the World, 2004).

URINALS/100 FLOWERS

Los Angeles punk band founded in 1978 that was very influential on the minimalist sounds of punk bands of the time such as the **Minutemen.** The original lineup for the Urinals was Delia Frankel on vocals and Steve Willard on guitars, who quickly left, and the band stabilized as John Talley Jones on vocals and bass, Kjehl Johansen on guitar, and Kevin Barrett on drums. The band's first EP was produced by Vitus Matare, keyboardist for the legendary Los Angeles pop punk band the Last, and was released on the band's own label, Happy Squid. Their second EP was recorded in a film-storing soundstage at UCLA, where the original lineup met and where they played several talent shows before starting to gig in Los Angeles. In 1981, the band changed its name to 100 Flowers (after a quote from Chairman Mao that stated, "Let 100 flowers bloom and 100 schools of thought contend") and continued to play sporadically. Johansen left in 1998 and was replaced by David Nolte (from the Last) and then by Rod Barker. In 1997, some of their earliest material was released on the *Negative Capability* CD.

Discography: *Urinal* EP (Happy Squid, 1979); *Another* EP (Happy Squid, 1979). **As 100 Flowers:** *Negative Capability? Check It Out!* (Amphetamine Reptile, 1997; Warning Label, 2003); *What Is Real and What Is Not* (Warning Label, 2003).

U.S. CHAOS

Early U.S. **hardcore** band from New Jersey that originally formed in 1982 as the Radicals and toured and played the **New York** scene. The band broke up for the first time in 1987 but reformed for reunions after 1992. The original lineup featured Gary Rightmeyer on guitar, Jack Gibson on bass, Spike Chaos on drums, and vocalist Ron. Ron was replaced quickly by vocalist Skully Chaos. The lineup changed drastically over the years, with bassists and drummers leaving constantly. The current lineup includes Skully Chaos, Gary Rightmeyer on guitar, Jack Gibson on bass, and drummer Eddie. Their first U.S. Chaos single was pressed in 1984 and released in 1996, but early pressings are rare and worth quite a bit of money in punk rock collectible circles.

Discography: *Blame It on Sam* (Punkrockrecords, 1998); *Complete Chaos Anthology* (Punkrockrecords, 1998); *We Are Your Enemy* (split release with Statch & the Rapes; Punkrockrecords, 2001); *You Can't Hear a Picture* (Pure Impact Records/Razorwire Records, 2003; Punkrockrecords, 2003); *We've Got the Weapons* (Punkrockrecords, 2003).

VANDALS

Los Angeles punk band from the **hardcore** days that continued with many personnel changes. The original lineup featured Stevo on vocals, Jan Nils Ackerman on guitar, Steve Pfauter on bass, and Joseph Escalante on drums. The band was quickly successful, including a stint in Penelope Spheeris's movie *Suburbia,* and even played a joking benefit for the Young Republicans in 1984. A time of turmoil, however, saw the original singer Stevo replaced by vocalist Dave Quackenbush, bassist Pfauter replaced by drummer Escalante (who moved from drums to bass), guitarist Ackerman replaced by Warren Fitzgerald, and Josh Freese join on drums, so by 1989 the only original member still in the band was Escalante on a new instrument. The band toured extensively and recorded albums that ranged from fast melodic pop to twisted country to a Christmas record. After a stint on several labels, Escalante and Fitzgerald formed Kung Fu Records, which released records by the Vandals and other bands. Freese remained in demand as a session drummer and played with A Perfect Circle and Guns and Roses.

Discography: *Peace through Vandalism* EP (Epitaph, 1983); *When in Rome, Do as the Vandals* (National Trust, 1984); *Fear of a Punk Planet* (Restless, 1991); *Slippery When III* (Restless, 1993); *Sweating to the Oldies: The Vandals Live* (Triple X, 1994); *Live Fast, Diahrea* (Nitro, 1996); *Quickening* (Nitro, 1996); *Christmas with the Vandals: Oi to the World* (Kung Fu, 1996); *Hitler Bad, Vandals Good* (Nitro, 1998); *Play Really Bad Original Country Tunes* (Kung Fu, 1999); *Look What I Almost Stepped In* (Nitro, 2000); *Internet Dating Superstuds* (Kung Fu, 2002); *Hollywood Potato Chips* (Kung Fu, 2004).

VANS WARPED TOUR

The Vans Warped tour is a huge touring festival of **punk** and **hardcore** bands (with occasional rap and **reggae** artists thrown in) that also promotes skate culture, political activism, and the Vans product line. The tour usually features bands from the **Epitaph** label or **Fat Wreck Chords,** such as **Bad Religion** or **NOFX,** as the headliner and also features older punk bands such as the **Damned** during the day. The Warped tour has helped launch many pop punk bands such as **Good Charlotte** and Yellowcard.

VATICAN COMMANDOES

Connecticut-based **hardcore** band from the early 1980s that featured a young Moby (billed as M. H.) on guitar, along with Chuck Wheat on vocals, Jim Spar on bass, and Charles Moody on drums. Moby went on to become Moby.

Discography: *Hit Squad for God* EP7 (Pregnant Nun, 1983).

VEGANS

Vegans in general are those who not only eat no meat but also consume no dairy products or eggs or use any kind of animal products in their food. The term goes back to 1944 when the British vegan society was founded. Living a true vegan lifestyle has inherent difficulties because many foods that are labeled vegetarian often contain milk and cheese. Many punks who became vegetarian or **straight edge** often became vegans in a natural continuance of the philosophy that advocates doing less harm to the environment. Many vegan punks help sponsor communal meals or food kitchens that help vegans stay healthy. Touring is particularly difficult for vegan punks because there are few places to get healthful vegan food on highways crowded with fast-food restaurants such as McDonald's and Taco Bell. The vegan philosophy is strongly connected to the loosely based **punk** ethos and many punks decide to go vegan less for health reasons than to not contribute to policies that harm the planet.

VEGETARIANS

Many punks espouse a vegetarian lifestyle (without going to the extreme that **vegans** do) for philosophical or ideological reasons. Some punks oppose eating meat from a perspective that sees the exploitation of animals as a larger symptom of capitalist culture, and others do not eat meat because they look upon animals as spiritual beings. Many punks relate a vegetarian lifestyle with the **punk** ethos because of its political and moral implications, and numerous punks, such as the members of **Crass** and **MDC,** as well as **Ian MacKaye** and even Fat Mike from **NOFX,** are vegetarians.

VELVET UNDERGROUND

The Velvet Underground was a groundbreaking, albeit ignored, group of the 1960s, an enormous influence on numerous **punk** and indie bands, as well as the birthing place of the careers of punk icon **Lou Reed** and **Nico** and John Cale. The Velvet Underground started as an experimental band created by literature student Lou Reed on guitar and vocals along with John Cale (who had previously worked with minimalist composer and musician Lamonte Young) on viola and bass, Sterling Morrison on guitar, and Angus Maclise on percussion. They played their first experimental drone music (influenced both by Reed's pop sensibility, honed as a songwriter for hire for Pickwick Records, where he wrote the novelty hit "The Ostrich," and Cale's work with Lamonte Young) as early as July 1965. Maclise, who hated the thought of the rampant commercialism involved in actually playing a gig for money, was replaced by Maureen Tucker on drums. After spending several years in India, Maclise died in 1979 in Kathmandu. The band was championed, managed, and "produced" by artist Andy Warhol, who packaged them as a collective with Nico (an icy European model and sometime singer), dancers, and a light show as the Exploding Plastic Inevitable, although the band was not enamored of the idea. Nico soon began singing songs with the band, such as "All Tomorrow's Parties," "Femme Fatale," and "I'll Be Your Mirror." Nico left the Velvet Underground after the first record and soon began a career as a solo artist; he died in 1988. After Nico left, Warhol more or less began to lose interest and eventually left the band to its own devices. The second record was the more acerbic and even less commercial *White Light/White Heat*. It contained the ultimate anticommercial epic "Sister Ray" and other classics. After the record, tensions between Cale and Reed came to a boiling point, and Cale was forced out of the band in September 1968 and replaced by bassist Doug Yule. For their third record, simply titled *The Velvet Underground*, the band abandoned some of their more abstract and confrontational music and ended up producing a work of quiet beauty that revealed that despite the layers of feedback and cacophony, Reed had an instinctive gift for telling stories though song. The band continued to struggle to find a foothold in the United States, where it was ignored by commercial radio, lambasted in the few reviews that actually came out in mainstream media, and generally was comfortable only playing in towns with a vibrant music scene, such as San Francisco, **Boston,** and in **New York** at places such as **Max's Kansas City,** where the bohemians gathered. The band was let go by MGM after the release of *The Velvet Underground*, and their last official album, *Loaded,* was a conscious effort to get radio play, an effort that, despite the band's best attempts, would not pay off during the lifetime of the band. The Velvet Underground returned to play an extended residence at Max's Kansas City, minus Maureen Tucker, who had left the band to have a child, and by the end of the residence, Reed had had his fill and departed as well. Yule kept the band going for an unwise album without any of the major players but with his brother Billy (who had played on *Loaded,* although Ian Paice would play on *Squeeze*), bassist Walter Powers, and guitarist Willie Alexander. By that time, the Velvet Underground had become a rapidly growing legend, one that would inspire musicians for years to come.

Lou Reed went on to a successful career as a solo artist, releasing landmark albums such as *Transformer, Coney Island Baby,* and *Berlin*. After Cale and Reed reunited to record "Songs for Drella," a tribute to the late Andy Warhol, and after Sterling Morrison and Reed had joined Cale live on stage, the Velvet Underground reunited for a reunion tour in 1993, but plans for future tours and recordings ended when Sterling Morrison died of cancer in 1995. Lou Reed, Cale, and Maureen Tucker continued solo careers of varying success. The Velvet Underground was one of the most important bands in punk rock and in rock and roll in general, and Brian Eno was quoted as remarking that everyone that saw them formed a band.

Discography: *The Velvet Underground & Nico* (Verve, 1967, 1985); *White Light/White Heat* (Verve, 1968, 1985); *The Velvet Underground* (MGM, 1969; Verve, 1985); *Loaded* (Cotillion, 1970); *The Velvet Underground Live at Max's Kansas City* (Cotillion, 1972); *Lou Reed and the Velvet Underground* (Pride, 1973); *Squeeze* (UK Polydor, 1973); *1969 Velvet Underground Live with Lou Reed* (Mercury, 1974); *VU* (Verve, 1985); *Velvet Underground* (Polydor, 1986); *Another View* (Verve, 1986); *The Best of the Velvet Underground* (Verve, 1989); *Live MCMXCIII* (Sire/Warner Bros., 1993); *The Best Of* (UK Global Television, 1995); *Peel Slowly and See* (Polydor, 1995); *Loaded (Fully Loaded Edition)* (Rhino, 1997); *Bootleg Series Volume 1: The Quine Tapes* (Polydor, 2001).

VERBAL ASSAULT

Influential U.S. **hardcore** band from Newport, Rhode Island, that formed in 1981 and broke up in 1991. The *Learn* record was produced by **Ian MacKaye** and is considered a punk classic by many. The band featured Pete Chramiec on guitar, Chris Jones on bass and vocals, and Doug Ernest on drums. Numerous drummers and bass players came and went over the years, but the band soldiered on with primary members Jones and Chramiec. Chramiec later formed Rain Like the Sound of Trains and toured with Lois and Not from Space.

Discography: *The Masses Demo* (self-released, 1985); *Learn* EP (Positive Force, 1985); *Trial* (Positive, 1988); *On* (Groove, 1989); *Verbal Assault* (Groove, 1991); *Exit/On* (Groove, 1992); *On* EP (Razorwire, 2003); *Volume One: Masses and Learn* (Mendit, 2003).

VIBRATORS

The Vibrators were more of an English power-pop band that was in the right place at the right time to be swept into the **punk** scene. The original band was formed in 1976 and consisted of Ian "Knox" Carnochran on lead vocals, Pat Collier on bass (replaced by Gary Tibbs for the second record), John Ellis on guitar, and John "Eddie the Drummer" Edwards on drums. Prior to the Vibrators, Knox had been a veteran of the rhythm-and-blues and pub-rock scenes and brought some of the lessons he had learned on the pub circuit with him to the band. Collier and Ellis had previously played in a local band called Bazooka Joe before meeting Knox and deciding to form an edgier band. In 1977, the band released its first album, *Pure Mania*, which contained their best-known song, "Baby Baby." The Vibrators were on the bill for the famous **100 Club** punk rock festival along the **Sex Pistols, Subway Sect,** the **Buzzcocks,** the **Damned,** Stinky Toys, and the **Clash** but remained largely outsiders to the punk scene, possibly due to their generic look and propensity for power pop as opposed to raunchy punk rock. The band went through several breakups (first in 1980 and then reuniting in 1982) and reformations (including the addition of Mark Duncan and, later, Nick Peckham on bass, Mickie Owen, and Nigel Bennet and then Darell Bath on guitar) and continued to tour in a new lineup. Collier went on to become a prolific record producer, working with bands as disparate as the Soup Dragons, Katrina and the Waves (which also featured Kimberly Rew of the Soft Boys), and House of Love.

Discography: *Pure Mania* (Columbia, 1977; Sony, 1990); *V2* (UK Epic, 1978; Sony, 1999); *UK Batteries Included* (CBS, 1980); *Guilty* (UK Anagram, 1983); *Alaska 127* (UK Ram,) 1984); *Fifth Amendment* (UK Ram, 1985; Anagram Punk UK, 2001); *Live* (UK FM/Revolver, 1986); *Recharged* (UK FM/Revolver, 1988); *Meltdown* (UK FM/Revolver, 1988); *Disco in Moscow EP* (UK FM/Revolver, 1988); *Vicious Circle* (UK FM/Revolver, 1989); *Volume 10* (UK FM/Revolver, 1990); *The Power of Money: The Best of the Vibrators* (Continuum, 1992); *BBC Radio 1 Live in Concert* (Windsong, 1993); *Hunting for You* (Dojo, 1994); *Unpunked* (Vibes, 1996; Orchard, 1998); *We Vibrate: Best of the Vibrators* (Cleopatra, 1997); *French Lessons with Correction* (Anagram, 1997, 2003); *Rip up the City Live* (Receiver, 1999); *Best of the Vibrators* (Anagram Punk UK, 1999); *The BBC Punk Sessions* (live; Captain Oi!, 2000); *Live at the Marquee 1977* (Orchard, 2000); *Public Enemy #1* (Harry May, 1999, 2000); *Demos and Rarities* (Orchard, 2000); *Noise Boys* (Receiver, 2000); *Guilty Alaska 127* (Anagram Punk UK, 2001); *Buzzin'* (Ripe and Ready, 2001); *Punk Rock Rarities* (Captain Oi!, 2001); *Live at CBGB's (Gig) 2002* (Almafame, 2001); *Meltdown/Vicious Circle* (Anagram Punk UK, 2002); *The Independent Punk Singles* (Anagram Punk UK, 2002); *Energize* (Track, 2002); *Live at the Nashville and 100 Club* (Overground, 2003); *Live at the Cortex* (Overground, 2003); *Live: Near the Seedy Mill Golf Club* (Invisible Hands Music, 2004). **Knox:** *Plutonium Express* (UK Razor, 1983).

VICE SQUAD

British **punk** band formed in Bristol in 1978 that helped pioneer punk's second and more politicized wave in England. The band was led by lead singer Becky Bondage (Rebecca Louise Bond), and the original lineup featured Dave Bateman on guitar, Mark Hambly on bass, and Shane Baldwin on drums. The band started out of the ashes of two local bands, the Contingent and TV Brakes, and released its first album in 1980 on their own label, RiotCity. The band was extremely popular, but internal dissention tore the band apart in 1985 when Bondage left the band over an argument about the issue of animal rights. After the departure of Bondage, the other band members went on to form the band Ligotage with new singer Lia. In 1998, Bondage decided to revive the Vice Squad name for a new generation of punks and toured the punk festival circuit with a new lineup featuring Paul Rooney on guitar, Michael Gianquinto on bass, and Tone Piper on drums. The band released new material as well as various collections and live records.

Discography: *Last Rockers* EP (UK Riot City, 1980); *Resurrection* EP (UK Riot City, 1981; Rhythm Vicar, 1999); *No Cause for Concern* (UK Zonophone/EMI, 1981; with bonus tracks, Captain Oi!, 2000); *Live in Sheffield* (tape; UK Live, 1981); *Stand Strong Stand Proud* (UK Zonophone/EMI, 1982); *Stand Strong* EP (UK Riot City, 1982; Captain Oi!, 2000); *State of the Nation* EP (UK Riot City, 1982); *Shot Away* (UK Anagram, 1985; Anagram Punk UK, 2002); *Live and Loud!!* (UK Link, 1988; Cleopatra, 1995); *Lavender Hill Mob* (Combat Rock, 1995); *Get a Life* (Rhythm Vicar, 1999; High Speed Recording, 2001); *The Complete Punk Singles Collection* (Anagram [Cherry Red], 1999); *Lo-Fi Life* (Sudden Death, 2000); *The Very Best of Vice Squad* (Anagram Punk UK, 2000); *The Rarities* (Captain Oi!, 2000); *Bang to Rights* (EMI, 2001); *BBC Sessions* (live; Anagram Punk UK, 2002); *Rich and Famous* (EMI, 2004); *Riot City Years* (Phantom, 2005).

VICIOUS, SID

Sid Vicious was the bass player for the seminal English band the **Sex Pistols,** and his chaotic life and early, messy death made him a public icon and one of the faces of **punk** rock to most people outside of punk. He was a school friend of **John Lydon (Johnny Rotten),** and Simon Beverly was renamed Sid in tribute to Lydon's hamster. After the Pistols and the recording of the "My Way" single, he and girlfriend Nancy Spungen relocated to New York City, where they lived at the fabled Chelsea Hotel on 23rd Street (previously home to such lost souls as Irish writer Brendan Behan and Welsh poet Dylan Thomas and future home of **Dee Dee Ramone**). While in New York City in September 1978, Sid Vicious played a few dates at **Max's Kansas City** with a backing band featuring Steve Dior, Jerry Nolan, and Arthur Kane (from the **New York Dolls**) and Mick Jones from the **Clash,** who was in town recording the album *Give 'em Enough Rope*. The impromptu supergroup ended up playing five songs for about 20 minutes before Sid's addled state ended the gig prematurely. After the few abortive gigs, Sid decided to concentrate more on his addiction. On October 12, 1978, Sid Vicious was arrested for the stabbing death of Nancy Spungen and was arraigned in a New York City court that morning. **Malcolm McLaren** bailed Sid out a week later, but Sid attempted suicide via a methadone overdose and slashing his arms on October 22. Sid survived this attempt but was arrested in November for fighting with **Patti Smith's** brother Todd at Hurrahs disco. He was returned to Rikers Island, where he underwent forcible detox for seven weeks. After his release on bail, Sid Vicious returned to a friend's Greenwich Village apartment and overdosed on **heroin** apparently provided by his mother. Vicious lives on as a punk icon, sort of a romanticized version of the junkie as James Dean, with an image almost as iconic and visually arresting as Dean's or Marilyn Monroe's. Vicious was portrayed by actor Gary Oldman in the 1986 Alex Cox biopic *Sid and Nancy*.

VING, LEE

Lead singer of **Fear** and actor in movies and television shows through the 1980s and 1990s. Ving's most notable performance was in the movie **Clue,** in which he played the quickly murdered misogynist Mr. Body, overall not much of a stretch. Ving frequently reunited with Fear for reunion tours.

VINYL

Despite the prevalence of compact discs (and before that cassette tapes and eight-track cassettes), many punks have chosen vinyl records as a "purer" and more "authentic" way for music to be produced, and to this day there is a vibrant and diverse array of music released every year solely on vinyl records. How much longer this will last is open to debate because new formats make the storage and transmission of music much more easy and accessible. *See also* Punk and Technology.

VIOLENCE

One of the key myths (perpetuated both through sensationalistic media coverage and by certain members of the punk movement) was that punk rock shows were a hotbed of violence. Certain TV shows (such as the notorious *Quincy* episode) and movies (such as *Class of 1984* and *Return of the Living Dead*) presented punks as violent gang members ready to attack those not involved in the punk scene. Although it is certainly true that some bands had more violent followings than others and in England many shows were marred by attacks from the violent fascist goons of the **National Front** or right-wing **skinheads,** this was not true of the vast majority of punk rock shows during the 1970s or afterward. In the United States, there were also instances (as indicated in Mark Spitz and Brendan Mullen's *We Got the Neutron Bomb* and Mark Andersen and Mark Jenkins's *Dance of Days*, the books that detailed the **Los Angeles** and **Washington, D.C.,** punk scenes) in which **hardcore** led to a more violent form of dancing. This does not indicate that anything but a small minority engaged in violent actions, however, and many punks that started out participating in mindless violence changed their ways after others in the scene remarked that their behavior was counterproductive. During his days in the **Teen Idles** and up to his early days in **Minor Threat, Ian MacKaye** was known to be a notorious fighter (as indicated both in *Dance of Days* and Michael Azerad's *Our Band Could Be Your Life*) who would instigate violence at shows as a sign of machismo. By the time he was in **Fugazi,** however, MacKaye was much better known for his efforts toward peace and unity in the scene and would often stop Fugazi shows if the **pit** was getting too violent. The **New York** scene was also identified as being violent during the 1980s, especially at shows by skinhead bands or bands such as the **Cro-Mags,** where a certain level of intensity in the pit was considered to be the norm. Many punks identified themselves as **peace punks** or pacifists and refused to engage in violence, and in many cases tried to set up dialogues with the more violent elements in the local scene. Certainly, violence has occurred at many punk shows, and at many shows women and openly gay punks are made to feel unwelcome (*see* Gender and Punk), but, overall, there are instances (as detailed in numerous books on punk, such as **Get in the Van** by **Henry Rollins**) in which police attacked punk shows without provocation, leading to even more sensationalistic media accounts of punk violence. Although skinheads are often seen as the most prone to violence, many skinheads reject violence and racism. Ultimately, although violence has been a problem in the punk community, it is certainly not the only public relations problem that punk has, and much of punk's reputation may have more to with how it is presented in films and on television, where punks are as ubiquitous as thugs and gang members.

VIOLENT CHILDREN

Early **hardcore** band from the early 1980s that served as a breeding ground for future members of influential hardcore bands. John Porcell later went on to play in **Youth of Today, Shelter,** Young Republicans, Project X, and **Judge.** Ray Cappo went on to work with Porcell in many of those bands and later, along with Porcell, went on to join Krishna Consciousness and helped to bring a feeling of spirituality to hardcore punk during the late 1980s and early 1990s.
Discography: *Violent Children* EP (United Nutmeg, 1984); *Rock against Spindlers* (United Nutmeg, 1984, 1993); *S/t* (United Nutmeg, 1984); *Skate Straight* (Violent Records, 1991).

VOIDOIDS

The Voidoids were **Richard Hell's** backing band and consisted of Robert Quine and Ivan Julian on guitars and Marc Bell on drums. After the Voidoids broke up, Marc Bell joined the **Ramones** (as Marky Ramone) and toured with them for the next 16 years, with a brief hiatus for rehab. Robert Quine recorded several jazzy solo records and played as a session man for many artists, such as Mathew Sweet, before killing himself in 2004.

Discography: Richard Hell & the Voidoids: *Richard Hell* EP (Ork, 1976); *Blank Generation* (Sire, 1977; Sire/Warner Bros., 1990); *Richard Hell/Neon Boys* EP (Shake, 1980); *Destiny Street* (Red Star, 1982; UK ID, 1988; Razor & Tie, 1995); *Funhunt: Live at the CBGB's & Max's* (tape, Roir, 1990; Roir/Important, 1990, 1995).

WARZONE

New York City **hardcore** band of the 1980s and 1990s formed in 1982. Warzone went through numerous personnel changes before recording a seminal album five years later that promoted unity (at times), **straight edge** values, and tolerance for those who were not part of the immediate scene. The band featured lead singer Raybeez (Raymond James Barbieri), a New York City street punk from the Lower East Side and briefly a drummer for the early version of **Agnostic Front,** along with Todd the Kid on guitar, J-Sin on bass, and Vinny Value on drums. Warzone played a confrontational version of hardcore that simply changed from one militant stance to another when the band became straight edge in the mid-1980s. Warzone and Raybeez are best known for opposing the corporatization of hardcore music, as epitomized by the first album and defining slogan, *Don't Forget the Struggle, Don't Forget the Streets* (in which Raybeez admonished the kids to "keep the faith," despite the many temptations of corporate rock). Lead singer Raybeez died of pneumonia in 1997, ending a long and prolific career as an elder statesman of the **New York** hardcore scene. After Warzone, Todd went on to join **Murphy's Law,** Chrome Locust, and punk metal band Danzig, and Vinny later played in Grey Value. Warzone was among the most electrifying hardcore bands of the New York City scene of the 1980s and 1990s.

Discography: *Don't Forget the Struggle, Don't Forget the Streets* (Caroline, 1987; Another Planet, 1994); *Open Your Eyes* (Caroline, 1989); *Warzone* (Caroline, 1992); *Old School to the New School* (Victory, 1994); *Lower East Side* (Victory, 1996); *Sound of Revolution* (Victory, 1996); *Fight for Justice* (Victory, 1997); *Victory Years* (Victory, 1998).

WASHINGTON, D.C.

The Washington, D.C., scene of the late 1970s to the mid- to late 1990s stands as one of the most fertile and diverse scenes in the history of **punk** rock. Numerous bands, such as **Minor Threat, Bad Brains,** Urban Verbs, **SOA, Teen Idles, Fugazi, Bikini Kill,** Black Market Baby, and Rites of Spring, came from or were closely associated with the Washington, D.C., scene, and **Dischord Records,** one of the key independent labels in punk history, was founded and still operates just across the river from Washington, D.C. The original Washington, D.C., scene from the late 1970s was full of experimental art bands such as the Slinkees, Urban Verbs (featuring Roddy Frantz, the brother of drummer Chris Franz from the **Talking Heads**), White Boy (which featured father James Kowalski, who later went to jail on charges of child abuse, and his son Glenn), and early hardcore heroes Black Market Baby. Even though Washington, D.C.'s, main club, the 9:30 Club, initially refused to let most punk and hardcore bands play there, a thriving scene started to develop in the early 1980s, informally known as harDCore (after the district's initials), when **Ian MacKaye** began playing in a band called the Slinkees, which eventually evolved into the Teen Idles featuring MacKaye on bass, Jeff Nelson on drums, Geordie Grindel on guitar, and Nathan Strejcek on vocals. The Teen Idles inspired many on the scene by playing as many shows as possible and touring as far as **Los Angeles**, accompanied by faithful roadie Henry Garfield, who was inspired by the band and changed his name to **Henry Rollins** and started SOA (State of Alert). Rollins and MacKaye, who basically started the Washington, D.C., hardcore movement, also brought more violence to the scene, picking fights and even exporting their violence to **New York** shows. The Teen Idles did not last long, breaking up in 1981 after releasing the *Minor Disturbance* EP. Nelson, MacKaye, and Strejcek financed and released the EP via their new record label, Dischord Records, which Nelson and MacKaye built over the next two decades into one of the key independent labels in U.S. punk history. After the demise of the Teen Idles, numerous bands formed, such as SOA, **Government Issue** (featuring John Stabb), Youth Brigade (not to be confused with the Youth Brigade from California), and the band that defined Washington, D.C., hardcore, Minor Threat, which became an almost instant sensation and soon became local favorites. Minor Threat had been influenced by Bad Brains, which divided its time between Washington, D.C., and New York, and between the two bands they almost single-handedly defined U.S. hardcore. MacKaye and Minor Threat were also responsible through their songs "Straight Edge" and "Out of Step with the World" for the **straight edge** movement, in which participants foreswore drinking, drugs, and overindulgence, leading to a movement that continues today. After touring relentlessly and becoming one of the key hardcore bands in the United States, Minor Threat disbanded in 1983. Other Washington, D.C., bands included Faith (Alec MacKaye's, Ian's brother's, band); Iron Cross, a quasi-Nazi band led by skinhead Sab Prausnitz; and the extremely popular Scream, featuring Pete Stahl on vocals, Franz Stahl on guitar, Skeeter Thomson (one of the few black members of the hardcore scene) on bass, and Kent Stax on drums, who was later replaced by Dave Grohl, later of **Nirvana** and the Foo Fighters. Other key bands included metal-tinged bands such as Void and the Obsessed, which featured vocalist Scott "Wino" Weinrich, who later sang in St. Vitus and played on Probot, Dave Grohl's metal side project from the Foo Fighters. Go-go music was also a huge part of the Washington, D.C., scene, and numerous punk bands played with local go-go bands such as Chuck Brown and the Soul Searchers and Trouble Funk, which played extended live jams. Outside of music, one of the key things that marked the Washington, D.C., scene was it intense politicization during the mid-1980s. Led by members of Dischord bands and local activist group **Positive Force,** many in the scene decided to engage in a form of social protest, culminating in the famous **Revolution Summer** of 1985, during which numerous punks protested against apartheid and the **Ronald Reagan** administration's policies. New bands in the **emo** style grew up around the newly politicized scene such as Rites of Spring, **Beefeater,** and **Dag Nasty.** As Dischord became more prominent, other more emotionally intense and less hardcore band such as Shudder to Think, **Jawbox,** and **Nation of Ulysses** became mainstays of the Washington, D.C., scene, as did a transplanted Bikini Kill, which moved to Washington, D.C., because of the relative openness of the scene.

WASTED YOUTH

Early **hardcore** band that eventually went metal and inspired the members of Guns N' Roses. The band featured Danny Spira on vocals, Chet Lehrer on guitar, Jeff Long on bass, Allen Stiritz on drums, and Danny Kushner on guitar, who later went on to play in Velvet Revolver with Slash and Duff from Guns N' Roses.

Discography: *Reagan's In* (Sanoblast, 1981; Restless, 1990, 1993); *Black Daze* (Medusa, 1988; Restless, 1993); *Get out of My Yard* (Medusa, 1990).

WATT, MIKE

Key figure in the U.S. **punk** scene as the bassist in the **Minutemen** and Firehose, solo artist, and proponent of touring econo style. (Touring econo style is the punk concept of booking your own tours and playing as many shows as possible while driving cross-country in a van, crashing at the local **squats** or on the floors of accommodating fans, and living essentially hand to mouth in order to play as many shows as possible.) Watt also released several solo records and had a minor radio hit with the Eddie Vedder song "Against the 1970s" on the *Ball-Hog or Tugboat?* record. Watt played bass on a tour of the reconstituted **Iggy and the Stooges,** backing up **Iggy Pop** onstage. Overall, Mike Watt was among the most beloved and respected figures in U.S. punk rock.

Discography: *Ball-Hog or Tugboat?* (Columbia, 1994); *Contemplating the Engine Room* (Columbia, 1997).

WE GOT THE NEUTRON BOMB

This book (full title, *We Got the Neutron Bomb: The Untold Story of L.A. Punk*) contains an oral history of the early **Los Angeles punk** scene by writers Brendan Mullen and Marc Spitz and details the development of the early scene mostly before **hardcore** punk became predominant. The book features interviews with most of the surviving key players and assorted hangers-on. The book is a rich oral history that details how the Los Angeles punk scene started as an artistic movement fueled by revolutionaries and those dissatisfied with the vagaries of life and that included bands as diverse as the **Weirdos,** the **Screamers, X,** the **Dils,** and the **Bags.** The book details the rise and spectacular fall of the legendary **Germs** and the charismatic and twisted **Darby Crash** and also notes that as the scene developed and the music gradually evolved into hardcore punk, the early adherents began to feel marginalized by the violence and machismo that gradually began to permeate the Los Angeles scene as the 1980s began. The book features a wide variety of interviews with most of the original members of the Los Angeles punk scene, both living and dead. Cowriter Brendan Mullen ran the legendary club the **Masque** and also wrote the books *Lexicon Devil: The Fast Times and Short Life of Darby Crash and the Germs* and *Whores: An Oral Biography of Perry Farrell and Jane's Addiction.*

WEIRDOS

Key early **Los Angeles** band and Dadaist performance artists from the 1970s that wrote the classic Los Angeles anthem "We Got the Neutron Bomb" and helped pioneer the ripped clothing and outrageous look that dominated early **punk fashion.** The band broke up in the early 1980s but reformed for the *Condor* album in 1990. After that, the band went on a lengthy hiatus but continued to re-form sporadically for tours. The original lineup formed in 1976 and featured brothers John and Dix Denny on vocals and guitar, respectively, Dave Trout on guitar, and bassist Cliff Roman. The Weirdos were drummerless for their first gigs, until they located Nicky Beat (replaced briefly by Danny Benair, later of the paisley pop band the Three O'Clock, although Beat returned for the *Condor* album in 1990). One of the things that marked the Weirdos as outside the local scene was that they designed and created their own clothing, **flyers,** merchandise, and T-shirts in the pursuit of their philosophy of "weirdoism." Although initially reluctant to take on the label of *punk rock,* the Weirdos eventually became accustomed to the label when they were shown with various other punk bands in a *Time* magazine story on punk rock and were particularly inspired by the first **Ramones** record, which affirmed to them that they were working in the right direction. The band was also far more intelligent than the average punk band of the time and was known for its intentional Dadaist tendencies and love of Marcel Duchamp and the music of Stockhausen, **Captain Beefheart,** and Miles Davis. For their timeliness and fashion sense, the Weirdos epitomized the artistic ideal of the early Los Angeles punk scene and remained one of the pivotal bands from that period, demonstrating that punk could be both adventurous and extremely intelligent.

Discography: *Who? What? When? Where? Why?* EP (Bomp!, 1979); *Action Design* EP (Rhino, 1980); *Condor* (Frontier, 1990); *Weird World 1977–1981 Time Capsule Volume One* (Frontier, 1991).

WESTWOOD, VIVIENNE

Vivienne Westwood is a prolific fashion designer and former partner and wife of **Malcolm McLaren.** She invented, adopted, or created many of the key punk clothing forms during the mid-1970s and sold them at Let It Rock, Too Fast to Live, and **Sex,** the stores she ran with partner and ex-husband Malcolm McLaren at 430 Kings Road in London. Westwood started out designing Teddy-boy outfits (essentially British 1950s revivalists) but soon moved on to zoot suits, revival clothes, and situationist-slogan inspired clothing. After she and McLaren exhibited in **New York** in 1973, they met the **New York Dolls** (who McLaren went on to manage) and were inspired by the U.S. glitter and glam scenes and the clothing worn by **Richard Hell.** When they returned to London, Westwood started designing clothing based on the torn outfits and bondage gear that had inspired her and McLaren. The two broke up acrimoniously in 1983, and she continued to work as a designer. Westwood had a son with McLaren in 1967 and is best remembered for her partnership with him and the groundbreaking work they did in punk fashion.

WHISKEY a-GO-GO

Los Angeles club located in West Hollywood on Sunset Strip where numerous 1960s and 1970s punk bands played. The Whiskey opened in 1963 and was billed as a discotheque, and from its opening it had bands and women dancing in cages; this was allegedly the birthplace of go-go dancers. The club was a center for the Sunset Strip riots of the 1960s, and important national acts played there in the 1960s, including Jimi Hendrix, Otis Redding, the Who, Led Zeppelin, Roxy Music, and the Kinks. The Doors performed as the house band for a time. After initial resistance to the local **punk** scene, the Whiskey eventually relented and allowed bands such as the **Germs** and X to play and hosted touring punk bands such as the **Ramones,** Elvis Costello, XTC, and **the Jam.** The club closed in 1982 but reopened in 1986 as one of the centers of the mid-1980s metal explosion. It continued to be an epicenter of the Los Angeles metal scene.

WHITE FLAG

U.S. punk band from Sunnymead, California, known for its quirky sense of humor and melodic **pop punk.** The band started in 1982 with original members Al Bum on vocals (who left the band after the live *Feeding Frenzy* record), Jello B. Afro on bass, and Pick Stix on drums. Later members (the family tree is confusing as the band constantly revolved and members occasionally changed names) included Pat Fear (Bill Bartell), Trace Element, Doug Graves, and El Fee. White Flag went through numerous lineup changes and had a plethora of guest musicians who played in the band at one point or another, including the MacDonald brothers from **Red Kross (Red Cross),** Dale Crover from **the Melvins,** Greg Hetson from **Bad Religion** and the **Circle Jerks,** and Ken Stringfellow and Jon Auer of the Posies. The band is equally famous for the "Police Story" T-shirts that parodied the **Raymond Pettibon** design of **Black Flag's** "Police Story" logo, which for White Flag featured a friendly cop who had just helped a young child rescue a kitten from a tree. White Flag were one the premier satirists of the early **hardcore** scene.

Discography: *S Is for Space* (Gastanka, 1982); *Third Strike* (Gastanka, 1984); *Desperate Teenage Lovedolls* (Gastanka, 1984; SST, 1984s); *(WFO)* (Starving Missile, 1985); *Peace* (split LP with "F"; Gastanka, 1985); *Feeding Frenzy: Live in the City of Gold* (Bootleg Records, 1986); *Lead* (Bootleg Records, 1986); *Zero Hour* (Starving Missile, 1986); *Please Stand By* EP (Baratos Afins, 1986); *Wild Kingdom* (Positive Force, 1986); *Sgt. Pepper* (Wet Spots, 1987); *Jail Jello* (split 12" with the Necros; Gastanka, 1987); *Thru the Trash, Darkly (Best of Compilation)* (Munster Records, 1992); *Step Back 10* (Just 4 Fun, 1994); *Sator vs. White Flag* (split CD; Warner Bros., 1994); *Skate across America* (Mystic, 1995); *Empty Heaven* (Houston Party, 1999); *Eternally Undone* (Houston Party, 2002); *History Is Fiction* (Tuti, 2002; Phantom, 2003).

WIPERS

Portland, Oregon, band led by the enigmatic Greg Sage that paved the way for the grunge movement of the Pacific Northwest. The Wipers helped keep the flame alive for U.S. independent and **punk** music during the dark days of the late 1980s and put out challenging music since their first single in 1978. In addition to Sage, members included Dave Koupal on bass (who left in 1981 and was replaced by Brad Davidson and later joined the Jesus and Mary Chain) and Sam Henry on drums (who left in 1981 to join Napalm Beach and was replaced by Brad Nasih and later Steve Plouf). The Wipers played with some of Portland's other punk bands but did not really fit in as part of a scene, largely due to Sage's creativity and stylistic refusal to fit into any one formula. After numerous personnel changes, the Wipers continued to release music sporadically. Sage released two solo records before re-forming the Wipers as a duo with drummer Steve Plouf. He recorded new material before deciding to retire the Wipers name in 1996 and simply record under his own name. The Wipers were also a favorite of Kurt Cobain of **Nirvana,** and he championed them in numerous interviews, leading to a smattering of commercial success for the band in the mid-1990s. A tribute record of major bands such as Nirvana, Hole, and **Sonic Youth** was released in 1993. The Wipers, mostly thanks to Sage's reluctance to publicize the band and refusal to be involved in the machinery of stardom, despite his growing influence, remained one of the key bands in U.S. independent music.

Discography: *Is This Real?* (Park Ave., 1980; Sub Pop, 1993); *Alien Boy* EP7 (Park Ave., 1980); *Youth of America* EP (Park Avenue, 1981; Restless, 1990); *Over the Edge* (Brain Eater, 1983; Restless, 1987); *Wipers* (Enigma, 1985); *Land of the Lost* (Restless, 1986); *Follow Blind* (Restless, 1987; Dead Line, 1992; Gift of Life, 1995); *The Circle* (Restless, 1988); *The Best of Wipers and Greg Sage* (Restless, 1990); *Silver Sail* (Tim/Kerr, 1993); *The Herd* (Tim/Kerr, 1996); *Power in One* (Zeno, 1999); *3 CD Box Set: Is This Real?—Youth of America—Over the Edge* (Zeno, 2001). **Greg Sage:** *Straight Ahead* (Enigma, 1985); *Sacrifice (For Love)* (Restless, 1991). **Various Artists:** *Eight Songs for Greg Sage and the Wipers* EP7 (Tim/Kerr, 1992); *Fourteen Songs for Greg Sage and the Wipers* (Tim/Kerr, 1993).

WIRE

Wire is one of the most interesting bands of the **punk** movement and one of the few original British punk bands to stretch the parameters of punk in unexpected directions, paving the way for the infusion of synthesizers and dance rhythms into **postpunk** and **New Wave.** The band consisted of Robert Gotobed (Robert Gray) on drums (except for the bands' recordings as WIR, when it used a drum machine), Colin Newman on guitar and vocals, Bruce Gilbert on guitar, and Graham Lewis on bass. The band formed in late 1976 and released its seminal first album, *Pink Flag,* in late 1977. That album featured 21 songs that basically deconstructed punk rock much in the way groups like Can and Brian Eno had deconstructed rock and roll years earlier. Although *Pink Flag* did have "traditional" punk moments, such as the protohardcore song "12XU," later covered by **Minor Threat** (REM also covered the song "Strange" from **Pink Flag**), most Wire songs were haiku-like bursts of mysterious lyrics surrounded by buzzing guitars and the cryptic sound design of producer Mike Thorne (who also worked on Wire's other two albums, *Chairs Missing* and *154,* before the band's hiatus in the mid-1980s). If *Pink Flag* was a revelation, it is interesting to think of how far stylistically Wire advanced by their next album, *Chairs Missing,* which took the experiments of *Pink Flag* and further stripped down the songs to their skeletal structures before rebuilding them from a map known only to the members of Wire. Their third album, *154,* was a further step in a direction that was years ahead of its time. Seemingly conflicted about where to go next after they had left both punk and traditional rock and roll templates far behind, Wire took a six-year hiatus during which the various members of the band busied themselves with solo projects. (An entire book could be written about the various permutations under which members of Wire performed and recorded since the 1980s. Luckily, this is not that book.) In 1987, the band resumed, but instead of the old experimentation, Wire moved in a dance rhythm direction, reminiscent of many of the British New Wave bands of the 1980s, although they also continued their experiments in drones and bizarre soundscapes. Wire continued to record and tour, although, having been slightly older than most punks even during the 1970s, the band concentrated on short sets in which old favorites (such as "I Am the Fly") are reworked wildly. Part of Wire's rich legacy was that it was a key influence on bands as diverse as REM and most of the New Wave movement as well as Elastica, which had to pay Wire royalties for "borrowing" certain musical ideas.

Select Discography: *Pink Flag* (Harvest, 1977); *Chairs Missing* (UK Harvest, 1978); *154* (Automatic/Warner Bros., 1979).

X

The foremost and certainly the most popular band from the Los Angeles scene, X was known for blending roots rock, **rockabilly,** blues, and gospel in their potent and poetic punk songs. Led by charismatic poet Exene Cervenka and her ex-husband **John Doe** (along with guitarist Billy Zoom and drummer D.J. Bonebrake), X set the standard in combining roots rock and punk that would be followed by numerous other bands in the 1980s and 1990s. Formed during the early **Los Angeles** punk scene, X was one of the first bands to put out a major record in 1980 with *Los Angeles*, which was produced by Ray Manzarek of the Doors. He saw in X some of the poetic resonance he had previously seen in Jim Morrison. The first record is a brilliant summary of the dangers and joys of living in Los Angeles during the early punk scene and highlights the harmony vocals of Cervenka and Doe and Zoom's rockabilly mastery. (Zoom was a decade older than the rest of the band and had played in various rockabilly combos.) The first three records, produced by Manzarek, are priceless tales of love, loss, and debauchery and established X as one of the premier U.S. punk bands. By the fourth album, *Ain't Love Grand*, the production values had grown slicker, Cervenka and Doe's relationship had become unworkable, and Zoom was clearly growing tired of the increasingly less rocking material and left after the record. The rest of the band reunited with guitarist David Alvin from the Blasters (later replaced by Tony Gilkyson), with whom they had worked on the Knitters side project. After an uninspired live album with Gilkyson, the band went on hiatus for several years, with Doe acting and working on roots music and Cervenka working on her poetry and writing. The band (with Gilkyson) resumed in 1993 with *Hey Zeus!*, a slower, more thoughtful set that found the band aging with grace, as seen on the acoustic, unclogged record. The various members of X continued in various side projects, and X periodically continues to re-form and tour, sometimes with Zoom.

Discography: *Los Angeles* (Slash, 1980; Slash/Rhino, 2001); *Wild Gift* (Slash, 1981; Slash/Rhino, 2001); *Under the Big Black Sun* (Elektra, 1982; Elektra/Rhino, 2001); *More Fun in the New World* (Elektra, 1983; Elektra/Rhino, 2002); *Ain't Love Grand* (Elektra, 1985; Elektra/Rhino; 2002); *See How We Are* (Elektra, 1987; Elektra/Rhino, 2002); *Live at the Whisky A Go-Go on the Fabulous Sunset Strip* (Elektra, 1988); *Los Angeles/Wild Gift* (Slash, 1988); *Hey Zeus!* (Big Life/Mercury, 1993); *Unclogged* (Infidelity/Sunset

X's Exene Cervenka and John Doe not only led the roots rock and punk music era but also starred in movies, such as the 1981 film *The Decline of Western Civilization*. Photofest.

Blvd., 1995); *Beyond & Back: The X Anthology* (Elektra, 1997). **Exene Cervenka and Wanda Coleman:** *Twin Sisters* (Freeway, 1985). **Exene Cervenka:** *Old Wives' Tales* (Rhino, 1989); *Running Scared* (RNA, 1990); *Rage* EP7 (Kill Rock Stars, 1994); *Surface to Air Serpents* (213CD, 1996). **Exene Cervenkova:** *Excerpts from the Unabomber Manifesto* (Year One, 1995). **Lydia Lunch/Exene Cervenka:** *Rude Hieroglyphics* (Rykodisc, 1995). **Auntie Christ:** *Life Could Be a Dream* (Lookout!, 1997). **Original Sinners:** *Original Sinners* (Nitro, 2002). **John Doe:** *Meet John Doe* (DGC, 1990); *Dim Stars, Bright Sky* (Imusic, 2002). **John Doe Thing:** *Kissingsohard* (Forward, 1995); *For the Rest of Us* EP (Kill Rock Stars, 1998); *Freedom Is . . .* (spinART, 2000). **Knitters:** *Poor Little Critter on the Road* (Slash, 1985).

X-RAY SPEX

Although they were best known for their classic punk song "Oh Bondage, up Yours!," which was released in October 1977, X-Ray Spex were a short-lived but very influential punk band led by the dynamic Poly Styrene (Marion Elliot) on lead vocals (who allegedly was the one person **Johnny Rotten** was scared of) and originally contained famed punk saxophone player Laura Logic. The rest of the lineup consisted of Jak Airport on guitar, Paul Dean on bass, B. P. Hurding on drums, and Logic on sax. Logic left the band early (or was fired, depending upon which version of the story one believes) and went on to form her own group, Essential Logic, and was replaced by Rudi Thompson. In October 1978, the band released its debut album *Germfree Adolescents*, which featured the classic singles "The World Turned Day-Glo" and "Oh Bondage, up Yours!" Much of the album was a concentrated attack on consumer culture (as epitomized on songs such as "Art-I-Ficial" and "Warrior in Woolworth"), although Styrene later distanced herself from that narrow a perspective of the band's ideology. Due to mounting pressures and what some saw as Styrene's instability (she told an interviewer that she had been warned by a pink flying saucer to spread warnings about the "synthetic life"), the band disbanded around 1980, and Styrene released subsequent sporadic solo work. A reunion album, *Conscious Consumer*, with Logic and Dean continued the critique in 1995 and also highlighted Styrene's devotion to the **Hare Krishna** faith. In 2005, Styrene released an album called *Flower Aeroplane*, a collection of tracks she had recorded over the previous three decades, and started an organization called Fair Music to provide support for the various musicians who had played with her over time.

Discography: *Germfree Adolescents* (UK EMI Int'l, 1978; Caroline Blue Plate, 1991). **Poly Styrene:** *God's & Goddesses* EP (UK Awesome, 1986); *Translucence* (UK UA, 1980; UK Receiver, 1990).

YOHANON, TIM

One of the most influential Americans involved in the **DIY** movement of the 1970s and 1980s, Tim Yohanon was an ex-hippie and longtime publisher of the influential zine *Maximum Rock 'n' Roll,* which he organized in 1982 and kept going for more than 20 years, as well as the original radio show *Maximum Rock 'n' Roll,* which started in 1977, based on the Who's original idea of doing maximum rock and roll. Yohanon was also instrumental in the founding of the **Gilman Street** collective and the Epicenter Record Collective. Yohanon was known for his uncompromising ideological stance on what his magazine considered punk and what it did not, and this caused enormous controversy in the punk communities of the United States. Yohanon was instrumental though *MRR* in creating and maintaining a punk scene without the use of mainstream media and corporate consumer culture. Although his detractors thought him too ideologically uncompromising, he nonetheless is one of the people largely responsible for punk's continuing underground success during the 1980s and 1990s. Yohanon, who had a day job for many years in shipping and receiving at the University of California at Berkeley while running the magazine simultaneously, died of lymphoma in 1998, and Jen Angel of *Fucktooth* took over *MRR* for a year before leaving to found *Clamor* magazine. *See also* DIY; *Maximum Rock 'n' Roll*; Zines.

YOUNG AND THE USELESS

New York City **hardcore** band from the early 1980s that featured future Beastie Boy Adam Horovitz, who apparently did hardcore versions of AOR songs (e.g., songs by Journey, Boston, the Eagles, etc.) and even the soundtrack of *Grease*. The band originally featured Adam Horovitz, Adam Trese, Arthur Africano, and David Scilken. The band, which was largely an artistic parody on contemporary hardcore, was roughly active from 1982 to 1984, before Horovitz went on to superstardom with the Beastie Boys in the later 1980s and the 1990s. **Discography:** *Real Men Don't Floss* (Ratcage Records, 1982).

Youth Brigade proved that skins can be a positive force for change. © *Robert Barry Francos.*

YOUTH BRIGADE

Hardcore band from **Los Angeles** featuring the Stern brothers, Adam, Shawn, and Mark, who founded the **Better Youth Organization** in late 1979. The band was formed by Mark and Shawn in the infamous Skinhead Manor (which was a squat, flophouse, and rehearsal space used by bands such as Black Flag and the **Circle Jerks**), where Mark and Shawn decided to start a punk collective called the Better Youth Organization (BYO). Originally a six-piece **ska** band, Youth Brigade settled on a coherent lineup when younger brother Adam joined the band on drums and helped with running BYO. After Skinhead Manor was closed, the band briefly ran shows at the Godzilla club, before it, too, was closed. After a short time, BYO decided to release records, and in 1982 the Stern brothers released the *Some Got Their Head Kicked In* compilation (the title was taken from an incident at a show in which a skinhead attack left a fan in a coma), which featured **Bad Religion, Adolescents, Social Distortion,** and Youth Brigade. After the success of that release, Youth Brigade went on the BYO tour with Social Distortion, which was hilariously documented in the movie *Another State of Mind.* In 1985, the original group disbanded for the first time with Adam Stern's departure for school, but the other two brothers kept the band going as the much more commercial sounding Brigade for a few years. BYO continued, and Youth Brigade continue to re-form for tours and recording.

Discography: *Someone Got Their Head Kicked In* (BYO, 1982); *Sound and Fury* (BYO, 1982); *What Price?* EP (BYO, 1984); *Sink with Kalifornija* (BYO, 1985, 1994); *Happy Hour* (BYO, 1994); *Come Again* (BYO, 1995); *To Sell the Truth* (BYO, 1996); *Out of Print* (BYO, 1998); *BYO Split Series, Vol. 2* (Split with Swingin' Utters; BYO, 1999).

YOUTH BRIGADE

Washington, D.C., hardcore band featuring Nathan Strejeck, the former lead singer of the **Teen Idles** and a partner in early **Dischord,** along with guitarist Tom Clinton, Danny Ingram on drums, and Bert Querioz on bass. (The band is not to be confused with the similarly named and long-lasting Los Angeles band **Youth Brigade.**) The band was featured on the early Dischord single "Possible" in 1981 and was featured on the *Flex Your Head* compilation as well.

Discography: *Possible e.p.* (Dischord, 1981).

YOUTH OF TODAY

Seminal **New York straight edge** band most responsible for the rise of straight edge hardcore in New York City in the mid-1980s and that later espoused Krishna Consciousness and mutated into the Krishna core band **Shelter.** The original band went though many personnel changes but featured Craig on bass, Richie on second guitar, and Drew Thomas on drums (Thomas later went on to play drums with **Bold** and Into Another). The band was originally formed in 1985 by singer Ray Cappo and guitarist John Porcell, who had previously played together in the band **Violent Children** and were dedicated to the original hardcore scene as epitomized by such bands as **Seven Seconds** and **Negative Approach** and were ardent followers of the straight edge movement. The band was one of the earliest New York City hardcore bands to tour cross-country and overseas and was a major force in spreading the straight edge, and later the Krishna message to a new audience. Ray Cappo, the lead singer, broke up Youth of Today several times due to his inherent conflict over how to lead a spiritual life and still play to the adulation of the audience. He now lives a life of spiritual devotion in the Krishna Consciousness movement. *See also* Hardcore; Krishna, Hare; New York; Shelter; Straight Edge.

Discography: *Can't Close my Eyes* (Caroline, 1985); *Break down the Walls* (Revelation, 1986); *We're Not in This Alone* (Caroline, 1988); *Take a Stand Live* (Lost and Found, 1995).

ZAPPA, FRANK

Musically adventurous and bizarre musician who, along with **Captain Beefheart,** is seen aesthetically as predicting the origins of punk rock and especially **postpunk.** Zappa's experiments with rhythm and sound demonstrated that musicians did not have to stick with the template provided by the **Sex Pistols** but could radically experiment, which is the reason why many punk bands broke up or changed their sounds, feeling trapped by the limitations of the genre and questioning why a movement that espoused the experimental had become formulaic. Zappa's influence is not especially overt, but echoes of his work can be found in many of the British postpunk bands of the late 1970s and early 1980s and the U.S. indie rock scene of the 1980s and 1990s.

ZEDD, NICK

Although it may be somewhat difficult to define exactly what punk film is, Nick Zedd has been long regarded as one of the key innovators in that genre. Zedd started out emulating schlock filmmakers such as Hershell Gordon Lewis in films such as *Geek Maggot Bingo* with New York locals. Starting in 1985, Zedd pioneered what he called the "cinema of transgression" and created stark and violent films with Cassandra Stark, Richard Kern, and others. Zedd is also the author of two autobiographical books, *Bleed* (Hanuman Books, 1992) and *Totem of the Depraved* (2.13.61 Publications, 1997), as well as independent manifestos such as "Cinema of Transgression Manifesto" and the "Theory of Xenomorphisis" (relating to achieving transcendence through cognitive dissonance), published in the *Underground Film Bulletin*.
Filmography: *They Eat Scum* (1979) [Zedd says he invented death rock with this film]; *The Bogus Man* (1980); *The Wild World of Lydia Lunch* (1983); *Totem of the Depraved* (1983); *Geek Maggot Bingo* (1983); *School of Shame* (1984); *Thrust in Me* (1985); Kiss Me Goodbye (1986); *Go to Hell* (1986); *Police State* (1987); *Whoregasm* (1988); *War Is Menstrual Envy* (1992); *Smiling Faces Tell Lies* (1995); *Screen Test 98* (1998); *Ecstasy in Entropy* (1998); *Tom Thumb in the Land of the Giants* (1999); Elf Panties: The Movie (2001); *Thus Spake Zarathustra* (2001); *Lord of the Cockrings* (2002); *I Was a Quality of Life Violation* (2002); *Electra Elf* (2004).

ZERO BOYS

Indianapolis punk band formed in 1979 and led by Paul Mahern on guitar and vocals along with Terry Hollywood on guitar, Mark Cutsinger on drums, and John Mitchell on bass (Mitchell was replaced by David "Tufty" Clough in 1980). The Zero Boys played melodic **Ramones**-influenced pop punk before speeding up slightly into a poppy hardcore band. Mahern also ran the local indie label Affirmation Records. The band broke up several times, and Mahern formed the band Datura Seeds. He reformed the Zero Boys with Vess Ruthenberg, replacing Hollywood on guitar, but this lineup broke up in 1993. The band reunited for several shows, including benefit shows to save **CBGB's** in 2005.

Discography: *Livin' in the 80s* (Z-Disc, 1980; Lookout, 2000); *Vicious Circle* (Nimrod, 1982; Toxic Shock, 1988; Lookout/Panic Button, 2000); *History Of* (Affirmation, 1984); *Split 7"* (with Toxic Reasons; Self-less, 1991); *Make It Stop* (Bitzcore, 1992); *The Heimlich Maneuver* (Skyclad, 1993). **Datura Seeds**: *Who Do You Want It to Be?* (Toxic Shock, 1990).

ZERO CLUB

Los Angeles after-hours performance space and bar, partially financed by David Lee Roth of Van Halen. Many in the **Los Angeles** scene were attendees at after-hours parties at the Zero Club.

ZEROES

Los Angles punk band of the 1970s. The band was formed in 1976 by high school students Javier Escovedo on vocals and guitar (his brother Alejandro played with the **Nuns** and later played with the Kinman brothers from the **Dils** in the band Rank and File and went on to a prolific solo career) along with Robert Lopez on guitar and vocals (who quit the band in 1978), Hector Peñalosa on bass (later briefly replaced by Guy Lopez), and Baba Chenelle on drums. The Zeros were called the "Mexican **Ramones,**" although it is unclear if this was always a compliment. The band played extensively in the early Los Angeles punk scene alongside band such as **X, the Germs,** Dils, and the **Weirdos,** and compatriots the Plugz. Lopez later went on to become El Vez, the Latino homage/parody of Elvis Presley for a successful career in the eighties and nineties.

Discography: *Knockin' Me Dead* (Rockville, 1994); *Don't Push Me Around* (Bomp!, 1995); *Right Now!* (Bomp!, 1999).

ZINES

Although zines predate the punk movement and have been around in some form or another for at least 50 years, they became extremely popular during the early punk movement as a noncorporatized way for punks to communicate with one another and the outside community. Early British and European punk zines included Mark Perry's *Sniffin' Glue* and Shane MacGowan's (of the **Pogues**) *Bondage*. Other key zines of the early punk movement were *Ripped and Torn* from Glasgow and *I Wanna Be Your Dog* from Paris. Key U.S. zines from the early days of punk include the seminal zine *Punk,* founded by John Holmstrom and Legs McNeil (which coined the term *punk* from New York), as well as Greg Shaw's *Who Put the Bomp*. Later influential zines from the midperiod include the seminal **Maximum Rock 'n' Roll, Flipside, Punk Planet, Profane Existence,** and thousands or others, many of which have never been collected or cataloged. (Because of this, and despite the best efforts of *Factsheet 5* and others that try to cover the zine world, there has never been an adequate catalog of even North American zines, and the numbers of individual zines is almost impossible to catalog, although it is certainly in the tens of thousands, if not more.) There is a major collection of zines kept at the State University of New York at Albany as well as another collection kept at the collective **ABC No Rio** in New York City. Zines are essentially one of the clearest manifestations and continuing examples of the **DIY** (Do It Yourself) movement in action. Zines (except in some cases in which zines are bought out or fake zines are manufactured by record labels as promotional tools) usually have no financial backing and are produced by small groups of individuals (or sometimes one individual) based on a criteria not determined by sales but instead on a criteria determined on what the editor or editors of the specific zines think important. Although many zines are specifically related to music, and there have been numerous zines over the last 30 years dedicated to punk rock, not all zines are specifically about music. Many zines are about local movements or scenes and chronicle the artistic endeavors of a local community. Many zines are political in that they espouse a particular set of political beliefs or an agenda, such as **Queercore** zines, such as *Slander,* which offers a queer Asian American perspective on punk, and zines devoted to **vegans,** radical politics, or anticorporate behavior. Some zines such as *Chin Music* and *Zisk* are devoted to sports, albeit with a punk rock sensibility, and some such as *Go Metric,* *Chunklet,* and *Law of Inertia* deal with music in the larger context of popular culture. There are also distinctions within zines themselves, with some zines supported by advertising and others supported by sales, but most zines, even the ones with copious advertising, rarely make any kind of a profit and often simply are supported by the wallet of the zine editor or sometimes by the resale of review CDs sent by record companies.

ZOLAR X

A prepunk **Los Angeles** band whose members dressed in elaborate and bizarre space alien costumes and played the Sunset Strip clubs during the early 1970s. Their use of props, space images, and elaborate costumes and their habit of staying in character as aliens on- and off-stage made them stand out from the early Los Angeles scene. Although they dissolved by the late 1970s, they were an influence on the art punk scene that started in Los Angeles in the 1970s and epitomized how the U.S. scene was largely an artistic movement as opposed to

Punk fans communicated to each other through zines, especially during the early years of the punk movement. Here are two covers of *Go Metric,* a popular zine. *Collection of the author.*

the working-class-based movement in the United Kingdom. An album of their material was released by **Alternative Tentacles** records in 2005.

ZOOM, BILLY

Rockabilly guitarist, best known for his work with the band **X** from **Los Angeles.** Zoom had been a guitarist for a considerable length of time before he joined X and had previously played with other rockabilly bands. He is well known for his distinctive haircut.

ZOUNDS

British anarchist band form the early 1980s that recorded on the **Crass Records** label. They are considered by many fans to be one of the best of the **crust punk,** or street punk, bands, which were devoted to anarchism and smashing what was considered an unjust system in England at the time.

Discography: *The Curse of Zounds* (UK Rough Trade, 1982).

SELECTED BIBLIOGRAPHY

It should be noted that this is not an exhaustive listing of books and articles on punk rock; it is simply a listing of those that are most reader friendly to the general public, or at least the ones most easily accessible to a popular audience. This does not list every book on the subject and many more Web sites and zines contain valuable information about punk rock and the subjects discussed in this volume.

Alexander, Allison, and Cheryl Harris, eds. *Theorizing Fandom: Fans, Subculture and Identity*. Cresskill, NJ: Hampton Press, 1998.

Alleyne, Mike. "White Reggae: Cultural Dilution in the Record Industry." *Popular Music and Society* 24, no. 1 (spring 2000): 15–31.

Andersen, Mark. *All the Power: Revolution without Illusion*. New York: Akashic Books, 2004.

Andersen, Mark, and Mark Jenkins. *Dance of Days: Two Decades of Punk in the Nation's Capital*. New York: Soft Skull Press, 2001.

Antonio, Nina. "Johnny Thunders: A Reason to Believe." *Mojo Special Edition: Punk: The Whole Truth*, April 2005, 14–20.

Arnold, Gina. *Kiss the Girls: Punk in the Present Tense*. New York: St. Martin's Press, 1997.

Auslander, Philip. "Seeing Is Believing: Live Performance and the Discourse of Authenticity in Rock Culture." *Literature and Psychology* 44, no. 4 (1998): 1–26.

Azerad, Michael. *Our Band Could Be Your Life: Scenes from the American Indie Underground*. Boston: Back Bay Books, 2002.

Bacelin, Jason. "Hard Day's Fight: Rancid Overcomes Death, Divorce and a Sore Back to Deliver Its Most Personal Album." *Scene Entertainment Weekly*, 19 November 2003, p. 32.

Back, Les. "Voice of Hate, Sounds of Hybridity: Black Music and the Complexities of Racism." *Black Music Research Journal* 20, no. 2 (autumn 2000): 127–49.

Bangs. Lester. "Innocents in Babylon." In *Mainlines, Bloodfeasts, and Bad Taste: A Lester Bangs Reader*, edited by John Morthland, 259–299. New York: Anchor Books, 2003.

———. *Psychotic Reactions and Carburetor Dung*. Edited by Greil Marcus. New York: Vintage Books, 1988.

Barrett, Leonard E., Sr. *The Rastafarians: Sounds of Cultural Dissonance*. Boston: Beacon Press, 1988.

Bayer, Jonah. "The State of Punk to Come." *Alternative Press* 18, no. 189 (April 2004).

Beaujon, Andrew. "Out of Step with the World." *Spin* 19, no. 5 (May 2003): 84–86.

Black, Johnny. "Oh Shit!" *Mojo Special Edition: Punk: The Whole Truth*, April 2005, 88–89.

Blush, Steven. *American Hardcore: A Tribal History*. Los Angeles: Feral House, 2001.

Bourdieu, Pierre. *Distinction: A Social Critique of Taste*. Cambridge, MA: Harvard University Press, 1984.

Brannigan, Paul. "A Riot of Our Own." *Mojo Special Edition: Punk: The Whole Truth*, April 2005, 124–28.

Bushell, Gary. "Ain't That a Kick in the Head." *Mojo Special Edition: Punk: The Whole Truth*, April 2005, 102–4.

Bushszpan, Daniel. *The Encyclopedia of Heavy Metal*. New York: Barnes and Noble Books, 2003.

Cameron, Keith. "Something's Gone Wrong Again." *Mojo Special Edition: Punk: The Whole Truth*, April 2005, 36–41.

Cartledge, Frank. "Distress to Impress?: Local Punk Fashion and Commodity Exchange." In *Punk Rock: So What*, edited by Roger Sabin, 143–54. London: Routledge, 1999.

Chanel, Kevin. "From Joey Cora to Joey Ramone: The Connection between Baseball and Punk Rock." *Zisk* no. 2 (fall 1999).

———. Interview by Brian Cogan. 5 January 2003.

Colgreave, Stephen, and Chris Sullivan. *Punk*. New York: Thunder's Mouth Press, 2001.

Curtis, Deborah. *Touching from a Distance: Ian Curtis and Joy Division*. London: Faber and Faber, 1995.

D'Ambrosio, Antonino, ed. *Let Fury Have the Hour: The Punk Rock Politics of Joe Strummer*. New York: Norton Books, 2004.

Davies, Jude. "The Future of No Future: Punk Rock and Postmodern Theory." *Journal of Popular Culture* 29, no. 4 (spring 1988): 3–26.

De Whalley, Chas. "Lift Off!" *Mojo Special Edition: Punk: The Whole Truth*, April 2005, 32–35.

Duncombe, Stephen. *Notes from Underground: Zines and the Politics of Alternative Culture*. London: Verso, 1997.

El Hefe. Personal interview by Brian Cogan via email. 6 May 2004.

Ewen, Stewart. *All Consuming Images: The Politics of Style in Contemporary Culture*. New York: Basic Books, 1988.

Faloon, Michael. Personal interview by Brian Cogan. 22 December 2002.

Fish, Stanley. *Is There a Text in This Class?: The Authority of Interpretive Communities*. Cambridge, MA: Harvard University Press, 1980.

Foehr, Stephen. *Jamaican Warriors: Reggae, Roots and Culture*. London: MPG Books, 2000.

Ford, Simon. *Wreckers of Civilization: The Story of Coum Transmissions and Throbbing Gristle*. London: Black Dog, 1999.

Fox, Jeff. "How Publicly Admitting You Like the Dead Milkmen Can Destroy Your Professional Baseball Career! An Interview with Ex-Detroit Tigers Infielder Jim Walewander by Jeff Fox." *Chin Music*, no. 2 (1998).

Friedman, R. Seth. *The Fact Sheet Five Zine Reader*. New York: Three Rivers Press, 1997.

Frith, Simon. *Music for Pleasure: Essays in the Sociology of Pop*. New York: Routledge, 1988.

———. *Performing Rites: On the Value of Popular Music*, Cambridge, MA: Harvard University Press, 1996.

———. *Sound Effects: Youth, Leisure and the Politics of Rock and Roll*. New York: Random House, 1982.

Gencarelli, Thomas. "Reading Heavy Metal Music: An Interpretive Communities Approach to Popular Music as Education." Ph.D. diss., New York University, 1993.

Gimarc, George. *Punk Diary: 1970–1979*. New York: St. Martins' Press, 1994.

Goldman, Vivien. "Achtung Baby!: Siouxsie and the Banshees." *Mojo Special Edition: Punk: The Whole Truth*, April 2005, 62–65.

Gordon, Devin. "Car Tunes for New Grownups: Advertisers Tap the Music of a Previously Jilted Generation." *Spin* 16, no. 6 (June 2000): p. 60.

Gorman, Paul. "Dressed to Kill." *Mojo Special Edition: Punk: The Whole Truth*, April 2005, 46–49.

Gray, Marcus. *Last Gang in Town: The Story and Myth of the Clash*. New York: Henry Holt, 1995.

Grossberg, Lawrence. "Reflections of a Disappointed Popular Music Scholar." In *Rock over the Edge*, edited by Roger Beebe, Denise Fulbrook, and Ben Saunders, 25–59. Durham, NC: Duke University Press, 2002.

Gunderloy, Mike, and Carri Goldberg Janic., eds. *The World of Zines: A Guide to the Independent Magazine Revolution*. New York: Penguin Books, 1992.

Harrison, Ian. "The Naked Truth." *Mojo Special Edition: Punk: The Whole Truth,* April 2005, 70–75.

Hasted, Nick. "Back to the Planet of Sound." *Uncut* Take 91, December 2004, 82–96.

Heathcott, Joseph. "Urban Spaces and Working Class Expressions across the Black Atlantic: Tracing the Routes of Ska." *Radical History Review* 87 (2003): 183–206.

Hebdige, Dick. *Cut 'n' Mix: Culture, Identity and Caribbean Music.* London: Comedia, 1987.

———. *Subculture: The Meaning of Style.* London: Routledge, 1979.

Heylin, Clinton, ed. *All Yesterday's Parties: The Velvet Underground in Print 1966–1971.* Cambridge, MA: Da Capo Press, 2005.

———. *From the Velvets to the Voidoids: A Pre-Punk History for a Post-Punk World.* London: Penguin Books, 1993.

Hillsbery, Kief. *What We Do Is Secret.* New York: Villard, 2005.

Holmstom, John. Interview with Brian Cogan. 11 August 2005.

———, ed. *Punk: The Original.* New York: Trans-High, 1996.

Keithley, Joey. *I, Shithead: A Life in Punk.* Vancouver, BC: Arsenal Pulp Press, 2003.

Kellner, Douglas. "Advertising and Consumer Culture." In *Questioning the Media: A Critical Introduction,* edited by Roger Dowling and Ali Mohammadi, 329–344. Thousand Oaks, CA:Sage, 1995.

Kent, Nick. "The Lost Pistol." *Mojo Special Edition: Punk: The Whole Truth,* April 2005, 8–12.

King, Stephen A. "International Reggae, Democratic Socialism and the Secularization of the Rastafarian Movement, 1972–1980." *Popular Music and Society* 22, no. 3 (fall 1998): 39–61.

King, Stephen, and Richard Jensen. "Bob Marley's 'Redemption Song': The Rhetoric of Reggae and Rastafari." *Journal of Popular Culture* 29. no. 3 (winter 1995): 17–37.

Lahickey, Beth, ed. *All Ages: Reflections on Straight Edge.* Huntingon Beach, CA: Revelation Books, 1997.

Leblanc, Lauraine. *Pretty in Punk: Girl's Resistance in a Boy's Subculture.* New Brunswick, NJ: Rutgers University Press, 2002.

Levine, Noah. *Dharma Punx: A Memoir.* New York: Harper, 2003.

Levine, Robert. "A Nike Poster Upsets Fans of the Punk Rock Band Minor Threat in A Major Way." *New York Times,* 4 July 2005, C4.

Lisa, John. Interview with Brian Cogan via email. 31 August 2005.

Lydon, John, Keith Zimmerman, Kent Zimmerman. *Rotten: No Irish, No Blacks, No Dogs.* New York: St. Martin's Press, 1994.

Marcus, Greil. *In the Fascist Bathroom: Punk in Pop Music, 1977–1992.* Cambridge, MA: Harvard University Press, 1999.

———. *Lipstick Traces: A Secret History of the Twentieth Century.* Cambridge, MA: Harvard University Press, 1989.

McNeil, Legs. Telephone interview with Brian Cogan. 9 June 2005.

McNeil, Legs, and Gillian McCain. *Please Kill Me: The Uncensored Oral History of Punk.* New York: Grove Press, 1996.

McNeil, Legs, and Jennifer Osborne. *The Other Hollywood: The Uncensored Oral History of the Porn Film Industry.* New York: Regan Books, 2005.

McPeace, Shon. "Bad Brains Confound Categorization." *Arkansas Democrat-Gazette,* 27 July 2003, 54.

Medehurst, Andy. "What Did I Get: Punk, Memory and Autobiography." In *Punk Rock So What? The Cultural Legacy of Punk,* edited by Roger Sabin, 219–231. London: Routledge, 1999.

Middleton, Jasson. "D.C. Punk and the Production of Authenticity." In *Rock over the Edge,* edited by Roger Beebee, Denise Fulbrook, and Ben Saunders, 25–59. Durham, NC: Duke University Press, 2002.

Miles, Milo. "Rolling Stone Hall of Fame: The Clash." *Rolling Stone Magazine,* 20 June 2002, 87.

Miller, Steve. "Johnny Ramone: Rebel in a Rebel's World." *Washington Times,* 12 March 2004, http://www.Washingtontimes.com.

Mullen, Brendan. *Whores: An Oral Biography of Perry Farrell and Jane's Addiction.* New York: Da Capo, 2005.

Mullen, Brendan, and Don Bolles. *Lexicon Devil: The Fast Times and Short Life of Darby Crash and the Germs.* New York: Feral House, 2002.

Mulvaney, Becky Michelle. "Rhythms of Resistance: On Rhetoric and Reggae Music." Ph.D. diss., University of Iowa, 1985.

Murray, Noel. "Los Brothers Henandez." *The Onion* 41, no. 3 (September 2005): 14–16.

Negus, Keith. "Popular Music: Inbetween Celebration and Despair." In *Questioning the Media: A Critical Introduction*, edited by Roger Dowling and Ali Mohammadi, 379–393. Thousand Oaks, CA: Sage, 1995.

NOFX. *Flipside*, 1997 July/August. http://www.NOFX.org/oldint/flipside97.html.

NOFX. *Maximum Rock 'n' Roll*, 1991 June. http://www.NOFX.org/oldint/mrr91.html.

O'Hara, Craig. *The Philosophy of Punk: More Than Noise*. San Francisco: AK Press, 1999.

Perry, Andrew. "The Nutters's Club." *Mojo Special Edition: Punk: The Whole Truth*, April 2005, 114–20.

Perry, Mark. *Sniffin' Glue: The Essential Punk Accessory*. London: Sanctuary, 2000.

Radaway, Janice. *Reading the Romance: Women, Patriarchy and Popular Literature*, Chapel Hill: University of North Carolina Press, 1984.

Raha, Maria. *Cinderella's Big Score: Women of the Punk and Indie Underground*. Emeryville, CA: Seal Press, 2005.

Rimbaud, Penny (JJ Ratter). *Shibboleth: My Revolting Life*. London: AK Press, 1998.

———. *The Diamond Signature*. London: AK Press, 1999.

Rivett, Miriam. "Misfit Lit: 'Punk Writing' and Representations of Punk through Writing and Publishing." In *Punk Rock: So What?*, edited by Roger Sabin, 31–48. London: Routledge, year.

Robbins, Ira. "Clubbed!" *Spin* 21, no. 6 (August 2005): 78–82.

———. "How the West Was Lost." *Mojo Special Edition: Punk: The Whole Truth*, April 2005, 92–98.

———, ed. *The Trouser Press Guide to '90's Rock*. New York: Fireside/Simon & Schuster, 1997.

Rushkof, Douglas. *Media Virus: Hidden Agendas in Popular Culture*. New York: Ballantine, 1994.

Ruskin, Yvonne Sewell. *High on Rebellion: Inside the Underground at Max's Kansas City*. New York: Thunder's Mouth Press, 1998.

Ryan, Kyle. "Jon Langford." *The Onion* 41, no. 14 (November 2005): 14–15.

Sabin, Roger. "Introduction." In *Punk Rock So What? The Cultural Legacy of Punk*, edited by Roger Sabin, 1–14. London: Routledge, 1999.

———. "I Won't Let That Dago By: Rethinking Punk and Racism." In *Punk Rock So What? The Cultural Legacy of punk*, edited by Roger Sabin, 199–218. London: Routledge, 1999.

Sarig, Roni. *The Secret History of Rock: The Most Influential Bands You've Never Heard*. New York: Billboard Books, 1998.

Savage, Jon. *England's Dreaming: Anarchy, Sex Pistols, Punk Rock and Beyond*. New York: St. Martin's Press, 1992.

———. "In Search of Space." *Mojo*, January 2004, p. 85.

———. "Savage Jukebox." *Mojo Special Edition: Punk: The Whole Truth*, April 2005, 82–86.

Scabies, Rat, and Christopher Dawes. *Rat Scabies and the Holy Grail*. New York: Thunder's Mouth Press, forthcoming.

Shaw, Thomas Edward. *Black Monk Time: Coming of the Anti-Beatle*. Reno, NV: Carson Street Publishing, 1995.

Spitz, Marc, and Brendan Mullen, eds. *We Got the Neutron Bomb: The Untold Story of L.A. Punk*. New York: Three Rivers Press, 2001.

Sprague, David. "Rancid". In *Trouser Press Guide to 90's Rock*, edited by Ira Robbins, 595–596. New York: Fireside, 1997.

St. John, Warren. "A Bush Surprise: Fright-Wing Support." *New York Times*, 21 March 2004, http://www.nytimes.com.

Straugsbaugh, John. *Rock till You Drop: The decline from Rebellion to Nostalgia*. London: Verso, 2001.

Strauss, Neil. "Yep, the Clash was Musical, but Don't Tell Anyone." *New York Times*, 5 January 2003, sec. 2, 32.

Tabb, George. *Playing Right Field, A Jew Grows in Greenwich*. New York: Soft Skull Press, 2004.

———. *Surfing Armageddon: A Memoir*. New York: Soft Skull Press, 2006.

Taylor, Steven. *False Prophet: Field Notes from the Punk Underground*. Middletown, CT: Wesleyan University Press, 2003.

Taylor, Todd. *Born to Rock: Heavy Drinkers and Thinker*. Los Angeles: Gorsky Press, 2004.

Thompson, Dave. *Alternative Rock*. San Francisco: Miller Freeman Books, 2000.

Thompson, Stacey. *Punk Productions: Unfinished Business*. Albany: State University of New York Press, 2004.

Traber, Daniel. "L.A.'s 'White Minority': Punk and the Contradictions of Self-Marginalization." *Cultural Critique* 48, no. 1 (2001): 30–64.

True, Everett. *Hey Ho Let's Go: The Story of the Ramones*. London: Omnibus Press, 2002.

Turcotte, Bryan Ray, and Christopher Miller. *Fucked up and Photocopied: Instant Art of the Punk Rock Movement*. Corte Madera, CA: Ginko Press, 1999.

Tyler, Kieron. "Idiot Box!" *Mojo Special Edition: Punk: The Whole Truth*, April 2005, 106–9.

Unterberger, Richie. *Unknown Legends of Rock 'n' Roll: Psychedelic Unknowns, Mad Geniuses, Punk Pioneers, Lo-Fi Mavericks & More*. San Francisco: Miller Freeman, 1998.

Ward, Ed. "No Second Acts in Punk? Says Who?" *New York Times*, 29 December 2002, sec. 4, 7.

Warner, Charles. "Jah as Genre: The Interface of Reggae and American Popular Music." Ph.D. diss., Bowling Green State University, 1993.

Wilson, Lois. "Punk Smashers!" *Mojo Special Edition: Punk: The Whole Truth*, April 2005, 133–43.

Web Sites Consulted

Not all of the Web sites mentioned have up-to-date or even accurate information outside of the official band sites and Trouser Press and All Music. Many band sites and fan sites in particular tend to change URLs or become outdated quickly.

Allmusic, http://www.allmusic.com

All Official Website, http://www.allcentral.com

Alternativetentacles.com, http://www.alternativetentacles.com

Angelic Upstarts, http://www.angelicupstarts.co.uk

Anti-Nowhere League, http://www.antinowhereleague.com

The Art of Jamie Reid, http://www.jamiereid.uk.net/home.html

Celibate Rifles, http://www.celibaterifles.com

Dischord Records, http://www.dischord.com

Emplive.org, "Riot Girl Retrospective," http://www.emplive.org/explore/riot_grrrl/index.asp

Empty Records U.S., http://www.emptyrecords.com/

Nick Zedd Website, http://www.nickzedd.com

Punknews.org, http://punknews.org

Punknews U.K., http://www.punknews.co.uk/

Punk History Canada, http://www.punkhistorycanada.ca/

Punk Rock in My Veins, http://punkandoi.free.fr

Punk 77, http://www.punk77.co.uk

The Punk Vault, http://www.punkvinyl.com

Roir, http://www.roir-usa.com/

Search & Destroy, http://www.trashsurfin.de/

Slapshot Official Website, http://wwww.oldtimehardcore.com

Trouser Press Online, http:www.trouserpress.com

Wikipedia Encyclopedia, http://en.wikipedia.org

Liner Notes

Fricke, David. Liner notes for the Velvet Underground, *Peel Slowly and See* (Polydor, 1995).

Hitchcock, Doug. Liner notes for the Embarrassment, *The Embarrassment* (Bar None, 1995).

Hudson, Mike. Liner notes for the Pagans, *Shit Street* (Crypt, 2001).

Liner Notes for Wayne/Jayne County and the Electric Chairs, *Rock 'n' Roll Cleopatra* (Royalty Records, 1993).

Piccarella, John. Liner notes for Richard Hell and the Voidoids, *Blank Generation* (Sire/Warner Brothers, 1990).

Smith, TV. Liner notes from *The Adverts Anthology* (The Devil's Own Jukebox, 2003).

INDEX

Note: **Boldfaced** page locators refer to main entries in the encyclopedia.

About the Author

BRIAN COGAN is a writer and professor who has written extensively on music and popular culture as well as music criticism. He received his Ph.D. in Media Ecology in 2002 from New York University. He teaches at Molloy College and has taught at New York University and the College of Staten Island. Dr. Cogan has been a member of the punk scene for over twenty years and has written for a variety of zines as well as journals, newspapers, and magazines, and has performed and recorded with his band In Crowd since 1987.